T0305906

Technology and Engineering Strategies

This pioneering book is the first-ever practical guide to developing and communicating technology and engineering strategies.

It presents a unique step-by-step method for creating a robust, evidence-based strategy, known as the Five Dimensions Process (or 5DP). The book also introduces a host of original insights, including a new theory of technology, a novel approach to product innovation, and groundbreaking contributions to our understanding of technological risk. It describes many easy-to-use tools, both new and established, for supporting activities such as solution design, system monitoring, risk identification, project management, the development of personnel, and ethical decision making. The book brims with strategic and tactical advice on such topics as university collaboration, technical compatibility, data utilisation, product design, project cancellations, outsourcing, knowledge management, and risk mitigation.

It is essential reading for technologists and engineers across all disciplines, technology and engineering leaders, and professional strategy consultants.

P.J. Moar practises as an independent management and technology consultant and has been working with technologists, engineers, educationalists, and risk professionals for three decades. He was formerly an infrastructure manager with General Electric (GE). Moar was awarded the 1991 J. Elizabeth Morris Prize by the University of Wales, and in 2005 received a Letter of Commendation from the University of Cambridge. He later undertook research in technology policy and engineering theory both at MIT and Cambridge, work subsequently published by the Royal Academy of Engineering.

Technology and Engineering Strategies

Step-by-Step from Theory into Practice

P.J. Moar

Routledge
Taylor & Francis Group

LONDON AND NEW YORK

Designed cover image: © National Maritime Museum, Greenwich, London

First published 2025
by Routledge
4 Park Square, Milton Park, Abingdon, Oxon OX14 4RN

and by Routledge
605 Third Avenue, New York, NY 10158

Routledge is an imprint of the Taylor & Francis Group, an informa business

© 2025 P.J. Moar

British Library Cataloguing-in-Publication Data
A catalogue record for this book is available from the British Library

ISBN: 978-1-032-75202-0 (hbk)
ISBN: 978-1-032-73440-8 (pbk)
ISBN: 978-1-003-47291-9 (ebk)

DOI: 10.4324/9781003472919

Typeset in Sabon
by MPS Limited, Dehradun

This book is dedicated to all current and former employees of General Electric Corporation. It was GE that first introduced me to technology and engineering in a professional context, and their generous commitment to my training and personal development was genuinely transformative.

Contents

Preface

We can be fairly certain that people have been thinking strategically about technology for 300,000 years, because that's when the first simple technologies were developed.[1] However, the first *technology strategists*, in any professional sense, probably emerged around four or five thousand years ago, as humans carved early civilisations from the rocks beneath their feet. The names of these pioneering individuals will never be known.

The first great technology strategist of the modern era was probably the Birmingham (UK) entrepreneur and manufacturer Matthew Boulton (1728–1809). Not only did Boulton have the good sense to form a partnership with the talented young engineer James Watt, but he also had the vision to translate Watt's creative output into highly productive (and profitable) machinery. By the early 1780s, with Boulton's encouragement, Watt had developed a rotative steam engine, critical to the delivery of continuous power. Hitherto, steam power had been deployed mainly to pump water from deep mines, but Boulton had seen an opportunity. In a message that would shape modern civilisation, he suggested to Watt that "the most likely line for the consumption of our engines is the application of them to mills, which is certainly an extensive field."[2] This strategy would transform Boulton and Watt's fortunes. It also enriched many of their soon-to-be customers and suppliers and catapulted the United Kingdom towards a century of industrial leadership.

But you are probably not here for a history lesson, and this is certainly not a history book. In fact, it's an examination of strategic thinking and strategy development throughout the 'technological realm', a phrase I use to encapsulate the activities and outputs of all technical and engineering disciplines. Within this diverse realm, we observe technological devices and systems of all kinds. We also find high-value skills, countless stakeholders, intellectual property, international standards, foresight techniques, risk models, and much more besides.

This book has been written primarily for hard working, hard thinking technologists and engineers. It should also appeal to anyone with managerial or supervisory responsibilities in technology-oriented organisations. The central premise is that anyone can learn or be trained to think strategically, and this book is designed to support that process. Here are some teaser questions to challenge your own strategic thinking:

- Given that the Japanese Shinkansen 'bullet train' network has eliminated all fatalities and serious injuries since 1964, why has no other rail company been able to emulate this success?
- Is it possible, in the 21st century, to develop an entirely new form of technology without scientific support?
- What type of reasoning encouraged the Pirelli tyre company to start manufacturing fibre optic cables in the mid-1980s?
- After failing in its transition to digital photography, could the mighty Kodak Corporation have reinvented itself as a chemicals business?
- In the 1980s, when the steel firm Sheffield Forgemasters received an order from Iraq for 'pipes' made to extremely high specifications, did they have a duty to ask the customer how they would be used?
- If a team of the world's best engineers were given unlimited time and resources, could they build a 100% reliable machine?

How did you respond to those questions? Were they intriguing, inspiring, or neither? In varying degrees, they were all strategic questions. Do you see yourself as a naturally strategic thinker?

I believe that my own strategic thinking has developed substantially since I was first asked by a client to develop a technology strategy for an international engineering consultancy. In preparation for this task, I was struck by the absence of any published guidance for developing and writing such strategies. Furthermore, because technology strategies are, by their nature, commercially sensitive, only a few examples could be found in the public domain. Those published strategies were inconsistent; each had a unique structure and style. It seemed that there was no standard methodology for producing one. Consequently, I was able to develop a technology strategy for my client unhindered by presentational expectations. The outcome was a document written for a mixed audience of executives and frontline staff. It was well received. By default, I had become a technology strategist.

A year later, I was engaged in conversation with some network support engineers. We were attempting to reach a decision with significant long-term technical implications. Frustratingly, the options we had to choose from were diametrically opposed. It was a classic dichotomy, an engineering dilemma resembling a fork in the road. The choice is simple and stark – go left, or go right? After the commitment has been made, it's hard to reverse. Most readers will be aware of such dichotomies. For example: Is it better to build in-house, or buy off-the-shelf? Should we configure in series, or in parallel? Do we concentrate operations on a single site, or distribute activities across multiple sites in order to mitigate risks? Should we obtain new skills by recruiting, or train our existing employees? And the list goes on. These dichotomies are often strategic in nature.

At that moment it dawned on me that professional people who work with technologies would benefit from a book dedicated to strategic decision making. Moreover, the provision of a template for developing a formal technology strategy would also save time for those called upon (as I had been) to produce a strategy for an employer or client.

A more thorough literature survey confirmed my previous observations - the absence of any books for technologists and engineers dedicated to the step-by-step production of formal technology strategies and to the development of a strategic mindset in engineering. This type of book would surely be helpful because strategic challenges emerge daily, particularly in large organisations, and, in the words of Grant and Jordan, "the difference between massive value creation and ignominious failure may be the result of small errors of timing or technological choices."[3]

Over recent decades, much has been written about the administration of specific technologies and general technology management. The world is also drowning in a sea of books and articles about general business strategy. However, nothing bridges the identified gap - **enabling technical people in technological environments to make good strategic decisions at the right time and for the right reasons.**

So this is not a book about business strategy for technologists and engineers. Nor is it a book on technology strategy for general business readers. It is, quite deliberately, a book on forward thinking and strategy development for professionals with responsibilities for the design and management of their technological environments.

There will be occasions when the divide between traditional business strategy and technology strategy becomes indistinct. This is because overlaps exist, especially in technology-dominant organisations (e.g. NASA, Sony, Shell) where the same people will be involved in the creation and implementation of both types of strategy. Nevertheless, **it is my hypothesis that technology strategy can be perceived and analysed as a stand-alone topic, almost as a professional discipline in its own right.**

Furthermore, I believe that the principles of technology strategy are, for the most part, technology-neutral. In other words, one can apply the ideas described in this book to any technological domain or engineering discipline. A professional technology strategist in the aerospace sector, for instance, could transfer seamlessly to civil engineering, or electronics manufacturing. Consequently, the content is both multi-disciplinary and cross-disciplinary.

Although this book has a practical bent, it does introduce some theoretical and philosophical ideas. From experience, I know that many technologists are reluctant to engage with such matters, but it can be important both for greater understanding of the working environment and for personal development. Forthcoming chapters will therefore examine topics such as complexity science, utilitarian ethics, technical paradigms, even Donald Rumsfeld's 'unknown unknowns'. I believe it is vital to weave these more abstract ideas into the narrative, but when doing so I will always accompany them with practical insights or historical examples.

At times my writing will be informal in style, but the reader can be assured that strict academic rigour has been observed during the process of selecting, scrutinising, and recording sources. I am not an academic by profession, and this book is not designed for formal teaching purposes. However, the content will be compatible with some academic modules in engineering, such as those addressing innovation, ethics, and entrepreneurship. Student engineers may also gain valuable career insights, particularly in relation to systems engineering, explored in the final part.

When planning this book, I had no preconceived ideas about what it should contain. The various parts and chapters emerged only from the research. More than 200 sources had been studied before the shape of the book became clear – a potential narrative had emerged, linking ideas together. Upon completion, 350 sources had been used.

I should also emphasise that this book is not the product of any particular belief system or philosophy of technology. There is no 'hidden hand' at work. It is simply a presentation of the most important strategic ideas, as I perceive them, organised to the best of my ability in the spirit of sharing a fascinating subject with readers.

So, to summarise, this is a book about strategic thinking and strategy development in the technological realm. It has been written primarily for technologists, engineers, and anyone with an interest in, or responsibility for, the design and management of technical environments or technology-driven organisations. Its aim is to encourage new patterns of thinking, enabling its readers to write world-leading technology strategies, and to make faster, more effective short-term tactical decisions.

Notes

1 Harari, Y.N. (2015) *Sapiens: A Brief History of Humankind*. London: Penguin. 10–13.
2 Miller, D.P. (2019) *The Life and Legend of James Watt*. Pittsburgh: University of Pittsburgh Press. 100 [Note: These words marked the beginning of the Industrial Revolution. An early source for this quote is Samuel Smiles' *Lives of Boulton and Watt* (1865), published by John Murray, available online via Project Gutenberg.]
3 Grant, R.M. and Jordan, J. (2015) *Foundations of Strategy*. Chichester: Wiley. 223.

Parts and chapter summaries

This book consists of 13 chapters organised in three parts. The text progresses from foundational and theoretical concepts, through to more practical information and ideas. A template for producing an organisation's technology or engineering strategy is then presented. The book concludes with some recommendations for improving the practice of developing and implementing strategies.

A number of novel methods, insights, and ideas will be presented. These include the new five dimensions theory of technology, which supports innovation activities, risk analysis, technology foresight, and the strategy development process. Additional concepts, such as *analytical risk, paradigm risk*, and *entropic technical risk*, emerge from the examination of uncertainty. Chapter 6 describes 18 so-called 'origins of uncertainty'. It's possible that this is the first-ever attempt at identifying 'the root causes of the root causes' within technology and engineering. A later chapter introduces a new form of ethical decision making known as Ethical Due Process. Finally, Chapter 11 describes innovations in the management of risk and foresight analysis, including Positive Risk diagrams and the 5D Risk Radar horizon scan.

In Part I, *Definitions, scoping, and challenges*, the core concepts of strategy, technology, and engineering will be examined and defined. Firstly, a number of published technology and engineering strategies from major organisations are reviewed. This is probably the first-ever review and analysis of formal technology strategies. How are they structured and how useful are they? This will lead to a discussion of what we mean by 'strategy', 'technology', and 'technology strategy'. Next, the critical concept of 'uncertainty' (which underpins, and often undermines, all strategic thinking) is given substantial treatment. Here the focus is on the origins, or fundamental causes, of uncertainty. Finally, in order to act strategically, it is necessary to think strategically, so the psychological dimension of decision making will be explored.

In Part II, *Strategy in practice*, the more tangible aspects of this book begin to emerge. Strategising inevitably involves stakeholders, so the role of employees, suppliers, users, collaborators, regulators, and so on, will be discussed. This stakeholder focus leads to an examination of the ethical challenges raised by technology decisions. We then change tack in order to address the ever-popular topic of innovation. Does innovation lie at the heart of strategy development? No, it does not, and I will explain why. Part II then draws to a close by addressing the core concept of uncertainty for a second time. Here, we look at some practical methods for navigating the threats and opportunities presented by uncertainty.

Part III, *Something to take away*, presents the reader with a blueprint for creating a formal technology or engineering strategy. This is based on a novel method called the Five Dimensions Process developed, in part, from the author's experience of writing real-world strategies and studying countless more examples. In the final chapter, some broad conclusions will be drawn. Here, recommendations will be made which readers are invited to consider, and perhaps implement for the benefit of their own organisations (and careers).

The first three parts also include a number of break-out boxes. These feature stand-alone content intended to be both informative and thought-provoking. Most of the break-out boxes are presented under one of three headings: *Analytical tools and techniques*, *Strategic and tactical moves*, and *Strategic dichotomies*.

Analytical tools and techniques: These boxes describe useful analytical methods for making decisions and developing strategies. Dozens of tools and techniques, mostly qualitative, were documented and developed during the research. Eleven are presented here.

Strategic and tactical moves: No book on strategy would be complete without suggestions for some strategic and tactical moves. These will include the new concept of *dennovation*, plus more traditional approaches, including university collaboration, knowledge management, 'vanilla' solutions, technical compatibility, and future-proofing. Of the many strategic and tactical moves identified during the research, 12 are explained in the chapters that follow.

Strategic dichotomies: As mentioned earlier, anyone with decision making responsibilities in the technological realm knows that the route to progress often arrives at a fork in the road. The decision to go left or right has significant long-term implications. Occasionally there will be an acceptable middle way, but often the choice is stark and brutal. I call these *strategic dichotomies*. Consider the following familiar dilemmas: to centralise or decentralise a solution; to use people or machines; to move first, or wait and move second; to locate in a technology cluster or maintain geographical separation; to satisfy client wants or client needs; and so on. There are scores of these dichotomies, and reading or thinking about them helps to train the strategist's mind. Twelve dichotomies are shared in the pages that follow.

Appendix 4 itemises each of the tools, techniques, strategies, tactics, and dichotomies presented in the book.

Part I

Definitions, scoping, and challenges

This is a book about the strategic management of the technological realm. It's about the systems, tools, and devices we design, build, test, implement, monitor, maintain, repair, upgrade, retire, repurpose, decommission, and scrap. It's also about the ways we organise ourselves to do these things.

There is an abundance of historical evidence to show that strategic decisions about technologies can make or break both companies and careers. This book is concerned with developing methods to control these existential challenges.

This first part presents a primer, underpinning the later parts. To this end, it will include definitions of what we mean by *strategy*, *technology*, and *technology strategy*. Some of these will be new definitions developed specifically for this book.

Arguably the critical chapters in this part are those addressing the ubiquitous concept of *uncertainty*, the bane of every strategist's professional life.

This is the most cerebral of the three parts, framing the book using key theories and concepts. In order to maintain the interest of a broad readership, the academic content is counter-balanced with relevant examples and unusual cases.

DOI: 10.4324/9781003472919-1

1 The formalities

How organisations communicate strategies

This chapter presents

- A review of some real-world technology strategies.
- An examination of what we mean by 'strategy'.

This chapter establishes

- Inconsistencies in the content and presentation of formal organisational strategies.
- A clear definition of 'strategy'.

It may be a paradox, but sometimes it's logical to begin at the end. If we know where we're going, we're more likely to arrive.

Our destination is the acquisition of greater skills and confidence in the development of technology strategies to support the aims and ambitions of organisations – our employers and clients. In the final section of this book, I will present a method for producing a formal technology strategy (Chapter 12). It's called the *Five Dimensions Process* and it draws upon the contents of the next 11 chapters, in which a wide array of historical cases, novel ideas, tools, theories, and insights will be explored. The output of the Five Dimensions Process will be a strategy document ready for distribution to an organisation's key stakeholders.

There's a lot to examine, so let's switch on and power up.

Let's "begin at the end" by reviewing some real-world examples of published technology strategies. Due to the commercial sensitivities associated with most strategy development, the majority of organisations, especially those in the private sector, reserve their strategic thinking for internal eyes only. This secrecy is understandable, although frustrating for those of us wanting to learn more about the ways that strategies are designed and communicated. Fortunately, a small number of formal technology strategies can be found in the public domain. These are reviewed below.

DOI: 10.4324/9781003472919-2

During my latest trawl for strategies, I discovered around 20 documents. Table 1.1 itemises 14 of these and lists some of their attributes. Presumably, we can learn something from these documents. Who were they written for? What information or ideas do they contain? Are there any similarities in style and structure, and how do they differ?

My assumption is that a review of real-world examples will help us to produce better technology strategies for our own organisations. It may not be the only way to develop those skills, but it's a good first step.

The 14 listed examples were published by 6 different types of organisation in North America, Europe, and Australasia. They have been selected for review because they reflect, as far as possible, a cross-section of presentational styles and organisational types. Should you wish to read them yourself, it's likely that many are still available online (see the Notes after this chapter).

As noted above, companies in the private sector are reticent about placing their technology strategies in the public domain. This is evidenced by the fact that only one of the documents was produced by a private company (Toshiba). The others have been issued by non-profit organisations, including government departments, local authorities, and charities. It seems likely that the transparency expected of 'non-profits' renders them more likely to share their strategies publicly. However, as a consequence of this sampling bias, the review is skewed towards less competitive management cultures, whose perspectives will differ substantially from those in the private sector. These differences between public and private organisations could be significant, e.g. in their attitudes towards innovation. This may become clearer as the book progresses. However, it would be wrong to assume that there are only two broad approaches, public and private. The fact is that each organisation's strategy will be shaped by its unique internal culture and operating environment, combined with the talents of its strategic thinkers.

Despite their wide geographical spread, each of the 14 strategies has been published in English. With the exception of Toshiba, they all originate in countries where English is the most widely spoken language. In order to redress this imbalance, and to enable a more comparative approach, I would encourage readers to acquire and read technology strategies published in other languages. It would be interesting to know whether cultural differences affect the content, structure, and confidentiality of the strategy documents. For example, are private companies in Japan more likely to share their strategies in public, as Toshiba has done? Do public authorities in some countries recommend a standard template for such documents?

Table 1.1 The 14 published technology and engineering strategies examined in this chapter[1]

Organisation	Organisation type	Location	Document title	Year released	Pages or slides
Australian Department of Defence	National government department	Australia	*Defence Science and Technology Strategy 2030*	Not specified	20
City of Coquitlam, Canada	Local or regional government	Canada	*2019–2024 Coquitlam Technology Strategy*	2018	10
Toshiba	Business (for-profit)	Japan	*Technology Strategy*	2018	37
UK Space Agency CEOI	National public service institution	UK	*Technology Strategy*	2019	31
European Space Agency	International public service institution	International	*Technology Strategy*	2022	68
NASA	National public service institution	USA	*Strategic Plan 2022*	Not specified	73 + appendices
Dundee City Council	Local or regional government	UK	*Information Technology Strategy [2018–2023]*	Not specified	13
City and County of San Francisco	Local or regional government	USA	*Information and Communication Technology Plan FY 2022–26*	Not specified	28 + appendices
Social Security Scotland	National government department	UK	*Digital and Technology Strategy 2022–2025*	2022	32
UK Home Office	National government department	UK	*Digital, Data and Technology 2024 Strategy*	2021	33

(Continued)

Table 1.1 (Continued)

Organisation	Organisation type	Location	Document title	Year released	Pages or slides
Irish Department of Agriculture, Food and the Marine	National government department	Ireland	*Information and Management Technology Strategy 2021–24*	2021	13
New Zealand Ministry of Social Development	National government department	New Zealand	*Technology Strategy 2022*	2022	25
National Highways	National public service institution	UK	*Operational Technology: our 2035 strategy*	2022	32
MSI Reproductive Choices	Charity	UK	*Digital and Technology Strategy* (summary version)	2021	4

Unfortunately, it won't be possible to answer these questions from the current sample, but these 14 examples should be informative.

General observations

Firstly, let's consider the document titles. All except one use the word 'strategy', although this could be a consequence of the search algorithms used to compile the sample. However, it seems more appropriate for organisations to use this term rather than 'plan', for instance. This is because there are significant differences between strategies and plans, a fact which should become clearer as this book progresses. It is notable that the City and County of San Francisco opted to use the latter term, and their document is also particularly long, at over 200 pages. Are plans inevitably longer than strategies? I will argue later that strategies require brevity to be effective, whereas plans serve a different purpose, requiring greater detail (and consequently greater length). Where strategies and plans are mixed in a single document, as we see in the San Francisco case, this probably diminishes the impact of the strategic message, overwhelming it with information about delivery methods, dates, teams, projects, risk factors, and so on. It supports the argument for separating the publication of a strategy from its execution plan.

Only three of the document titles make specific mention of the type of technology under consideration, and in all of these, the reference is to information technology. A further three titles refer to both a digital *and* a technology strategy (e.g. Social Security Scotland), suggesting a document addressing both IT and other technologies of relevance to the organisation. What other technologies might these be? Operational machinery? Vehicle fleets? Heating and ventilation? Confusingly, though, the documents mentioning both digital *and* technology are exclusively devoted *only* to digital services. In the interests of clarity, it would surely help readers if titles were more explicit about the type of technologies addressed within the strategy.

A further five documents are labelled simply "Technology Strategy". One assumes that these documents will be addressing all areas of technology and engineering vital to the organisation's success. Reassuringly, four of the five do just that. They refer to a wide range of non-digital technologies ranging from space engineering to industrial products.

The City of Coquitlam (a district of Vancouver) opens its generically titled "Technology Strategy" with the following helpful statement:

For the purposes of the 2019–2024 Coquitlam Technology Strategy, the technology sector is inclusive of a number of technology-related subsectors such as information and communications technology, digital media and wireless, robotics, automation, artificial intelligence, health and life sciences and clean-tech as well as the creative sector, which encompasses subsectors such as software development, research and development, design, arts and culture, etc.[2]

Here, the scope has been clearly laid out for the reader. However, this particular document does *not* contain a strategy for the organisation's internal technologies, such as finance systems or neighbourhood waste recycling. Instead, it describes Coquitlam's approach to the economic development of its local industrial and employment sectors. Elsewhere this might be referred to as an 'industrial strategy', 'industrial policy', or 'technology policy'. Their "Vision Statement" expresses a desire to "foster a climate that supports growing our technology sector ..." In other words, it's not about actually managing technologies, but about "fostering" or facilitating local economic activity. This difference between 'doing' technology and merely encouraging it (which we typically associate with political institutions), is discussed further in Chapter 3.

None of the strategies under review refer to 'engineering' within their titles. Does this mean that "technology" also implies engineering? For example, Toshiba's *Technology Strategy* devotes around 50% of its content to digital, including AI, and the remainder to a wide range of other engineering activities: gas turbines, batteries, robotics, precision medicine, and so on. The relationship between the terms 'technology' and 'engineering' needs further clarification, and will therefore be explored in the next chapter.

However, we can't escape the fact that the technologies addressed by these 14 strategy documents are overwhelmingly in the digital realm. This is hardly surprising because there are few organisations in the 21st century that are not constantly examining the opportunities presented by digitalisation. Nevertheless, it seems clear that there is more to the meaning of 'technology' than merely digital goods and services, a fact which many organisations appear to be ignorant of. This raises a serious question. If a so-called 'technology strategy' only addresses digital technologies, then where are the strategies for other technologies, such as lighting, construction, clean rooms, physical security, and so on? Most organisations appear to have no interest in them.

In Chapter 2, I will analyse *technology* as a concept. This will culminate in a new definition of the term. As the book progresses, this new definition will be used to help us improve the process of developing and implementing technology and engineering strategies.

Communication

The target audience for strategy documents is often ambiguous. Which stakeholders are expected to read them? Those issued by private companies could be written for owners, shareholders, investors, creditors, employees, suppliers, customers, and even regulators. Public bodies need to share their strategic thinking with service users, politicians, and voters, in addition to employees, suppliers, and regulators.

It's likely that most organisations would prefer to produce a single strategy document, but that may not be feasible. For example, sensitive or controversial strategic thinking may only be found in versions of the strategy circulated among senior leaders. Information about new product ranges, acquisition targets, patentable inventions, and plant closures are unlikely to be shared beyond the board room. Hence, we should not assume that strategies in the public domain are a true reflection of an organisation's intentions.

Clues about the intended audience may be found in the time and effort expended on the production of the document. Simpler, word-processed examples, such as those from Dundee County Council or the UK Space Agency Centre for Earth Observation Instrumentation (the CEOI), were probably not intended for wider dissemination. Their shorter, more matter-of-fact style indicates a strictly functional, business-like approach intended for consumption by internal stakeholders. By contrast, strategies published in presentation format (e.g. National Highways) are much more conscious of the need to impress their audiences with a strong visual message. These may have been designed both for internal presentation to employees and to external groups, such as investors or political funders.

The longer and more impressively produced documents, such as those by Social Security Scotland, the European Space Agency, NASA, and the City and County of San Francisco, are more difficult to interpret. Their readership (i.e. people prepared to read most or all of the document) is likely to be extremely limited in number. Does this justify the expense of producing such elaborate documents? Perhaps not. However, all of these organisations have budgets large enough to employ strategy consultants and document designers, so this probably leads to bloated publications. It should be noted, though, that many public institutions are dependent upon a small number of influential political funders (who may have little technical knowledge). Therefore a large, glossily-produced document could be perceived as a proxy for competence. The technical content is unlikely to be either read or understood. Such documents might be described as performative, costly, and frankly pointless.

Arguably the people who most need to read, comprehend, and act upon a technology strategy are frontline technologists and engineers. Yet, in my experience such people are generally unwilling to engage with these types of long and elaborate documents.

Eben Hewitt, a leading business architect and author of *Technology Strategy Patterns* (2018) writes that "once you've devised a strategy, it languishes on the shelf if you can't make people excited to hear it, understand it, care about it, approve it, and execute it."[3]

Clearly, communication is one of the key dilemmas facing technology strategists. A strategy is worthless without a keenly interested readership, but which audience should this be? What do they need to know and how should it be presented to them? These are questions which this book will endeavour to answer.

Content

Thus far we have only made a superficial examination of the 14 strategy documents. This has included their titles, their technological scope, and their readerships. However, we have not yet explored their contents. Let's look at the way the strategies have been structured and the types of information they contain.

Contextual information

Most documents describe the context within which each strategy has been developed, including current technologies and other underlying factors. For example, the City and County of San Francisco reveal the budget allocations and quantify the number and range of digital services currently offered to internal and external users. In the appendices, hundreds of these services are described, along with their Digital Maturity scores. They also use the appendices to specify, perhaps unnecessarily, the supporting legislation and administrative codes, along with descriptions of other related strategies, including their *Cybersecurity Strategic Plan*. The San Francisco document is unusual in the large volume of information provided. Most of the other documents offer similar types of contextual data, although with greater brevity.

Business strategies

It seems reasonable to expect that the developers of a technology strategy will both study and directly reference their organisation's highest-level strategy, often known as the business strategy. However, surprisingly only 3 of the 14 documents did this. For example, Social Security Scotland refers to their *Corporate Plan 2020–2023* which "sets out who we are, what we do and how we will do it." They describe how two of the four main themes in the Corporate Plan relate directly to the technology strategy. NASA refers its readers to the *Agency Priority Goals* (APGs) which "reflect the top NASA and national performance priorities." These include climate change research, the Artemis programme, and "space technology leadership". One wonders how many of the other strategy development teams went to the trouble of seeking out, and synchronising with, their organisation's top-level strategy? It's difficult to ascertain this from the evidence, but it's an important topic which I will return to later in the book.

Box 1.1 STRATEGIC AND TACTICAL MOVES

Collaborating with universities

Does your organisation have a working relationship with any universities? If not, you may be missing opportunities to improve your products, processes, and people. The costs of collaborating with universities are generally low, while the benefits can be transformative. Here are some suggestions:

Research: Use the facilities and expertise of a university to deliver technical studies. NASA's early successes under its first Administrator, Thomas Keith Glennan, were partly built upon his policy of contracting out research to universities.[4] For substantial work there will be costs, of course, but a lot of research is free. Most graduate students need to deliver short dissertations, so universities encourage external parties to suggest projects.

A source of ideas: There is much to be gained from simply observing university outputs and talking to their staff. Read their research output and attend public events.

Locating within university technology clusters: One beneficiary commented: "The advantage of being close to the university is the ability for people from both sides just to walk across the road, so from a hands-on collaboration point of view it is very quick and it is very easy. Basically our time-to-solution has been much quicker working in that way, rather than working by correspondence all the time with remote partners."[5]

Networks: By collaborating with a university you become part of its network. This includes other research institutions, funding bodies, alumni, and companies with similar interests to your own (who might even become future clients).

Product development: Try offering your latest products to universities, either free or at a discount. You will gain valuable feedback. At the same time, you will be building a business ecosystem of future customers and suppliers (i.e. former staff and students of the university). Sun Microsystems did this successfully in the 1970s and 80s with their computer hardware.[6]

Recruitment: Supporting research students is a highly effective way to recruit. If you're impressed by their work ethic and the quality of output, offer them a job! Your organisation will get first pick of the brightest graduates.

University engagement is a low risk, high reward activity.

Values and principles

All organisations have core values and/or principles, although these are not always expressed in written form. Nevertheless, the strategic direction of an organisation is surely influenced by them. Values/principles reflect what is culturally, ethically, and philosophically important, either to the organisation's owners, political funders, or its senior leadership. Around half of the 14 strategy documents listed key underlying values and principles. Many of these were non-technical in nature, such as equity, respect, privacy, and inclusivity.[7] However, some organisations presented more technically focused statements. The UK Home Office, for instance, explains their "six principles of change", which include a preference for converging existing technologies, embracing innovation, being "product-centric over programme-centric", and using data to drive decision making. NASA describes its "Core Values", which include safety, multi-disciplinary teamworking, and engineering excellence. It would be misleading to say that these statements are an essential feature of an effective strategy, but if they truly reflect the organisational culture and are drafted carefully (i.e. succinctly), then they will help to explain some of the strategic choices that have been made. This could be useful, even motivational, for the personnel expected to execute them.

Challenges

Each strategy development team faces, and responds to, a unique set of challenges and uncertainties. These challenges were described in around half of the 14 documents under review. For instance, Dundee City Council's *Information Technology Strategy* lists the following unremarkable challenges: budget pressures, leadership changes, increasing demand from service users, regulatory changes, and potentially disruptive technologies. The Irish Department of Agriculture, Food and the Marine itemise key technical risks, including the presence of legacy IT systems, cyber attacks, and an over-dependence upon contract staff. Each risk is then mapped to a mitigation measure. This focus on mitigation appears to be good practice, because if challenges and uncertainties are to be reflected in a strategy, then surely each must be addressed within the document.

Technological futures

How should organisations respond to the latest scientific and technological developments? Is it necessary for a strategy to address the 'state of the art'? For example, we might expect strategy developers to assess the market for emerging technologies. Organisations engaged in research and development, or with formal innovation policies, might also feel the need to incorporate details of these within the strategy.

Technological futures were only mentioned in half of the surveyed documents, notably those from organisations engaged in commercial engineering or with particularly ambitious technical goals (e.g. Toshiba, the European Space Agency). National Highways, the UK's road authority presents a useful table mapping technological innovations to different classes of road vehicles. The cells within the table are used to quantify technology readiness levels (TRLs), commercial maturity levels (CMLs), and estimates of the year when each technology is expected to become a standard feature for each class of vehicle.

Around half of the organisations under review deliver public services, so perhaps we should not be surprised to find that their strategies pay little attention to research, innovation, and emerging technologies. One government department, the UK Home Office, admits that "It's not always useful for us to try to be at the leading edge of change."[8] In general, it seems that public authorities at the national, regional, and local levels have little interest in either developing, acquiring, or anticipating the state of the art.

Box 1.2   STRATEGIC DICHOTOMIES

Technology stick OR Technology twist?

Mature technologies or 'state of the art'? Stick or twist? This is a familiar dilemma for many organisations.

When new technologies emerge, should you stick with what you have and what you know, or should your organisation make the transition immediately? Historically, these questions will have been asked many times during the great technological transitions, e.g. from sail to steam, from horse to motor vehicle, and from analogue to digital. Transitions on a smaller scale will be more frequent, but often just as significant.

Some reasons to stick: There is a cost to writing-off current assets, including the experience and skills associated with older technologies. Staff will need to be retrained. Many longer-serving personnel will choose to leave in order to continue working with the older technology. Costly redundancies may be necessary. A technology switch also cannibalises current products, processes, IP, and trade secrets. Relationships with established suppliers could be lost. The true operating costs, reliability, and public safety of the new technology may be unknown, perhaps for decades. Meanwhile, your business model might need to change, a high-risk activity for any established business, e.g. during the early years of the internet, the retail sector became consumed in a debate over 'clicks versus bricks'.

Two decades ago the Kodak Corporation, specialists in chemical-based photography, chose to twist by going digital. They didn't survive. Jobs were lost and investments ruined. Grant and Jordan ask this question: "Might Kodak have been better off by sticking with its chemical know-how, allowing its photographic business to decline while developing its interests in specialty chemicals, pharmaceuticals and healthcare?"[9] We'll never know whether that would have worked.

Some reasons to twist: In the 20th century GE used the slogan, "Progress is our most important product."[10] As a former employee I can vouch for the fact that there was little sentimentality for yesterday's technologies. The desire to progress was part of GE's DNA. Nevertheless, technological changes were only undertaken if deemed commercially viable. The business case was paramount.

New technologies are undoubtedly seductive. They enable organisations to present a positive, go-getting image. Meanwhile, employees are motivated by the prospect of developing new technical skills. Recruitment becomes easier. 'Twisting' may force competitors to respond by adopting the same technologies, perhaps disrupting their own strategic plans and budgets. Technology transitions can be spectacularly successful. Contracted to design an aircraft invisible to enemy defences, Lockheed's management at the secretive Skunk Works facility in California, opted to twist. Peter Westwick explains:

> Against the protests of Skunk Works stalwarts steeped in traditional aerodynamics, Lockheed put radar experts in charge, leaned on computer codes to design the plane, and turned to fly-by-wire flight controls to tame the unwieldy craft that resulted.[11]

What emerged was the paradigm-shifting F-117 stealth fighter.

Weighing the arguments: It's comfortable to stick with mature technologies that perform well, but this introduces the opportunity cost of not using something that may be technically better. Historians of technology, Derry and Williams, noted that sometimes "the good is the enemy of the best."[12] The philosopher of scientific revolutions, Thomas Kuhn, wrote that "retooling is an extravagance to be reserved for the occasion that demands it."[13] As a technology strategist, you must decide whether that occasion is now, later, or perhaps never. In *Mastering the Dynamics of Innovation* (1994), Utterback warns:

> To avoid the grim reaper that has carried off so many proud and prosperous firms over the past century, modern managers must develop and nourish organizational capabilities that will carry them successfully from one generation of product and process technology to the next. This may be the ultimate managerial challenge.[14]

Visions and objectives

Is it possible to write a strategy without a high-level vision? A vision describes some future state for the organisation and its technologies. We might, therefore, expect every technology strategy document to contain a vision statement. This was indeed true for most of those under review. At times, however, the distinction between visions and delivery objectives became blurred.

For example, the New Zealand Ministry of Social Development presents vision statements for each of its six "strategic themes". Its "enabling better insights" theme offers the vision that "We will extend our data platform to operational data, capable of processing high volumes of unstructured data from across a broad range [of] external sources to deliver real time and predictive analytics." The Australian Department of Defence encapsulates most of its ten-year vision statements within a feature called "STaR Shots" (where STaR is an acronym for science, technology, and research). One of these visions, for undersea surveillance systems, involves "Developing above/below water sensors ... and data fusion systems to provide remote surveillance of undersea environments over Australia's area of maritime responsibility." Vision statements are indelibly bound up with each strategy's specific time horizon. Some strategies look only a few years ahead, while others are written for a distant horizon of ten years or more. These timescales are important and will be discussed further in Chapter 3.

Objectives, on the other hand, are expected to be more detailed, specific, and measurable than visions. Thirteen of the documents presented a range of technological objectives. Good examples were provided by two organisations: the UK Space Agency CEOI and MSI Reproductive Choices.

The CEOI lists four particular objectives relating to: economic gains from earth observation (EO) technology development and sales; innovating EO technologies; strengthening EO capabilities and competences; and focusing on the benefits to be gained from close collaboration with the European Space Agency. Although these may sound like visions, a series of bullet points beneath each one provides the detail.

The charity MSI Reproductive Choices presents their technical objectives in a clear, visually impressive format. These include equipping frontline teams with digital tools to improve efficiency and clinical safety and collaborating with partners to improve the capture and use of quality data.

Interestingly, MSI describes their technical objectives as 'strategies', listing them as Strategy 1, Strategy 2, and so on. Later in this chapter, I will explain why I disagree with this terminology. Indeed, throughout my years of research, it has become clear that words such as *vision*, *goal*, *aim*, *objective*, *strategy*, and *tactic* are used in surprisingly different ways, and often interchangeably. Let's be realistic: we can't have a productive conversation about technology strategies if one person's 'vision' is another person's 'goal', or if the words 'objective' and 'strategy' are used interchangeably. This book will achieve greater consistency by developing and imposing terminological simplicity.

Of the 14 strategies under review, only the Australian Department of Defence failed to clearly enunciate a set of objectives. Instead, they were implicitly interwoven within vision statements and a section on workforce development. However, this absence of clarity may be explained by the fact that defence organisations in democratic states walk a tightrope of public accountability above a chasm of state secrets and technological uncertainty. Perhaps we should not be surprised by the absence of transparent objectives in their document.

Actions

Around one-third of the documents translated their objectives into specific actions. For example, both the City and County of San Francisco and Dundee City Council include a combination of actions and roadmaps. San Francisco's roadmaps are presented in tabular form, while Dundee uses the traditional horizontal bar graph. The European Space Agency provides a roadmap showing the application of critical technologies over three phases: "Today" (at the International Space Station), "Near-Future" (on the Moon), and "Future" (towards Mars). Toshiba's Technology Strategy offers a surprisingly low level of detail, although it's more opaque about specific responsibilities and timescales. None of the aforementioned organisations identify the teams or individuals assigned for the delivery of each action, which seems sensible given the need for confidentiality in a public document, and the frequency with which individuals and teams are likely to change.

This reveals a fundamental concern with the publication of strategies. The more detail they contain, the sooner they 'age'. Throughout this book, I will use the term *depreciation* when referring to the devaluing effects of age. The weightier strategies are likely to be out of date before they've been edited, approved, and shared with stakeholders. Arguably strategies that are lighter on detail have both greater longevity and a greater potential for real impact. When evaluating the quality of published organisational strategies, there may be truth in the dictum that 'less is more'.

What has been learned?

This concludes my brief survey of real-world technology strategies. Since 2018 I have probably studied around 40 published strategies. Here are some observations:

1 The diversity of format, length, content, and terminology across the 14 documents implies an absence of any recognised standard for the presentation of technology strategies.
2 In general, strategy documents don't have a clearly defined target audience. Were the strategy developers writing for internal stakeholders, external stakeholders, both of these groups, or for a narrow sub-group, such as investors or employees?
3 Background or contextual information was patchy, varying in both depth and quality. For example, there were few direct references to the primary organisational strategy (the business strategy).

4 Limited interest was shown in state of the art technologies. Most strategies adopted a conservative approach. Only the largest organisations showed a desire to participate in technological advances, typically through R&D, e.g. Toshiba, NASA. (Chapter 10 will examine innovation.)

5 The thought processes translating high-level organisational strategies into lower-level technology objectives were rarely explained. In fact, structured thinking was not always in evidence. This probably explains the diversity of documentation formats.

6 Most organisations avoided including implementation roadmaps or details of actions being taken. Arguably this is good practice due to concerns about document 'depreciation' caused by the dynamic nature of technological environments.

7 No single document emerged as exemplary, either in presentation or content. A 'best practice' technology strategy, if one could be established, would bear little resemblance to any of those reviewed here. (My recommendation for a strategy development process, including documentation ideas, will be introduced in Chapter 3 and described more fully in Chapter 12.)

Something we can begin to rectify immediately is the confusing terminology. In particular, what do we really mean by words such as "strategy"?

Box 1.3 ANALYTICAL TOOLS AND TECHNIQUES

Value chain analysis

Value chain analysis examines how organisations deliver value. The theory is attributed to Harvard's Michael Porter, emerging from his groundbreaking book, *Competitive Advantage* (1985).

A value chain (see Figure 1.1) illustrates the linked production stages within an organisation. Each stage is a so-called *primary activity* in the process of delivering value. These activities constitute the chronological stages of value creation, beginning with *inbound logistics*, then *operations*, *outbound logistics*, *marketing/sales*, and finally *after-sales service*. In order to be useful for analysts, each stage is broken down into constituent processes or actions. By studying the value chain, we can ensure that a technology strategy is tightly focused on an organisation's principal value-adding activities.

There are also four *support activities* which enable the value chain to function. They are listed as *firm infrastructure, HR management, technology development,* and *procurement*. Strategically, these are less critical than the primary activities.

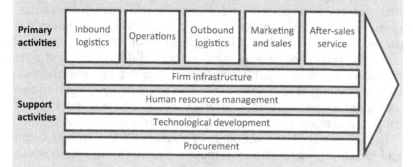

Figure 1.1 The value chain

Defining *strategy*

So much has been written about strategy in the past 50 years, especially business strategy, that if every book and article were laid end-to-end they would probably stretch half way around the world. However, this book is different because its focus is upon the strategies pursued by technologists and engineers, rather than those by business leaders and entrepreneurs.

Napoleon Bonaparte claimed that learning about strategy was "the only means" of becoming a great military leader, writing that, "Your own genius will be enlightened and improved by this study".[15] The modern fascination with strategy owes a considerable debt to such military men as Napoleon, Clausewitz, and Eisenhower. Indeed, the word itself is of Greek origin meaning "generalship".[16] However, our interests lie outside the military realm.

In the course of preparing this book, I have collected many definitions of strategy. Here, I will look at a few authoritative examples, then settle upon a working definition. In Colin Gray's *Theory of Strategy* (2018) we are offered probably the most succinct of all the definitions. Strategy's "basic structure" consists of "Ends, Ways, Means, and Assumptions."[17] In other words, it's about knowing where we want to go, which methods to adopt, and which resources to use, ensuring that the ends, ways, and means are all consistent with a set of assumptions about the operating environment. Later, Gray emphasises that a strategy can only be characterised as good or successful "with reference to its consequences".[18] In other words, it is unwise to proclaim the merits of a strategy before it has even been executed. It might *look* good when produced, but only *becomes* good in retrospect.

In *Good Strategy, Bad Strategy* (2017), Richard Rumelt provides a comprehensive analysis, including criticisms of the way that strategy is developed and communicated in many organisations. He offers this definition: "The core content of a strategy is a *diagnosis* of the situation at hand, the creation or identification of a *guiding policy* for dealing with the critical difficulties, and a set of *coherent actions*."[19] He emphasises that "A good strategy ... creates strength through the coherence of its design."[20] From this we might conclude that a strategy needs to be a package of proposed actions, each designed to complement the others.

In their textbook, *Foundations of Strategy* (2015), Robert Grant and Judith Jordan remind us of the dynamic environments in which strategies are made. As a consequence, strategic plans are always incomplete. "It is during the implementation phase that the gaps are filled in and, because circumstances change and unforeseen issues arise, inevitably the strategy changes."[21] This uncertainty could influence the way that strategies are formulated. Perhaps there is some merit in the argument that strategies should be less prescriptive about the precise direction of travel, emphasising instead the creation of opportunities, so that a strategy becomes "the management of a portfolio of options".[22] This tension between the production of comprehensively detailed strategies, and the fluid environment within which those strategies are deployed, will become clear later when *uncertainty* is examined.

A couple of other terms which may be worth clarifying at this stage are *grand strategy* and *tactics*. The former is a rarely used label for a concise statement of high-level strategy. It typically has a long time horizon and describes objectives in limited detail. If, in the late 1990s, Google had written a grand strategy for the company (which they probably didn't) it might have been something like this: *To create a natural monopoly of engaged users attracted initially to a comprehensive internet search facility, then introduced to complementary online products, enabling real-time monetisation of the data acquired.* There is no detail in that grand strategy, but it would have been good enough to energise the operational team and point them in a particular direction. (Of course, I wrote that Google example with the benefit of hindsight. A new company's grand strategy is unlikely to correlate with its evolution over the longer term.)

Tactics, on the other hand, may be very short-lived. A tactic is an action or initiative taken in support of a strategy.[23] It is sometimes said that 'tactics win battles, strategies win wars.'

Tactics may be devised and undertaken by frontline staff without any direct input from the strategists. In theory, if your 'troops' understand the organisational strategy, then they ought to be capable of both devising and executing appropriate tactics. This frontline empowerment is influenced by the way that a strategy is communicated to staff (assuming it is communicated at all). This is something we will explore later, in Chapter 12, when a practical guide to the development and communication of technology strategies is presented.

Although we tend to associate strategies with larger organisations, such as armies and companies, it is also possible to use them in other contexts. Of particular interest here are *product strategies*. These involve longer-term thinking about individual solutions, product ranges, and end-user services. Product strategies are concerned with quality standards, service accessibility, compatibility with complementary products, licensing, sourcing, maintainability, ethical use, and much, much more. Consequently, in order to give our full attention to strategy as a concept, we need to remember that it can be applied both to organisations *and* their products. It might be argued that product strategy is an alternative name for a tactic in support of an organisational strategy, but that would be misleading because it's possible to think strategically both at the organisational level *and* at the product level. Tactics may also be devised for both levels.

Henry Mintzberg has been one of the leading strategic thinkers of recent times. His writings include an observation that the vast majority of projected strategic outcomes never materialise and that only 10% of actions within most companies can be attributed to formal strategies. The other 90% of what companies do is 'emergent strategy'.[24]

Explained by Julia Sloan, author of *Learning to Think Strategically* (2020), emergent strategy is "the accumulation of day-to-day decisions, disjointed initiatives, and actions taken by managers in response to everyday work demands, without any master plan or comprehensive strategic concept to guide them."[25] In summarising Mintzberg's work, Grant and Jordan explain that "In practice, strategy making almost always involves a combination of centrally driven rational design and decentralized adaptation." The adaptation is the "realized strategy".[26] It is difficult to disagree with this analysis. Figure 1.2 presents my visual representation of how an original strategy, denoted by three simple shapes, could be substantially transformed during implementation.

It is because of this uncertainty of outcomes that some readers may already be sceptical about the merits of developing any strategy at all. Indeed there are plenty of detractors willing to extol the

Original strategy   Emerging strategy   Realised strategy

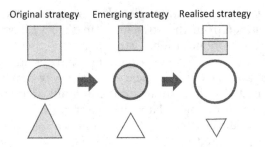

Figure 1.2 The evolution of a strategy during implementation

virtues of a strategy-free zone, although business architect, Eben Hewitt, is scathing about those who under-value strategising:

> Executives in some organizations may ignore or even show outright contempt for strategy. They proudly act on instinct and inspiration, and consider any strategy as the work of bureaucrats or dreamers disconnected from the real world, or as something quaint and cute that best belongs on the shelf to collect dust with the rest of the stuffed animals. People can enjoy the freewheeling lifestyle and moderate success that sometimes accompany this mode, but this is not how market leaders are typically made[27]

One of the aims of this book is to overcome this scepticism among technologists and engineers. It will explain why a thoughtfully presented strategy, however flawed, is better than no strategy at all. It costs relatively little to produce a credible strategy, yet the potential long-run benefits (the return on investment) may be substantial, in fact *very* substantial. Rumelt points out that a company's strategy "merely has to be *more right* than those of its rivals. If you can peer into the fog of change and see 10 percent more clearly than others see, then you may gain an edge."[28] I would put it this way: in competitive environments margins are tight, so if a technology strategy is able to deliver a 2 or 3% improvement over your strategy-free opponent, then that translates into a substantial uplift, particularly if those improvements 'compound' year on year.

Earlier I asked this question: What do we really mean by the word *strategy*? To obtain a definition, let's briefly review what has emerged so far, some of which may be inferred from the discussion above:

- Strategies involve ends, ways, and means, and the quality of a strategy can only be judged retrospectively.
- There must be a common purpose, such as the sustainable

growth of a business, the success of a product, or the long-term stability of an organisation.

- Strategy development involves some form of diagnosis, which leads to options.
- A vision for the future enables the identification of objectives.
- Objectives must be met through a set of concerted actions – coordinated, coherent, and non-conflicting.
- Tactics are discrete actions which support the strategy, often devised by professionals on the frontline.
- All strategies are executed within dynamic operational environments, and this dynamism devalues or depreciates those strategies which fail to adapt or evolve.

DEFINITIONS FOR *STRATEGY* AND *TACTIC*

A strategy is an evolving package of concerted actions, designed with a common purpose.

A tactic is a discrete action executed in support of a strategy.

The development process

How are strategies developed? Is there a method?

Yes there is, or more accurately, yes there *are*; in fact, too many to document here. Most of the established models, tools, or frameworks for developing strategies have been devised either within business consultancies (for supporting clients) or business schools (for publishing and graduate-level teaching). Ironically, despite this superabundance of methods, or perhaps because of it, there is no internationally recognised or standard procedure for producing business or technology strategies.

Let's look briefly at two typical models used in the business world: APIC and SOSTAC. The former is a simple four-stage process, attributed to the American academic and marketing theorist, Philip Kotler.[29] APIC is an acronym representing each of four stages: 1) Audit and analysis, 2) Planning, 3) Implementation, and 4) Control and evaluation. On a superficial level, this clearly describes the stages one goes through in preparing, executing, and assessing a strategy. However, one wonders which part or parts of this process constitute the strategy. Is it simply the plan? Or is the strategy a combination of the plan and its subsequent implementation? Or perhaps a strategy is the collective term for the entire process.

SOSTAC is a proprietary tool developed in the 1990s by PR Smith (a marketing consultancy). Like APIC, the SOSTAC name is an acronym for six procedural steps: 1) Situation analysis, 2) Objectives, 3) Strategy, 4) Tactics, 5) Actions, and 6) Control. In the SOSTAC model the third step, 'strategy', follows the development of objectives. Indeed strategy is defined as "how you are going to fulfil the objectives".[30] Therefore SOSTAC separates the 'objectives' from the 'strategy'. This contrasts with my earlier definition, where I concluded that a strategy is the collective term for *an evolving package of concerted actions, designed with a common purpose*. I therefore see the objectives as an intrinsic part of the strategy. In fact the SOSTAC definition of strategy is what I will later call the *Statement of Delivery*, an important feature of any formal strategy document.

Many decades ago it was believed that strategies could be developed using 'scientific management' techniques of data gathering and analysis. Organisations could *plan* their futures. Indeed plans were almost synonymous with strategies. However, the emergence of a faster moving, more complex, and uncertain world has led to so-called "post-modernist" and "new modernist" approaches to strategy development.[31] Strategies are now required to be more flexible and responsive to change. Strategy development has become less top-down and hierarchical. Instead, it relies upon middle management and frontline staff to identify strategic requirements and to devise the tactics needed to pursue objectives. This historical generalisation reflects the way that organisational cultures have also evolved in recent decades.

However, at no point during this research have I encountered any standard frameworks or processes for developing technology strategies. This puts an obligation on me to propose such a method, which will be one of this book's key deliverables.

The strategists

To be valuable, a strategy needs to be viable. This means that the people who create strategies should have substantial organisational knowledge and experience. They must understand what they are strategising for and its internal capabilities. A non-viable strategy will not only fail, but it could undermine an organisation's confidence in the strategy-making process. If frontline staff don't have faith in the strategy, their enthusiasm for its delivery will falter.

This raises questions about the effectiveness of using external consultants or new employees (e.g. a recently recruited CTO) to lead the strategy development. Will these outsiders know enough about the organisation and its culture to make the right choices?

One of the conclusions emerging from my research is that an employer's most experienced technologists and engineers hold the key to the successful production of technology strategies. The remaining chapters are therefore dedicated to the development of this expertise.

Glossary for this chapter (Items in bold are also defined in the same table)

business strategy	The primary or top-level **strategy** issued by an organisation. It is usually designed with the aim of securing the organisation's long-term future while delivering benefits to key stakeholders.
depreciation	The devaluation of a documented **strategy** as its contents are gradually invalidated by changes in the operational environment.
grand strategy	A rarely used label for a concise statement of high-level **strategy**. It typically has a long **time horizon** and describes objectives in limited detail.
objective	One of many specific ways that an organisation will deliver on its **vision**. An objective ought to be unambiguous. Either it is achieved, or it isn't.
primary activities	The stages of value creation in a **value chain**. According to Porter's theory, they consist of inbound logistics, operations, outbound logistics, marketing/sales, and after-sales service.
product strategy	A **strategy** developed for a particular commercial solution, such as a consumer good, an end-user service, or an entire product range.
strategy	An evolving package of concerted actions, designed with a common purpose (such as the success and longevity of an organisation or product).
tactic	A discrete action executed in support of a **strategy**.
time horizon	The execution period for which a **strategy** has been designed. In the technological realm horizons are typically three to five years, but can be much longer.
value chain	A series of linked stages within a production system. Each link represents a so-called **primary activity** in the process of delivering value to stakeholders.
vision	A description of some future state for an organisation, its products and technologies.

Notes

1 The strategy documents listed in Table 1.1 are as follows:

- Australian Department of Defence (undated) *Defence Science and Technology Strategy 2030*, available at https://www.dst.defence.gov.au/strategy/defence-science-and-technology-strategy-2030 (Accessed: 31 August 2022).

- City of Coquitlam (2018) *2019–2024 Coquitlam Technology Strategy*, available at https://www.coquitlam.ca/620/Coquitlam-Technology-Strategy (Accessed: 31 August 2022).
- Toshiba Corporation (2018) *Technology Strategy*, available at https://www.toshiba.co.jp/about/ir/en/pr/pdf/tpr20181122e_1.pdf (Accessed: 09 September 2022).
- UK Space Agency, Centre for Earth Observation Instrumentation (2019) *Technology Strategy*, available at https://www.gov.uk/government/publications/uk-earth-observation-technology-strategy (Accessed: 31 August 2022).
- European Space Agency (2022) *Technology Strategy*, available at: https://esamultimedia.esa.int/docs/technology/ESA_Technology_Strategy_Version_1_0.pdf (Accessed: 06 October 2023).
- NASA (undated) *Strategic Plan 2022*, available at https://www.nasa.gov/sites/default/files/atoms/files/fy_22_strategic_plan.pdf (Accessed: 02 September 2022).
- Dundee City Council (undated) *Information Technology Strategy*, available at https://www.dundeecity.gov.uk/sites/default/files/publications/dcc_it_strategy_final.docx (Accessed: 03 September 2022).
- City and County of San Francisco (undated) *Information and Communication Technology Plan FY 2022–26*, available at https://sf.gov/coit-strategy (Accessed: 03 September 2022).
- Social Security Scotland (2022) *Digital and Technology Strategy 2022–2025*, available at https://www.socialsecurity.gov.scot/asset-storage/production/downloads/Digital-and-Technology-Strategy-2022-%E2%80%93-25.pdf (Accessed: 03 September 2022).
- UK Home Office (2021) *Digital, Data and Technology 2024 Strategy*, available at https://www.gov.uk/government/publications/home-office-digital-data-and-technology-strategy-2024 (Accessed: 04 September 2022).
- Irish Department of Agriculture, Food and the Marine (2021) *Information Management and Technology Strategy 2021–2024*, available at https://assets.gov.ie/133805/f322bfba-c5fa-4ac5-915e-bdabe280f6e5.pptx (Accessed: 04 September 2022).
- New Zealand Ministry of Social Development (2022) *Technology Strategy*, available at https://www.msd.govt.nz/about-msd-and-our-work/publications-resources/corporate/msd-technology-strategy.html (Accessed: 04 September 2022).
- National Highways (2022) *Operational Technology: our 2035 strategy*, available at: https://nationalhighways.co.uk/media/n1edbo0z/operational_technology_strategy_2035_issue-may-2022.pdf (Accessed: 05 September 2022).
- MSI Reproductive Choices (2021) *Digital and Technology Strategy* (summary version), available at https://www.msichoices.org/news-and-insights/resources/choice-in-a-digital-age-msi-choices-digital-and-technology-strategy/ (Accessed: 05 September 2022).

2 City of Coquitlam, *2019–2024 Coquitlam Technology Strategy*.
3 Hewitt, E. (2018) *Technology Strategy Patterns*. Sebastopol, CA: O'Reilly. xvii.
4 McDougall, W.A. (1997) *The Heavens and the Earth*. Baltimore: Johns Hopkins University Press. 196.

5 National Centre for Universities and Business (NCUB) (2012) *Enhancing Collaboration, Creating Value: Business Interaction with the UK Research Base in Four Sectors*, available at https://www.ncub.co.uk/insight/enhancing-collaboration-creating-value-business-interaction-with-the-uk-research-base-in-four-sectors/ (Accessed: 05 October 2022).

6 Afuah, A. (2003) *Innovation Management*. New York: OUP. 163–165.

7 New Zealand Ministry of Social Development, *Technology Strategy*.

8 UK Home Office, *Digital, Data and Technology 2024 Strategy*.

9 Grant, R.M. and Jordan, J. (2015) *Foundations of Strategy*. Chichester: Wiley. 88.

10 McDougall, *The Heavens and the Earth*. 69.

11 Westwick, P. (2020) *Stealth: The Secret Contest to Invent Invisible Aircraft*. New York: OUP. 192.

12 Derry, T.K. and Williams, T.I. (1961) *A Short History of Technology*. London (UK): OUP. 277.

13 Kuhn, T.S. (1996) *The Structure of Scientific Revolutions*. Chicago: University of Chicago Press. 76.

14 Utterback, J.M. (1994) *Mastering the Dynamics of Innovation*. Harvard: HBS Press. xix.

15 Bonaparte, N. (2015) *The Officer's Manual: Napoleon's Maxims of War*, available at https://www.gutenberg.org/files/50750/50750-h/50750-h.htm#MAXIM_LXXVIII (Accessed: 21 January 2022).

16 Grant and Jordan, *Foundations of Strategy*. 8.

17 Gray, C.S. (2018) *Theory of Strategy*. Oxford: OUP. 4–5.

18 Gray, *Theory of Strategy*. 48.

19 Rumelt, R. (2017) *Good Strategy, Bad Strategy*. London: Profile Books. 79.

20 Rumelt, *Good Strategy, Bad Strategy*. 9.

21 Grant and Jordan. 313.

22 Grant and Jordan. 352.

23 Gray. 48.

24 Grant and Jordan. 15–16.

25 Sloan, J. (2020) *Learning to Think Strategically*. Abingdon: Routledge. 64.

26 Grant and Jordan. 16.

27 Hewitt, *Technology Strategy Patterns*. 101.

28 Rumelt. 193.

29 Blümelhuber, C. (2007) 'Goodbye and good luck, Mr Kotler'. *Expertise*. Available at http://www.iot.ntnu.no/innovation/norsi-pims-courses/Service-Innovation-Pedersen-Kristensson/Bl%C3%BCmelhuber%20(2007).pdf (Accessed: 30 September 2022).

30 PR Smith, 'SOSTAC Official Site' Available at: https://prsmith.org (Accessed: 01 October 2022).

31 McGrath, J. and Bates, B. (2013) *The Little Book of Big Management Theories*. Edinburgh: Pearson. 152–155.

2 Key components
The parts that make the whole

This chapter presents

- An examination of the book's key underlying concepts.

This chapter establishes

- Important relationships between *design*, *systems*, *technology*, and *engineering*.
- A new definition of 'technology'.

Before constructing any complex device or machine, it's wise to lay out the components on a workbench or floor. This chapter aims to do something similar with the book's core concepts, which include *design, artificiality, systems, technology,* and *engineering*.

It is my view that we can produce better technology strategies if we have a better understanding of these concepts.

This chapter is therefore largely theoretical, although it will be interspersed with plenty of insights and practical examples. For the non-theoretical reader (or even the skim reader), a Glossary is supplied at the end.

Design is unnatural

The work of technologists and engineers is frequently associated with the term *design*. For example, we have design thinking, design life, design for manufacturing, human-centred design, dominant design, open design, and design for inclusion. Projects are often subject to a formal design phase, perhaps involving product designers or design engineers. So-called 'elegant design' is often synonymous with engineering excellence. It would seem, therefore, that design is inseparable from technology and engineering.

Objectively, however, design is not an exclusively technical activity. In fact, *everyone* is engaged in designing. Donald Norman, a leading design theorist, notes that "All artificial things are designed" and that people have therefore been designing things since prehistoric times.[1] In a similar vein Nigel Cross, author of

DOI: 10.4324/9781003472919-3

Engineering Design Methods, observes that "Everything around us that is not a simple, untouched piece of nature has been designed by someone."[2] As a species we've been busy designing, both as amateurs and professionals, for hundreds of thousands of years. Guru Madhavan of the US National Academy of Engineering urges us to "Look down from an airplane 4 miles above the ground and all you see are systems of nature and engineering. The same is true of the view from the ground, and on into the heavens."[3] Design is perhaps synonymous with the human urge to satisfy needs and solve problems by shaping, changing, and making things. The work of technologists and engineers always creates artificiality. Technologists and engineers are therefore designers.

Let's establish a working definition. Cross describes designing as "proceeding from the statement of the problem to a statement of the solution".[4] This feels a little too abstract for our purposes. A more generic definition is offered by the *McGraw-Hill Dictionary of Scientific and Technical Terms* (2003) where design is "The act of conceiving and planning the structure and parameter values of a system, device, process, or work of art."[5] Writing in 2010 John Turnbull, a chemical engineer and Fellow of the UK's Royal Academy of Engineering, said that design is "the really core and fundamental engineering activity".[6] Another Fellow of the Academy, aerospace engineer Chris Elliott, agrees: "The element that makes engineering different from science and craft is design. That is not popular with university departments, which are mostly made up either of physicists or of people who are actually trying to pursue the craft of making things ... but my thesis remains that engineering is design."[7] We will look more closely at engineering as a professional and academic discipline later in this chapter.

Box 2.1 ANALYTICAL TOOLS AND TECHNIQUES

The Double Diamond Design Process Model

In 2004 the UK Design Council introduced the *Double Diamond Design Process Model*, described as "a clear, comprehensive and visual description of the design process."[8] The model (Figure 2.1) illustrates best practice in the design of almost any *thing*, from consumer devices to technology strategies.

A designer must first discover the true nature of the challenge or problem. That's not always obvious at the beginning of the process. Customers or managers don't always know what they *really* want or need, but once the problem has been defined, designers can move on to developing ideas. This leads to the delivery of a solution.

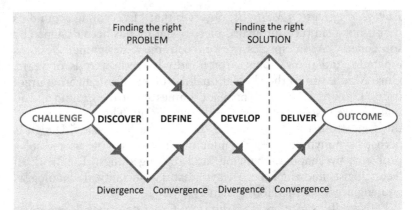

Figure 2.1 The double diamond design process model

The illustration of this process consists of two successive 'diamonds'. Each diamond combines divergent and convergent thinking. The former involves research and the exploration of possibilities, while the latter leads to a focus upon either the problem definition or a solution and outcome.

The divergent phases sometimes create the impression that a designer lacks the self-discipline to reach a solution, but the model explains why this initial divergence is necessary for achieving the best outcome. **Have faith in professional designers and engineers. There is a purpose to their seemingly wayward, divergent thinking.**

Let's briefly consider a hypothetical (though very likely) event 300,000 years ago. An early human wants to break open a coconut. She realises that a pounding stone is needed. It must be weighty, but fit comfortably within her hand. One side of the stone should be pointed for piercing the shell. She walks among the randomly strewn rocks and only stops when she sees the correct size and shape. She picks it up. It feels right. The subsequent pounding successfully yields the coconut's milk and flesh. In a similar vein, technologists and engineers in the 21st century regularly deliver products and outcomes by starting with a specification (not always in writing). From this they *design* a path to delivery, such as a project plan, creating a product, sometimes called a 'solution'. If all goes well, this yields satisfaction for the client. The early human in our example also began with an unwritten specification, subsequently designing and executing a solution. Although made only of a natural material, the 'hammer' was *artificial* because the stone had been carefully selected according to the specification, and also because it required human intelligence and action to transform it into a functioning tool. That particular rock, and the way it was handled, became the solution to the problem. It was pure engineering.

Hence, we can say that all technological solutions are engineered (designed) in order to yield some value for one or more stakeholders, e.g. our employers, our clients, or simply ourselves. The significance of this statement will become clearer later in the chapter as we look more closely at the meaning of 'technology'.

Box 2.2   Exceptional people

Human beings are *natural*. We are part of nature. In that sense, we have the same status as trees, insects, and clouds. Consequently, everything we do – eating, talking, designing, and destroying – are natural activities. To believe otherwise is to suggest that people are unnatural, or exceptional. All technologies may therefore be perceived as works of nature. The Golden Gate Bridge is a work of nature, and so is the neutron bomb.

However, we could be described as 'exceptional' in one sense. We are unusually intelligent, and something unique happens when we use that intelligence to create value by adapting other natural entities. This is what is meant by *artificiality*.

Something adapted by a human being becomes, in common parlance, artificial and unnatural. This is the context in which these terms are used in this book.

Artefacts and artificiality

We can divide our environment into two groups of entities. The natural and the artificial. Everything unchanged by humans could be described as being natural, e.g. imagine the Earth before humans existed. Everything subsequently manipulated by human design could therefore be described as artificial, e.g. the things we make such as shoes, furniture, canals, gardens, and televisions. Some of these artificial entities we call 'technologies'.

There is an overlap between the untouched, natural world and the world of artificiality. This is the set of natural entities *adapted* to our needs. This set includes the rock/hammer described earlier, also selectively bred plants and animals, plus the use of animals (including people) to perform technological tasks, such as train drivers, or sniffer dogs at airports. We can represent these ideas in a simple diagram. See Figure 2.2.

It is not entirely clear why we refer to some entities as technologies, but not others. Most readers would probably agree

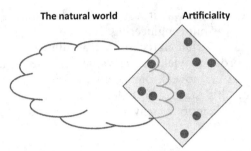

Figure 2.2 The distribution of 'technologies' among the natural and artificial environments

that a television is a technology, but what about an item of furniture, or a garden, or a sniffer dog?

In reality, there are no *rules* about how to use the word 'technology'. If we want to call a sniffer dog a technology, we can. It's our choice. This may sound arbitrary. Indeed, precise definitions of technology are elusive, as my research will show. However, if we can understand what is meant by this word it might provide insights during the process of developing technology and engineering strategies.

By the end of this chapter, I hope to bring more clarity to these issues with a new definition of technology, but before then we need to explore another important theme: the *system*.

Systems unlimited

Most of us use the term 'system' in daily conversation, but do we really know what it means? How might our understanding of this term be important for the development of technology and engineering strategies?

ISO 15288, an international standard addressing engineered systems, defines them as "an arrangement of parts or elements that together exhibit behavior or meaning that the individual constituents do not."[9] Alternatively, a team at the Massachusetts Institute of Technology (MIT) describes them as "organised constructs for creating value over time."[10] I like to think of systems as multi-component entities creating value by transforming inputs into outputs. Washing machines, aeroplanes, and postal systems all satisfy these criteria. Furthermore, each of these is an artificial entity, purposely designed by humans. Does this imply that all systems are technologies?

Confusingly, some 'systems' don't have an engineered history or designed purpose. Consider the Solar System or a natural ecosystem.

Even a 'national transportation system' is not a purposely designed system; it's a collective term for various smaller-scale, independently managed systems, often poorly coordinated. We might describe these types of systems as non-engineered networks of interactions. Given that this book is concerned with the work of technologists and engineers, it seems reasonable to focus here upon the former meaning of the word. In other words, systems are much more than uncoordinated networks of interactions. For our purposes, **systems are consciously designed, they feature components, inputs and outputs, and they create value over time.**

An important question now emerges: Where does a system begin or, more importantly, where does it end? What are the system boundaries? Sometimes multiple systems will be integrated into a system of subsystems. The undercarriage of an airliner is a system of multiple hydraulic, mechanical, and electronic components, some of which are clearly systems in their own right. So an undercarriage is, at the very least, a system of subsystems. Within the same hierarchy of systems, the undercarriage is a subsystem of the aircraft, which in turn performs a function within the global system of civil aviation.

So, a single system may actually be a multi-tiered hierarchy of other systems. There will also be some stand-alone systems that are not integrated with the hierarchy, but which interact with it.

An environment in which independent systems are interacting is often known as a 'system of systems'. This is an extremely complex phenomenon, but something which nevertheless needs to be understood and managed by people.

Engineers face the challenge of melding all these systems of subsystems into one comprehensible unit in order to generate and deliver value. Normally they do an extremely good job, but the problem of identifying boundaries between systems can be problematic. For the civil aviation industry, this problem was exposed tragically in 2002. In July of that year, two aircraft collided over Überlingen (Germany) with many fatalities. The cause was found to be a discrepancy between the instructions issued by an aircraft subsystem, the Traffic Collision Avoidance System (or TCAS), and the instructions from air traffic control (ATC) using internationally recognised working practices. In a nutshell, the system boundaries for the TCAS were not those of the ATC. This resulted in a conflict of instructions and consequent disaster.[11] Was anyone to blame here, or is a world of overlapping systems of systems simply too difficult to fully comprehend and manage?

The civil aviation industry may be described as a 'socio-technical system', a complex web of people interacting with multiple technologies. The pilots, air traffic controllers, freight handlers, refuellers, and maintenance engineers work with aircraft, ground radar, flight scheduling software, service vehicles, and precision tools. The aviation industry is clearly a system of systems. These almost boundary-less, multi-layered phenomena have immense implications for the competencies, expectations, and responsibilities of technologists and engineers. **For strategists, they represent the greatest challenge of all.**

The analysis of technological interactions and their boundaries is often referred to as 'systems thinking', and might be regarded as a key skill for technology strategists. Later in the book, we will return to the theme of systems thinking while exploring related topics, including complexity science and the discipline known as systems engineering.

Before then, let's get back to basics. If this is a book about technology strategy, then we need to establish a definition of 'technology'. This quest for definitions is not a purely academic exercise because, as this book will demonstrate, getting these right will help us to improve forecasting, innovate more successfully, and ultimately to produce better strategies.

Technology and technologists

If any politicians or journalists are reading this, they might wish to take note: the word 'technology' is not shorthand for digital consumer products and services. In recent decades, the extraordinary growth and impact of digital technologies have encouraged this lazy misnomer. We need to be more precise with our words because, as economist W.B. Arthur explains (and this should interest both politicians and journalists), "More than anything else technology creates our world. It creates our wealth, our economy, our very way of being."[12] Arthur isn't referring specifically to computers or the internet. His list of technologies includes toilets, stoves, cars, buildings, steam engines, agriculture, and printing presses. We could add many more to this list, including coffee grinders, fusion reactors, bicycles, antibiotics, bridges, laser surgery, screwdrivers, rockets, distilleries, and books. Technology is, without doubt, a vast field of study. We therefore need to impose some sort of order and structure to our analysis.

On the first occasion that I was asked to produce a technology strategy, the client was an international engineering consultancy, with hundreds of professional staff working both in company offices and on client sites. Here, the technology was mainly digital: networks, desktop computers, laptops, peripherals, servers, and so on. The strategy which emerged was divided into provisions for *hardware, software, architecture, data,* and *people.* The latter category related to matters of recruitment, skills, training, and so on. This arrangement seemed to work and was well received, but it raised an interesting question: How should a strategy for non-digital technologies (e.g. for a shipbuilder, railway operator, or chemical plant) be structured? Does each type of technology require a unique approach?

Inevitably, this led to a deeper dive into the concept of technology itself. In what ways do technologies differ from one another, and what commonalities do they share? The answers to these questions might help us to improve the process of developing strategies, enabling a generic or standardised approach.

This line of thinking has led to a new definition of technology and an original method for developing technology strategies. How I got there is revealed within this chapter and beyond.

Artists and artisans

In 1855, George Wilson became the University of Edinburgh's first Professor of Technology. Indeed he was probably the first person to hold that title in the English-speaking world. In his inaugural lecture, he admitted that the word 'technology' might be "unfamiliar to English ears".[13]

The meaning of this word evolved through the late 18th and 19th centuries. According to the philosopher of science and technology, Sven Hansson, it originally denoted "knowledge about the skills and devices of craftspeople", but by the dawn of the 20th century it meant "the actual tools, machines, and procedures, rather than ... knowledge about them."[14]

Technology was also considered to be an artistic endeavour or a branch of the arts. Indeed it translates from the Greek as "Science of the Arts".[15] This might seem alien to us today, but the terms "industrial arts" and "useful arts" were commonly used when referring to tools and machinery. Article 1 of the US Constitution, for instance, explicitly protects intellectual property in order "to promote the progress of science and useful arts."[16]

In his lecture, Professor Wilson explained that all of the craft-based arts serve humanity. Therefore, just as the crafts of music and painting provide people with pleasure or psychological needs, so the crafts of the industrial arts provide for our physical needs. Technologies serve to "fill the hungry stomach with food or to clothe the naked body". By this definition, **artists and artisans are in the same business: meeting the needs of humanity.**

In 1901, the aeronautical pioneer Wilbur Wright was explaining that humans had hitherto failed to master powered flight because "the art must be highly developed before any flight of any considerable duration at all can be obtained."[17] Eight years later, with record-breaking flights regularly making the news, the journal *Scientific American* called it a "new art".[18] Therefore, Professor Wilson's general interpretation of the arts, including technology, as 'craft-based activities serving humanity' (to paraphrase him) sounds reasonable. As a definition of technology, however, it's too imprecise.

In the quest for more precise language we might define the arts, both aesthetic and industrial, as *intelligent combinations of components, the whole delivering greater value than the sum of the parts.* Here 'value' is an important term, because where there is value, there must also be a beneficiary. These components of art can include musical notes, dance moves, canvases, and paints (i.e. the aesthetic arts) or they can be electric motors, chemical catalysts, or gear mechanisms (i.e. the 'useful arts', or technologies).

The idea that any successful technology is the work of 'artists' also suggests that a complex engineered product, such as an aeroplane, metaphorically resembles a great symphony, a ballet, or perhaps a large and impressive oil painting. Each of the discrete elements or components may be appreciated for its particular virtues, but most of the value is created from the balance and harmony of the overall piece. Arthur makes the following observation:

> The reason engineering is held in less esteem than other creative fields is that unlike music or architecture, the public has not been trained to appreciate a particularly well-executed piece of technology.[19]

We might therefore conclude that **the aesthetic arts and the useful arts (technologies) are compositions or assemblages of things, designed to yield value.** This takes us a little closer to a precise definition of technology.

Definitions, categories, and types

There are, however, other ways to examine what is meant by *technology*. It could be viewed more holistically as, in Arthur's words, "the entire collection of devices and engineering practices available to a culture."[20] This resembles my use of the phrase "technological realm" earlier in the book. People often remark that they are "interested in technology", without specifying any particular examples, and many news organisations have web pages or printed supplements simply entitled *Technology*. What is that supposed to mean? What's included? What's excluded?

Fortunately, these vague meanings are rarely found in scientific, engineering, or manufacturing environments, where most communications are characterised by greater precision and purpose. This is essential for technology strategists, who need to have a more granular focus on their subject.

Somewhat closer to the strategist's remit is the suggestion by management researcher Bishnu Sharma that "A firm's technology is defined as the knowledge, tools/equipment, people, procedures/ techniques and activities used to transform organizational inputs into outputs."[21] Here, the organisation and its technologies are almost a single entity. Similarly, economist Giovanni Dosi describes technology in terms of knowledge, methods, and procedures.[22] Sharma and Dosi are both defining technology as possessing material (physical) and non-material characteristics.

It is undoubtedly true that there is more to technologies than visible, material components. For example, a radio is useless without the electromagnetic spectrum, and a computer network is merely a jumble of cables and routers without a designed architecture. So technologies need to be understood as **a conflation of both material and non-material elements, or components.**

Some of the sources used for this book propose categorisations or types of technologies, though not always successfully. A relatively unconvincing classification is presented by the physicist and specialist in the application of technologies, Ernest Braun. In his book *Technology in Context* (1998), he identified three types of technology in commercial environments: *production, product,* and *ancillary.*[23] A production technology is one used in manufacturing processes. This includes both tools and machines. A product technology, on the other hand, is the output from a manufacturing process – the product itself. The third category, ancillary technologies, are those which support the manufacturing process: heating, power, ventilation, and so on. This disintegrates under scrutiny because, of course, many production technologies (such as tools) emerge firstly as product technologies before being integrated within a manufacturing process. Meanwhile, all ancillary technologies are also likely to be manufactured products. It's surely easier to say that *all* technologies are produced or created in some way (i.e. they are designed and assembled from components) and that some products are for use in manufacturing, some are for consumption or 'end use', while others are for ancillary use. That makes slightly more sense, but it feels clumsy.

A special category of technology, mentioned by many commentators, is one that facilitates the growth of yet more technologies. These are usually known as *enabling* technologies, although we might also classify them as *disruptive technologies*. The steam engine, electricity, and the computer have been among the most enabling/disruptive technologies of the past 300 years, each spawning thousands of related innovations.

Does this mean that some technologies should be classified as 'non-enabling'? I would suggest not, because surely we can never know what future uses may be found for any technology. Therefore, each has the *potential* to become an enabling technology. So, once again, this is not a helpful categorisation.

Consequently, after nearly four years of study, I have concluded that there is little to be gained from placing technologies into categories. All typologies evaporate under scrutiny. However, I do believe that we are capable of distinguishing between a technology and a non-technology. This is a more useful activity and something which will become intrinsic to the theory of technology described below.

Technology and science

Let's now explore technology's relationship with science, because this could lead to further insights. Allan Afuah, a researcher and writer on business strategy and innovation, describes the classic "unidirectional model" according to which "basic science yields discoveries, which then lead to applied research, which in turn leads to invention and commercialization."[24]

There are plenty of examples to support this idea that technology is a form of applied science. In the 19th century, the chemist Ludwig Mond was able to create some of the world's largest and most successful chemical manufacturing operations, supported by his teams of dedicated scientists. In 1889, Mond claimed that "The slow methodical investigation of natural phenomena is the father of industrial progress."[25] Technology historian Daniel Headrick also describes how, in the 1970s, the scientists Herbert Boyer and Stanley Cohen developed gene splicing techniques and the associated equipment necessary for DNA replication on an industrial scale. This led to the founding of Genentech for manufacturing insulin, "thereby launching the biotechnology industry."[26]

The Mond and Genentech examples are just two of many which support the 'unidirectional' idea that technology is merely the application of science. It's important to note, however, that the chemical, pharmaceutical, and biotech industries are, unlike most other sectors, much more likely to employ scientists in dedicated laboratories. So perhaps this model is being selective with the facts; it sees 'applied science' only where science is being applied. In other words, it may not be a universal rule.

The main reason for this linkage between science and technology is that the latter relies upon the exploitation of natural phenomena.[27] For example, accurate timekeeping is facilitated by the oscillation of quartz crystals, while radar uses the phenomenon of electromagnetic wave reflections.[28] Indeed, it's quite easy to compile a listing of the natural phenomena upon which technologies depend. These include gravity, magnetism, momentum, chemical properties, the lifecycle of plants, inertia, atmospheric pressure, radiation, the four states of matter, geological characteristics, and many, many more. Hence the observation by science historian George Basalla that many modern artefacts "could not have been produced without the theoretical understanding of natural materials and forces provided by science."[29]

However, this 'applied science' hypothesis is easily debunked. Historians usually date the emergence of science as a serious professional discipline to the Renaissance era, coinciding with the careers of da Vinci, Copernicus, Galileo, and many others. Yet technologies have clearly been with us since the dawn of time, e.g. stone tools. Indeed, thousands of years before the Renaissance, in Egypt and Greece, sophisticated metal tools and even concrete were in use. Furthermore, many of the early scientists actually *relied upon* technologies for their discoveries. We can't imagine Newton without his set of scales, or Galileo without his telescope. In a sharp reversal of the unidirectional model, we could realistically, if impolitely, define science as 'a branch of applied technology'.

Indeed science and technology often function independently of one another. Much theoretical science relies upon mathematics, which in the pre-digital era required little more than brain power. Conversely, many 20th-century technologists have made substantial progress without any assistance from scientists. For instance, according to Basalla, in developing wireless communications, "Marconi was not applying scientific knowledge to the solution of technical problems, he was providing technological solutions for problems not yet comprehended by the scientific community."[30] Around the same time, the Wright brothers were learning how to conquer the air using only empirical techniques. Wilbur could not have been more blunt in remarking, "I know that an ounce of fact outweighs a pound of theory."[31]

An important turning point in this relationship between science and technology was probably the Industrial Revolution. Historians T.K. Derry and Terry Williams suggest that "On the whole, up to 1750 science probably gained more from technology than vice versa."[32] It was then that the maturing scientific disciplines, particularly physics and chemistry, became more closely entwined with technology. Arthur agrees:

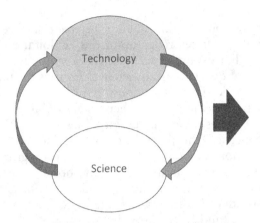

Figure 2.3 A bi-directional model of joint technological and scientific progress

The reason science arrived in technology about this time was not just that it provided more insight and better prediction of results. It was that the families of phenomena beginning to be exploited then – the electrical and chemical ones, for example – acted on a scale or in a world not accessible to direct human observation without the methods and instruments of science.[33]

This evidence points to a bi-directional model – what Arthur calls "a symbiotic relationship" between the scientific and technological realms.[34] **Technologies introduce tools which are often quickly adopted by research scientists, while scientists deliver insights, such as theoretical limits on scale or performance, highly valued by technologists.** Figure 2.3 illustrates this relationship.

Basalla observes that science "does not prescribe the final form of the artifact; Ohm's law did not dictate the shape and details of Edison's lighting system nor did Maxwell's equations determine the precise form taken by circuitry in a modern radio receiver."[35] **This 'precise form' is a design or architectural task that remains the remit of engineers.**

This idea of a designed architecture, consisting of both physical and logical components, seems to be a significant differentiator between technologies and non-technologies. This will now be explored, as a new theory of technology is presented.

Defining *technology*

Thus far we have seen that there are many different analytical approaches to technology, although none appears to be definitive. We might *think* we know what a technology is, but is that good enough?

To develop effective technology strategies we need to have a more precise understanding. We can then use this knowledge to better exploit the attributes of any technologies we are required to operate or manage. If we get this definition of technology right, we can improve our decision-making, innovate more successfully, perhaps see further into the future, and therefore produce more robust technology strategies. So let's take hold of the first technology, a hammer, and knock this nail on the head.

I began working in technical environments nearly three decades ago. In that time I've interacted with hundreds of technology and engineering professionals across Europe, Asia, and North America and had the good fortune to study and research at some of the world's finest academic institutions. Later I gained further insights while managing training and education programmes for engineers. Along the way, I've learned a great deal from both my mistakes and my successes. So now, drawing upon all of this experience, and after many years researching this book, I believe that I have a solid understanding of **what a technology is and what a technology isn't**.

In Appendix 1, the theory of technology developed for this book is explained in full. Within the context of this chapter, however, it is only necessary to outline the theory and the definition of technology that emerges from it.

It is my assertion that all technologies are 'designed' entities. By this, I mean that they bear the imprint of human agency. They have been created by people. They are artificial. They are unnatural. Furthermore, all technologies possess five key attributes or 'dimensions'. These are **the necessary and sufficient conditions for any entity to be called a technology**. They are as follows:

1 Physical
2 Logical
3 Architectural
4 Yield
5 Stakeholder.

The acronym **PLAYS** may be used as a shortcut. These five dimensions are not mutually exclusive. There are some overlaps. However, it seems evident that all technologies possess all five dimensions. If a single dimension is missing, the entity cannot be called a technology.

Let me explain the theory in a single paragraph. Firstly, every technology has a **physical** dimension. It exists in the material world. It has mass. Also, every technology has a **logical** dimension. This represents the core functionality, often exploiting natural phenomena, such as friction, conductivity, or chemical reactions. A technology functions in a particular way, and that "particular way" is its logic. Thirdly, every technology has an **architectural** dimension. An architecture emerges from the intelligent combination and integration of both the physical and logical dimensions to produce a functioning arrangement. A single technology or technological product may be available in multiple architectural arrangements, e.g. the various types of hammer, such as a pounding rock, a sledgehammer, and a pile driver. Fourth, every technology has a **yield** dimension. This is the technology's output as it delivers value to stakeholders. It should be possible to quantify the yield in some way. Fifth and finally, every technology has a **stakeholder** dimension. These are the beneficiaries of the technology's yield, such as owners and users.

This theory leads to the following definition:

A DEFINITION FOR *TECHNOLOGY*

A technology is a designed entity consisting of an integrated physical and logical architecture yielding stakeholder value.

Its five 'dimensions' have the acronym **PLAYS**. These are the necessary and sufficient conditions for being a technology. Therefore, any entity possessing all of the PLAYS attributes *must* be a technology. For this theory to be valid, there can be no exceptions.

So, according to this definition, the following may be called technologies: electric motor, antibiotic medicine, office building, written language, ship, mouse trap, computer. The following are **not** technologies: patent application, spoken language, ship sitting in dry dock for repairs, dinosaur trap, software application. These differences are fully explained in Appendix 1.

The five dimensions theory will appear later in this book as a tool to support technology strategy development. For example, the five dimensions help us to dissect technologies with the aim of innovating enhancements to them. PLAYS is also central to the template for producing formal technology strategies. This is called the *Five Dimensions Process* (see Chapters 3 and 12).

A *system* was previously described as *multi-component entities creating value by transforming inputs into outputs.* That held true for washing machines, aeroplanes, and even postal systems. It might also hold true for anything we call a technology. According to the five dimensions theory, every technology consists of multiple elements or 'components'. At least one of these will be physical, and another logical. It could even be argued that the architecture is another type of component, because it often takes different forms. Consequently, if every technology has at least two components, and if it also receives inputs (such as energy or data) and outputs (the value that it yields), then a technology *must* be a system. In summary, all technologies are systems, though, as we saw earlier, not all 'systems' are technologies, e.g. the Solar System.

Box 2.3   STRATEGIC AND TACTICAL MOVES

Exploiting compatibility

One cannot overestimate the importance of technical compatibility in strategic thinking. Products, systems, and processes can be compatible or incompatible with other products, systems, and processes. International or industry-wide standards and protocols are developed to support compatibility, especially where all parties are likely to benefit. System boundaries may determine where technical compatibility begins and ends. There are broadly two types of compatibility, vertical and horizontal. Vertical is further divided into backward and forward compatibility:

Backward compatibility: This is a design strategy enabling the continued use of older products or systems by ensuring that they work with the latest version, e.g. enabling ageing software to run on new computers. Backward compatibility involves compromises which slow the take-up of new technologies, because older products continue to function and therefore retain some value. For example, digital radios incorporate FM receivers for backward compatibility. Consequently, some stations continue to broadcast on FM, holding back the digital transition. Backward compatibility is often withdrawn after a specified gap, measured either in years or versions.

Forward compatibility: If designers are armed with knowledge about how a technology will progress, especially concerning forthcoming changes to standards or protocols, they can ensure that a current product will serve its users well into the future. This increased design life may encourage hesitant buyers. For example, a mobile phone which is compatible with the *next* generation of wireless communication standards will be more desirable to buy than one which lacks this feature. The ability to foresee changes in society or the law, for instance, could also facilitate forward compatibility.

Horizontal compatibility: Products and systems may be designed to integrate with complementary technologies or to avoid conflicts with unrelated products operating in the same environment. Combustion fuels, for instance, are refined to standards compatible with complementary engines. Double-A and triple-A batteries are compatible for use in consumer electronic products. The railway 'gauge wars' of the 19th century arose due to the incompatibility of adjacent railway networks, preventing total network integration. Horizontal compatibility is particularly important in safety-critical environments, in order that devices work well together. Technical platforms, such as the UNIX operating system, or an AC power distribution network, provide a foundation upon which complementors can place their compatible products, e.g. software applications, electrical devices. Some systems deliberately evade broader horizontal compatibility with the aim of locking in customers to a proprietary product range. Think of Apple's control over its range of desktop devices and peripherals.

Compatibility comes at a cost, however. It takes longer to design and test for compatibility. Also, such products tend to be more complex and prone to perceived faults (e.g. from unforeseen incompatibilities). A very lean and efficient design, such as an MVP (minimum viable product), avoids the costs associated with compatibility, but only by offering minimal functionality and experiencing isolation within the product ecosystem. Compatibility also undermines product sales because it increases the operational life of older products, and facilitates easier switching to competitors.

Technologists

Finally, let's take a moment to consider the technologist. Anyone who works directly with technologies in a decision-making capacity (e.g. designing, deploying, managing) could reasonably be called a technologist. Many technologists are formally-educated engineers, but a substantial number will have established their careers via work experience and self-directed study.

Any technologist, regardless of age, experience, or professional status will, from time to time, find themselves making strategically important decisions. The more senior the role, the more frequently these decisions will be made. The day may come when a technologist is asked to produce a formal technology strategy for their employer or even a client. This first experience may prove uncomfortable. They will be expected to look beyond the boundaries of familiar technical systems in order to consider unfamiliar technologies and more abstract entities, such as laws, markets, and the natural environment.

To aid these inexperienced strategists, a structured process for producing a technology strategy is presented in Chapter 12's *Five Dimensions Process*.

A special category of technologist is the professional engineer, a person who will typically be working both directly and indirectly with technologies. How do we differentiate professional engineers from the many other types of technologists? This question is answered below.

Engineering and engineers

If I say that I am going to "engineer a meeting" between two people, I'm using the term *engineer* to imply a conscious act of creating a favourable outcome using the resources at my disposal. I will not be relying upon nature or the vagaries of chance to deliver the desired result. I am creating an artificiality.

Our earlier examination of design included Donald Norman's assertion that "All artificial things are designed."[36] This alerts us to the links between engineering and design, as expressed earlier by the Royal Academy of Engineering's John Turnbull and Chris Elliott. In a similar vein, two leading figures in American engineering, W. Hammack and J. Anderson refer to the "engineering method", which they describe as "an attitude or approach, or even a philosophy of creating a solution to a problem".[37] **Engineering is therefore a solution-oriented, creative design activity.** In France, the profession we call engineering is known as *ingénierie*, in Spain it is *ingeniería* and in Germany *Ingenieurwesen*. Engineers are literally ingenious. They're expected to show ingenuity. That's the etymological connection between the term *engineering* and solution design.

In the year 2000, the US National Academy of Engineering decided to look back upon "the 20 greatest engineering achievements of the twentieth century." Apart from such obvious candidates as electrification and aviation, the list also included water supply and distribution, agricultural mechanisation, the internet, household appliances, health technologies, and high-performance materials.[38] The scope of professional engineering is therefore very broad, but importantly it is closely associated with the technological realm.

The professional branches or disciplines of engineering are well established. For example, three of the world's leading engineering universities, Massachusetts Institute of Technology (MIT), Imperial College London (ICL), and the Indian Institute of Technology Bombay, offer a broadly similar array of under-graduate engineering programmes with titles such as: Aeronautics and Astronautics, Biological, Chemical, Civil and Environmental, Electrical, Computer Science, Medical, Materials, Mechanical, and Nuclear.[39] These programme titles offer clues to their relationships with specific technologies, or technological 'domains'. (This idea of domains will be examined in the next chapter.)

One discipline not listed among those undergraduate programmes is *systems engineering*. This relatively young branch of the profession could be described as a meta discipline because of the way it straddles the others. Systems engineering takes an overarching, holistic view of engineering solutions. It explores the relationship between individual technologies and higher-level systems, their lifecycles, and their stakeholders, both internal and external. Systems engineering opti-mises the design of system-based solutions by examining and seeking to rein in their inherent complexity. This is a rare but valuable skillset, captured comprehensively in the book *The Paradoxical Mindset of Systems Engineers* (2018) by Arthur Pyster, Nicole Hutchison, and Devanandham Henry.[40] The International Council on Systems Engineering (INCOSE) is the leading professional body for this discipline, offering formal certification in systems engineering to traditional engineers, but only those with substantial breadth and depth of experience.[41] I will be arguing later that systems engineers make particularly effective technology strategists.

Box 2.4   STRATEGIC DICHOTOMIES

People OR Machines?

Human beings have multiple capabilities. These include sensors, data stores, cognition, power sources, and levers. A human being is a very capable 'machine', but often more capable than needed, and sometimes undesirably complex. Technological machines are often able to deliver the same outputs as people, so machines can be their substitutes. Why use workers?

It is factors such as quality of output, speed, and unit costs that influence choices between people and machines, but this dichotomy is not solely within the accountants' remit. It is also a challenge for technology strategists, for whom decisions con-cerning the recruitment, training, and retention of personnel must be weighed against the operational implications of automation.

The argument for people: Humans tend to be more flexible and adaptable than machines. Indeed, machines are often 'one trick ponies', de-valuing rapidly when processes, products, or markets change. People can usually be recruited and deployed quickly, whereas complex machinery often requires custom manufacturing and configuration, followed by testing. Furthermore, people are generally smarter than machines. They can innovate and see the 'bigger picture', helping organisations to progress and adapt. It is only people that can determine the architectures and processes needed to optimise overall performance. Finally, machines don't do strategy or tactics; you need people for that. If we replace too many good people with machines, where will our future strategic thinkers come from?

The argument for machines: People have limitations of strength, speed, and stamina relative to machines. People need to rest, have fun (sometimes at work), and sleep (sometimes at work). They produce outputs of variable quality, whereas well-designed and well-maintained machines will work consistently for days, weeks, and even months. Automation delivers a reliability premium, enabling more confident planning. Machines can be managed by a small number of semi-skilled technicians, whereas non-automated production processes require both skilled craftspeople and well-paid managers capable of coordinating large teams.

Human-machine augmentation: There is a hybrid approach. Automation can be more closely integrated with people, increasing productivity and improving job satisfaction by eliminating some of the more tedious, dirty, or dangerous tasks, e.g. manual data processing, waste recycling, or visual inspections in hazardous environments. This is sometimes called human-machine augmentation. It is a topic which often arises in discussions about the future role of AI, because it is not expected that AI will be sufficiently advanced to *completely* replace workers for many decades. However, where AI is designed to support people in their jobs, it should prove beneficial for all parties.

In 2009, the Board of Trustees of the Ohio Academy of Science published a short white paper entitled *What are technology and engineering?* In their definition, "Engineering is design under constraint that develops and applies technology to satisfy human needs and wants." Later, they elaborate on the phrase "design under constraint", explaining that engineering practice is constrained by, amongst other things, cost, safety, reliability, the laws of nature, and manufacturability.[42] A practical example of these constraints is offered by G. Madhavan. "For an airplane design, a typical trade-off could be to balance the demands of cost, weight, wingspan, and lavatory dimensions within the constraints of the given performance specifications." He notes that there is also an aesthetic constraint because "This type of selection pressure even trickles down to the question of whether passengers like the airplane they're flying in."[43] Here, "pressure" is the operative word, because not only is engineering technically challenging, but it also involves working with stakeholders who sometimes present even greater challenges than the technologies. In fact negotiation skills are often found near the top of an engineer's toolbox. Willy Messerschmitt is reported to have said, "We can build any aircraft that the aviation ministry calls for, with any requirement satisfied. Of course, it will not fly."[44] Try telling that to a government minister preparing for war! The best engineers are skilled diplomats and communicators.

In most commercial engineering activities, the greatest constraint of all is cost. Warren East, CEO of Rolls-Royce and a former engineer himself, asserted that "It is all very well to do fantastic designs, but if you can't make them economically then in my mind that is not very good engineering."[45] This echoes the famous remark of American railroad engineer, Arthur Wellington, who wrote that engineering "is the art of doing that well with one dollar, which any bungler can do with two".[46] In other words, if it's inefficient, it's inelegant. **Good engineering is not about achieving perfection or being showy, it's about achieving the best possible solutions via negotiation, compromise and optimisation.**

According to everything we have seen so far, professional engineering is fundamentally about the design of solutions. If so, why are locomotive drivers and the people who repair washing machines also called engineers? Is this a correct use of the term? Probably not, and for two good reasons: 1) they have not had the same type of formal training and peer-reviewed assessment as conventional professional engineers; 2) locomotive 'engineers' and washing machine service 'engineers' specialise in operations and maintenance; they do not make creative design decisions about the technologies they work with. Turnbull makes a related point: "Many years ago I was responsible for running a petrochemical complex and the last thing I wanted was an engineer to actually run the plant ... we want pilots to fly aeroplanes, not aeronautical engineers."[47] Designing, operating, and maintaining are three very different technical skillsets performed by people with very different interests and training backgrounds. It is only by convention that some technicians are referred to as engineers. However, whether 'real' engineers or not, they clearly work 'hands on' within the technological realm. They are technologists. As such, they will occasionally need to think strategically and tactically during the course of their work. The mindset promoted by this book should still be useful to them.

We mustn't conclude that a professional engineer is wholly preoccupied with design. In fact the role involves many ancillary, non-design activities. The engineer's mathematical and analytical skillset may lead to work supporting fellow engineers, for example, by performing calculations or testing solutions. One of the ancillary skillsets in high demand is risk management, sometimes called risk engineering or safety engineering. Here, engineers use specialised techniques for identifying, quantifying, and mitigating risk. Usually, this does not involve design work. However, if a risk engineer creates or recommends a safer solution, such as re-configuring machinery or changing a production process, then that creative input is, of course, a form of design. Risk management is examined further in Chapter 11.

As the world becomes increasingly dependent upon engineering solutions, the role of engineers in society is changing. There are many high-profile figures within the profession urging it to become more eclectic, pro-active, and leadership-oriented. Roland Clift and Jo da Silva, both Fellows of the Royal Society of Engineering, are forthright in their wish to see the engineering profession evolve and grow intellectually. Clift, an environmental systems engineer, argues that "engineers are not just problem solvers; they have to become engaged in framing the problems which are to be solved."[48] Similarly da Silva, a senior Arup civil engineer, reminds her peers that "We, as engineers, create the stage set on which the play happens", arguing that a broader mix of expertise is needed in order to better deal with the world's challenges. "Life isn't just about technical parameters. You need to understand the environmental parameters, the social parameters, the economics behind what we are doing."[49]

Calls for the engineering profession to go both deeper and broader have implications, not only for the way that engineers are taught, but also for the drawing of boundaries in professional practice. As noted earlier in this chapter, technical solutions often introduce multiple system layers. How many layers of hierarchical systems should be in scope? Where exactly does responsibility end? We might also question whether the design and management of engineering solutions should continue to be demarcated by the traditional discipline boundaries. Perhaps the broader skillset of systems engineering, described above, offers a clue to the profession's future.

That concludes our brief look at the fundamentals of the engineering profession. The reader is advised that throughout this book references to *technology* and *technology strategy* are each intended to imply the inclusion of engineering practices and solutions. For instance, technology strategy is largely synonymous with engineering strategy because all professional engineering is heavily dependent upon technologies, and all technologies are, in the purest sense, engineered. Furthermore, many best practices within the technological realm are associated with core engineering methodologies, such as requirements analysis, project planning, and testing regimes. Occasionally I will use the stock phrase "technology and engineering" to emphasise these connections, but they must never be viewed as discrete realms. They're interwoven and inseparable.

In Chapter 1, a number of authors talked about the "design" of strategies. Indeed Rumelt stated that "a master strategist is a designer."[50] Strategies are designed via processes involving negotiations over constraints and subsequent trade-offs. In other words, strategies are *engineered*. So, who better to develop technology and engineering strategies than the technologists and engineers themselves? This book aims to support them in performing that role.

Glossary for this chapter (Items in bold are also defined in the same table)

architecture	The intelligent combination and integration of both the physical and logical dimensions resulting in a functioning, purposeful arrangement.
beneficiary stakeholder	Any entity gaining value from a **technology**. The beneficiary 'reaps' the technology's **yield**. Beneficiaries can include people, companies, even animals. A beneficiary can also be another technology, receiving the yield as an input, such as the next machine in a continuous flow operation.
compatibility	An attribute of **products** and **systems** enabling them to integrate or co-exist with other products and systems. There are two types of compatibility: horizontal and vertical, the latter of which may be forward or backward facing.
component	A constituent part of a **product**, **system**, or **technology**. Components may be physical or virtual. A virtual component can be a product's logic, or even its architecture.
design	The act of conceiving and planning the creation of any entity in response to a specification, which may be written or unwritten. All **technologies** are, in the first instance, designed.
engineering	An array of professional activities leading to the **design** and delivery of solutions. Engineering work is frequently supported by **technologies**. Engineering solutions are **products**, and many of these are regarded as technologies.
product	A discrete entity emerging from a production process. A product has economic value to one or more parties. It may be a physical item or a service. Organisations produce and support products. Some physical products are **technologies**.

(Continued)

socio-technical system	A complex web of people and **technologies**.
system	A **designed** multi-component entity creating value by transforming inputs into outputs.
systems engineering	A meta discipline of the **engineering** profession which takes an overarching or holistic view of **system**-based solutions. It optimises the **design** and performance of systems by examining and reining-in their inherent complexity.
technological realm	A collective term for the activities and artefacts associated with *all* technical and **engineering** disciplines.
technology	A **designed** entity consisting of an integrated physical and logical architecture **yielding** stakeholder value. (Also, more generically, the entire collection of technologies and **engineering** practices available to a culture or organisation.)
yield	A **technology's** quantifiable output, which delivers value to one or more **beneficiary stakeholders**.

Notes

1 Norman, D.A. (2013) *The Design of Everyday Things*. Cambridge (MA): MIT Press. 4.
2 Cross, N. (2008) *Engineering Design Methods: Strategies for Product Design*. Chichester: Wiley. 3.
3 Madhavan, G. (2016) *Think Like an Engineer*. London: Oneworld. 12.
4 Cross, *Engineering Design Methods*. 13.
5 *McGraw-Hill Dictionary of Scientific and Technical Terms* (2003). Sixth Edition. USA: McGraw-Hill.
6 Turnbull, J. (2010) 'The Context and Nature of Engineering Design'. *Philosophy of Engineering*, Vol. 1. Royal Academy of Engineering, London, June 2010. Available at: https://www.raeng.org.uk/publications/reports/philosophy-of-engineering-volume-1, 30–34.
7 Elliott, C. (2010) 'Engineering as Synthesis – Doing Right Things and Doing Things Right'. *Philosophy of Engineering*, Vol. 1. Royal Academy of Engineering, London, June 2010. Available at: https://www.raeng.org.uk/publications/reports/philosophy-of-engineering-volume-1, 54–57.
8 Design Council, *'Framework for Innovation: Design Council's evolved Double Diamond'*. Available at: https://www.designcouncil.org.uk/our-work/skills-learning/tools-frameworks/framework-for-innovation-design-councils-evolved-double-diamond/ (Accessed: 06 October 2022).
9 International Council on Systems Engineering (2023) *Systems Engineering Handbook: A Guide for System Life Cycle Process and Activities* (5th ed.). Hoboken: Wiley. 2.
10 Ross, A., Rhodes, D. and Hastings, D. (2008) 'Defining Changeability: Reconciling Flexibility, Adaptability, Scalability, Modifiability, and Robustness for Maintaining System Lifecycle Value'. *Systems Engineering*, Vol. 11, Issue 3, 246–262.
11 Franssen, M. (2010) 'Roles and Rules and the Modelling of Socio-Technical Systems'. *Philosophy of Engineering*, Vol. 1. Royal Academy

of Engineering, London, June 2010. Available at: https://www.raeng.org.uk/publications/reports/philosophy-of-engineering-volume-1, 45–53.

12 Arthur, W.B. (2010) *The Nature of Technology*. London: Penguin. 10.

13 Wilson, G. (2017) *What is Technology?* Online: CreateSpace Publishing.

14 Hansson, S.O. (ed.) (2017) *The Ethics of Technology*. London: Rowman & Littlefield. 1–2.

15 Wilson, *What is Technology?*

16 Afuah, A. (2003) *Innovation Management*. New York: OUP. 313.

17 Tobin, J. (2003) *To Conquer the Air*. New York: Free Press. 121.

18 Tobin, *To Conquer the Air*. 345.

19 Arthur, *The Nature of Technology*. 98.

20 Arthur. 28.

21 Sharma, B. (2008) 'Technology Strategy, Contextual Factors and Business Performance: An Investigation of Their Relationship'. *South Asian Journal of Management*, Vol. 15, Issue 3, 19–39.

22 Dosi, G. (1982) 'Technological Paradigms and Technological Trajectories'. *Research Policy*, Vol. 11, Issue 3, 147–162.

23 Braun, E. (1998) *Technology in Context*. London: Routledge. 60–61.

24 Afuah, *Innovation Management*. 84.

25 Derry, T.K. and Williams, T.I. (1961) *A Short History of Technology*. London (UK): OUP. 280.

26 Headrick, D.R. (2009) *Technology: A World History*. New York: OUP. 145.

27 Arthur. 22.

28 Arthur. 49.

29 Basalla, G. (1988) *The Evolution of Technology*. Cambridge (UK): CUP. 27.

30 Basalla, *The Evolution of Technology*. 101.

31 Tobin. 174.

32 Derry and Williams, *A Short History of Technology*. 42.

33 Arthur. 60.

34 Arthur. 64.

35 Basalla. 92.

36 Norman, *The Design of Everyday Things*. 4.

37 Hammack, W.S. and Anderson, J.L. (2022) 'Working in the Penumbra of Understanding'. *Issues in Science and Technology*. Available at https://issues.org/penumbra-engineering-perspective-hammack-anderson/ (Accessed: 16 February 2022).

38 Wulf, W.A. (2000) '*Great Achievements and Grand Challenges*'. Available at: https://www.nae.edu/7461/GreatAchievementsandGrandChallenges (Accessed: 29 January 2022).

39 Massachusetts Institute of Technology, School of Engineering '*Departments*'. Available at https://engineering.mit.edu/departments/ (Accessed: 29 January 2022).

40 Pyster, A., Hutchison, N. and Henry, D. (2018) *The Paradoxical Mindset of Systems Engineers*. Hoboken: Wiley.

41 International Council on Systems Engineering (INCOSE). Available at https://www.incose.org/ (Accessed: 30 January 2022).

42 Anon (2009) 'What are Technology and Engineering?'. *Ohio Journal of Science*, Vol. 109, Issue 2, 40.

43 Madhavan, *Think Like an Engineer*. 26.

44 Elliot, *Philosophy of Engineering*, Vol. 1.

45 Kenward, M. (2016) 'Taking Engineering to Industry'. *Ingenia*, Issue 69, 42–46.

46 Wellington, A. M. (undated) '*Arthur Mellen Wellington*'. Available at: https://todayinsci.com/W/Wellington_Arthur/WellingtonArthur-Quotations. htm (Accessed: 13 January 2022).

47 Turnbull, *Philosophy of Engineering*, Vol. 1.

48 Clift, R. (2011) 'Children of Martha: On Being an Engineer in the Environment'. *Philosophy of Engineering*, Vol. 2. Royal Academy of Engineering, London, October 2011. Available at: https://www.raeng. org.uk/publications/reports/philosophy-of-engineering-vol-2, 48–55.

49 Kenward, M. (2019) 'Structures for a Sustainable Society'. *Ingenia*, Issue 80, 38–42.

50 Rumelt, R. (2017) *Good Strategy, Bad Strategy*. London: Profile Books. 130.

3 Scoping the subject
What should we expect from a strategy?

This chapter presents

- A high-level introduction to the scope and purpose of technology strategy.

This chapter establishes

- The relationship between business strategies and technology strategies.
- A process for developing a technology strategy.
- A new definition of 'technology strategy'.

In the opening chapters, we have examined some of the key 'components' of this book. We gained some clarity around the meaning of strategy and explored the nature of engineering, particularly its inseparability from design. This was complemented by a brief look at the nature of systems, especially their nebulous boundaries. A theory of technology was also presented, explaining its five constituent 'dimensions'. It is now time to put the focus on *technology strategy*.

Strategies are created by organisations with the intention of securing a more successful future, both for themselves and their stakeholders. A technology strategy can be used, for example, to rescue a failing company and its products, or to propel a thriving company to even greater heights. Technology strategies are therefore high-value commodities.

Strategy in practice

We don't have to look very far to find examples of both successful and unsuccessful strategies in the technological realm. It may be helpful to briefly examine some of these cases.

One famous example, often discussed, concerns the Xerox corporation which, in the 1970s, had a near monopoly on the photocopier market. "Xerox" actually became a verb meaning 'to copy'. Their machines were large, heavy, complex, and very,

DOI: 10.4324/9781003472919-4

very expensive. Only larger organisations could afford them, supported by an army of mobile Xerox engineers. Then Japanese disrupters emerged, notably Canon, who were masters of both optics and microelectronics. Canon copiers were compact, inexpensive, modular, and could even be maintained by their owners.[1] It was a blow to Xerox's position within the copier market, from which they never fully recovered. Their product strategy of centralised, high volume, high-speed copying, contrasted with Canon's distributed desktop machines, operating more reliably but at lower speeds. Xerox could have launched a fightback, but complacency had set in. Their attempt to pivot into computer hardware was ultimately unsuccessful.[2] The Xerox story is an excellent example of the complex interdependencies between business strategies and technology strategies, and these two distinct strategic threads will be disentangled later in this chapter.

Also in Japan, at roughly the same time that Canon was disrupting the copier market, Toyota was transforming industrial manufacturing. The soon-to-be-famous Toyota Production System (TPS) sought to improve output and maximise quality through low-level innovation by frontline workers. In the process, Toyota, along with other Japanese companies, created what Braun has called a new "techno-economic paradigm".[3] The traditional engineering trade-off of quality versus quantity was no longer valid. High quality and low prices could co-exist.[4] Despite its focus upon people and their often low-tech solutions to manufacturing problems, the TPS has been hugely influential within the technology strategies of many organisations, along with other quality methodologies, such as Six Sigma and Total Quality Management (TQM).

By the 1980s computers were beginning to feature heavily in the strategies of most large organisations, although the desktop computing revolution was still a few years away. In fact it was mainframe and mid-range systems, located in head offices, which were transforming commercial practices. At the forefront of exploiting these promising technologies was Walmart, the US retail giant. Among their many initiatives were the early adoption of bar coding and the use of electronic data interchange (EDI) to manage the flow of merchandise between suppliers and stores. Later, the launch of a bespoke system known as *Retail Link* enabled continuous, real-time interactions between Walmart management, stores, and suppliers. The use of Retail Link became mandatory for any company hoping to see its products on a Walmart shelf.[5] The boundaries of Walmart's technical systems now had no geographical limits.

A leading manufacturer of the computers transforming US corporations at that time was Digital Equipment Corporation (DEC). Culturally DEC were wedded to the model of large, expensive devices supporting centralised architectures. Desktop-based computers were, however, beginning to emerge and the trend towards more distributed architectures had begun. Fortunately, DEC were well placed to capitalise on their strengths. Internally, they were already making use of local-area and wide-area networks, email, an intranet of bulletin boards, and an information-sharing solution called *Notes* (an idea later reborn as Lotus Notes).[6] Despite such solid foundations DEC were slow to adapt to the 32-bit micro revolution, and by the 1990s were in the final phases of a corporate death spiral. Conflicting interests within the organisation were pulling in different directions. Traditionalists favoured established products for established clients. Those with more foresight wanted new products for a new era. Prior to the company's demise, a 1992 strategy discussion among senior personnel resulted in a bland compromise statement: "DEC is committed to providing high-quality products and services and being a leader in data processing." Rumelt's verdict is excoriating:

> This fluffy, amorphous statement was, of course, not a strategy. It was a political outcome reached by individuals who, forced to reach a consensus, could not agree on which interests and concepts to forgo. So they avoided the hard work of choice, set nothing aside, hurt no interest groups or individual egos, but crippled the whole.[7]

The lesson here is simple. **Strategy is about *making choices* from the range of options available, then grasping the selected opportunities firmly and committing to them with energy.** DEC didn't survive into the 21st century.

Digital has had plenty of attention here, so let's take to the skies. We have already touched upon the origins of powered flight with the Wright brothers and their "new art", but how does strategic thinking influence today's airborne businesses, the commercial airlines? The era of state-controlled companies, operating at high cost and low efficiency, has been in decline for decades. Dozens of more nimble disrupters have emerged to capture the public's imagination with inexpensive flights to popular destinations on remarkably safe aircraft. The commercial margins in this industry have always been tight, so the smallest improvements reap significant benefits. Europe's most commercially successful airline, Ryanair, is not only recognised for its short turnaround times, but also for its strategic decision to standardise on just one aircraft, the Boeing 737. The benefits of using one aircraft type are clear:

familiarity for crews and maintenance personnel, the need for a limited range of spares, and bulk purchasing discounts from the manufacturer, Boeing. It helps that Ryanair operates only short-haul flights conducive to the 737, but that's the niche they have chosen to fill. State-owned, and formerly state-owned airlines, such as British Airways, tend towards mixed fleets of long and short-haul aircraft, often acquired from multiple manufacturers. They have never been able to compete directly with the low-cost disrupters.

Another state-controlled carrier, Singapore Airlines, has built an enviable reputation for service. Nevertheless, by operating out of a hub airport (Changi, Singapore), they too must run a mixed fleet, of five different aircraft types from two different manufacturers, Boeing and Airbus.[8] Despite this technical burden, according to Grant and Jordan, they have managed to gain a competitive edge from their strategy of operating only younger aircraft. The Singapore Airlines fleet had an average age of 81 months in 2014, compared with an industry average of 128 months. These newer aircraft are both more fuel efficient and require less maintenance. Perhaps as a consequence of this, they spent more time in the air: 13 hours per day compared with an industry average of 11.3 hours. Data from 2008 also showed that repairs accounted for just 4% of Singapore's total costs, compared with nearly 5% for American Airlines and nearly 6% for United.[9] In the absence of contemporary data, it's unclear whether Singapore has continued with this strategy, but its benefits seem self-evident and the underlying logic is strong.

However, we are assuming that the accountants are getting their numbers right because, for example, newer aircraft experience depreciation more quickly. Hence, what the airline gains in fuel efficiency and increased flying time, they may be losing on the premium being paid for new aircraft. Is this a sound technology strategy or a bad business strategy? Could it be both? Is it a better practice to 'sweat' older assets for maximum returns, or off-load them in favour of the latest equipment? This question could be asked of any physical asset.

To end this brief review of strategy in practice, let's consider how the US Department of Defense (DoD) is now looking towards its technological future. In 2017 Mary Miller, then the acting Assistant Secretary of Defense for Research and Engineering, gave a talk in Washington D.C. on the future of defence systems. During her speech, she mentioned 14 areas of research and development favoured by the DoD. These included hypersonics, directed energy, novel materials, and artificial intelligence. From our perspective, a more interesting aspect of Miller's speech was the list of fundamental ways that DoD systems are expected to change, including:

- From systems built to last to systems built to evolve.
- From deeply integrated architectures to layered, modular architectures.
- From hierarchical development organisations to ecosystems of partners and agile teams.
- From automated systems to learning systems.[10]

These are profound technological shifts, revealing a technology strategy that will influence R&D, purchasing policies, and the practice of warfare for decades to come.

This strategy will have been the product of thousands of hours of deliberation within the Pentagon. Communicated in this way, the strategy engages its listeners and readers without overwhelming them with technical detail. Could this relatively high level of engagement succeed in encouraging the DoD's stakeholders to undertake the necessary internal cultural changes and innovation activities? The way that strategic messages are delivered is clearly something we will need to consider when planning our own technology strategies. Strategy communications will be explored later.

Business before technology

Organisations come in many forms: startups, global corporations, corporate divisions, family firms, universities, charities, and so on. The highest level of strategy developed by these organisations will often be known as the *business strategy*. Referring back to our definition of strategy in Chapter 1, we would expect a business strategy to consist of *an evolving package of concerted actions, designed with a common purpose*. That common purpose will typically reflect a concern for the longevity and prosperity of the organisation.

A business strategy might consist of a leadership vision, along with plans or proposals relating to finance, marketing, personnel, product ranges, stakeholder relations, and so on. There may be references to technology, although it's possible that this content won't have been produced in collaboration with frontline technologists and engineers (as arguably it should). In some circumstances, this will be explained, or excused, by technology's limited role within the organisation. For instance, the sport, leisure, and non-profit sectors may not feel the need to expend time and resources on the development of a detailed technology strategy. By contrast, some energy businesses, telecoms providers, and social media platforms will struggle to separate technologies from their core business. For such companies, one combined strategy will often suffice. For most organisations,

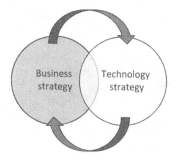

Figure 3.1 A closely coupled relationship between a business strategy and a technology strategy

however, business and technology strategies will be treated as two interdependent, but entirely separate entities.

So, rather like the relationship between science and technology discussed in the previous chapter, we might conclude that business strategies and technology strategies are also interwoven in a symbiotic relationship. This is illustrated in Figure 3.1.

The precise nature of that relationship will vary, of course, according to many factors, including:

- The extent to which business operations are currently dependent upon technology.
- The likely impact of technologies on future prospects.
- The proportion of business overheads attributed to technology.
- The enthusiasm for technology among business leaders.
- The closeness of the working relationship between business and technology leaders.
- The assertiveness and proactivity of technology leaders.

This is not an exhaustive list by any means, but in relation to the diagram above, the factors I have mentioned will all influence the relative size of each strategy 'bubble' and the degree of overlap or separation between them. For example, the diagram for a company like Tesla would consist of a near 'total eclipse' as one bubble overlaps the other. On the other hand, the diagram for an institution like the British Museum might feature a smaller technology bubble some distance from the business strategy and wholly dependent upon the latter for its content and direction. These two examples are illustrated in Figure 3.2.

The key message here is that **business strategies either precede or shape an organisation's technology strategy**. Technology is the

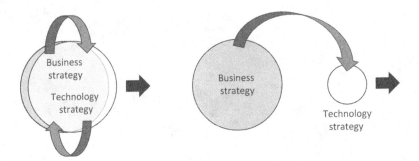

Figure 3.2 Two scenarios depicting (left) the progress of an organisation wholly wedded to technology, and (right) one in which technology has little or no influence over the business strategy

servant. You can't put the cart before the horse. The welfare of the business always comes first, and technology strategies promote that welfare.

It is inconceivable that a technology strategy would be developed either in advance of, or without any reference to, the business strategy.

What's in scope?

What should we expect from a technology strategy? What does it look like? I will use the following eight headings to examine these issues of scope:

1 The degree of formality
2 Value chains
3 Technology domains
4 Internal and external environments
5 The *five dimensions* of technology
6 Timescales
7 Internal and external communications
8 The business strategy.

The degree of formality

Earlier, Eben Hewitt, the author of *Technology Strategy Patterns*, noted that some people view formal strategy documents as "something quaint and cute that best belongs on the shelf to collect dust".[11] Many staff pay little attention to corporate diktat in written form. However, whether we like it or not, the formally documented technology strategy, of the type reviewed in Chapter 1, is the archetypal form. We associate these documented strategies with the highest level of decision making in organisations, often bearing the signature of a CEO or CTO.

By contrast, the least formal strategic decision making occurs at lower levels of the organisation – on the frontline. This is characterised by intuitive (or barely researched) decisions executed quickly, often with the aim of clearing backlogs, exploiting opportunities, or simply getting home after another ten-hour day. However, the long-term implications of such low-level decisions can be substantial. What starts as a 'quick win' for the team could end with the emergence of a so-called 'technical debt' many years later. (Technical debt is defined in the Glossary at the end of this chapter.) These extremes of formality and informality, and all points in between, are captured in Table 3.1.

Technology strategies may be both formal and informal. They are developed and executed at all levels of the organisation.

Table 3.1 The formality of strategic decision making within organisations

Organisational tier	Degree of formality	
	More formal: more likely to be part of a process, documented and shared	**Less formal (informal):** day-to-day decisions with strategic implications, rarely published
High level	**Organisation-wide technology strategies** (regularly revised)	**Senior leadership strategy** (probably shared or discussed with peers, followed by occasional public announcements)
Mid level	**Divisional or departmental strategies** (regularly revised)	**Middle management strategies** (probably shared or discussed with senior leadership, peers, and sometimes frontline staff)
Low level	**Individual product strategies** (for manufactured goods, technical services, or other engineered solutions)	**Strategic and tactical decisions made by small teams or individual technologists/engineers** (probably shared or discussed with managers and peers)
Always underpinned (and sometimes undermined) by the quality of strategic thinking		

Value chains

Technologies permeate the whole organisation. The marketing department, the post room, HR, the shop floor, logistics, accounts, sales, the warehouse, and the facilities manager all adopt gadgets, widgets, gizmos, and machines to make their work more productive. Consequently, the prospect of producing a technology strategy for any medium or large-sized organisation seems daunting at first. Where do we begin our analysis? Where should it end? This is where scoping comes to our rescue, particularly if we use *value* as a guide.

Organisations exist to create value for various stakeholders. Although we might question the organisation's ultimate value to society, there will always be one or more stakeholders expecting, or hoping, to gain some benefit. The mechanism by which organisations produce and deliver this value to beneficiaries is called the *value chain*. Box 1.3 *Value chain analysis* (in Chapter 1) provides a brief explanation of this concept, distinguishing in particular between so-called *primary* and *support* activities.

Primary activities are *critical* to the success of the organisation. Therefore, we might say that the technologies used by primary activities are more likely to be strategic in nature. They will probably be listed as strategic assets (see Box 3.1 *Strategic asset audit*). Technologies associated with support activities will be less critical, although their users and internal evangelists may disagree. Support activities are often easier to purchase 'off-the-shelf', for instance, or simply to outsource. It is therefore vital that the development of a technology strategy is not waylaid by assertive or well-connected managers promoting their internal support functions. **To achieve a strategic focus, primary technologies should always be at the forefront of the strategist's mind.**

Box 3.1   ANALYTICAL TOOLS AND TECHNIQUES

Strategic asset audit

A strategic asset audit is the process of identifying all assets of strategic value and examining their current status.

In general, an organisation's assets are any entities within its direct control deemed to be of current or future economic value. Such assets may be *tangible* (e.g. laboratories, vehicles, land) or *intangible* (e.g. intellectual property, brand reputation, bespoke software).

However, only a subset of assets are critical to the implementation of strategy. These so-called *strategic assets* (or strategic resources) have been defined as "Any asset that provides the basis for core competence, distinctive performance or sustainable competitive advantage, or which allows a business unit to participate in business opportunities."[12]

These assets are special and should be protected from loss, interruption, and over-zealous cost-cutting.

It is therefore beneficial to identify all strategic assets via an audit. Here are two suggested methods:

1 List all assets with strategic *potential*, both current and future. This could include all assets used within the 'primary activities' of the value chain, plus strategic products under development. Strategic assets at the organisational level may differ from those at the product level.
2 A quicker approach is to examine the current strategy and simply look for references to strategically significant products, clients, and operational facilities. Next, identify all associated assets. This is less comprehensive than method 1) and could exclude potential *future* strategic assets in need of advance protection.

Technology domains

In Chapter 2, we saw how biotechnology emerged from the research of Boyer and Cohen in the 1970s. Today we think of biotechnology as being a distinct branch or *domain* of technology. Indeed it seems reasonable to argue that all technologies belong to a specific domain. Consider these collective terms: electronics, telecommunications, hydraulics, energy, computing, medicine, construction, and so on. These domains are clearly not mutually exclusive. We've already seen how multiple technologies are often tightly integrated within a single device, such as the aeroplane.

Interestingly, there is also a strong correlation between the names of these technology domains and many of the university-taught engineering disciplines listed in Chapter 2. This is yet another example, and further evidence, of the ties that bind technology with engineering.

In his book *The Nature of Technology* (2010), W.B. Arthur describes domains as "families of devices, methods, and practices". He notes that "They are not invented; they emerge, crystallizing around a set of phenomena or a novel enabling technology".[13] Elsewhere he says that domains combine "a family of effects" and "a common purpose".[14] As an example Arthur describes the automotive technologies domain:

> The automobile in 1900 created a set of ancillary needs ... for assembly line manufacture, for paved roads and properly refined gasoline, for repair facilities and gas stations. And gasoline in turn set up further needs for refineries, for the importation of crude oil, and for the exploration of oil deposits.[15]

These ideas are useful because they should help us to scope our technology strategies. **The concept of domains can perhaps be used to contain strategy development in such a way that the output is packaged in a coherent and easily communicated structure, targeted at the primary audience.**

With no international standard or formal definition to guide us, we can define domains to suit our own strategic needs. For example, it may be helpful to think of both domains and sub-domains. An information technology strategy might benefit from delineation into such sub-domains as *software*, *hardware*, *security*, and *data management*. The published strategy for the UK's National Highways agency (reviewed in Chapter 1) refers to three separate domains: corporate technologies (mainly digital admin systems), construction technologies, and operational technologies (consisting of road network management systems and digital signage).[16]

Let's explore a hypothetical example. You have been asked to lead the development of a technology strategy for a large shipbuilder. It's clearly a challenging assignment. Where should you begin? Here are some of the domains you will need to examine:

- At the highest level, the shipbuilding domain (consisting of many sub-domains)
- Shipyard manufacturing technologies (a subdomain of shipbuilding)
- Marine engineering (another subdomain of shipbuilding)
- Marine propulsion (a subdomain of marine engineering)
- Marine navigation and communication technologies (two standalone domains)
- On-board information technology (a subdomain of marine engineering)
- Information technology in the shipyard offices (a standalone domain).

We can see that a domain-led approach enables us to structure our strategy development for the shipbuilder. Each of these domains and sub-domains is associated with one or more dedicated teams of engineers, technicians, and managers. Not only will the strategy development involve consulting with these specialists, but the primary audience for the resulting strategy should be the same people. Of course, it's true that most of the domains overlap in various ways, but it would be inconceivable to develop a single, unifying strategy for the shipbuilding organisation without requiring multiple, tightly coordinated development teams working in parallel, generating enormous volumes of work. We might call that the 'Big Bang' approach to strategy development. It sounds unworkable.

An alternative and more incremental approach involves working through the hierarchy of dependencies, one domain at a time. Although this could take many months to complete, it would be an efficient process. It would also ensure compatibility between each of the domain and subdomain strategies.

Therefore, domains help us by suggesting a methodology for the strategy development process. In a later chapter, we will be comparing the concept of domains with technological 'paradigms' and considering how these might become susceptible to disruptive 'paradigm shifts'.

Internal and external environments

An organisation's technology strategy is incomplete if it does not address its wider operating environment. It therefore has both internal and external scope.

Internally there will be multiple assets and processes, especially in the digital domain. The organisation might also be involved in designing technical products or producing them using industrial techniques. Personnel matters will also need to be considered, such as up-skilling, recruiting, and team structures.

Externally, there might be a dependence upon technologies belonging to suppliers and partners, and there will usually be some kind of regulatory oversight, e.g. data protection. The organisation's products are also in daily use by clients and customers (or service users). An organisation often has responsibility, both legal and ethical, for its products after their sale or release into the public domain. Meanwhile, governments or regulators may need to be lobbied for favourable laws and favourable interpretations of existing laws. Economic conditions, if ignored, might impact the supply of key components. At the same time, impending demographic changes could have implications for the supply of skilled workers. The possibilities are endless.

All of the aforementioned activities will be outside the organisation's direct control, but this absence of control does not equate to the absence of strategic considerations. The fact is that we operate within complex socio-technical environments, so these matters cannot be ignored by strategists.

In summary, the scope of a technology or engineering strategy is considerably broader than we might have originally assumed. The people tasked with developing these strategies will need to be smart and multi-skilled; they might also benefit from access to specialised resources, including consultants in legal, environmental, and economic matters.

The reader may feel daunted by this breadth of scope. However, the express purpose of this book is to inspire and enable *all* readers to become better strategists by offering practical suggestions, ideas, and advice. A strategist doesn't have to be a genius, but it's important to know the work involved in producing strategies. What we don't know, we can delegate or outsource. **The best strategists are facilitators, not autocrats.**

The *five dimensions* of technology

Chapter 2 introduced the theory that all technologies are composed of five 'dimensions': physical, logical, architectural, yield, and stakeholder. Extrapolating from this idea we should be able to develop a comprehensive technology strategy structured around these five dimensions. In doing so, we can be confident that all aspects (dimensions) of our technological environment have been taken into consideration. For example, improved physical materials or new techniques may now be available. Perhaps the architecture can be altered for greater efficiency. Similarly, mechanisms for distributing the yield to beneficiaries could be re-designed to reduce waste or increase speed of delivery.

Without considering these possibilities, a strategist could be missing a high-value opportunity. In short, all five dimensions must be consciously and thoroughly examined during strategy development.

Timescales

How far into the future should we plan our strategies? 5 months? 5 years? 50 years? Of course, much depends upon context, but there are constraints determining both a *minimum useful timescale* and a *maximum realistic timescale*.

Referring to strategy development in general, business educators James McGrath and Bob Bates suggest that "any plan over three years contains more conjecture and wishful thinking than useful information."[17] However, five and ten-year strategies are relatively common. My research for this book encountered a number of technology strategies in the public domain, most of which commit to a specific time horizon. Some even include a *vision* spanning multiple decades. Table 3.2 captures this information

Table 3.2 The time horizons of some real-world technology strategies[18]

Organisation	Location	Document title	Start year	Strategic horizon	Extended vision
Australian Department of Defence	Australia	*Defence Science and Technology Strategy 2030*	2020	10 years	-
City of Coquitlam, Canada	Canada	*2019–2024 Coquitlam Technology Strategy*	2019	5 years	-
Toshiba	Japan	*Technology Strategy*	2018	5 years	12 years
UK Space Agency CEOI	UK	*Technology Strategy*	2019	10 years	21 years
European Space Agency	International	*Technology Strategy*	2022	13 years	28 years
NASA	USA	*Strategic Plan 2022*	2022	4 years	10 years
Dundee City Council	UK	*Information Technology Strategy*	2018	5 years	-
City and County of San Francisco	USA	*Information and Communication Technology Plan FY 2022–26*	2021	5 years	
Social Security Scotland	UK	*Digital and Technology Strategy 2022–2025*	2022	3 years	-
UK Home Office	UK	*Digital, Data and Technology 2024 Strategy*	2021	3 years	-
Irish Department of Agriculture, Food and the Marine	Ireland	*Information and Management Technology Strategy 2021–24*	2021	3 years	-
New Zealand Ministry of Social Development	New Zealand	*Technology Strategy 2022*	2022	Not specified	-
National Highways	UK	*Operational Technology: our 2035 strategy*	2022	13 years	-
MSI Reproductive Choices	UK	*Digital and Technology Strategy (summary version)*	2021	9 years	-

from the same 14 real-world technology and engineering strategies reviewed in Chapter 1. The first six strategies in this list address both digital and non-digital technologies. The final eight strategies, from Dundee City Council through to MSI, are digital only.

Table 3.2 reveals that the time horizons for published technology strategies vary from 3 to 13 years. However, the strategies which address only digital products and services tend to be shorter. Is it feasible to have a ten-year IT strategy, given the current rate of innovation? Probably not, although National Highways and MSI have been bold enough to try. In general, the longer timescales are addressing a more diverse range of technologies, notably aerospace and defence engineering.

Some organisations also offer extended visions, typically more than twice the length of their main strategy timescales. All four of the examples in Table 3.2 are focused on non-digital products, including industrial processes and devices (Toshiba) and spacecraft (NASA, UK Space Agency, ESA). Perhaps the rate of technological innovation correlates with the time horizons, i.e. digital = shorter, non-digital = longer.

We might conclude that strategic time horizons are influenced by a wide range of factors, including:

- Technological uncertainty and the rate of innovation.
- The length of major projects, with the space sector in particular requiring upwards of 15 years for delivery.
- Financing periods for large investments (e.g. a 25-year loan repayment may necessitate strategies that address long-term maintenance and decommissioning).
- Organisational stability and confidence in the organisation's future; present-day instability will stifle the urge for long-term thinking, resulting in shorter strategic horizons.

As a general rule, volatile technology domains, shorter projects, shorter asset lifecycles, and organisational instability, all correlate with shorter strategic horizons. Hence, timescales are very context specific and need to be agreed by the strategist in consultation with key stakeholders.

Internal and external communications

The way that strategies are shared will depend upon the intended audience and the sensitivity of the content. As we saw earlier in Table 3.1, a lot of strategising is informal, involving discussions in meetings or decisions communicated to colleagues by conversation or email. This strategy content remains private to the organisation and can therefore address sensitive commercial matters, such as targeted R&D, new product ranges, major reorganisations, and technology choices.

However, a small number of strategy communications are clearly designed for the public domain. The organisations that choose to do this are often non-profits, less concerned with gaining a competitive edge via technology than with demonstrating their accountability to taxpayers, donors, politicians, and other stakeholders. Also, companies with monopoly powers, and therefore few competitors, may be less fearful of sharing their technology plans in public.

It's reasonable to assume that all published strategies feature *highly selective content*. In part, this is because the unvarnished truth is rarely seen as palatable for outsiders, but it would also be impractical to share every strategic idea, no matter how small. A published technology strategy is therefore an exercise in both skilful writing and judicious editing.

Between these two extremes (of informal internal discussions and formally published documents) there lies a middle ground of formally agreed technology strategies communicated internally to all engineering staff. Such communications are likely to take place in large group meetings, perhaps presented by a CTO or CIO. These events can be remarkably candid, notifying the entire workforce of the strategy they will be expected to support and execute. One of the primary benefits of this communication method is the empowerment it gives to frontline personnel. It is now incumbent upon them to act in ways that will support the strategy. Think back to those troops in Chapter 1 who make tactical decisions in battle without needing the approval of generals. This is an efficient form of strategy execution because, in the heat of battle, empowered troops may be the only way to achieve strategic aims.

It is therefore important to employ frontline technologists and engineers with good strategic/tactical thinking skills so that organisational strategies can be shared directly with them and delivered skilfully while 'under fire'. (One of the aims of this book is to support the training of engineers in the development of these skills.)

The business strategy

Earlier in this chapter we looked at the relationship between business strategies and technology strategies. Within most organisations, the business strategy represents the highest level of strategic thinking. It is the cock that rules the roost. Technologies, however, are often the chickens that lay the eggs, underpinning the economic integrity of an organisation. This fact empowers the technologists and engineers.

A good technology strategy should therefore **always** make direct reference to the business strategy. A failure to do this would undermine the organisation's ability to deliver on its primary mission.

In a 2008 study of 225 leaders of Australian manufacturing firms, Bishnu Sharma found examples of how technology strategies respond to business strategies. The study referred to business strategies associated with the work of Harvard's Michael Porter, including *cost leadership* and *differentiation*. It was found that organisations aiming to be cost leaders were averse to the unpredictable costs of developing technologies in-house. Presumably, they preferred to procure from specialists or buy off-the-shelf. Those with a differentiation strategy (i.e. making products that stand out in the market) placed significantly more emphasis on the potential benefits of technology than the cost leaders.[19] Now think about your own work experience. Is there a discernible and direct relationship between your organisation's strategic business goals and the strategic management of your technologies? Is the latter a response to the former? If not, why not?

The business strategy is therefore the first place to look when developing a technology strategy. Everything proposed or planned by the business should be examined from a technological perspective. Then, after the business strategy has been given full consideration, engineering teams may feel empowered to go one step further, generating additional value by innovating new options for the business. This is both creative and fulfilling for technical staff. In this way, a business-focused, solution-oriented engineer can become a valuable strategic asset for the organisation.

Detailed actions

In developing a technology or engineering strategy, an organisation's entire operational environment, both internal and external, will be in scope. Here are some examples of the many thousands of detailed actions which could emerge from a carefully designed strategy:

- Abandon a project no longer compatible with the business strategy.
- Open a technology incubator for employee-led innovations.
- Search for a partner company with which to develop a next-generation product.
- Licence a proprietary technology to a third party if there is no internal appetite to develop it.

- Build stronger relationships between the business department heads and technical support teams.
- Join an industry standards body to gain prior knowledge of future changes and to influence outcomes.
- Acquire a small business already employing the skills needed for an emerging technology.
- Partner with a local university to engage in targeted research and recruit their most talented graduates.
- Work with the sourcing department to avoid dependence upon a dominant supplier for critical components.
- Design future products with 'self-service' features, reducing customer demand upon technical support teams.
- Evaluate the costs/benefits of relocating the R&D function to a thriving high-technology cluster.
- Aim to achieve forward compatibility of at least X years across all products.
- Invest in the technical changes needed to deliver a 'zero harm' safety management system.
- Lobby government to raise concerns about legislation affecting the import of essential materials.
- Engage consultants to advise on the transition from batch to continuous flow processing.
- Undertake research in design for recycling and re-use across all product ranges.

This list could go on and on, but these give a flavour of the actions which might emerge.

Box 3.2 STRATEGIC AND TACTICAL MOVES

Terminating projects

One of the most difficult decisions any manager (or board) can make is to terminate a live project, especially one at a relatively advanced stage of development. There are many reasons to choose termination, including:

- The *business case* is no longer convincing. It might have been strong initially, but the operating environment has probably changed. Business cases are also frequently (sometimes even fraudulently) over-optimistic.
- The project cannot be completed by the *deadline*, and the deadline cannot be moved.
- There are *insufficient funds* to continue. This is not always due to project overspending. Competing demands may have emerged.

- The technology has already been *superseded* by something better.
- Some of the key project resources (e.g. specialist engineers or assets) are needed elsewhere. In other words, the *opportunity cost* of continuing could damage a higher-value activity.

When projects are terminated there will always be winners and losers. Expect potential losers to put up a fight. Indeed, some projects will prove hard to terminate. J. Avery in the *HBR Guide to Thinking Strategically* calls these "zombie projects ... creating less and less value over time but refusing to die."[20] Here are some justifications for 'zombie' projects.

- "We have spent so much already – we cannot just write off the investment." This is known as the *sunk costs fallacy*, throwing good money after bad.
- "The business case might recover again if the context or environment moves in a more favourable direction, so let's keep going and hope for the best." This is a form of gambling.
- "As the management team, we are going to lose face. We approved this project, so now we must see it through." This is sometimes called 'kicking the can down the road'. It's an example of cowardly inaction by people happy to receive leadership salaries, but unwilling to do what's best for their employers.

How can we mitigate for the impact of projects that fail?

- *Monitoring* and *reviews* must identify emerging problems. The earlier the better.
- Delay starting projects until the business case is watertight, then *execute at speed* to minimise the impact of an evolving environment (e.g. the economy, the market, or the actions of a competitor).
- Defer the costliest tasks until later in the project. This delays the onset of the sunk costs fallacy, enabling earlier termination, if required.
- Rather than terminate the entire project, try salvaging it. Identify sub-projects or discrete work packages that still offer value for money. Keep those alive, but shut everything else down.
- Avoid creating large, high-profile 'marquee' projects. These are more susceptible to achieving 'zombie' status. Break them down into more granular, lower profile, more easily terminated deliverables.

What's not in scope?

Thus far, we have only considered the scope of a typical technology or engineering strategy. But what might be out of scope? I will consider some exclusions under four headings:

1 Standalone initiatives and reactions to events
2 The pursuit of technology trends
3 Industrial strategies
4 Technology policies.

Standalone initiatives and reactions to events

It was established in Chapter 1 that a strategy is *an evolving package of concerted actions, designed with a common purpose,* and also that a tactic is *a discrete action executed in support of a strategy.* Consequently, any actions that are executed independently, without reference to other technology initiatives or agreed strategies, are neither strategic nor tactical.

For example, the pursuit of cost-cutting can have a profound impact upon an organisation's technological environment. Yet despite this, cost-cutting is unlikely to be classed as a technology strategy. Greg Carmichael, a former COO and CIO, has called cost-cutting "optimizing something that is already in place. This is not strategic."[21] And in a similar vein, the General Manager of an Italian machinery manufacturer quoted by Rumelt says, "I left the cost-cutting to the last because I wanted the cost-reduction campaign to work with, but not define, the type of machines we build."[22] The *type* of machines would, of course, be determined by the strategy, but not the subsequent cost-cutting.

When James Dyson opted to build a manufacturing operation for his vacuum cleaners, it ran contrary to his original strategy of licensing the patented designs to an established manufacturer. The absence of reliable licensing partners had left him with no option.[23] No option = no strategy.

In 1956 when the Suez Canal was unexpectedly closed by the Egyptian Government, it became necessary for oil to be shipped around Africa and the Cape of Good Hope. Royal Dutch Shell realised that it was no longer necessary for its ships to be limited in scale in order to pass through the shallow Canal. This led to the construction of *Serenia*, their first of many supertankers.[24] The rest of the industry followed suit. Neither the Cape route nor the supertanker designs had been part of anyone's strategy at the time.

Twenty years later, in the economically-disrupted 1970s, when auto makers instructed their designers and engineers to focus on fuel efficiency, this wasn't part of a business strategy to make their vehicles more appealing to customers. It was a knee-jerk response to yet another oil crisis and the sudden quadrupling of prices.

A large proportion of decisions within the technological realm are simply reactive. They are not strategic.

The pursuit of trends

Industry journals thrive on the presentation of technological breakthroughs and exciting new products, confusingly described as either 'hot' or 'cool'. All technological domains experience this phenomenon. Here are some memorable examples from the 1990s and beyond: virtual reality, mobile apps, artificial intelligence, 3D printing, IoT, electric vehicles, fusion energy, quantum computing, and so on. Sometimes, in the absence of any objective analysis or justification, an organisation will introduce one of these technologies for 'fear of missing out' or because it's fashionable.

Of course, the adoption of a fashionable new technology is not necessarily wrong, but the decision to deploy it may *not* have been made in support of any agreed strategy, nor might there be a strong enough business case. Business professor Amrit Tiwana of the University of Georgia reminds decision makers that "You do not need a Cadillac when a Chevy will do."[25] In his analysis of educational technologies, Webster describes this mentality as *"Keep up with technology (or be left behind)"*.[26] Compounding this problem is the fact that the newest technologies are likely to be both expensive to acquire and unreliable once deployed. There are many factors that should influence the development of a technology strategy, but fashion isn't one of them.

There's nothing wrong with using any technology, new or old, providing it is deployed for the right reasons, in the right place, at the right time.

Industrial strategies

An 'industrial strategy' sounds like a technology strategy, but it's not. Governments of all hues manage their economies through various forms of intervention. Their macroeconomic policies are typically geared towards outcomes such as export growth, reduced dependency upon imports, achieving high levels of employment, and attracting inward investment. In order to do this, they set out a package of ideas for improving industrial performance. Here 'industrial' usually means business activities in general, although policies sometimes target a specific industrial sector.

These industrial strategies may support or encourage innovation practices, vocational training, international cooperation, better transport infrastructures, and so on. Specific measures can include changes to legislation, overseas trade missions, and a broad range of financial incentives such as grants, loans, or tax breaks. A contemporary example is the promotion of low carbon technologies.

In this book, we have considered three very different types of strategy: *military*, *business*, and *technology*. In these examples, the strategy developers are also the strategy-doers. Those who make the strategy, also execute the strategy. But industrial strategies do not follow this pattern. Democratic governments rarely have the desire to get directly involved in their delivery. Instead, they incentivise and encourage independent companies and frontline public institutions to perform the work.

Although national industrial strategies are not technology strategies, they remain of interest to us because they present both opportunities and threats to our own strategy development. **We also have the ability to influence industrial strategy through campaigning, lobbying, and the democratic process.**

Technology policies

Some years ago I had the good fortune to attend the Technology Policy programme developed jointly by the universities of Cambridge and MIT. There is no doubt that its curriculum addressed many topics of interest to technology strategists. Over the course of nine months, I studied subjects as diverse as system dynamics, intellectual property, complexity theory, engineering ethics, sustainable construction techniques, and the design life of structures. The programme at Cambridge has described itself as developing skills "integrating technology, management, economics, and policy" with "a focus on business-government interaction".[27]

Clearly *policy* is the operative word here because the Technology Policy programme was largely concerned with matters of *public policy* and the way that companies or entrepreneurs navigate their way through a world of laws and regulations.

We often associate policies with governments, but companies have them, too, often with technological implications. For example, most large organisations have security policies, procurement policies, data privacy policies, and so on. Hence, for all practical purposes the phrase 'technology policy' encapsulates policies in both the public and private sectors.

So, what are the main differences between a policy and a strategy? A policy is often defined as a 'principle' or a 'framework' for action. Policies tend to be more rigid or durable, whereas strategies are fundamentally dynamic. Policies often remain in place for years without revision or amendment and, more importantly, they rarely consist of specific actions with assigned responsibilities or deadlines. Strategies however are both action-oriented and begin to depreciate (become outdated and lose validity) as soon as they are issued; hence, strategies need constant attention and frequent revisions.

Therefore, **we should not confuse a technology policy with a technology strategy**, although it might be argued that each is capable of influencing the shape and contents of the other.

What's the point?

There is an overriding question here which we have not yet fully addressed. Why should organisations go to the trouble of developing technology strategies, especially in a fast-moving world? Why not rely upon day-to-day management decision making, supported by the skills and experience of frontline staff? The answer to this question should become obvious if we try listing some advantages of a well-designed, formal technology strategy:

- It strengthens the business strategy, encouraging a focus on the technologies which support primary business activities.
- It improves overall financial performance through more confident long-term planning, enabling contracting, bulk purchasing, and so on.
- It increases the involvement and, therefore, the job satisfaction of technical personnel.
- It provides greater accountability and transparency for stakeholders.
- It enables stakeholders to plan their parallel or complementary activities with greater confidence.
- It demonstrates effective control and good governance of engineering functions and technical teams.
- It adds tangible value to the organisation through the skilful management of technology assets.
- It helps to navigate ethical challenges associated with technology, thereby avoiding reputational damage.
- It minimises future technical debt (thereby delivering intangible benefits over the longer term).
- It helps to manage uncertainty and control risk.

To *prove* the true worth of a technology strategy one would need to demonstrate a direct relationship between the strategy and its intended benefits. We noted earlier that there are plenty of cynics with little time for formal strategy development. However, my research did find some evidence to support the thesis that technology strategies deliver net benefits to organisations.

For example, strategy research conducted by the *MIT Sloan Management Review*, in conjunction with Deloitte, found that in 'early-stage' digital organisations, more than half of respondents to their survey cited "lack of strategy" as a significant barrier for their organisation. In the more mature 'developing' digital organisations, this absence of strategy was still regarded as a challenge by one-third of respondents.[28] Some years earlier, in a survey of Australian manufacturing CEOs, Sharma looked at seven types of functional strategy, concluding that "technology strategy was the second most effective strategy after operations strategy". This supported *Hypothesis 1b* of the research, specifically that "Technology strategy adopted in Australian manufacturing industry is effective."[29] There must be more research out there, but I have yet to find it. None of this is conclusive, but it gives the anti-strategists something to think about.

Even cynics would surely agree that the process one goes through when developing a strategy supports organisational learning. It challenges the assumptions of everyone involved and exposes the strategy developers to new information and ideas. This can only be beneficial in the long run.

Technology strategies are needed. QED.

Box 3.3   STRATEGIC DICHOTOMIES

Co-location OR Cloistering?

Technologists and engineers are passionate about their craft. They thrive in purely technical environments alongside their peers. Hours are often long, overtime rarely paid, and personal thanks from stakeholders virtually unheard of. When 'recognition' does come, it's usually in the form of criticism: either something has failed or isn't meeting expectations. Consequently, the relationship between technical people and their internal stakeholders often constitutes a 'them and us' culture. This divide may be reflected organisationally, because technical teams are often physically separated from their non-technical colleagues. Sometimes *co-location*, bringing everyone together, is offered as a solution.

The theory is that co-location enables greater day-to-day interaction. Technical work becomes demystified and appreciated, while technologists and engineers are more exposed to the broader organisational culture and its principal challenges. Business writer and anthropologist, Gillian Tett, advocates this breaking down of 'silos' with the aim of enabling more "social collisions".[30] For example, the integrated design-build teams (DBTs), used by Boeing during development of the 777 airliner, provide a successful example of cross-functional integration and co-location.[31]

However, co-location can be detrimental. Technical activities not only require immense concentration, but errors or distractions can have disastrous consequences. Furthermore, technical environments often contain sensitive material protected under law, such as customer data or commercially sensitive plans. So maybe it's better to keep technologists and engineers physically separated from the rest of the organisation.

This is what I call *cloistering*: physically isolating the offices or workshops of technical teams. One of the most famous and successful examples of cloistering has been the Lockheed Skunk Works facility in California. It was set up to enable aerospace engineers and manufacturing technicians to design and build, in secrecy, the world's fastest, stealthiest aircraft. For decades these workers have been thriving in a collegiate environment, unmolested by auditors and corporate bureaucrats.[32] Similarly, when IBM opted to develop a desktop computer in the 1970s, one commentator suggested it would be "like teaching an elephant to tap dance." IBM's solution was to set up an independent unit in Florida which, in Grant and Jordan's words, was "freed from the usual organizational constraints".[33] What emerged was the all-conquering PC. It's also common for outsourcing and offshoring arrangements (see Box 8.2) to involve purely technical teams, perhaps to enable the same degree of focus.

There is also a middle way between co-location and cloistering. The use of *secondments* involves rotating the best or most promising business and technical personnel within an organisation, broadening their knowledge, skills, and internal networks. This benefits all parties, breaking down internal barriers without significant disruption to the work of the technical and engineering teams.

Where are we going, why, and how?

As we saw in Chapter 1, there is no agreed format, model, or template for creating a technology strategy. It's likely that large corporations and consultancies will each have their own methodology, although there will be variations in approach. What follows is a synopsis of my method for developing an effective technology strategy. This will be developed in full towards the end of the book.

Throughout the strategy development process, I will refer to the *five dimensions* of technology introduced in Chapter 2. **This is the only way to be certain that we are taking into consideration all of the factors affecting technologies.** We must always be conscious of the physical dimension (materials, hardware), the logical dimension (how things work), the architectural dimension (arrangements and combinations), the yield dimension (outputs, the distribution of value), and the stakeholder dimension (users, direct beneficiaries).

We begin by asking the question *Where are we today?* If we can't answer that, then we can't propose a way forward. A baseline is needed. This should be a summary of the current technological environment we are developing the strategy for. It needs just enough detail to support the analysis. It must start with a listing of the technologies in scope and the systems they contribute to. In addition, we need to know about the technical staff (employees and contractors), the customers or users, the product and service offerings (of both the company and its competitors), the legal and regulatory environment, and any other relevant factors.[34]

Concurrent with this data gathering, we should be examining the business strategy. This will be the driver for most of the new technology strategy. Amrit Tiwana writes specifically about information technology, but his ideas are sufficiently generic for us to apply them more broadly. Tiwana emphasises the importance of engaging with the business throughout the strategy development process, arguing that "Lack of business involvement is *the* primary reason that IT is often uneconomical and strategically feeble."[35] You will therefore need business representation on the development team for the new technology strategy.

What if there is no formal business strategy to refer to? How will that impact the development? Is it possible to have a technology strategy without reference to a business strategy? In this situation, the input from your business representatives becomes even more important. They must act as proxies for the business strategy. Although this situation is far from ideal, do not allow the absence of a business strategy to prevent the development of a technology strategy. You need to discover and understand the organisation's medium and long-term goals and the mechanisms they will be using to achieve them.

We now have a baseline and an understanding of business needs. The next step is to review the 'state of the art'. As strategists, it is our job to ensure, in Braun's words "that the firm is aware of technological and scientific developments that might offer future opportunities for better production technologies or new/improved products."[36] We need to understand the latest innovations and any anticipated future versions of the technologies in current use. The state of the art also encompasses new and emerging practices, methodologies, theories, and so on. Don't forget to use the five dimensions as a guide during state of the art research.

Our next task is to consider the major challenges faced by both the business and technology or engineering teams. These challenges come in a variety of forms, too many to list here. Many will be concerned with the unknown – the various uncertainties ahead. (The concept of *uncertainty* is of fundamental importance to strategy development, so the next three chapters will be devoted to that subject.) It might even be necessary to use a *foresight* process for developing scenarios related to the future evolution of technology within the organisation. (Foresight processes will also be introduced in later chapters.) Finally, frontline technologists and engineers should introduce any ideas they have for the development of their operational practices and product lines.

The research phase is now over. It's time to produce a statement of the organisation's strategic vision for technology. We must answer the question, *Where are we going, and why?* In other words, the strategic vision lays down a description of the organisation's technological environment in X years' time, where X is the chosen time horizon (5 years, for example). I will argue that this statement should neither be lengthy, nor too specific in detail, but it needs to contain all of the organisation's key technological objectives. **Remember, the strategy is a communication to fellow practitioners and other stakeholders. In order for it to be effective, it must be easily understood, and hopefully remembered, by everyone.**

The following proverb is apposite here: "Vision without action is a daydream. Action without vision is a nightmare." So, in order to have any credibility or effectiveness, the strategic vision must be followed by a high-level statement of delivery answering the question *How are we going to get there?* It may be tempting to put a lot of detail into this section, but again this should be resisted. A detailed delivery statement will depreciate rapidly as the business and technology environments continue to evolve.

The statement of delivery might include proposals for new projects and product ranges, the adoption of standards, new or revised technology policies, trials of emerging technologies, and so on. It only needs a sentence or two on each item. It should mirror the definition from Chapter 1, of being a "package of concerted actions, designed with a common purpose."

And that's it! That's the strategy: a vision statement followed by a delivery statement.

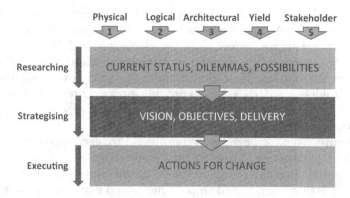

Figure 3.3 The Five Dimensions Process: a method for developing technology strategies

What follows next are the details, notably who's doing what and when? This action-oriented information does **not** belong in the formal strategy text, because it represents the day-to-day tactical work of delivery.

Hence, this strategy development and delivery process consists of three stages: 1) preparatory research; 2) production of a vision statement and delivery statement; and 3) the execution of the strategy.

I have just summarised what I call *The Five Dimensions Process*. All five of the PLAYS dimensions should be uppermost in the minds of strategists throughout the development. Figure 3.3 is a simplified illustration of this method. In Chapter 12, I will present a full description of the process.

Strategies are alive

A reasonable criticism of formally produced and documented strategies is that they depreciate rapidly. They have a short 'half-life'. Any proposals not enacted or implemented immediately are increasingly likely to be overtaken by events. The business environment is constantly evolving and so is the technological realm. Nothing stands still. Therefore, no strategy should be so tightly bound by words and prescriptive actions that it loses the capacity to flex. The best strategies are like living organisms. They must be allowed to breathe.

As explained earlier, both the vision statement and the statement of delivery should be concise. This helps with the longevity of the strategy. It also aids communication. Currency and validity can be maintained by undertaking periodic reviews. The details of how and when to perform this essential task should be decided by the leadership team. Two factors will determine the frequency of revisions: elapsed time and events.

Elapsed time: For how long should the wording of a strategy remain static? Many organisations opt for 12 months. That's a reasonable balance between half-life 'depletion' and the cost of the revision exercise. By contrast, quarterly revisions would overwhelm the strategy development team. It would also annoy those stakeholders regularly asked to provide inputs. Three years, on the other hand, is surely too long given the pace of change in the technological realm.

Events: Arguably, certain events should trigger a revision of the technology strategy. These include major corporate acquisitions, substantial internal reorganisations or divestments, withdrawal from a major market, and so on. One would expect each of these to result in an immediate revision of the business strategy, and this would of course impact the technology strategy. Technological events could include a lengthy supply chain interruption caused by a war, new technical legislation affecting a key product range, a major scientific discovery, the withdrawal of a technical partner, and so on.

A technology strategy must be as relevant and up-to-date as possible. An outdated strategy is one which staff will rapidly lose confidence in. However, there is an important balance to be struck between too many revisions and too few. Chapter 12 will look again at this topic and offer further advice.

A definition

We can now adapt the generic definition for a *strategy* (developed in Chapter 1) in order to define what we mean by a *technology strategy*. It seems reasonable to argue that it will possess the same basic attributes. However, its focus will be strictly within the technological realm, and subservient to organisational needs.

A DEFINITION FOR *TECHNOLOGY STRATEGY*

A technology strategy is an evolving package of concerted actions within the technological realm, supporting organisational goals.

The technology strategist

Finally, a word about the technology strategist. Who is this person? Could it be you? These questions are not difficult to answer because anyone directly involved in the development of a technology strategy, or devising a tactic to support that strategy, could be described as a technology strategist. It may not be a job title (although it can be), but it's clearly an important professional role.

According to Eben Hewitt, as a technology strategist, you may be expected to do some, or all, of the following:

- Survey the landscape across your industry, organisation, customers, stakeholders, competitors, and employees.
- Examine technology trends.
- Determine current priorities, problems, and possible opportunities.
- Analyse and synthesise these problems and opportunities into a course of action: decide what to do, and what not to do.
- Make strong recommendations for how to allocate your company's resources, in what way, in what places, to what extent, and to what end.[37]

Clearly, to be a technology strategist does require at least a moderate level of experience and expertise. It also helps to have a strategic mindset – to think strategically. (This mindset will be examined in Chapter 7.)

The next chapter examines *uncertainty*. This is arguably the primary justification for developing any kind of strategy, because without uncertainty we could simply make plans, and be confident in their successful delivery.

Glossary for this chapter (Items in bold are also defined in the same table)

business case	The economic justification for a course of action, such as starting a **project**. It includes consideration of both tangible and intangible factors.
cloistering	The physical isolation of specialist teams in order to create an unencumbered working environment. Contrast with **co-location**.
co-location	Bringing organisational functions together on a single site. It aims to improve knowledge sharing and cultural integration. Secondments are a more granular form of co-location. Contrast with **cloistering**.
industrial strategy	A public **policy** targeting macroeconomic outcomes such as export growth, reduced dependency upon imports, high levels of employment, and increased inward investment.

(Continued)

(Continued)

policy	A principle or framework for action. Unlike strategies, policies are unlikely to feature allocated tasks or deadlines.
project	A temporary organisational structure for delivering products or outcomes according to a formal set of requirements/specifications.
strategic asset	An asset critical to the implementation of current or future strategy. Physical or tangible strategic assets include machinery, specialist tools, or buildings. Non-physical or intangible assets include patents, skills, and trade secrets.
technical debt	A phrase often associated with software development, although the concept applies throughout the technological realm. The 'debt' analogy describes how poor quality work and inadequate documentation accumulate, generating 'interest' and overheads in the form of additional work. Once accumulated, technical debts are rarely 'settled'.
technology domain	An informal grouping or 'family' of related technologies, products, and ancillary activities, e.g. aviation, telecommunications. Larger domains may include sub-domains.
technology policy	A **policy** for the technological realm.
technology strategist	Anyone directly involved in the development of a **technology strategy** or devising tactics to support such a strategy.
technology strategy	An evolving package of concerted actions within the technological realm, supporting organisational goals. For clarity it is best expressed in written form.

Notes

1 Hewitt, E. (2018) *Technology Strategy Patterns*. Sebastopol, CA: O'Reilly. 5–7.
2 Rumelt, R. (2017) *Good Strategy, Bad Strategy*. London: Profile Books. 136.
3 Braun, E. (1998) *Technology in Context*. London: Routledge. 61.
4 Freeman, R.E., Harrison, J.S. and Wicks, A.C. (2007) *Managing for Stakeholders*. New Haven: Yale University Press. 30.
5 Grant, R.M. and Jordan, J. (2015) *Foundations of Strategy*. Chichester: Wiley. 115.
6 Afuah, A. (2003) *Innovation Management*. New York: OUP. 125.
7 Rumelt, *Good Strategy, Bad Strategy*. 61–62.
8 Singapore Airlines 'The Singapore Airlines Fleet'. Available at: https://www.singaporeair.com/en_UK/us/flying-withus/our-story/our-fleet/ (Accessed: 12 February 2022).
9 Grant and Jordan, *Foundations of Strategy*. 121–122.
10 Pyster, A., Hutchison, N. and Henry, D. (2018) *The Paradoxical Mindset of Systems Engineers*. Hoboken: Wiley. 220–221.
11 Hewitt, *Technology Strategy Patterns*. 101.

12 Axelos Limited (2011) *ITIL glossary and abbreviations*, available at: https://www.axelos.com/corporate/media/files/glossaries/itil_2011_glossary_gb-v1-0.pdf (Accessed: 19 March 2019).

13 Arthur, W.B. (2010) *The Nature of Technology*. London: Penguin. 145.

14 Arthur, *The Nature of Technology*. 70.

15 Arthur. 175–176.

16 National Highways (2022) *Operational Technology: Our 2035 Strategy*, available at https://nationalhighways.co.uk/media/n1edbo0z/operational_technology_strategy_2035_issue-may-2022.pdf (Accessed: 05 September 2022).

17 McGrath, J. and Bates, B. (2013) *The Little Book of Big Management Theories*. Edinburgh: Pearson. 148.

18 The strategy documents used in Table 3.2 are as follows:

- Australian Department of Defence (undated) *Defence Science and Technology Strategy 2030*, available at https://www.dst.defence.gov.au/strategy/defence-science-and-technology-strategy-2030 (Accessed: 31 August 2022).
- City of Coquitlam (2018) *2019–2024 Coquitlam Technology Strategy*, available at https://www.coquitlam.ca/620/Coquitlam-Technology-Strategy (Accessed: 31 August 2022).
- Toshiba Corporation (2018) *Technology Strategy*, available at https://www.toshiba.co.jp/about/ir/en/pr/pdf/tpr20181122e_1.pdf (Accessed: 09 September 2022).
- UK Space Agency, Centre for Earth Observation Instrumentation (2019) *Technology Strategy*, available at https://www.gov.uk/government/publications/uk-earth-observation-technology-strategy (Accessed: 31 August 2022).
- European Space Agency (2022) *Technology Strategy*, available at: https://esamultimedia.esa.int/docs/technology/ESA_Technology_Strategy_Version_1_0.pdf (Accessed: 06 October 2023).
- NASA (undated) *Strategic Plan 2022*, available at https://www.nasa.gov/sites/default/files/atoms/files/fy_22_strategic_plan.pdf (Accessed: 02 September 2022).
- Dundee City Council (undated) *Information Technology Strategy*, available at https://www.dundeecity.gov.uk/sites/default/files/publications/dcc_it_strategy_final.docx (Accessed: 03 September 2022).
- City and County of San Francisco (undated) *Information and Communication Technology Plan FY 2022–26*, available at https://sf.gov/coit-strategy (Accessed: 03 September 2022).
- Social Security Scotland (2022) *Digital and Technology Strategy 2022–2025*, available at https://www.socialsecurity.gov.scot/asset-storage/production/downloads/Digital-and-Technology-Strategy-2022-%E2%80%93-25.pdf (Accessed: 03 September 2022).
- UK Home Office (2021) *Digital, Data and Technology 2024 Strategy*, available at https://www.gov.uk/government/publications/home-office-digital-data-and-technology-strategy-2024 (Accessed: 04 September 2022).
- Irish Department of Agriculture, Food and the Marine (2021) *Information Management and Technology Strategy 2021–2024*, available at https://assets.gov.ie/133805/f322bfba-c5fa-4ac5-915e-bdabe280f6e5.pptx (Accessed: 04 September 2022).

- New Zealand Ministry of Social Development (2022) *Technology Strategy*, available at https://www.msd.govt.nz/about-msd-and-our-work/publications-resources/corporate/msd-technology-strategy.html (Accessed: 04 September 2022).
- National Highways, *Operational Technology: our 2035 strategy*.
- MSI Reproductive Choices (2021) *Digital and Technology Strategy* (summary version), available at https://www.msichoices.org/news-and-insights/resources/choice-in-a-digital-age-msi-choices-digital-and-technology-strategy/ (Accessed: 05 September 2022).

19 Sharma, B. (2008) 'Technology Strategy, Contextual Factors and Business Performance: An Investigation of Their Relationship'. *South Asian Journal of Management*, Vol. 15, Issue 3, 19–39.
20 Avery, J. (2019) 'Identify and Kill Outdated Objectives' in *HBR Guide to Thinking Strategically*. Boston (MA): HBR Press. 146.
21 High, P.A. (2014) *Implementing World Class IT Strategy*. San Francisco: Wiley. 13.
22 Rumelt. 121.
23 Dyson, J. (2011) *Against the Odds: An Autobiography*. Andover: Cengage Learning. 129.
24 Howarth, S. (1997) *A Century in Oil: the "Shell" Transport and Trading Company 1897–1997*. London: Weidenfeld & Nicolson. 255–256.
25 Tiwana, A. (2017) *IT Strategy for Non-IT Managers: Becoming an Engaged Contributor to Corporate IT Decisions*. Cambridge, MA: The MIT Press. 36–37.
26 Webster, M.D. (2017) 'Philosophy of Technology Assumptions in Educational Technology Leadership'. *Educational Technology & Society*, Vol. 20, Issue 1, 25–36.
27 Anon (2022) 'MPhil in Technology Policy'. Available at https://www.jbs.cam.ac.uk/programmes/mphil-technology-policy/ (Accessed: 18 February 2022).
28 Kane, G.C. *et al.* (2015) 'Strategy, not Technology, Drives Digital Transformation'. *MIT Sloan Management Review, Research Report*, Summer 2015. Available at https://www2.deloitte.com/content/dam/Deloitte/fr/Documents/strategy/dup_strategy-not-technology-drives-digital-transformation.pdf (Accessed: 28 August 2019).
29 Sharma, *South Asian Journal of Management*, Vol. 15, Issue 3, 19–39.
30 Tett, G. (2016) *The Silo Effect*. London: Little, Brown. 307.
31 Pyster, Hutchison, and Henry, *The Paradoxical Mindset of Systems Engineers*. 119.
32 Westwick, P. (2020) *Stealth: The Secret Contest to Invent Invisible Aircraft*. New York: OUP. 34, 112–113.
33 Grant and Jordan. 172.
34 High, *Implementing World Class IT Strategy*. 175–176.
35 Tiwana, *IT Strategy for Non-IT Managers*. 1.
36 Braun, *Technology in Context*. 83.
37 Hewitt. 28–29.

4 The unexpected
In the realm where uncertainty is King

This chapter presents

- An introduction to technological uncertainty and its strategic significance.

This chapter establishes

- The relationship between proximal and root causes.
- The impact of lifeforms (especially people) on uncertainty.
- A revised definition of 'strategy' in the context of uncertainty.

If we could see or predict the future, all events and their outcomes would be known in advance. Decision making would be taught in the language of Newtonian mechanics, of actions and reactions. Action A would be followed by reaction B, and B would precede C. The time, place, and characteristics of A, B, and C would always be known precisely. Certainty would prevail. Planning would be easy. We would have no need for strategists.

Understandably, this is how we want to manage our technical environments: "Let's do X at time T1 to enable Y at T2. This will give us Z at T3." In their book *Embracing Complexity* (2015), J. Boulton *et al.* note that "This pervasive mechanical worldview maintains its attraction as it provides a sense of order, purpose, and control."[1]

However, the real world of technology decision making is a long way from Newtonian ideals. In the technological realm uncertainty is King. The fact that futures are hazy is the principal justification for developing strategies. This challenges the notion that a strategy is a plan.

In his *Theory of Strategy* (2018), C. Gray refers to "the fragility of prediction", noting "the prominent role played by unintended consequences."[2] Thomas Chermack, a specialist in organisational decision making at Colorado State University, puts it more bluntly: "The future often acts like a drunken monkey stung by a bee".[3]

DOI: 10.4324/9781003472919-5

So, one of the ideas central to this book is captured in this simple statement: **A strategy is not a plan. It's a proposal for navigating uncertainty.**

In this chapter, and the two that follow, I will explore this concept of uncertainty, using many examples from technology and engineering history. I will then get beneath the skin of the topic, culminating in the identification of 18 *origins of uncertainty* within the technological realm. These origins could help us to develop better strategies by highlighting where our research and analysis of threats and opportunities need to be focused.

You win some, you lose some

For every technical decision there are four types of outcomes: 1) exactly as expected; 2) better than expected; 3) worse than expected; and 4) neither better nor worse but unexpectedly different. The first outcome is highly unlikely, particularly at the lowest level of detail. No future can be *exactly* as expected. This leaves three types of unexpected outcomes: better, worse, and merely different. Consequently, as professional technologists and engineers, we must expect the unexpected, and we have a duty to incorporate this thinking into our decision making.

Better than expected

Two examples. In the 1950s and 1960s when nuclear reactors were a novel technology, it was difficult, if not impossible, to determine how long each device would remain operational. In the US, reactor vessels were given a nominal design life of 40 years, but in the intervening period, knowledge of material ageing has improved. Consequently, some of these early vessels are now being licensed for periods of 60–80 years.[4]

More recently Adobe was faced with the uncertainty of transitioning from a traditional software licensing model to the now familiar software-as-a-service (or SaaS). The established model, involving single payments followed by support 'in perpetuity', was to be replaced by online access via annual subscriptions. Sunil Gupta of Harvard Business School uses a good metaphor to describe the challenge facing Adobe:

> It is like changing the engine of a plane while in flight. The plane is going to go down first before it goes up again – and that is a scary and uncertain time, when everyone in the organization starts questioning the company's strategy.

Unsurprisingly, Adobe experienced an immediate slump in business as the 'engines' of the old licensing model were changed, but this was only temporary. Within a few years, the company had more than doubled its pre-SaaS net income.[5]

Worse than expected

These types of unwanted events are more familiar to us, mainly because the media revels in tales of disastrous outcomes, particularly when the likes of Shell, NASA, or Kodak take the hit. Let's look at a few examples.

During the early days of rapid growth in the rail industry, track widths varied between independent lines. Each operating company favoured a particular gauge. I.K. Brunel, the British engineer, had selected a broad gauge for his Great Western Railway (GWR) project. At just over seven feet (2,140 mm), it would be technically superior to competing gauges, enabling a lower centre of gravity, higher speeds, and a smoother ride. Most other companies were opting for the narrower 'standard' gauge favoured by railway pioneer, George Stephenson. For Britain to have an integrated rail network, it was necessary for one gauge to prevail. This sparked a vigorous public and Parliamentary debate. A technical competition was even arranged to evaluate the options.[6] To his great frustration Brunel lost the so-called 'gauge war', though not on engineering grounds. The GWR was compelled to change all of its track in the west of England, at immense cost, so through-trains could then operate between north and south.

Sixty years later, the British Navy, the world's largest at that time, had successfully transitioned from sail to coal-powered steam. However, oil was emerging as a new and potentially superior fuel, emitting less smoke, occupying less space within ships, and requiring smaller crews. In 1902, the emerging oil company, Shell, arranged for a demonstration in Portsmouth harbour using the Navy ship *HMS Hannibal*. For Shell, the commercial stakes were extremely high, with the opportunity to secure a lucrative Navy contract. At the time, Shell's own tanker fleet was already using modern, virtually smoke-free atomising burners, but *HMS Hannibal*'s burners were vaporisers, not atomisers. This would be a costly oversight. The story of what happened is told by Shell's historian, Stephen Howarth:

Leaving harbour, the warship trailed light white smoke from her furnaces fired with Welsh coal. At a signal, the switch to liquid fuel was made; and within minutes, the funnel discharged large volumes of black soot, followed by thick clouds of black smoke ...

Navy observers, including an Admiral, were not impressed. According to Howarth, "this single demonstration delayed the introduction of fuel oil into the fleet for nearly 10 years."[7]

In the 1950s, the US military was designing a supersonic strategic bomber, the B-70, with the aim of defeating Soviet air defences by flying at high altitude. However, in 1960 a U2 reconnaissance plane was shot down. This revealed the inconvenient fact that Soviet surface-to-air missiles could reach these formerly invincible altitudes. It was therefore necessary to revise US military strategy, favouring missiles over bombers. Only two prototypes for the B-70 were ever built.[8]

Thirty years after the U2's ill-fated attempt to capture high-resolution photos of Soviet defences, the launch of the Hubble Space Telescope in 1990 promised pin-sharp views of distant galaxies. But the images transmitted to Earth were blurred. In the words of aerospace historian Thomas Heppenheimer, NASA's "billion-dollar blunder" was the product of too much faith being placed in the pre-launch testing, later found to have been seriously flawed.[9]

In the same year that Hubble was launched, MIT's James Utterback, in his book *Mastering the Dynamics of Innovation* (1994), was discussing the commercial potential of digital photography. He speculated that the new technology "may become the way people take pictures in the future – which raises the question of how the massive industry based on photosensitive film will respond."[10] Utterback mused over the fate of companies like Kodak and Fuji, plus the camera makers and thousands of independent film processors around the world. Kodak, for instance, was an iconic global brand, and the company was fortunate in having considerable knowledge of digital imaging based on early research. Utterback gave them fair warning:

> If electronic imaging represents the future, Kodak will have to leap from its century-old expertise in fine chemicals and the production of coated films and papers to a field in which expertise in electronics and digital technology is critical.[11]

The sales of digital cameras began to grow in the late 1990s and camera phones emerged soon after. Like Hubble, Kodak's vision was impaired. Despite the strength of their brand, Kodak's products failed to impress the market. Hopelessly out of focus, they filed for bankruptcy in 2011. Starting from such a promising position, Kodak's demise was genuinely unexpected.

The final example of disappointing outcomes concerns the extraction of gas via hydraulic fracturing (or fracking). This technique is well established and highly efficient, especially in the US. If geological conditions are conducive, an abundance of inexpensive gas is almost guaranteed. However, attempts to introduce this method outside the US have been problematic, despite the granting of drilling licenses in many countries.[12] To the surprise of both the operators and their government sponsors, strong public opposition has emerged, mainly in response to fears about ground water pollution, earth tremors, and the effects of gas production on climate change. The growth of fracking has now largely stalled outside North America, leaving a sense of bewilderment in the industry.

Unexpectedly different

Sometimes the outcomes are neither better nor worse, just different. These neutral outcomes may not make headlines, but they are just as likely to upset the smooth implementation of a strategy. Let's take just one example, which played out over many years at significant cost to an entire industrial sector.

The year 1951 saw the first of many post-war 'oil shocks' which re-shaped the economics of both the oil industry and its technologies.[13] In that year the assets of the Anglo-Iranian Oil Company were nationalised by the government of Iran. These assets included the Abadan refinery, at that time the largest in the world. Other major oil companies realised that this new type of commercial risk necessitated new thinking. A strategic shift was necessary. The geographical sources of oil could not be altered, of course. Therefore, in order to minimise the impact of hostile and unstable governments it was necessary to reconfigure the logistics of crude oil refining.

The original model involved refining oil at source, then transporting the refined products to global markets via specialist tankers. This became untenable after 1951. It was now more logical to ship the crude oil directly to those regions where it was wanted, and refine it there into the products demanded by local economies, such as gasoline optimised for regional climates and jet fuel piped directly to aviation hubs. Howarth explains:

> All told, this was to be a major shift in construction policy, but in addition to enhanced safety for refineries it had three other attractive aspects. Firstly, any interruption of supply from one source could more readily be made good by supply from another; secondly, transporting products from refinery to market-place

would be much cheaper; and thirdly, tankers would no longer have to be designed to carry several different grades of oil. Instead only one grade, raw crude, would need to be shipped. This too would be more economical – and even more so if new single-cargo tankers were bigger than traditional ones.[14]

These events played out over many years, hastened by further oil shocks. The net outcome, however, is the oil industry we see today, in which enormous ships transport crude oil around the globe to regional refineries.

The unexpected nationalisation of the Abadan refinery had precipitated a domino effect from which there were few substantial winners or losers among the major operators. However, the industry had fundamentally and permanently changed.

Clearly, uncertainty impinges upon both technologies and engineering practice in myriad ways. Perhaps we should take a closer look at the causes of this uncertainty.

Why?

For each of the examples above, it is relatively easy to attribute one or more causes or simple explanations for the unexpected event or outcome. Indeed the more we look for possible causes, the more we will find. When I was working in the financial services sector, all team leaders in our Infrastructure Group were required to complete a *Root Cause Analysis* in response to any unexpected events that had significantly impacted business operations. Fortunately, these were rare. Nevertheless, this was a useful exercise because it compelled busy analysts and engineers to pause and think deeply about why a particular problem had arisen. This process introduced two types of causes:

1 Those which are chronologically adjacent to the event, known as proximal causes (or sometimes 'proximate' causes).
2 Far deeper antecedents, which underly the proximal causes, often called "root causes".

If we adopt this simple approach we should be able to attribute causes for each of the events described (see Table 4.1). Arguably this two-tiered structure of proximal and root causes lacks analytical rigour, although it does make a small contribution to our understanding of unexpected events.

Let's not forget that there are often *multiple* proximal causes and *multiple* root causes. In industries with strong safety management cultures, such as aviation, accident investigations often find

Table 4.1 Unexpected events and possible causes

Event	'Proximal cause'	'Root cause'
Reactor life extensions	Regulatory approval	Slower than expected degradation
Adobe SaaS transition success	Customers adjusted to the new model	Good strategic choice and timing
Broad gauge hits the buffers	Consensus favoured narrower gauge	Failure to appreciate 'network effect'
Fuel hopes sink during demo	Unsuitable burner technology	Poor planning for a high-stakes event
Bomber vulnerability	The 'U2 incident'	Absence of missile intelligence
Hubble reflects NASA's flaws	Faulty test device and practices	Poor project oversight by management
Kodak loses focus	Unimpressive digital products	Weak and naïve business/tech strategy
Fracking cracks under pressure	Public objections to new technology	Insufficient early public engagement
Oil industry restructured	Political events in the Middle East	Flawed industry model

that serious incidents have multiple simultaneous causes (both proximal and root). For example, an aircraft's hydraulic failure, arising from a poorly written maintenance procedure, may be further compounded by an incorrect pilot response associated with poor cockpit design, resulting from inadequate evaluation during development, as a consequence of pressure from senior management to deliver a new aircraft version. This type of simultaneity is so difficult to foresee that even the best safety regimes remain vulnerable.

Some readers will be reminded of the so-called *Five Whys* technique for discovering underlying causes. This method requires the analyst to ask "why" up to five times, until a suitable explanation, cause or solution is found. However, in technical environments, the point at which analysts should stop asking "why" (i.e. settling upon a cause) is clearly problematic. In a complex world, how many layers of verifiable causes are there?

Influential product designer Donald Norman expresses dismay at the ease with which, when things go wrong, the causes are attributed to people rather than to the design of procedures or equipment.[15] The classic example, only too common, is when an accident is attributed to "operator error", but later found to have been caused by poor ergonomics or misleading data. Human error

is often the most convenient conclusion, because it diverts attention from flawed management practices and suspect engineering
quality, both of which trigger opposition from their professional
defenders. Nevertheless, **a great deal of uncertainty in technological environments must, inevitably, be attributed to human
behaviour, because the technological realm is entirely a human
construct.** We will come back to the role of people (and other
lifeforms) later.

An obvious question remains: What is the best method for
examining the causes of uncertainty in technological environments? Indeed, is there really a 'best method', or is it more prudent
to study each event from multiple perspectives, in the hope that a
discernible picture will emerge? This latter approach may be the
only option available. In Chapter 6, a compilation of 18 'origins of
uncertainty' will describe the starting points for such analyses.

It is my assertion that a comprehension of uncertainty is central
to the development of effective technology strategies, and for this
reason, I propose to examine uncertainty from four broad
perspectives: product; organisational; lifecycle; and knowledge.
These will be supplemented by short discussions of analytical risk,
technological paradigms, complexity science, and the concept of
entropy. The remainder of this chapter is dedicated to the product
and organisational perspectives, while the other topics will be
examined in the next chapter.

Product uncertainty

Technological products vary in size and complexity from the most
basic components (e.g. bolts, diodes, coatings) through to the most
complex systems imaginable (e.g. space stations, chemical plants,
genetically modified animals). The development and application of
each product is riven with uncertainty. I believe it helps to differentiate between the uncertainty that is intrinsic to a product and that
which is extrinsic, originating from the product's environment.

Intrinsic product uncertainty

The French philosopher of technology, Paul Virilio, said "When
you invent the ship, you also invent the shipwreck".[16] The clear
implication is this: in an environment of perpetual technological
innovation, uncertainty will exist in perpetuity. It's hard to
disagree with Virilio's argument.

One good example, among thousands, concerns the emergence of
the motor vehicle at the turn of the 20th century. The Pirelli Company
of Italy already had 30 years' experience in the manufacture of rubber

products, so the decision to supply tyres for automobiles was a logical transition into a rapidly growing sector. This happened around 1900, yet by 1909 Alberto Pirelli (son of the founder Giovanni Battista Pirelli) was clearly unhappy with the company's progress, complaining that "the difficulties that arise in the details of the manufacture of automobile tyres are far beyond any expectations." In 1946, Alberto reminisced about these early challenges:

> In the still primitive evolution of motoring, tyres continued to be an Achilles heel. And, alas, there were countless problems at the beginning due to the malfunctioning of those heels, creases in the fabric, blowouts of the frame, cracking, rapid wear and tear, tread detachments and early ageing. Getting half-way through a trip in a car without one or more blow-outs was a real miracle.[17]

However, in general, new technologies probably bring more joy than pain. For example, one assumes that the motor vehicle was already good news for the owners of rubber plantations and oil wells. As we saw earlier, uncertainty is not an overwhelmingly negative concept. Outcomes are often unexpectedly better, or merely unexpectedly different.

In 1950, when assigned the task of building the world's first nuclear-powered ships, Admiral H.G. Rickover of the US Navy recognised the uncertainties associated with novel technologies, not least the various types of coolants being proposed for nuclear reactors. Opting for speed of delivery and minimal project risk, Rickover made a portentous decision which is still felt today. Basalla, a science historian, explains:

> The choice of a so-called light-water reactor was a conservative one, made by an engineer who knew that more technical data were available on water than on some of the more exotic coolants and that the technology for water transfer already existed for steam boilers, turbines, and the like.

Rickover was therefore able to deliver his first vessel, the submarine *Nautilus*, ahead of schedule just five years later. However, the subsequent cancellation of a nuclear-powered aircraft carrier led, inadvertently, to Rickover managing the development of America's first civil nuclear power plant at Shippingport, Pennsylvania. Utilising the unused naval reactor, Shippingport inevitably became a water-cooled plant. As a direct consequence of Rickover's hurried and risk-averse decision for the *Nautilus* back in 1950, pressurised water reactors (PWRs) have since dominated the world's nuclear energy landscape, in spite of the fact that they're widely considered to be less efficient than other designs.[18,19] By 2022, more than 300 of the world's 441 operational reactors were PWRs.[20]

Rickover's conservatism was a manifestation of the aphorism that "What can't be tested, can't be trusted."[21] In recent decades, these sentiments have led to the development of highly sophisticated testing regimes in many sectors, most notably software development. However, in spite of this, according to Tony Hoare (a Fellow of the UK's Royal Society of Engineering), programming errors and the resources used to prevent them are costing the global economy tens of billions of dollars, most of which falls on the customers and users of software.[22] Another Fellow, Martyn Thomas of Gresham College in London, explained the fundamental problem in a 2016 letter to *Ingenia* magazine:

> … computer scientists and software engineers have known for at least 40 years that testing can only show that faults exist rather than that the software is safe or secure. Running a series of tests may show that the specific tests work, but even a small change to the test conditions will put the software in a different, untested state that may fail.[23]

In a similar vein, but writing in the context of structural engineering, Henry Petroski of Duke University, North Carolina, writes that "the absence of failure does not prove that a design is flawless, for a latent failure mode may be triggered by yet-unexperienced conditions."[24] Consequently, with or without testing, in engineered products uncertainty is always baked in.

Let's not forget that some engineering solutions are incompatible with comprehensive testing in controlled environments, such as laboratories. These products are generally large, highly bespoke, and very expensive. They include bridges, ocean liners, and scientific research assets such as the Large Hadron Collider (LHC) or the James Webb Space Telescope. It's true that they can be modelled physically or digitally, which obviously helps, but models do not have the scale or complexity of the final product, nor can they be submitted to testing in real-world conditions, such as South Atlantic storms or the freezing, irradiated vacuum of space. Even the design specifications may be incomplete until the product is finally available for the client to see and begin (tentatively) to use.

For example, the largest offshore wind turbines operate in wave and weather conditions which can neither be duplicated in the lab nor fully anticipated. Once erected, they are expected to function with minimal maintenance for decades. Research engineers designing blade coatings have no option but to work with limited data about localised temperatures, humidity, ultraviolet radiation levels, and rain droplet sizes, particularly their effects upon rotating equipment. The best information comes from oil and gas platforms (which, of course, don't rotate). The consequences of this data gap will not become evident for many years.[25] It may later be found that these data limitations were inconsequential, but it's also conceivable that some turbines will require early blade replacements or even premature decommissioning.

Although some technologies are designed from the outset as complex, multi-component systems, others may only achieve this level of complexity after successive cycles of upgrades and miscellaneous enhancements. Most technologists and engineers will be familiar with the disease of *featuritis*, the symptoms of which arise from adding more and more 'bells and whistles' to proven designs until they become almost too difficult to use and maintain (see Box 4.1 *Going 'lite', or dennovating*). Everyone can name at least one product 'victim' of featuritis. (Mine is the microwave oven. If there is such a thing as 'design pollution' it belongs to the user interface and never-used functionalities of modern microwave ovens.) Figure 4.1 illustrates the disease.

W.B. Arthur explains that new features may be added to enhance performance, improve monitoring, automate responses, and increase safety or reliability. He uses the example of modern aircraft engines. It's true that these have achieved substantial power increases relative to Frank Whittle's original design, but the number of component parts has also increased from just a few hundred to more than 22,000.[26] However, it's interesting to note that while aircraft engines have become more powerful and complex, they've also become more reliable, despite there being more things 'to go

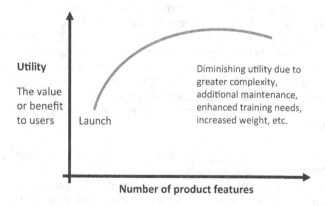

Figure 4.1 A graphical representation of featuritis

wrong'. Clearly, the modern jet engine is *not* a victim of featuritis. This particular example illustrates the fact that perceived causes of uncertainty will often be at variance with empirical insights. What we perceive as a downside could, upon closer inspection, be quite the opposite. This is why it's important to use good data, rationality, and objectivity when analysing uncertainty.

Box 4.1   STRATEGIC AND TACTICAL MOVES

Going 'lite', or *dennovating*

Successful products and systems often remain in high demand for decades. However, when we compare their earliest versions with current versions, they are usually found to have undergone significant change. The core functionality of version one has, over time, acquired a host of additional features. Some of these may be very desirable, but others, being of unknown purpose (or simply pointless), remain unused.

Compare the features in 'classic' cars with contemporary examples. Take the same critical eye to early microwave ovens, older word-processing applications, and ten-year-old smartphones. For every useful product innovation, there will be another meaningless menu option, pointless button, mysterious bleep, or extraneous knob.

This phenomenon is known pejoratively as 'feature creep' or 'featuritis'. According to designer Donald Norman, this disease is "unavoidable, with no known prevention" and "highly infectious."[27] Featuritis has many causes including a desire to justify higher prices, attempts to future-proof a product or improve its compatibility, the need to keep well-paid teams of internal designers and developers busy, an 'arms race' against competitors (suffering from the same affliction), the desire to force 'upgrade' purchases upon existing customers, or even 'design by committee' resulting in too many compromises.

These products and systems become increasingly difficult to use and maintain. There is both more to learn and more to go wrong. Many physical products are also less compact than the original versions and use more energy. The latest version, despite commanding a higher price for additional functionality, **may be perceived as inferior to earlier models**.

The disease of featuritis can be cured. Here are some prophylactics:

1 Obtain strong empirical evidence that there is a user demand for each proposed new feature.
2 Establish which current features are being rarely used and remove them. Transactional web services are particularly good at doing this, whereas manufacturers are not. Be ruthless.

3 Adopt a *one in, one out* rule for adding and removing features.
4 Improve customer choice by selling a less costly 'lite' version. This may attract a new cohort of users.
5 Enable more user opt-ins via modularity, plug-ins, and extensibility.

Clearly some innovation ideas do add value, but many do not. Defeating featuritis involves *innovation reversal*. I call it de-innovation or *dennovation*. It can be defined as **a focus upon the most desirable functionality while removing extraneous historical innovations, thereby increasing reliability and reducing the costs of production, maintenance, training, and operation.**

Another probable source of uncertainty emerges from the precision with which engineered solutions are specified and built. Accuracy in the specification or measurement of physical dimensions, for example, will often be critical to the performance and longevity of an engineered product. However, even with modern tools *absolute precision* in the purest sense can never be achieved. At the most granular level, two parts will never meet or join together *perfectly*. Furthermore, metering will never report with *100% accuracy*, and timings can never be *absolutely* synchronised. We can work to three decimal places, or to five decimal places, but that will be inferior to six or even ten decimal places. Clearly there is an economics of precision – a law of diminishing returns. The more precision we require, the more resources (skills, time, materials, and money) must be expended in order to achieve it. It's likely that this will be an exponential function, which partly explains the spiralling costs in modern precision engineering, such as scientific research devices and, yes, aircraft engines.

A related observation is that high-volume mass production techniques are incapable of producing two or more *identical* items. Basalla provides this example:

On close examination, supposedly identical beverage cans can be distinguished by the arbitrary marks left by the manufacturing process: a rougher or smoother finish on the pull tabs; variations in the incised and relief lettering on the can tops; a misshapen head on the rivet that attaches the pull tab to the top; differences of ink thickness in the wraparound lithographed label, especially where the ends overlap; and deviations in label coloring and lettering. Random variations in mass-produced objects underline the point that variability is the absolute rule in the made world.[28]

Our industrialised environment is therefore less uniform than we think. If the costs of precision really do increase exponentially, then this leads to an uncomfortable conclusion: it is an economic fact of life that we must learn to live with inconsistency, coupled with occasional, randomised failures due to imprecision.

More intrinsic uncertainty emerges from the processes of physical disintegration. These affect all technologies and are associated with such factors as erosion, chemical properties, and entropy. This topic will be explored further in subsequent chapters.

Finally, let's consider the elephant in the room, or to be more precise, the creatures on the planet. We can't ignore the fact that the greatest source of uncertainty in the technological realm is life itself: everything from bacteria to blue whales. This includes humans, of course.

Here are some ways that lifeforms exacerbate uncertainty:

As gremlins: Living things often get in the way, both literally and metaphorically. In the 1840s, I.K. Brunel's innovative South Devon Railway, along which trains were propelled by atmospheric pressure, was partly defeated by the local rat population which developed an appetite for the waxed leather flanges used to maintain the vacuum.[29] Elsewhere, wooden structures are riddled by termites and fungal rot, birds destroy engines in mid-flight, and deadly Legionella bacteria thrive in aircon systems. It's probably not an exaggeration to say that every time-served engineer will have been scuppered, at least once, by some kind of creature.

As users: Many technologies interface directly with end users. Designers often despair at the way their products are used, misused, and abused by free-thinking organisms (usually people). If engineers design and calibrate solutions within performance or operational envelopes, are they at fault if some creature chooses to 'push the envelope' a little too far? Often there is little that can be done, other than to ensure that good design practices have been followed and accurate instructions provided for operators. After that, it's anyone's guess what might happen.

As components: Let's bring the focus back to the technologies themselves. As I noted in Chapter 2, it's not unusual for the physical components of technologies to be alive. Amongst other things, live components can digest waste (bacteria), control machinery (people), and improve air quality (plants). Back in 2006, I researched the topic of organic machine components in the Engineering Department at the University of Cambridge.[30] Organisms would have little impact upon uncertainty if they acted like automatons, came in predictable shapes and sizes, and were resistant to disease – but they don't and they aren't. In recent years, having worked in the engineering sector alongside both consultants and educators, I've reached the conclusion that the most important of all living components are not bacteria, plants, fungi, insects, or algae, but people.

As human actors: People can do great things in engineering environments; they can innovate, they can control, they can even 'save the day'; these examples all belong with the upsides of uncertainty. However, we also associate people with poor communications, loss of situational awareness, stress, fatigue, and even falling asleep on the job.[31] They also have a reputation for misinterpreting data, failing to prepare, forgetting to act, and succumbing to illness. The role of human beings in technological uncertainty is therefore beyond dispute. There are many books exploring these 'human factors' in engineering, including *The Human Contribution* (2008) by the prolific writer on occupational psychology, James Reason.

Box 4.2   ANALYTICAL TOOLS AND TECHNIQUES

Leading indicators

Some people like surprises. Engineers don't. After all, they have a professional duty to meet or exceed client expectations. Fortunately for engineers, unexpected events can often be foreseen, and their impacts neutralised.

Various forms of indicators are used to better understand the status of engineering systems. These may be described as either 'lagging' or 'leading'.

Lagging indicators deliver historical information about the system. They don't anticipate, but they sometimes reveal future trends.

Leading indicators, on the other hand, are focused upon the anticipation of future events. This data enables actions to be taken which can either be preventative (for unwanted future events) or supportive (for desirable future events). Most leading indicators, it seems, are deployed for the avoidance of unwanted events, probably because risk aversion predominates in engineering, as in so many other professions.

Here are some examples of leading indicators: an electronic fuel-level gauge showing the time or distance remaining given current engine usage; vibration sensors detecting the emergence of abnormal machine conditions in advance of a failure; wear sensors in brake pads indicating when they will be due for replacement; near-miss reporting of incidents in medical or aviation environments, enabling mitigation for possible, or probable, future events; the number of professionals enroling on a certification programme, indicating the number who will be qualified in X months' time.

Leading indicators are therefore valuable, but often difficult to design and implement. Today's abundance of low-cost chemical, biological, electrical, and mechanical sensors, combined with wireless connectivity, enables high-quality data to be more easily captured for analysis. Increasingly, machine learning is used to identify relationships within data which human analysts are incapable of perceiving. For instance, this approach is used by Rolls-Royce in their 'digital twin' aero engines, which capture data from aircraft in flight.[32]

Recently the new Queensferry Bridge was opened in Scotland. It is a 2.7-kilometre, three-towered cable-stayed construction containing several thousand monitoring devices. These include accelerometers, anemometers, GPS/biaxial tilt meters, and dynamic strain gauges.[33] With such an abundance of data available, the likelihood of an undesirable mechanical failure in the future is, presumably, close to zero.

A leading indicator capable of initiating corrective actions, without human intervention, might sound like a very advanced engineering solution, but in fact such devices have been with us for centuries. At the dawn of the industrial revolution, James Watt patented his 'governor', which used rotating weights to automatically regulate the flow of steam into engines, thereby preventing catastrophic mechanical failures.

Leading indicators are effective weapons in our war on uncertainty.

Extrinsic product uncertainty

In contrast with the intrinsic view of uncertainty, it's helpful also to look at the wider environment. This is the extrinsic view of product uncertainty. It concerns the actions of customers, competitors, and suppliers, plus the existence of other external factors, such as market pricing.

For example, when commercial products or technologies are new, the market's likely response is unknown. Passionate entrepreneurs are likely to overestimate early demand, confident that they already know who their buyers will be and the type of products they want. When these innovators are professional engineers, they may feel inclined to focus upon the quality of their products, thereby raising costs and prices. The target market may then reject the product on the basis of price, rather than quality. The ideal product-market fit can take time to emerge. In his book

The Lean Startup (2011), Eric Ries warns entrepreneurs that "If we do not know who the customer is, we do not know what quality is." He argues that even a low-quality early version of a product, delivered quickly, will accumulate market intelligence which might later justify the development of a higher-quality final version. Equally, it could demonstrate the market's preference for lower quality at a correspondingly lower price.[34] Suffice to say, our assumptions about the behaviour of economic actors, including their likes and dislikes, are frequently incorrect.

Sometimes we may have established who the buyers are, but their response to our new, superior product may be much slower than anticipated. A famous research study in 1930s USA by Bryce Ryan and Neal Gross explored the adoption of a new breed of hybrid corn in Greene County, Iowa. This breed was so good that its substantial benefits to farmers were beyond dispute. Yet it took an astonishing 22 years for the corn to be fully adopted by the county's conservative farmers.[35]

More recently, the principal hindrance to the growth of modified foods has not been reluctant farmers, but political interventions in response to public fears. For example, the Golden Rice Project was a public health initiative to introduce rice enhanced with Vitamin A (beta-carotene). It aimed to rectify this specific vitamin deficiency within poorer countries. Originating in the Swiss Federal Institute of Technology and the University of Freiburg, the product took 24 years to develop prior to its launch in 2004, yet its widespread use has since been delayed by various biosafety concerns. One explanation for this slow diffusion of an excellent product is that the researchers had failed to engage at an early stage with key stakeholders.[36] The health impacts arising from this delay are incalculable. (Stakeholder engagements will be explored more thoroughly in Chapter 8.)

As evidenced above, a product or technology may satisfy market requirements, but this won't necessarily lead to widespread adoption. Sometimes a less impressive solution emerges as the so-called *dominant design*. According to one of the originators of this idea, James Utterback, a dominant design is a product architecture that "wins the allegiance of the marketplace" and "that competitors and innovators must adhere to if they hope to command significant market following."[37] Grant and Jordan explain that a dominant design "defines the look, functionality and production method for the product and becomes accepted by the industry as a whole."[38] In other words, new technologies may take time to become established, but when they do, one specific architecture will tend to dominate. The success of this design will be attributed to some combination of price, aesthetics, ease of use, compatibility, complementarity, brand associations, and so on. However, it won't necessarily be the 'best' design according to any objective analysis, even though its widespread acceptance may create that impression.

In the business literature, two of the most frequently cited dominant designs are the IBM PC (among desktop computers) and the VHS standard (among video recording technologies). Some dominant designs are so hard-wired into our collective consciousness that we forget just how specific they are and how many variants there have been over the decades, or even centuries. For example, the clock face with two hands is one of numerous ways to display time, but it achieved dominance many centuries ago and remains popular today. In the early days of the motor vehicle, there was much experimentation with features, such as the position of the engine (front, middle, rear), the sources of motive power (gas, electric, steam, diesel), and the number of wheels (three or four). Eventually, the internal combustion, front-engined, four-wheeled vehicle became the dominant design. More recently, the dominant design for smartphones has become so ubiquitous that it's difficult to distinguish between manufacturers without close inspection of each device. In all cases, the production of a significant design variant, such as single-handed clocks, three-wheeled cars, or folding smartphone screens, is seen as a very bold move and becomes the subject of much debate.

Until the dominant design emerges, there will be much uncertainty within a product category. For example, a decision to invest in an expensive manufacturing plant before the emergence of the market's preferred design constitutes a substantial business risk. What can a technology owner do in order to increase the likelihood of being associated with the dominant design? One of the most likely routes is via scale and reputation. There is some evidence that larger organisations with established brands have a higher than average probability of winning the race to dominance. Hence, IBM's worldwide reputation within corporate computing gave it credibility when promoting its personal computer standard. Yet, the market power of leading brands can sometimes be defeated by clever competitors. This was demonstrated when Sony's Betamax video recording system was outsold by the VHS format, the product of a multi-business collaboration, ably led by JVC.[39]

The verdict of history is that Apple desktop computers were superior to the IBM PC and that Sony Betamax was the better video recording system. However, that couldn't save them from the tyranny of the dominant design.

There is a tendency here to focus on physical products, especially consumer goods, but it should be noted that technical services also favour particular ways of doing things, which can then become orthodoxies. For instance, there are 'dominant designs' for the consulting process, drug development methods, and so on. Hence, there are no grounds for complacency. Most technological domains and engineering sectors are susceptible to dominant designs. The impossibility of knowing which design or architecture will predominate in the future underpins that uncertainty.

It's worth noting that bespoke and lower-volume products are much less likely to face this challenge. There are no dominant designs in bridges or office buildings, despite the fact that hundreds are delivered each year. It is therefore decision makers working with higher volume products who should be most concerned about this phenomenon.

Another extrinsic consideration is the presence of a *substitute* technology. To economists, substitutes are products which deliver the same (or similar) outcomes, but by different means. In other words, although substitutes are a different *type* of product, they can steal market share and severely undermine a technology's long-term prospects. Mobile phone networks are substitutes for landlines, short-haul flights for trains, nuclear power generation for gas-fired plants, gene editing for pharmaceutical products, and home entertainment via cable for home entertainment via satellite.

Typically, substitutes co-exist and compete, but they also have the potential to become disruptive technologies. When a technology disappears altogether, it is often due to the emergence of a superior substitute. Cars replaced horses. Semiconductors replaced vacuum tubes. Digital streaming replaced CDs. LEDs are replacing incandescent light bulbs. This substitute replacement often plays out over decades. Once started, reversals are rare, but they do happen. For example, in the transport sector, we are currently seeing a revival in long-distance rail travel, in preference to flying, and a resurgence in trams, in response to the urban pollution caused by fossil-fuelled buses.

The supply chain is another cause for concern. Most technologies are reliant upon components and skilled labour, neither of which can be 100% assured for consistency, quality or regulatory compliance. In recent years we have seen the fragility of supply chains across many sectors due to pandemics and wars, although there are many other reasons to harbour doubts. This problem is hardly new. Matthew Boulton's new factory in Birmingham experienced similar challenges in the 1790s. It was here that Boulton and Watt wanted to create the first production line for steam engines, but they lacked confidence in iron foundries and fabricators, believing them incapable of meeting their technical demands. Of particular concern was the cylinders, which needed to be bored with great accuracy. A decision was therefore taken to manufacture these onsite rather than trust third parties.[40]

Whether or not the supply chains are robust, if critical supplies become too costly, the prospects for a particular product or technology could be jeopardised. This is a fundamental economic problem which, due to globalisation, is difficult both to predict and control. The prices of raw materials, specialised components, and key skills can change substantially in a matter of weeks. Sometimes these changes will be favourable, with falling costs passed on to customers as lower prices, and to business owners as profits. However, when costs rise to unprecedented levels this can signal a technology's demise, as substitutes become more attractive.

The source of these price fluctuations may be the aforementioned wars and pandemics, but it can also be surprisingly obscure. For example, if an unrelated sector is experiencing rapid growth, it has the economic power to persuade both component suppliers and workers to change their sector allegiances in order to meet its needs. Component factories can be re-tooled and people retrained in order to satisfy this new, voracious sector. During the COVID-19 lockdown, there was a substantial increase in demand for domestic electronic consumer products. This shifted the demand for microchips away from car manufacturers, who were simultaneously cancelling their orders due to the decline in demand for new cars. As economies returned to normal in 2021, the car makers were then unable to reinstate their chip supplies. This hindered production, causing the prices of new and used vehicles to rise substantially. Another example may be found in the UK where the London-based financial services sector offers highly paid jobs to mathematically skilled graduates. This has proved attractive to many young engineers, contributing to the significant skills shortage in UK engineering. **You may be confident that you understand your own industrial sector, but it's nearly impossible to foresee how other sectors will impact yours.**

The future costs of production will always be a source of uncertainty. For example, in recent years there has been much speculation about the potential for generating electricity from fusion energy. It has been argued that because this will be an abundant energy source, it will also be inexpensive. However, this belief is now being challenged by more realistic analyses. Although dozens of companies are developing fusion technologies, none has yet demonstrated a sustained net power output. Whichever technology wins the race, the resulting power plants are likely to be operating at very high cost, at least until the sector has scaled up and matured. The massive research and development costs, some dating back to the 1990s, will either need to be written off by funders (notably governments) or recovered from the prices charged to consumers. Commercial investors will also want to see substantial rewards for the financial risks they have taken. These economic factors were considered in Arthur Turrel's book, *The Star Builders*,[41] and in a report produced jointly by the Institution of Mechanical Engineers and Assystem:

> It is not a question of whether there is sufficient demand for electricity from nuclear fusion, it is a question of whether nuclear fusion is able to produce electricity at a low enough cost to meet the demand.[42]

Beyond the uncertainty of the science lies a more practical economic uncertainty. It's a heady mix which could scupper the long-term viability of the fusion sector, despite its wondrous potential.

Let's take one final example of extrinsic product uncertainty: intellectual property (or IP). Once created, how can this be protected, especially from theft and legal challenges? In addition to the administrative and legal costs of securing IP, owners must then be prepared to defend their property in court against challengers or transgressors. The resources consumed by securing and defending IP might be better deployed elsewhere, particularly within fledgling businesses.

Another source of uncertainty arises from the fact that the patenting process involves a requirement to publish, in detail, the proposed technological breakthrough or invention. From that moment onwards anyone may scrutinise the invention and begin devising workarounds. The applicant is now much more exposed to potential competitors. Furthermore, the legal clock has already begun to tick, counting down to the moment when IP ownership lapses, which for patents is typically after 20 years.

Given all of this uncertainty, we shouldn't be surprised by the approach taken by one UK startup seeking to conquer the holy grail of fusion energy production. First Light Fusion specialise in a method known as inertial confinement fusion (ICF). Their IP policy is based upon maximum secrecy for the maximum length of time.[43] This tactic enables them to refrain from patenting until they have a fully proven and marketable technique for generating energy. First Light Fusion's finances and management energies are therefore focused on the science and technology of fusion energy, rather than on the distractions and uncertainties of securing their IP through legal routes. Maximum secrecy will, in theory, give them a long head start over any challengers. Maintaining IP as a 'trade secret' is a commonly used and relatively low-cost alternative to legal IP

Table 4.2 Some 'causes' of technological uncertainty at the product level

Intrinsic uncertainty	Extrinsic uncertainty
Undiscovered latent faults, weaknesses, or even strengths. For instance, the durability or longevity of a novel product may be unknown.	The market response to a product or technology, including susceptibility to cultural shifts or fashions.
The inability to test due to large scale, or the impossibility of replicating the operating environment.	The emergence of a dominant design for the product class.
Product 'degradation' caused by the gradual addition of more features and components, leading to ever-greater maintenance challenges (i.e. *featuritis*).	Substitute products emerging to compete for the same customers.
Imprecision in assembly or calibration. Imperfections between manufactured 'duplicates'.	Supply chain reliability, perhaps including new sources of supply suddenly becoming available.
Pushing the envelope. Using a technology in ways not originally specified or considered by designers.	Changes in production costs influencing product viability and attractiveness.
Human factors – the performance of human components within systems.	Legal recognition and defensibility of intellectual property.

protection, especially patents. However, if the secret escapes, it's nearly impossible to obtain legal protection thereafter.

Table 4.2 itemises some of the causes of product and technological uncertainty, introduced above.

Uncertainty may also be analysed according to the 'five dimensions' of technology, explained in Chapter 2. Table 4.3 offers examples.

Table 4.3 Some 'causes' of uncertainty associated with each of the five dimensions of technology

Dimension		Some causes of uncertainty
P	Physical	Rate of material ageing and degradation; chemical reactivity between novel materials
L	Logical	Confidence in underlying assumptions or theories; software bugs
A	Architectural	Efficiency of the chosen architecture; flexibility in response to new operating conditions
Y	Yield	Accuracy of output measures; effectiveness in delivering outputs to beneficiaries
S	Stakeholder	Social or political changes causing a decline in the number of beneficiaries; simply going out of fashion

Organisational uncertainty

Most organisations use engineered solutions in their business critical activities. We should therefore take this opportunity to examine technological uncertainty at the organisational level.

Organisations vary in size and complexity from small teams, such as those delivering projects, through to the most Byzantine of arrangements, notably global corporations. Uncertainty permeates both the creation and long-term management of these organisations. In the same way that products are riven with technological uncertainty, so are the organisations that produce them and use them.

At the start of the 21st century, the leading internet search engine was called Alta Vista. Meanwhile, SixDegrees, a ground-breaking social network, was attracting millions of subscribers. Apple Corporation, on the other hand, was dying on its feet. Yet, within five years, Alta Vista had been squished by Google, SixDegrees was six feet under, and a frat house startup called Facebook was on track to world domination. Apple, however, was resurgent, soon to become the world's most valuable company. This trend towards organisational tumult is particularly prevalent in the digital industries, but many other sectors are similarly afflicted.

Here, I believe it helps to differentiate between uncertainty that is internal to the organisation and that which originates from the organisation's external environment. Again, as with the product analysis, I will refer to these as *intrinsic uncertainty* and *extrinsic uncertainty*.

Intrinsic organisational uncertainty

If our technological futures could be planned, complete with schedules, assigned teams, and known costs, organisations would operate in conditions of great certainty. Any published strategy would remain valid for the duration of the planning period. However, as we noted in Chapter 1 and explained in Chapter 3, technology strategies begin to lose value (or depreciate) from the moment they are created. What emerges is a so-called 'realised strategy', a pragmatic response to the ongoing evolution of the technological environment. Henry Mintzberg has estimated that only between 10 and 30% of 'intended' strategy becomes realised strategy.[44] For technologists and engineers, this means that any strategy more than a few months old could now be unreliable. Unable to read the minds of senior leaders, workers guided by ageing strategies could innocently be taking actions that undermine the best interests of the organisation. We must therefore recognise that **an organisation's *current* strategic needs are uncertain, or even** unknowable, unless they have recently been revised and communicated by the leadership team.

Another source of uncertainty is the technical project, something we should all be familiar with. Here it is common for delivery dates to slip and budgets to bloat. Furthermore, because slippage lengthens the project even further, it has the effect of accentuating the problems of strategy depreciation associated with evolving environments. The longer a project takes, the more likely it is that the business case will lose its validity. Slippage also reduces the time window within which, upon completion, future value can be earned (e.g. via a new revenue stream). To compound these effects, the personnel involved in project conception and sponsorship may no longer be in the team. They might have already been promoted, 'jumped ship', or been head-hunted. In short, although uncertainty is embedded in all projects, the longer a project takes, the greater this uncertainty will be.

So-called 'cash cows' are successful products which, like their namesakes, can be milked every day for easy revenue. Such products generate large returns with little effort, offering a rare form of certainty to business leaders. Cash cows are often protected by intellectual property or trade secrets, defying any attempts by would-be competitors to replicate their success. In recent decades, Apple Corp has benefited from two cash cows, the iPod and iPhone. Boeing's short-haul aircraft, the 737, first flown in the 1960s, is another, with thousands having already been produced. And when Xerox had their monopoly over paper copiers in the latter half of the 20th century, it was probably a good time to own Xerox shares or to be a senior executive. In many cases, the certainty offered by cash cows can lead to complacency, and complacency increases the exposure to uncertainty.

Many cash cows fall into the category of 'strategic asset', or 'strategic resource' (see Box 3.1 *Strategic asset audit*, in Chapter 3). Richard Rumelt defines a strategic resource as "a kind of property that is fairly long lasting ... and that competitors cannot duplicate without suffering a net economic loss." A robust IP portfolio protecting a lucrative product range would be one example of a strategic resource. Rumelt observes that, once established, profits from strategic resources can be maintained "without genius".[45] This is where complacency can set in, leaving the organisation without a clear plan for dealing with the eventual demise of the resource. This could arise, for example, from a change in consumer behaviour, or because of a disruptive new substitute technology. Fortunately for Apple, they were able to follow the iPod with the iPhone, but after the iPhone's demise, will Apple be able to continue milking the consumer electronics market? Maybe not. How long will the Boeing 737 continue to be produced, particularly with the onset of new engine types, alternative fuel sources, and changing customer preferences? Do Boeing have another huge seller in their product range? If not, will it precipitate Boeing's corporate decline? As for Xerox, their photocopying cash cow expired decades ago (as described in Chapter 3). So the question for the strategist to ask is this: "Do we have any cash cows or strategic resources? If so, am I placing too much reliance on their future value to my organisation? How should I prepare for their eventual demise?"

A very different type of economic impact arises from the occasional technological revolutions that transform the size and shape of industries. Rumelt likens these events to changes in the wind direction during a yacht race.[46] Every skipper must make an immediate adjustment to the new conditions. The most skilful and experienced racers emerge from this transition in the lead. However, in the technological realm, a lot more than skill is needed to survive the change in direction caused by a disruptive technology. Often the costs of transition will be staggering, involving investments in research and development, new plant, new personnel, extensive re-training, and so on. Rumelt offers the example of the photographic film industry in the 1960s, as it undertook the difficult transformation from black-and-white to colour film:

> As the costs of color-film R & D escalated, many firms were forced out of the market, including Ilford in the United Kingdom and Ansco in the United States. That wave of change left behind a consolidated industry of fewer but larger firms, dominated by Kodak and Fuji.

Also in the 1960s, aircraft engine manufacturing was transitioning away from the piston engine towards the jet. As a consequence, just three private companies successfully navigated the disruption to dominate the engine market: GE, Pratt & Whitney, and Rolls-Royce.[47]

Earlier, we considered the role of 'human factors' in relation to products. When looking at organisations we shouldn't be surprised to discover that the people who work within them contribute to much of their prevailing uncertainty. As always there is both an upside and a downside. For example, we know that great teams can do great things. They can put people on the Moon or, in the case of Apollo 13, bring them safely back to Earth. Dysfunctional teams, though, are more likely to make the headlines, because such teams bring down airliners and sink ships. The safety engineering literature on human factors explains many of these cases in detail, often focusing on the psychological dimensions of team working. See, for example, *Safety at the Sharp End: A Guide to Non-Technical Skills* (2008) by Rhona Flin *et al*.

When examining human factors in engineering, one area that is easily overlooked is organisational cultures. This might be because 'culture' feels too nebulous and therefore beyond analysis. However, anyone who has experienced the merger of two organisations can usually attest to the stark differences between their cultures and the subsequent impact upon performance. I once had experience of a newly merged European company where technical personnel remained fiercely loyal to their former employers' operational systems. These two cultures were even distinguishable by styles of clothing, regional accents, and mannerisms. Corporate staff at all levels continued to be known as an 'X-person' or a 'Y-person' depending upon which of the two legacy IT systems they favoured. This resulted in a delay of over ten years before a new, fully integrated business platform could be built. Ten years!

Formal collaborations between firms, such as joint ventures and partnerships, also face merger-like challenges. In his examination of the failed TSR2 bomber project, The Open University's Bill Nuttall has described how two long-established engineering companies, Vickers and English Electric, were required to work together. Vickers was responsible for the forward fuselage, weapons systems, and overall budget control, while English Electric was focused on aerodynamics, notably the wings and rear fuselage.

> The firms involved in these mergers had been bitter rivals with quite different histories, philosophies and sources of institutional pride. These differences also operated at the level of individuals. George Edwards of Vickers is quoted as saying: 'never had it been less likely that such personalities would willingly have become subservient to each other ...[48]

As a national defence project at the height of the Cold War, this culture clash might have been amusing if it wasn't so serious. In fact, it became a contributory factor in the TSR2 project's demise.

A similar tale is told by Allan Afuah about the experiences of engineers from Siemens, IBM, and Toshiba collaborating in the development of a new memory chip. Some of the challenges related to office layouts, smoking policies, and the so-called 'not invented here' syndrome, but management styles also clashed:

> Siemens described the way American managers criticize their subordinates as America's "hamburger style of management." Managers start with sweet talk – the top of the hamburger bun. Then the criticism is slipped in – the meat. Finally, some

encouraging words – the bottom bun. With the Germans, all one gets is the meat. With the Japanese, all one gets is the buns; one has to smell the meat.[49]

Leadership, though, is probably more influential than culture. Leaders exercise authority, maintain standards, and prioritise workloads. The fate of an entire organisation is in the hands of a few senior people, some of whom may be brilliant. Others, however, will be incompetent, and occasionally criminal. It's not only their decisions that matter. Sometimes it's their 'non-decisions'. Of particular interest to us is the failure to produce a formal technology strategy or, having successfully developed a strategy, failing to communicate it to frontline staff. This then creates a tactical vacuum leading either to inaction or, perhaps more dangerously, to tactical decisions based on little more than assumptions about the strategic preferences of the leadership team.

As every technologist and engineer knows, the current leader is not always the best person for the job. The technological evolution of organisations is rarely matched by the evolution of its leaders. The talented inventor of a blockbuster product may be better suited to laboratories than besuited in the boardroom. Chermack remarks that the 'mental map' of someone in high office may have been drawn during an earlier phase in the organisation's development. They may be incapable of adjusting to life in the boardroom, because "the map that got them to the top is unlikely to be the map that they need for the future."[50] Should they, perhaps, be shown the door?

The consequence of the examples given above is that we cannot underestimate the significance of human factors across the entire technological realm. I have already described many examples, although I've barely scratched the surface. Anyone who believes that technology and engineering can be studied and practised without reference to the human dimension is utterly deluded, and in organisations with safety-critical processes, such deluded in-dividuals are a danger, both to themselves and to others.

Box 4.3 STRATEGIC DICHOTOMIES

First mover advantage OR Second mover advantage?

Inventors and pioneering entrepreneurs are widely admired. It's often assumed that their creative energies lead inexorably to success. But is this true? In the business literature, the phrase 'first mover advantage' appears regularly. What exactly is the advantage of being first?

First mover advantage We sometimes say, "It's the early bird that catches the worm." Pioneers gain a head start of months, sometimes years, over their potential rivals. For example, inventors can obtain legal protection via patents and design rights. The pioneer gains deep technical insights by solving the science and engineering challenges of a new product or process. Many technologies depend upon a 'network effect' to succeed; the first mover creates the platform and establishes 'standards' for this network. It seems that those who go first cannot fail.

Examples: 1) James Dyson invented and patented the dual-cyclone vacuum cleaner, which became a worldwide success; the Dyson company has since evolved into a major manufacturer of domestic appliances. 2) Through its pioneering auction site, the eBay company used the network effect to build and dominate a new form of online market. 3) The so-called 'standard' railway gauge, introduced by George Stephenson, was already widely adopted when Brunel introduced the technically superior 'broad' gauge. Nevertheless, in the subsequent 'gauge war' Stephenson's standard was able to claim victory.

Second mover advantage However, it's also easy to find successful companies, products, and technologies that have *followed*, rather than led. Here are some explanations for this 'second mover advantage'. For instance, followers can evade or ignore patents, and even overturn them in the courts. Indeed, often the first mover has no defensible IP at all, their only advantage being the head start; followers may eventually catch up and overtake them. The pioneer expends much time and expense on foundational R&D, but these costs are felt less by second movers, who also benefit from the first mover's investments in marketing costs, especially 'educating' the market in the new technology. The pioneer also develops employees with new skills, while the second mover can simply poach the pioneer's experienced staff. The network effect, which supposedly benefits first movers, can sometimes be evaded by creating a new, alternative network, and investing heavily in its promotion. Indeed, two or three separate platforms can often co-exist in the same market. First movers may also encounter regulators objecting to the new technology, or to their early dominance of the market. In general, second movers benefit from greater certainty and fewer financial risks than pioneers.

Examples: 1) Nestlé's Nespresso coffee machine was protected by multiple patents, but competitors have simply re-engineered the basic idea in order to grab a substantial share of the market.[51] 2) The de Havilland Comet was the world's first jet airliner, but design flaws damaged its reputation; the 'second moving' Boeing 707 then captured the market. 3) EMI's X-ray body scanner revolutionised medical imaging in the 1970s, but within a few years, GE's superior manufacturing, sales, and servicing capabilities had overtaken them.[52] 4) Apple Corporation was able to quietly observe the early development of smartphones before launching the all-conquering iPhone in 2007.[53]

The first mouse smells the cheese, then sees the cheese. The second mouse hears the sound of a trap snapping shut. The second mouse steps over the body of the first mouse and eats the cheese.

Extrinsic organisational uncertainty

In George Basalla's *The Evolution of Technology* (1988) we are introduced to the arguments of socio-technical theorist Langdon Winner, who sees technological progress as an autonomous force subverting our decision-making processes.[54] Basalla paraphrases Winner's ideas:

> The freedom to develop technology primarily to serve human needs was lost with the spread of industrialization and the growth of modern megatechnical systems in communications, transportation, power production, and manufacturing. These gigantic, complex, interconnected technological systems overwhelm human values and defy human control. Change is possible in the system only if it does not conflict with primary technical values such as efficiency or large-scale integration.

Basalla uses the example of electricity generation upon which we are increasingly dependent. Its reliability has become one of our primary concerns, because prolonged power outages cause chaos and threaten social order:

> Therefore, we cannot undertake any radical changes in our electrical system for fear of disrupting its technological integrity. Men and women may sit at the control panels of electric generating plants and on the governing boards of electric power companies, but their freedom of action is restricted by the technological master they serve ... they are unable to reorganize it or replace it with a different system.

Another familiar megatechnical system is, of course, the Internet. Such systems introduce uncertainty to the organisations aiming to navigate them. Like ships without sails, they drift at the mercy of currents, winds, and waves. Their captains may issue commands, but to little discernible effect.

In the previous chapter, government technology policies were discussed, and I explored the key differences between technology policies and technology strategies. However, there are also some causal relationships between them. In other words, public technology policies (emerging from the political process) can influence the content of organisational technology strategies. This public policy dimension fuels uncertainty. For example, the 1990 Clean Air Act in the United States is believed to have cost US refiners around $20 billion over the subsequent five years, and there were concerns that they would struggle to recover these costs.[55] At around the same time, the post-Cold War defence needs of the United States were being re-evaluated. Substantial budget cuts followed. According to historian Peter Westwick of the University of Southern California, major defence contractors soon realised that they would either have to "merge or perish", an unwelcome choice. Some companies looked beyond the US military for new markets, but they were ill-suited to such radical realignments. Norman Augustine, President of Martin Marietta, the missile manufacturer, expressed his frustration: "Why is it rocket scientists can't sell toothpaste? Because we don't know the market, or how to research, or how to market the product. Other than that, we're in good shape."[56] Not long after Augustine's comments, Martin Marietta ceased to exist as an independent entity following its merger with Lockheed.

Let's not forget, however, that during periods of upheaval, the loudest voices will always be those preaching doom and gloom. By contrast, the upsides of uncertainty will also be there in equal measure, but usually below the radar. A change in government policy or new legislation can bring a wealth of opportunities to organisations, especially those lucky or smart enough to be in the right place at the right time.

The Martin Marietta example leads us to another important topic: mergers and acquisitions (M&A). It's the uncertainty prior to the formal merger that concerns us here, rather than the often chaotic aftermath as two organisations are squeezed into one. We associate these situations with the process known as *due diligence*, the intelligence gathering activity which seeks to understand the less visible capabilities and assets of the acquisition target. One area of focus for any due diligence team will be projects in development. The purpose and status of each project must be understood, in particular how they're likely to sit within the newly combined organisation. For example, most medium or large-sized companies will have live IT projects related either to functionality (requiring software development) or performance (requiring infrastructure change). Christopher Wright and Bryan Altimas address this topic in their book *Reviewing IT in Due Diligence* (2015). They list some of the many questions which need to be asked about live projects, including:

- Will the solution be scalable to the merged organisation?
- Will the project team survive the transition? Are they in line for redundancy?[57]

During my time with General Electric, I participated in around eight acquisitions, mostly involving European companies. The mergers generally passed off without significant disruption, either to operations or projects in development. This absence of organisational trauma was mainly due to legacy systems being left intact during the active phase of the merger. Most technical projects were allowed to continue. No attempts were made to combine legacy systems until all of the people had been successfully integrated together, often in the same building. This was a successful formula. However, the M&A process is, more generally, seen as notoriously difficult, with high failure rates. Around 10% of mergers are cancelled before completion,[58] and more than 70% of those that go ahead fail in some significant way.[59] Organisations seeking certainty would be well advised to avoid the M&A process altogether, although many boardrooms have an insatiable appetite for acquisition and the unpredictability that brings.

Readers familiar with business school curricula will have already encountered the ideas of Michael Porter. His famous 'five forces' model of the external business environment provides a framework for devising corporate business strategy. Porter identified these five forces as: 1) the bargaining power of buyers; 2) the bargaining power of suppliers; 3) the threat of substitute products; 4) the threat of new entrants to the sector; and 5) the intensity of rivalry between existing competitors.[60] Each of these forces is a source of uncertainty, and one would expect a company's business strategy to address all of them. In later chapters, some of the technological and engineering responses to these forces will be considered. These can include product differentiation, 'locking in' customers, acquiring companies for their technical expertise, and cutting out suppliers altogether by opting to 'make' rather than 'buy'.

One of Porter's forces, the threat posed by new entrants, could account for the way that Compaq, one of the world's leading early PC manufacturers, went into a slow but inexorable decline through the 1990s. The company had grown rapidly through the previous decade manufacturing innovative IBM 'clone' PCs.

Their profits rose from $3 million in 1983 to $455 million by 1990. However, by this stage, there were many equally capable competitors producing PCs. Afuah describes the circumstances leading to Compaq's demise:

> Unfortunately ... it neither controlled any standard nor possessed any core copyrights like Microsoft. Moreover, the competences it had used to introduce the first portable and the first 80386-based PC were neither unique nor inimitable. It had utilized its capabilities in logic design, circuit design, miniaturization, component assembly, and testing, all of which hundreds of other computer companies already had or could quickly put together.

In this weakened state Compaq was acquired by Hewlett Packard (HP) in 2002.[61] Its branding outlived the merger, but the Compaq name has now disappeared. Compaq had been weakened by at least two of Porter's five forces.

A final example of extrinsic organisational uncertainty involves the threat of highly disruptive, game-changing technologies capable of turning an industry upside down. It is inevitable that such paradigm-shifting technologies will emerge at some future moment. The uncertainty resides in the timing and nature of their arrival. Consider the following contemporary examples:

- Petroleum refineries facing the transition to all-electric vehicles.
- Factories and logistics operations challenged by localised 3D printing on-demand.
- Linear broadcasting losing audience share to on-demand services.

These processes tend to move more slowly than anticipated, often taking decades to progress from ideas to market transformation. This allows plenty of time for executives to make the right strategic decisions, but too frequently they get it wrong. In fact, the history of corporate failures is peppered with these periods of technological turmoil. We saw earlier how the mighty Kodak failed catastrophically to recognise the threats and opportunities presented by digital photography. They are not alone among the pantheon of former corporate stars extinguished by slow-moving, but highly disruptive technologies. Utterback despairs at "the disturbing regularity with which industrial leaders follow their core technologies into obsolescence and obscurity." And, by implication, it's often the disrupters who, decades later, succumb to the next generation of innovators. "Firms that ride an innovation to the heights of industrial leadership more often than not fail to shift to newer technologies."[62] This malaise of conservatism,

Table 4.4 Some 'causes' of technological uncertainty at the organisational level

Intrinsic uncertainty	Extrinsic uncertainty
Rate of strategy depreciation. The original strategy evolves into an unforeseen 'realised strategy'.	Megatechnical evolution beyond the control or foresight of organisations.
Long project lead times undermine confidence in the benefits claimed by the business case.	Legislation or political action capable of transforming an industry, both helpfully and detrimentally.
The timing and prospects for replacing strategic resources, such as 'cash cows'.	An acquisition target's technical prospects prior to its purchase and subsequent merger.
Capacity to absorb the costs of transitioning to an emerging technology within the sector, including R&D, re-tooling, re-training, recruiting, etc.	Porter's five forces: the power of customers and suppliers, plus the threat from substitutes, new entrants, and current competitors.
Relationships between team members and partner organisations, especially those with different working cultures.	Decisions by competitors to target the same markets using near-identical or substitute products.
Human factors associated with leadership skills, the structure of teams, internal coordination, and so on.	The emergence of a new, disruptive technology with potential to eliminate the industry or sector altogether.

defensiveness, and myopia at the heart of so many organisations guarantees a never-ending stream of failures for us to learn from. Some examples of organisational uncertainty are summarised in Table 4.4.

One tangible outcome from this chapter is an improved understanding of how uncertainty pervades strategic thinking and action. At the outset, I suggested that a strategy is not a plan, but a proposal for navigating uncertainty. Similarly, Rumelt has written that "A good strategy is, in the end, a hypothesis about what will work. Not a wild theory, but an educated judgment."[63] It therefore seems sensible to revise the definition of *strategy* introduced in Chapter 1.

DEFINITION OF *STRATEGY* (REVISED)

A proposal for navigating uncertainty, consisting of an evolving package of concerted actions, designed with a common purpose.

(The 'common purpose' may simply be the success and longevity of an organisation or product.)

The next chapter will continue with this examination of uncertainty, focusing on some new topics and discussion points. It will then lead to a description of the 18 *origins of uncertainty*, presented with the aim of simplifying this extremely diverse topic.

Glossary for this chapter (Items in bold are also defined in the same table)

dennovation	A process of 'reverse innovation' (i.e. de-innovating) involving the removal of extraneous functionality and features from products. A cure for **featuritis**.
dominant design	A product form, characterised by a particular architecture, appearance, functionality, and production method, which the market favours over alternative designs.
due diligence	An intelligence gathering activity which seeks to better understand the assets, capabilities, and liabilities of a future partner or acquisition target.
featuritis	A 'disease' of the product development process resulting in the incremental growth of generally unwanted or unused functionality and features. It may be cured by **dennovation**.
first mover advantage	The various benefits associated with being the first organisation to develop and launch a new product of some kind, e.g. securing early customers, acquiring patents. Contrast with **second mover advantage**.
Five Whys	A simple analytical technique for identifying the **root cause** of a problem via repeated use of the question *Why?*
human error	A commonly attributed cause of negative events. Many alleged human errors are later found to have **root causes** in management systems, workplace organisation, and the design of human-machine interfaces.
human factors	A specialist topic and professional field within the practice of technology risk management. It involves detailed consideration of human performance, especially in safety-critical environments.
lagging indicator	The output from a measuring or monitoring system which reports on events of interest, but only after they have occurred.
leading indicator	The output from a measuring or monitoring system which reports the possibility or probability of future events of interest.
megatechnical system	A large, complex, interconnected system which overwhelms human capabilities to redesign or control it, e.g. energy production and distribution, transportation networks, the internet.
proximal cause	The trigger for an event, though usually not the **root cause**.
root cause	The fundamental cause of an event. Generally a more thoughtful explanation than the **proximal cause**.

(Continued)

second mover advantage	The various benefits associated with *not* being the first organisation to launch a new product, e.g. minimal expenditure on R&D, proven market demand. Contrast with **first mover advantage**.
sensor	A data collection device supplying real-time information about operational environments. Sensors may help to reduce uncertainty, e.g. by pre-empting component failures. See **lagging indicator** and **leading indicator**.
strategy (revised definition)	A proposal for navigating uncertainty, consisting of an evolving package of concerted actions, designed with a common purpose.
substitute technology	A technology or product which delivers the same (or similar) outcomes, but by different technological means, e.g. mobile phones are substitutes for landlines.
trade secret	Intellectual property which is secured without public disclosure. Secrecy may be maintained by legal means, such as non-disclosure agreements, or by strict 'need to know' controls within an organisation.

Notes

1 Boulton, J.G., Allen, P.M. and Bowman, C. (2015) *Embracing Complexity.* Oxford: OUP. 1.
2 Gray, C.S. (2018) *Theory of Strategy.* Oxford: OUP. 63.
3 Chermack, T.J. (2011) *Scenario Planning in Organizations.* San Francisco: BerreATT-Koehler. xv.
4 Institution of Mechanical Engineers and Assystem (2021) *Fusion energy: A global effort – a UK opportunity*, available at https://www.imeche.org/policy-and-press/reports/detail/fusion-energy-a-global-effort-a-uk-opportunity (Accessed: 14 November 2021).
5 Gupta, S. (2018) *Driving Digital Strategy.* Boston, MA: Harvard Business School. 192–195.
6 Buchanan, A. (2006) *Brunel.* London: Continuum. 77–79.
7 Howarth, S. (1997) *A Century in Oil: the "Shell" Transport and Trading Company 1897–1997.* London: Weidenfeld & Nicolson. 64.
8 Nuttall, W.J. (2019) *Britain and the Bomb: Technology, Culture and the Cold War.* Dunbeath: Whittles. 157.
9 Heppenheimer, T.A. (1997) *Countdown: A History of Spaceflight.* New York: Wiley. 345.
10 Utterback, J.M. (1994) *Mastering the Dynamics of Innovation.* Harvard: HBS Press. 181.
11 Utterback, *Mastering the Dynamics of Innovation.* 185.
12 Mulder, K. (2016) 'Technology Assessment' in van der Duin, P. (ed.) *Foresight in Organizations.* Abingdon: Routledge. 117.
13 Howarth, *A Century in Oil.* 231–254.
14 Howarth. 254.
15 Norman, D.A. (2013) *The Design of Everyday Things.* Cambridge (MA): MIT Press. 167–168.

16 Hewitt, E. (2018) *Technology Strategy Patterns*. Sebastopol, CA: O'Reilly. 15.

17 Pellegrini, C.B. (2017) *Pirelli Technology and Passion 1872–2017*. London: Third Millenium. 16.

18 Basalla, G. (1988) *The Evolution of Technology*. Cambridge (UK): CUP. 163–166.

19 Arthur, W.B. (2010) *The Nature of Technology*. London: Penguin. 104–105.

20 International Atomic Energy Authority (IAEA), Power Reactor Information System (PRIS) '*Operational & Long-Term Shutdown Reactors*'. Available at https://pris.iaea.org/PRIS/WorldStatistics/OperationalReactorsByType. aspx (Accessed: 09 May 2022).

21 Heppenheimer, *Countdown*. 336.

22 Hoare, T. (2010) 'The Logic of Engineering Design'. *Philosophy of Engineering*, Vol.1. Royal Academy of Engineering, London, June 2010. Available at: https://www.raeng.org.uk/publications/reports/philosophy-of-engineering-volume-1, 14–20.

23 Thomas, M. (2016) 'Assuring Safety and Security in RAS' (Letter to the Editor). *Ingenia*, Issue 68, 8.

24 Petroski, H. (1994) *Design Paradigms: Case Histories of Error and Judgment in Engineering*. New York: CUP. 160.

25 Dyer, K. and Greaves, P. (2017) 'Futureproofing the Next Generation of Wind Turbine Blades'. *Ingenia*, Issue 70, 31–35.

26 Arthur, *The Nature of Technology*. 135–137.

27 Norman, *The Design of Everyday Things*. 261–262.

28 Basalla, *The Evolution of Technology*. 103–104.

29 Buchanan, *Brunel*. 110.

30 Moar, P. and Guthrie, P. (2006) 'Biocomponents: Bringing Life to Engineering'. *Ingenia*, Issue 27, 24–30.

31 Flin, R., O'Connor, P. and Crichton, M. (2008) *Safety at the Sharp End: A Guide to Non-Technical Skills*. Farnham: Ashgate.

32 Nathan, S. (2021) 'Creating a Virtual Replica'. *Ingenia*, Issue 87, 16–20.

33 Ferguson, H. (2017) 'World Record-Breaking Bridge'. *Ingenia*, Issue 71, 20–26.

34 Ries, E. (2011) *The Lean Startup*. London, UK: Penguin. 107.

35 Krogerus, M. and Tschäppeler, R. (2017) *The Decision Book*. London: Profile Books. 114.

36 Hall, J., Bachor, V. and Matos, S. (2014) 'Developing and Diffusing New Technologies: Strategies for Legitimization'. *California Management Review*, Vol. 56, Issue 3, 98–117.

37 Utterback. 24.

38 Grant, R.M. and Jordan, J. (2015) *Foundations of Strategy*. Chichester: Wiley. 158.

39 Afuah, A. (2003) *Innovation Management*. New York: OUP. 357.

40 Tann, J. and Burton, A. (2013) *Matthew Boulton: Industry's Great Innovator*. Stroud: History Press. 167–170.

41 Turrell, A. (2021) *The Star Builders*. London (UK): W & N. 231–239.

42 Institution of Mechanical Engineers and Assystem, *Fusion energy: A global effort – a UK opportunity*.

43 Turrell, *The Star Builders*. 156–157.

44 Grant and Jordan, *Foundations of Strategy*. 15–16.

45 Rumelt, R. (2017) *Good Strategy, Bad Strategy*. London: Profile Books. 136.

46 Rumelt, *Good Strategy, Bad Strategy*. 193–194.
47 Rumelt. 194.
48 Nuttall, *Britain and the Bomb*. 61.
49 Afuah, *Innovation Management*. 79.
50 Chermack, *Scenario Planning in Organizations*. 52.
51 Grant and Jordan. 228.
52 Grant and Jordan. 207–208.
53 Kingsnorth, S. (2016) *Digital Marketing Strategy*. London: Kogan Page. 48–49.
54 Basalla. 204-205.
55 Doshi, T. (1998) 'Oil Refining and Petroleum-Product Specifications in Asia,' in Stevens, P. (ed.) *Strategic Positioning in the Oil Industry*. Abu Dhabi: ECSSR, 80–99.
56 Westwick, P. (2020) *Stealth: The Secret Contest to Invent Invisible Aircraft*. New York: OUP. 186–187.
57 Wright, C. and Altimas, B. (2015) *Reviewing IT in Due Diligence*. Ely (UK): IT Governance Publishing. 70–71.
58 Bahreini, D., *et al.* (2019) '*Done deal? Why many large transactions fail to cross the finish line*'. Available at https://www.mckinsey.com/business-functions/strategy-and-corporate-finance/our-insights/done-deal-why-many-large-transactions-fail-to-cross-the-finish-line (Accessed: 20 May 2022).
59 Christensen, C., *et al.* (2011) 'The Big Idea: The New M&A Playbook'. *Harvard Business Review: Disruptive Innovation*. Available at https://hbr.org/2011/03/the-big-idea-the-new-ma-playbook (Accessed: 20 May 2022).
60 Cadle, J., Paul, D. and Turner P. (2014) *Business Analysis Techniques*. Swindon: BCS. 6–8.
61 Afuah. 148–149.
62 Utterback. 162.
63 Rumelt. 243.

5 A shadow of doubt
Why light rarely shines on the future

This chapter presents

- Various theoretical approaches to understanding uncertainty.

This chapter establishes

- Three new concepts – analytical risk, paradigm risk, and entropic technical risk.
- The fundamental challenges posed by complex systems to strategy development.

The previous chapter introduced uncertainty and its impact on the technological realm. Strategies were interpreted as 'proposals for navigating uncertainty'. Thus far we have only explored uncertainty from the product and organisational perspectives. In this chapter I want to explore six further perspectives: lifecycles, knowledge, analytical risk, technological paradigms, complexity science, and the concept of entropy.

Lifecycle perspective

The lifecycle is a widely used analytical tool for understanding entities. In the context of this book, our entities could be technical projects, individual products, or even product types (also called 'technologies'). Using the lifecycle method, uncertainties can be mapped to individual lifecycle stages. As in the previous chapter, I have categorised uncertainties between those that are intrinsic to the entity and those that are extrinsic.

Perhaps the best-known lifecycle is that of the project. In Figure 5.1 the project lifecycle is presented as four basic stages. Here, I suggest examples of how uncertainty might impinge upon the thinking of professional project managers. For example, at the first stage, *Initiation*, the business case is especially problematic because misjudgements here will have a disproportionate impact on the remainder of the project. As behavioural scientist Daniel

DOI: 10.4324/9781003472919-6

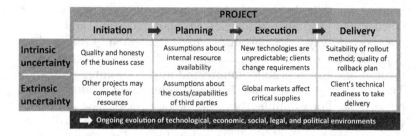

PROJECT			
Initiation ➡	**Planning** ➡	**Execution** ➡	**Delivery**
Intrinsic uncertainty	Quality and honesty of the business case	Assumptions about internal resource availability	New technologies are unpredictable; clients change requirements	Suitability of rollout method; quality of rollback plan
Extrinsic uncertainty	Other projects may compete for resources	Assumptions about the costs/capabilities of third parties	Global markets affect critical supplies	Client's technical readiness to take delivery
➡ Ongoing evolution of technological, economic, social, legal, and political environments			

Figure 5.1 Examples of uncertainty at each stage of the project lifecycle

Kahneman explains, business cases tend to embody the wishful (or deceitful) thinking of their sponsors, exploiting the fact that "projects are rarely abandoned unfinished merely because of overruns in costs or completion times."[1] The integrity of the business case is clearly a major source of uncertainty.

Another common source of uncertainty in projects is 'scope creep', the introduction of new requirements during a project's *Execution* stage. Every experienced project manager is familiar with this phenomenon. The longer the project, the greater the likelihood that scope creep will emerge. For example, in the 1970s the US Government had begun funding the development of radar-invisible 'stealth' aircraft. In 1981, however, the Air Force lost confidence in the likelihood of achieving stealth at high altitudes, so low altitude flying became a requirement. In response to this specification reversal, Northrop's engineers were required to reconfigure their designs, moving the cockpit forward, strengthening the wings (adding significant weight in the process), and creating new control surfaces resulting in the now familiar WW or "bat-wing" shape of the B-2 bomber.[2] Scope creep helps to explain why project managers are often the hardest working professionals in technical organisations.

Individual products are also subject to uncertainty throughout their lifecycle. Figure 5.2 captures the four basic stages of the

SINGLE PRODUCT			
Production ➡	**Distribution** ➡	**Utilisation** ➡	**Disposal**
Intrinsic uncertainty	Manufacturing consistency	Product robustness for the processes of delivery	Unanticipated usage outside the design envelope	Ease of technical decommissioning or recycling
Extrinsic uncertainty	Reliability of external resources, such as electricity supply	Quality of handling and storage	Availability of third party consumables	Public response to 'waste' or changes to regulations
➡ Ongoing ageing and erosion processes, plus 'wear and tear'			

Figure 5.2 Examples of uncertainty at each stage of the single product lifecycle

product lifecycle. In the previous chapter, reference was made to inaccuracies and inconsistencies in manufacturing and to the unexpected ways that products are used, often pushing them beyond their original design envelope. Such unexpected usage invariably leads to product failure and other unwanted outcomes. The fourth stage, end-of-life *Disposal*, often takes product owners by surprise. For example, they may be faced with new hazardous waste regulations, or an organisation may lack the skills and resources to dismantle its own custom-designed products, such as contaminated industrial facilities.

An individual product will typically be associated with a 'product type'. Many product types are distinct technologies. For example, an individual mountain bike is a member of the product type (or technology) we call 'bicycles'. When a new technology or product type is invented, its likelihood of achieving market success is relatively low. Even successful technologies can be short-lived. Many consumer technologies come and go within a few decades. It is therefore possible to think in terms of a technology lifecycle. This topic is regularly taught and researched within business schools across the world, mainly because there's a fascination with the progress of technological innovation leading to commercial success, or failure. Most technology lifecycle models contain more than the four stages I have used in Figure 5.3, but these should be sufficient to highlight some of the uncertainties involved.

Professor Brian Davies of Imperial College London has experienced many challenges while attempting to bring his robotic surgery technology to market. In 2014, he described some of these intrinsic and extrinsic challenges:

> Many of the barriers to the wider clinical use of robots lie not in the technology but in the broader context. The costs of robotic systems, not only capital but cost per procedure, are high and need to be justified by clearly demonstrated benefits. The

TECHNOLOGY (OR PRODUCT TYPE)			
Conception ➡	**R&D** ➡	**Production** ➡	**Decline**
Intrinsic uncertainty — Securing of IP	Challenges associated with recruitment and novel skills	Expected ROI from newproduction methods	Ease of transition or migration to the next technology
Extrinsic uncertainty — Future compatibility with complementary products	The availability and patience of investors	Public reaction, including possible ethical concerns	Willingness of suppliers to support a declining technology
➡ Ongoing presence of substitute technologies			

Figure 5.3 Examples of uncertainty at each stage of the technology (or product type) lifecycle

translation from R&D into products available for clinical use is also proving difficult. Recent legislation has made the move from early prototype to 'first in man' trials lengthier and more costly. Venture capital funds have been difficult to obtain, particularly with the threat of patent litigation from large aggressive competitors. Even when such litigation has no validity, contesting it can cost millions.[3]

At the time of Professor Davies' remarks medical robots were still at the R&D stage of their lifecycle, but their future looked promising, with many decades of productive use ahead. Nevertheless, even if they are adopted for use in mainstream healthcare, it's inevitable that medical robots will eventually reach the fourth stage, *Decline*. Robotic surgery will be superseded by … something as yet unknown. As with all technologies, the timing of the decline stage is never easy to predict because, for example, a new market may emerge to extend the production phase.[4]

This happened with digital video cameras, which were originally designed only for television companies, but soon made the transition to CCTV, domestic 'hobby' video, and finally to the smartphone. These new market opportunities are often enabled by lower costs of production, assisted by economies of scale and competition from producers in emerging markets. Using this logic, how soon will it be before specialised medical devices, currently found only in hospitals, are sold into the domestic market? Will every household possess a body scanner or one of Professor Davies' portable robotic surgeons? In short, given that technology lifecycles vary in length from a few years to many thousands of years, it's nearly impossible to predict their decline.

Before we leave lifecycles, it's worth noting that they're a useful method for illustrating the probabilities of success and failure, particularly for entrepreneurs. Basic probability theory reveals how events in series affect the probability of achieving an outcome. We simply multiply the probability of achieving each increment within the series. Hence, if the probability of progressing from Conception to R&D is 20%, and from R&D to Production is 35%, then the probability of taking a raw idea into production will be 0.2×0.35, which equals 7%. Admittedly, this is an over-simplification of the methodology, but by gaining an appreciation of uncertainty we are better equipped to moderate our hopes and expectations. It's better for us to establish an honest relationship with uncertainty than to be ignorant of its effects.

This leads us nicely to the subject of ignorance, e.g. to the things we know that we don't know. Yes, it's time for the Rumsfeld Matrix!

What do we know?

We can't discuss uncertainty without discussing knowledge, because the former implies some absence of the latter. In the field of strategy we are primarily concerned with the future, which is where most of the uncertainty resides. Technology strategists seek to understand as much as they can about how events will unfold. It is therefore important to differentiate between our current levels of knowledge and our current levels of ignorance.

Table 5.1 is a Rumsfeld Matrix, named after the former US Secretary of State for Defense, Donald Rumsfeld. During a Pentagon news briefing in February 2002 he famously said the following:

> ... as we know, there are known knowns; there are things we know we know. We also know there are known unknowns; that is to say we know there are some things we do not know. But there are also unknown unknowns – the ones we don't know we don't know.[5]

Table 5.1 A Rumsfeld Matrix associated with chemical manufacturing

	Known	Unknown
Known	**Known knowns – the things we know that we know:** The procedures for manufacturing each of our current products and their chemical properties at particular temperatures and pressures.	**Known unknowns – the things we know that we don't know:** The demand for particular products over the next five years and any technical investments which may be needed in response.
Unknown	**Unknown knowns – the things we don't know that we know:** What information is contained within the past X years of production data? It might reveal the under-utilisation of assets or patterns in the recurrence of maintenance shutdowns. Meanwhile, in planning for a new product, we might find that some of our engineers have prior experience of this technology, i.e. we already have the capability without needing to employ contractors.	**Unknown unknowns – the things we don't know that we don't know:** Are we prepared for the unforeseen and the unknowable? Do we have appropriate business continuity planning? Are we adaptable? For example, there may be some combination of operating conditions associated with new alloys being used at the plant that science is currently unaware of. Could the alloy's characteristics change over time, and over what timescales: months, years, decades?

Rumsfeld shouldn't take all the credit (or all the blame) for this formulation, because other commentators had used similar language. Nevertheless, his words are now regarded as a useful contribution to the study of decision-making under uncertainty.

Eagle-eyed readers will notice that Rumsfeld failed to mention the fourth permutation, "unknown knowns", i.e. the things we don't know that we know. In fact, unknown knowns are important, because they represent latent capabilities within our grasp, if only we knew where they existed and how to extract them. Table 5.1 has been completed with some examples of strategic thinking at a chemical manufacturing plant.

A Rumsfeld Matrix is not expected to capture all of the challenges faced by decision makers, but it's helpful in structuring our thinking. Let's look briefly at each of the four quadrants.

The known knowns

We take comfort in the things we know and understand, and this mindset feeds into technology strategies. For example, Highview Power in the UK are developing a novel cryogenic energy storage system using the Claude Cycle with liquefied air. It's a complex process, so in order to mitigate the degree of uncertainty in their demonstration plant, they have opted to use proven components from mature industries:

> The energy storage equipment that the company incorporates is already globally used for the bulk storage of liquid nitrogen, oxygen and LNG – such as heat exchangers, packed-bed storage units and cryogenic insulation. This way it can confidently state the lifespan and efficacy of each plant's hardware – Highview will guarantee a 30-year lifetime for its systems.[6]

Humans have many weaknesses, and one of these is a tendency to believe that we know more than we do, or to believe that certain facts are beyond dispute. One consequence of this is that our assumptions may be false, or fundamentally flawed in some way. For example, you might think that the boiling point of water at sea level is 100°C, yet an over-reliance on this staple 'fact' could induce errors. Apart from barometric pressure, the boiling point also varies according to the amount of dissolved air within the water. Science historian Professor Hasok Chang (University of Cambridge) explains how, without sophisticated equipment, the boiling point can be as low as 98.7°C (in a Teflon-coated pan) or up to 112°C, after extensive agitation within a container to remove most of the dissolved air. In the latter experiment, undertaken by

Jean-André de Luc in the 18th century, the absence of prior bubbling caused water to reach its boiling point instantaneously, i.e. explosively. In fact, this fate befell many early steam engines, until the phenomenon was better understood by engineers. Unquestioned assumptions can therefore be dangerous.[7] How much do you think you know about your technologies? Are you in denial about your own ignorance?

The known unknowns

It's much easier to simply accept that our knowledge is matched by our ignorance. The effects of a new drug on the human body consist of known unknowns. We know that we won't know these effects until the drug has been thoroughly tested.

Petroski makes the general observation that "Virtually all design is conducted in a state of relative ignorance of the full behavior of the system being designed."[8] This should be the default position for any technologist or engineer. It's for this reason that we have familiar design features, such as configurability, adaptability, and redundancy.

Where the knowledge gap involves skills or experience, rather than hardware and logic, this may be rectified by such obvious actions as training and recruitment. It can also be achieved, at greater cost, through the acquisition of companies already employing suitably skilled and experienced personnel.

Sometimes we know a great deal about the unknown. For example, although we have centuries of data on climate and weather conditions, we don't know precisely when or where a particular weather event will occur, or for how long it will last.

There are other unknowns about which we know almost nothing at all. Some years ago Robert High, CTO of IBM Watson, made the following observation about the development of artificial intelligence (AI):

> Economic value is going to drive the progression and evolution of these cognitive systems to a form of intelligence that I don't think we would recognize as being similar to human intelligence ... It's going to be a replication of some small portion of human intelligence, and then a whole bunch of other forms of intelligence that we don't necessarily recognize today but which will be more beneficial economically.[9]

This new form of intelligence may be unknown (and perhaps unknowable), but by foretelling the likelihood of its emergence we are at least partially prepared. Furthermore, we will now be unable to adopt the lazy excuse of calling it an "unknown unknown" (discussed below).

The unknown knowns

We often surprise ourselves with our own knowledge, perhaps when correctly answering a quiz question. The fact is that people, systems and organisations harbour a lot of latent and potentially valuable knowledge, sometimes called 'tacit knowledge'. The corporate silos described in Gillian Tett's book, *The Silo Effect* (2016), contribute to this problem of untapped potential within organisations. Extracting that knowledge may be achieved via numerous 'knowledge management' solutions. These can include mentoring, secondments, staff 'suggestion schemes', and searchable directories for locating colleagues with specific knowledge or experience. Another type of solution is the so-called 'expert system', designed to capture, codify and share the knowledge of experienced staff.

Unstructured data repositories also hold valuable untapped information. This data may be dispersed across corporate file systems or spreadsheets. Pulling this together into a single, dedicated management information system (MIS) has been a popular, though expensive, solution for many organisations. These powerful databases enable previously disconnected data to be combined and analysed. The advent of AI promises yet more opportunities for insightful analysis and the discovery of new knowledge from disparate data sources.

The unknown unknowns

When Boulton and Watt began selling their revolutionary, coal-powered steam engines in the late 18th century, it is inconceivable that they could have foreseen the onset of acid rain, lung diseases, depletion of the ozone layer, and global warming. These really were unknown unknowns until their scientific recognition many years later.

Similar sins of ignorance were committed through the widespread use of asbestos in manufacturing, which has been responsible for the deaths of many millions of people worldwide.[10] Less tragically, the material deficiency known as concrete cancer, caused by chemical reactions in particular formulations of concrete, has necessitated the premature demolition of many structures.

In fact, creating novel combinations of two or more materials always introduces the possibility that an incompatibility will emerge. On this basis, we could question whether concrete cancer was really an unknown unknown. Something similar may be argued for the Thalidomide drug which, despite improving the health of many patients, proved disastrous for pregnant women and their babies in the late 1950s. Engineers and scientists might ask, "How could we have known?" Yet it's a question that invites a critical answer: novelty invokes uncertainty, so perhaps the responsibility belongs with you.

Finally, let's not forget that there are always upsides in our relationship with uncertainty. It's not all doom and gloom. Outcomes are just as likely to be unexpectedly good as unexpectedly bad. That's what makes business, engineering, and life itself so enthralling to be part of.

Analytical doubts

To succeed within the technological realm, it's necessary to understand how entities perform, how they interact, how they fail, and so on. We need to logically deconstruct systems, devices, and data into basic forms which can then, if needed, be reconfigured or reformulated. These are the processes of analysis and synthesis. This is also the essence of design, because these same techniques enable discovery and creativity. Analysis also helps us to affirm truths and expose falsehoods.

In short, we can't function professionally without analytical methods. However, our reliance upon analysis and our faith in its efficacy is challenged by the following hypothesis: *all analysis is imperfect, and therefore all analytical outcomes are uncertain.* If this hypothesis is true, where might these imperfections reside?

Some of our most familiar analytical tools include statistics and modelling, both of which rely upon data. Julia Sloan, in her book *Learning to Think Strategically* (2020), suggests a number of questions we should be asking about data "in order to get the story and the context". For example: Whose data is it? Where does it come from? Why was it collected? Whose interests is it intended to serve? Why was it compiled in this way? Who funded its collection?[11] In short, how accurate or current is the data, and how do we know that its method of collection was well-designed and managed? Harbouring doubts like these is not cynicism or paranoia, it's fundamentally good practice.

What if we collected the data ourselves? Surely that would allay some concerns. However, like all humans we're susceptible to aberrations such as lost concentration, imperfect eyesight, 'fat finger' typing, and fatigue, all of which can introduce errors. Incidentally, when did you last test or calibrate your measurement tools, and how many decimal points have you opted to use? Are you rounding up or down?

One might reasonably ask whether there is enough data, for this is surely the single greatest weakness in statistical analysis. A large volume of data processed via recognised techniques may offer a high degree of confidence, perhaps 95%. That leaves 5% of doubt. This list of analytical weaknesses could go on. Furthermore, **they compound, one upon the other.**

Qualitative analysis is equally suspect. Much has been written about this, and the reader is encouraged to learn more about the pitfalls of qualitative research. Let's take one example, particularly pertinent to this book. We often study real-world 'cases', derived both from our own and other people's experience. However, as Kahneman reminds us, these cases tend to be outliers, such as notable successes and notable failures.[12] In other words, they may be 'noteworthy', but are they really worth noting? They're certainly not typical.

Arguably, 'typical' cases are more informative, but they're also the least interesting to study. Teachers and authors might argue that it's difficult to retain the attention of students, or attract publishers, via presentations of typicality. This is why the non-fiction bookshelves at airports reek of entertainment rather than serious analysis. Meanwhile, stories of quiet unrelenting progress go untold. This constitutes a hindrance to learning and intellectual progress. We owe it to ourselves to be more critical readers and listeners, ignoring hyperbole and sensation. It's the first step towards the rational analysis of any topic.

Another common form of analysis is modelling, often used by technologists and engineers in order to better understand future behaviours and outcomes. According to the physicist Ernest Braun:

> The essence of a model is a collection of postulated mathematical relationships between a number of variables that substitutes for and depicts real functional relationships. The model is only as good as the approximation of the postulated functional relationships to reality.[13]

Here Braun associates uncertainty with the "postulated" relationships which, unless we were involved in the model's design, we would have to accept on trust when using the output.

Braun goes on to remark that, when creating models of engineering systems, such as nuclear reactors, we should be able to predict their behaviour "provided we understand the system sufficiently well."[14] As the first few chapters of this book demonstrate, our ability to fully comprehend the characteristics of complex, multi-layered, almost boundaryless systems is a daunting (and perhaps impossible) challenge.

In a resource-constrained world, modelling has to be made as practicable as possible. We therefore use assumptions, exclude certain things, and establish workable boundaries for the model.[15] Yet, each of these will constitute further sources of doubt.

It also seems obvious that we can only model using information and variables that are *known* to us, and we can't model any factors or variables emerging *after* the design of the model. Boulton *et al.* explain:

> ... some of the things that will turn out to change possible futures most profoundly may concern new techniques and innovations, new tools, new knowledge, new materials ... and new, unexpected strategies of other actors in the field – not to mention how these interact with the factors in the current situation, which we have until now either not recognized or not seen as important enough to include.[16]

Despite these weaknesses, models do help to illustrate relationships and can, according to Joshua Epstein of Johns Hopkins University, be used to demonstrate trade-offs and suggest efficiencies. We might say that models are as informative as they are unreliable. Epstein defends modelling by observing that, "Simple models can be invaluable without being 'right', in an engineering sense". Even the best models are technically wrong, but "they are fruitfully wrong. They are illuminating abstractions."[17]

Let's now consider the assumptions which underlie all forms of analysis. Assumptions are 'truths' which, in the context of the task in hand, don't need to be proved or supported with evidence. In engineering, for instance, most established scientific principles are regarded as given: the speed of light, for instance. It's uncontroversial to do this. However, of some concern might be the use of assumptions when extrapolating from historical data. Here, it's assumed that the behaviour of some component or system will continue in the future as it did in the past.[18] Without these assumptions, simple extrapolation exercises cannot be performed.

Surely, some form of explicit explanation or justification is required when such bold assumptions are made. What evidence is there for the continuation of the modelled behaviour?

In situations where the stakes are particularly high, we have an even greater need to challenge the assumptions made by analysts. The safety of people and the integrity of assets cannot be compromised by the passive acceptance of assumptions. These risks are compounded when the outputs of one or more analyses become the inputs to other analyses. Boulton *et al.* warn that "mixing conclusions derived from different types of models can be extremely problematic and misleading."[19]

One of the more ruinous assumptions implicit within some models is that no adaptation or learning is taking place. Yet, this would cause agents in the model to alter their behaviour. Imagine modelling a system in which there are intelligent actors, such as animals or AI. How is it possible to model their responses to developments *within* the system?[20] Surely it's close to impossible. This goes to the very heart of complexity science, discussed later in this chapter.

Where artificial intelligence is involved, the quest for integrity is especially challenging. As AI is used more often for analytical work, we might expect to be rewarded with more effective insights. There is some evidence to suggest that this is already happening. But an AI system is a classic 'black box' of invisible interactions. To use an English proverb, 'the proof of the pudding will be in the eating'. We will know little of the pudding's ingredients, so we will judge it on taste alone. That's highly subjective, and therefore problematic.

By way of mitigation we could take a closer interest in the design of AI solutions. It's imperative that very high quality data is used during the 'training' and operational phases. We will, of course, have the same data concerns described earlier: How accurate and current is the data, and how do we know that the collection method was appropriately designed and effectively managed? In the hands of skilled practitioners, AI should produce tangible improvements over many conventional forms of analysis, so the uncertainty associated with AI outcomes will, one hopes, decrease over time. Yet this loss of processing transparency could neutralise any gains in confidence associated with AI's improved results.

To conclude, it seems clear that the use of analysis in the technological realm introduces multiple layers of uncertainty. It's probably better to think of these challenges as a type of intangible risk. We could call it *analytical risk*. I spent ten years either working in or observing the field of technology risk management, yet at no point did I see an explicit reference to 'analytical risk' or any similar concept. Perhaps I missed it, but I want to put it on record here:

A DEFINITION FOR *ANALYTICAL RISK*

The likelihood and severity of erroneous outputs arising from poorly selected, badly designed, or improperly used analytical tools.

It might be the intangibility of analytical risk that dissuades traditional risk management practitioners from fully acknowledging it. But ignoring a risk does not make it go away. Somehow we need to build analytical risk into our mainstream thinking, because only by raising awareness of its effects will we improve our chances of mitigating its potential threat to good professional practice.

In developing our strategies, how much confidence do we attach to the data we're using? Generally, this supports my assertion in the previous chapter that a strategy should be perceived as a proposal, rather than the pseudo-certainty of a plan.

Box 5.1   STRATEGIC DICHOTOMIES

Suppress failure OR Highlight failure?

How should we respond when things go wrong in technical environments? Should our actions differ depending upon the visibility of the event? How can we respond in a way that minimises the probability of a similar event occurring in the future?

For understandable reasons, professional people don't wish to be associated with errors or failures. Regardless of causes, there may be a sense of embarrassment or shame and a fear of professional consequences. Non-specialists, such as senior managers, may struggle to differentiate between a completely unforeseeable incident and your professional responsibility for the technology involved. You may be blamed unfairly.

Fortunately, many technical failures go unnoticed by outsiders. This presents an opportunity to 'brush the debris under the carpet' and carry on. Remaining silent is an attractive option.

However, in the interests of quality (and particularly safety) all errors should be acknowledged and understood. In many cases this necessitates a root cause analysis and the sharing of findings. Professional colleagues then have the opportunity to learn from the incident which you experienced.

The creation of a 'no-blame' culture within organisations and across industrial sectors is essential for this type of learning to succeed. The aviation sector probably has the world's most impressive no-blame reporting system. This has resulted in thousands of shared lessons, saving countless lives over many decades.

In particular, it's the 'near misses' that we need to learn about. Statistically, there are many more averted failures, or 'close calls', than actual impacts or losses. These should be the focus of all reporting mechanisms. From a professional perspective, there is considerably less shame in explaining a near miss and how a negative outcome was skilfully averted. We should take pride in our honesty and be recognised for it.

A no-blame culture of near-miss reporting is long overdue in many sectors, including medicine, the extractive industries, and information technology. Why not implement yours today?

It turns on a paradigm

Some years ago, while reading Thomas Kuhn's great work, *The Structure of Scientific Revolutions*, it became evident that Kuhn's ideas about science could be applied, with a little imagination, to the technological realm.

Thomas Kuhn is famous for laying bare the mechanisms by which an established scientific consensus and its associated 'facts' are overturned by the emergence of a new consensus with an alternative set of facts. These processes of overturning established theories were the 'revolutions' of the book's title.

Fundamental to Kuhn's hypothesis is the *paradigm*: the accepted scientific model or pattern. A paradigm must be coherent and logical. Two competing scientific paradigms cannot therefore co-exist without conflict between their proponents, whose views are described by Kuhn as being 'incommensurable'.[21] Each group will believe that there can only be one paradigm; there can only be one truth.

I believe Kuhn helps our understanding of uncertainty through ideas which can be adopted by technologists, engineers, and risk management professionals.

Coincidentally, the economist, W.B. Arthur also wrote about an association between Kuhn and technology in his book *The Nature of Technology* (2010). It's therefore possible that some of Arthur's ideas have subliminally influenced my thinking on this subject, described below.

In an article published posthumously by the Royal Academy of Engineering in 2010, Peter Lipton, former Department Head in the History and Philosophy of Science at the University of Cambridge, made the following "pessimistic argument against truth":

> The history of science is a graveyard of putative entities that turn out not to exist, of putative processes that turn out not to take place and of theories that turn out to be false ... it is very likely that all present theories and, probably, all future theories, will eventually be found to be false as well. Our best current

theories may look terrific at the moment, but that is because we are stuck in the present ... We will find out that we are wrong now, as we were in the past.[22]

Kuhn used the expression "paradigm shift" to describe the process whereupon one source of truth is usurped by another. The most famous of all paradigm shifts probably occurred when Einstein's theory of relativity disproved Newton's laws of motion for bodies travelling close to the speed of light. In the early 20th century, when the founder of modern astronautics, Konstantin Tsiolkovsky, began making his ground-breaking calculations for rocketry and space travel, his faith would have been placed in Newton's Laws.[23] One wonders how he reacted to Einstein's discoveries, which emerged during his own lifetime.

So what could be the next candidate for a scientific revolution? To take one example, the scientific consensus currently supports Darwin's theory of biological evolution, but if we follow Kuhn and Lipton's arguments, that consensus will eventually be challenged by a new explanatory paradigm. In the words of the great physicist and Nobel Prize winner, Richard Feynman, "People search for certainty. But there is no certainty."[24]

The concept of the paradigm is not exclusive to science, of course. Kuhn did not invent the term; he merely gave it a specific application to the scientific realm. For non-scientists, Kuhn's ideas can be both inspirational and practical. For example, we know that structures or organisations based on centralisation are incompatible (or 'incommensurable') with those based on decentralisation. They constitute different paradigms. Americans are only too familiar with the irreconcilability of centralised Federal and decentralised Confederal systems of government. It led to the Civil War (1861–65). One obvious technological example is found in business computing, where centralisation via the mainframe and mid-range systems was largely supplanted in the 1990s by more decentralised client-server architectures. This was a paradigm shift. It even involved internal tussles between technology teams as power shifted from the centralising traditionalists to the younger generation of decentralisers.

Transportation networks, especially road and rail, present a different form of paradigm. For example, those designed for travel on the right are wholly incommensurable with those designed for travel on the left. Any decision to transition or 'shift' from right to left would require one paradigm to instantaneously supersede the other, because a period of parallel working is infeasible. Hence, in 1967 the government of Sweden chose a particular moment on a particular day for the whole country to switch from driving on the left to the right.

In technology, we might consider the following to be incommensurable or competing paradigms:

- Electrical power distribution: alternating current versus direct current.
- Aircraft controls: cables and pulleys versus fly-by-wire electronics.
- Computation: digital versus analogue.
- Movies: celluloid chemical processing versus electronic video capture.
- Voice communications: wireless mobile versus wired landline.
- Medicine: chemical drugs versus gene editing.
- Project methodologies: Waterfall versus Agile.
- Data processing: algorithmic programming versus neural networks.
- Timekeeping: mechanical versus quartz.

In the technological realm a dominant paradigm emerges when a consensus of stakeholders demonstrates their support. These parties become committed to the pattern of industrial activity embodied in the new paradigm. Designers, operators, managers, suppliers, standards organisations, regulators, and customers are so deeply embedded in the paradigm that they become committed to its preservation. In the words of economist Giovanni Dosi, "they are, so to speak, "blind" with respect to other technological possibilities."[25] Hence, if a new paradigm emerges in the form of a disruptive technology, we witness an "era of ferment".[26] Typically, this period of conflict will play out over many decades, before the new paradigm achieves a consensus, thereby dominating the sector.

Technological paradigms become enveloped in supporting ecosystems. If the paradigm disappears, these supporting features become legacies, e.g. legacy skills, legacy hardware (including buildings), legacy ways of working (e.g. policies, procedures, algorithms), legacy products, even legacy attitudes. These legacies are both slow and expensive to dismantle. One of many examples concerns the design of factories during the shift from steam power to electricity. Apparently it took decades before architects had fully adapted to the new requirements.[27] Meanwhile, factories formerly reliant upon steam would have struggled with internal reorganisations, redundancies, recruitments, some retraining, and huge capital investments in electrical systems. Often, these costs of paradigm transition are insurmountable. New entrants to the sector have a clear advantage.

Sometimes new technological paradigms come and go in a short space of time. We may hear little of them, because an insurgent paradigm is often beaten quickly into submission. In the early 2000s, Dean Kamen's *Segway* machines were proclaimed as paradigm-busting personal transportation devices.[28] Despite the hype, they barely left a mark. Around the same time, e-readers were expected by some commentators to kill off the traditional book, but they couldn't compete against the consumer's love of paper and the emergence of new tablet devices, followed by the smartphone.

Other paradigms may simply be illusory. 3D printing has been hailed as a possible paradigm-shifter, but that seems unlikely at the moment. There is no obvious reason why localised 3D production can't operate successfully in the same geographical and commercial space as large-scale, centralised manufacturing. They may even be complementary technologies.

Sometimes competing paradigms are able to co-exist, providing they don't attempt to occupy the same 'space'. For instance, it's possible for an organisation to run two unrelated projects, one using the Waterfall development methodology and the other using an Agile method, such as Scrum. However, this would exclude any possibility of merging the projects at a future date. In the same way, many households retain landlines at home while using mobile devices on the move. In summary, competing paradigms are rarely found within the same product or system, but they can avoid conflict by occupying demarcated niches.

Some technological paradigms emerge without needing to challenge any established incumbents. These are the highly original, break-through ideas that make headlines around the world. For instance, when the Wright brothers discovered the secret to sustained flight, no paradigm shift was necessary. There was nothing to shift from. A potential contemporary example is the blockchain, an immutable (i.e. unchangeable) cloud-based, electronic ledger, which offers a techno-logical alternative to institutional forms of trust. According to Rachel Botsman, a blockchain advocate, the technology is destined to supplant the faith we place in various intermediary organisations, such as bankers, lawyers, solicitors, accountants, and estate agents: "Even though most people barely know what the blockchain is, a decade or so from now it will be like the internet: we'll wonder how society ever functioned without it."[29] The blockchain paradigm will have emerged without a technological paradigm shift.

Paradigms of scale

There is another type of paradigm which is much less tangible and therefore more difficult to analyse and describe. I'm referring to the so-called *scale effect*. Scientists and engineers might be familiar with scale effects from studies of fluid flows and aerodynamics. However, scale effects can be found in many technical disciplines. The expression is used to describe changes in the behaviour of entities as they increase or decrease in scale. A physical model being tested in a wind tunnel, for instance, does not experience the same effects as the full-size version in its real operating environment, because surface area friction does not change in proportion to the scale of the model. But how do scale effects relate to paradigms? **It is my assertion that during changes in scale, a point of transition is reached where the paradigm of performance changes, thereby introducing an unquantifiable risk.**

Henry Petroski explains that it was Galileo who first comprehensively studied scale effects in the 17th century. He observed and analysed these effects in physical structures, reporting variations in the strength of beams and explaining the bone shapes of different-sized animals.[30] Engineers who merely extrapolate their calculations without considering the effects of scale expose themselves to failure.

Petroski describes one case involving the collapse of the central span of the Quebec Bridge in 1907, which killed many construction workers. The engineers had been inspired by the success of the recently opened Forth Bridge in Scotland, so they chose the same paradigm of construction: the cantilever. However, they changed the scale of key structural members, not recognising the effect this would have. Consequently, "the bones of the bridge were too slender to carry its own weight."[31]

In the 1930s, the design of suspension bridges was evolving as they became longer and (like the Quebec Bridge) also more slender. The effects of wind then emerged as a significant engineering challenge. However, rather than undertaking a fundamental rethink, engineers applied what Petroski calls "ad-hoc patches":

> Retrofitted cables were employed to check the motions while the problem was studied, but in the meantime more slender bridges continued to be designed and constructed according to the prevailing paradigm, which did not include a consideration of aerodynamics.[32]

It took the collapse of the Tacoma Narrows bridge in 1940 to finally halt the madness.

In 1969 two of Shell's largest crude oil carriers, *Marpessa* and *Mactra*, were badly damaged by mysterious explosions just 15 days apart. Numerous lives were lost. The *Marpessa* sank. After two years of investigation it was concluded that the sheer scale of these ships had introduced a new phenomenon. During operations to clean their holds, water spray created an electrically charged mist within the vast interior spaces of the ship. These could form clouds and even sparks, effectively miniature thunderstorms, which would be catastrophic in the gaseous atmosphere of an empty tank.[33]

This was a classic scale effect, but at what point does the size of a ship's hold undergo this dangerous transition? Could the effect have been foreseen and mitigated? Where on the Rumsfeld Matrix should we place this phenomenon? Galileo had been dead for over 300 years, so we could argue that it was a 'known unknown' of the increase in scale. At the same time, the ships' designers probably argued that it was a less blameworthy 'unknown unknown'? This harks back to the earlier examples of concrete cancer, asbestos, and Thalidomide. Where does responsibility actually lie?

Today there are similar challenges with the design of wind turbine blades, which have reached unprecedented lengths.[34] Despite our awareness of structural scale effects, there remains uncertainty about the point at which these effects will emerge, possibly requiring a new type of design.

In the mid-1850s, when Brunel began planning the construction of the world's largest ship, *Great Eastern*, he found that its scale necessitated novel organisational solutions. Built from iron and at 211 metres in length (692 feet), a conventional longitudinal launch (i.e. stern first) raised the likelihood of blocking the busy River Thames in London, perhaps even striking the opposite bank. The launching of ships longitudinally is an ancient shipbuilding tradition, but the scale effect was now in play. A transition point had been reached and a paradigm shift occurred. Brunel made the pioneering decision to launch laterally, slipping the ship sideways into the river. Among the many changes this introduced, Brunel needed to design a lateral launch cradle.[35] Such lateral launches are now commonplace, even for smaller ships. However, Brunel's method did not entirely supplant the longitudinal technique. Today, both launch methods co-exist within the shipbuilding industry. It's important to note, however, that it's impossible to construct a ship while retaining the option of a longitudinal *or* lateral launch. To use Kuhn's terminology, the two methods are 'incommensurable'.

There are also paradigm shifts where technology intersects with economics. The viability of a technology changes in response to such factors as unit costs and productivity. For instance, if an order is placed for 100 specialist widgets, this might be fulfilled by skilled workers using hand tools. However, an order for 5,000 widgets may necessitate the customisation of some pre-existing machines. This will increase the rate of production while reducing unit costs. A subsequent order for 100,000 widgets would require the invention of a high volume 'widget-forming machine'.

In this example, the 'tipping points' between each production paradigm are difficult to identify. How many widgets need to be ordered before a widget-forming machine becomes economically viable? To complicate matters, these tipping points vary according to other economic factors. On one day the tipping point will be 20,000 widgets, but on another, changes in component costs or the price of energy could move the point down to 17,300, or up to 24,800.

Therefore, one of the factors determining the success of a new technology will be its economic profile relative to changes in the scale of production. This may help to explain the timing of technological transitions, and why some organisations survive this process through fortuitous timing, while others fail.

It's a risk

I doubt whether Thomas Kuhn would approve of these references to paradigm shifts in the technological realm. He was concerned only with the battle for scientific minds. Furthermore, in the natural sciences there is no possibility of two incompatible scientific paradigms co-existing, except during the fractious transition period, as one overcomes the other. In the technological realm, however, different paradigms *can* co-exist, but only when separated.

My focus has been less on the conflicts between rival groups of technologists, and more on the ways that new technological paradigms emerge and the transitions that follow.

This all implies a great deal of uncertainty, particularly in the timing of paradigm shifts and the speeds of transition.

We are therefore left with two unrelated forms of technological uncertainty associated with paradigms:

1 **The fragility of scientific truths.** These truths are often used to underpin our assumptions. Can we be sure that our calculations or conclusions have not been founded on a scientific paradigm that is about to shift? We must remain alert to the potential disruption this will cause.
2 **The fragility of technological paradigms.** Each technological paradigm is susceptible to being overturned and replaced by a new paradigm. This may be a consequence of radical innovation, or it could emerge spontaneously via physical or economic scale effects.

So, we now have a new category of risk, which I will call *paradigm risk*.

A DEFINITION FOR *PARADIGM RISK*

The likely impact (positive or negative) arising from the real-time emergence of a new scientific or technological paradigm.

It needs to be stated, as I often do, that all uncertainty involves both upsides and downsides. By remaining alert to paradigms we become aware of the opportunities they offer. Warren East, the former CEO of chip manufacturer ARM Holdings (as they were then known), has recalled how the firm's fortunes turned on a change of paradigms in the early 21st century, as mobile phone technology moved from analogue to digital signal processing. According to East, this good fortune meant that "ARM was poised to surf a wave that would change the face of electronics. The company had the right engineering at the right time."[36] By 2024, the company was valued at $130 billion.

One wonders whether Donald Rumsfeld would have classified paradigm risk as an unknown unknown or a known unknown? Following the discussion above, I favour the latter.

Emerging complexity

This quest for the origins of uncertainty feels relentless, and it doesn't end with paradigm risk. We can't do justice to this topic without considering *complexity science* and *complexity theory*. Philosophers, scientists, sociologists, and economists have been interested in complexity for centuries, often without realising it. However, it's relatively new as a recognised discipline. The evidence presented below will demonstrate that strategists must gain an intuitive understanding of complexity if their work is to have real value. I will begin with a brief explainer, then examine each of the main features of complexity using practical examples.

The theory

Complexity is primarily concerned with the behaviour of large systems of interacting entities. The latter are sometimes known as *agents*. An agent can be any entity with the capacity to respond or react to its environment, including the actions of other agents. This reactive, adaptive behaviour is described as being *reflexive*. The more agents that are interacting, the more difficult it becomes to comprehend or predict the system's behaviour, which collectively is known as a *complex adaptive system* (CAS). Such a system cannot be described using the language of linear cause and effect relationships. Instead, its behaviour is said to be *non-linear*.

We don't have to look hard to find complex adaptive systems. Any natural ecosystem of plants, insects, mammals, or bacteria may be interpreted and analysed in this way. Another obvious CAS is the economy, consisting of companies, products, resources, customers, and so on. In the technological realm, consider the multiplicity of cause-and-effect relationships between designers, machines, components, operators, suppliers, and so on.

The formal study of these complex systems is known as the discipline of 'complexity science'. On the other hand, 'complexity theory' explains the characteristic behaviours exhibited by such systems. **The uncertainty with such systems lies in the timing, rapidity, extent, and duration of the behaviours described. These characteristics not only enable us to recognise a complex system, but also to foresee how the system might behave in the future.**

Here, it may be helpful to distinguish between the terms complex and complicated when used in a technological context. The professional body for systems engineers, INCOSE, offers this helpful explanation:

> A complex system has elements, the relationship between the states of which are weaved together so that they are not fully comprehended, leading to insufficient certainty between cause and effect. Complicated systems are less challenging. A complicated system has elements, the relationship between the states of which can be unfolded and comprehended, leading to sufficient certainty between cause and effect.[37]

So, unlike complex systems, complicated systems are Newtonian in character and therefore relatively predictable. In general, complex systems can be recognised by their behavioural attributes.

First and foremost there will be periods of stability, punctuated by upheavals, then returns to stability, usually in a new arrangement or form. The specific moments of transition between relative stability and relative instability are variously known as *tipping points*, *lever points*, or *pivot points*. During periods of stability a degree of *self-organisation* may be observed, perhaps represented as patterns in the arrangement of the entities, or in the data that represents them. Stability also facilitates, and probably encourages, increased *specialisation* by the agents.[38] Recognisable *hierarchies* also develop, where "particular combinations of agents at one level become agents at the next level up."[39] All of the attributes described in this paragraph may be seen in both human societies and economies.

One of the most important ideas associated with complexity is *emergence*. An emergent property is a novel attribute which arises from the totality of interactions between the agents. Emergence is described by the phrase "the action of the whole is more than the sum of the actions of the parts."[40] In other words, a new quality emerges from a CAS which may not bear any obvious relationship to its inputs or the actions of its agents. In a market economy, we might say that prices emerge from the reflexive behaviour of buyers and sellers, so prices are emergent properties. An emergent property of human social interactions could be settlements – the clustering of homes into villages and cities.

Another important characteristic is *path dependency*. This concept is relatively difficult to explain, although it makes intuitive sense. Agents have history and so does the system, so every starting position (both time and place) is imbued with a unique pre-disposition. Furthermore, the agents are always adapting, not only to one another, but also to the emergent properties of the system, such as market prices or the creation of settlements, as described above.

Therefore, different starting points produce very different outcomes, all other things being equal. So on a practical level, we are unable to precisely replicate situations, such that they will lead to the same outcomes. **Every new starting point is on a unique path and therefore pursues a unique future path.**

So that's complexity theory in a nutshell. It's not an easy concept to grasp on first reading, but it's worth persevering (and there are plenty of learning materials online). Now let's apply complexity to the technological realm. If complexity theory is to provide valuable insights, it will need to be applicable to the vast array of products and systems we work with.

Do we observe such adaptive systems in our professional lives? Are we, as technologists, agents within these complex adaptive systems? It seems that the answer to both of these questions is "Yes".

Agents

Technical systems consist of multiple components, many of which are adaptive agents. In Chapter 2 *components* were defined in such a way that they could be physical, logical, or even architectural. Physical components could include 'intelligent' operators, e.g. one component of an aeroplane is its pilot. It is immediately obvious that all complex technological systems feature adaptive inputs of some kind, especially from people, including designers, maintenance staff, and users.

In relation to complex technological processes, such as projects, Amrit Tiwana explains that they frequently take longer than expected to complete because, "the more interdependencies a project's pieces have, the more a multiplier effect can derail its schedule".[41] I would argue that this "multiplier effect" is the reflexive behaviour of agents within the project. A large project is a type of open system, subject to both internal and external influences. The external agents, such as suppliers and competitors, compound the challenges presented by the internal agents, especially project staff, who could be adapting to the behaviour of their colleagues or even to outside influences, such as recruiters. Project personnel also have complex private lives outside the workplace which will occasionally affect their performance within the team. Management may attempt to 'contain' this complexity via internal discipline and defined working practices, such as policies and procedures. However, attempts to control the behaviour of people in organisations can trigger new forms of adaptivity. M. Franssen of Delft University of Technology makes a related point:

> A human decision to follow a particular rule requires first of all a judgement that the situation is one where the rule applies. But even when an operator decides that a particular rule applies, he or she can also be expected to make a judgement whether or not it is in the person's interest to follow the rule.[42]

The simple truth is that people cannot be converted from intelligent, reflexive animals into non-reflexive 'dumb' components within an organisational machine.

Antibiotics are a technology invented in response to human suffering caused by bacterial infections. When used, the technology becomes a participant within the bacterial CAS. Each antibiotic is therefore an agent, interacting in the same system as natural bacterial agents. In the words of D. Headrick, the growth of this technology during the 20th century marked the start of an "arms race" between humans and bacteria, resulting in antibiotic-resistant bacteria and a further round of countervailing antibiotic development.[43] Here we witness the uncertainty of agent behaviour in a real-world complex system. It's impossible to foresee where this path will lead, but bacterial evolution could defeat human ingenuity, plunging us into a global health crisis as antibiotic effectiveness declines.

Tipping points

Earlier I referred to a particular CAS characteristic involving "periods of stability, punctuated by upheavals, then returns to stability, usually in a new arrangement or form." One is immediately drawn to the idea of *disruptive technologies*. In previous chapters we have considered examples such as the steam engine, colour film, and the jet engine, to which we could also add electricity generation, the mobile phone, and of course the internet. These disruptors are known to trigger an 'era of ferment' within a particular industry or technological domain. Disruptions on this scale are rare events. However, we observe upheavals on a much smaller scale relatively frequently. These could be triggered by changes in government regulations, a new standard, a successful product launch, or increases in the price of key commodities. It's the sheer variety of tipping points that makes them hard to identify in advance.

Historically we tend to focus on the moment when the disrupting technology bursts on the scene. However, the innovation itself will almost certainly have been the product of incrementalism. By the time a technology is ready to disrupt, it will have already been available for many years in a less perfect form. A single incremental step, in the right place at the right time, is all that may be required to overturn the current technological order. How would we know which incremental step is going to trigger the next upheaval, especially when such steps are occurring every hour of every day? **In the context of history, we can only identify the disruptor with the benefit of hindsight.**

Changes to regulations or standards can tip stable systems into periods of instability. In the 1970s, technological dominance in Formula One motor racing was associated with engine performance. The McLaren team struggled to compete against their more capable competitors, notably Ferrari. But a rule change unexpectedly shifted the technical emphasis to aerodynamics, which favoured McLaren while disadvantaging those teams heavily invested in engine expertise.[44] McLaren went on to dominate the sport through the 1980s. Stability could only return when other teams had developed similar expertise.

A successful product launch may be another tipping point. The release of the iPhone in 2007 makes a compelling case. Almost overnight it became the sector's 'dominant design', forcing all other manufacturers to mirror its functionality and ease of use. The resulting turmoil caused immense damage to established manufacturers, notably Nokia, who had previously led the sector with its iconic push-button devices.

Box 5.2   ANALYTICAL TOOLS AND TECHNIQUES

Leavitt's Diamond

Organisations may be described as consisting of four elements: (1) a structure; (2) a set of tasks to be performed (the work); (3) the people who perform those tasks; and (4) various supporting technologies. However, when changes are made to one element in isolation, this can impact the others. For example, when there are changes to tasks it may also be necessary to make changes to the organisational structure, which will then affect the personnel. It's for this reason that the wider implications of each change should be thoroughly analysed and understood before being made.[45]

A simple tool to assist with this process is called Leavitt's Diamond (Figure 5.4). It is named after the management psychologist, Harold Leavitt. These interactions resemble the *reflexive* relationships of a complex adaptive system (CAS).

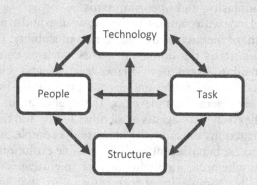

Figure 5.4 Leavitt's Diamond.

For technologists and engineers, not only does the Leavitt Diamond remind us to consider business tasks, structures and people when making changes to our technologies, but it also reminds people in the business to **always** consider the technological implications of their actions.

Periods of stability, self-organisation, specialisation, and hierarchies

Between their episodic upheavals, complex systems are characterised by periods of relative stability. This stability enables self-organisation, greater specialisation, and the establishment of agent hierarchies.

For example, the early years of network computing witnessed the instability and uncertainty of competing network protocols, such as IBM's SNA, DECnet, Microsoft's NetBIOS, and AppleTalk. It was only when the world settled on the non-proprietary Internet Protocol (IP), supported by Cisco, that stability was achieved. This coincided with the Internet boom. The rest is history.[46]

Stability encourages investment, technological specialisation, and the development of highly differentiated products. This desire for companies to differentiate themselves from competitors, occupying narrow technological niches, tends to drive innovation and build great companies.

However, the choice to specialise can be disastrous during the next phase of instability, the onset of which is impossible to predict. The realisation of this danger encourages risk mitigation methods, such as greater diversification of products and markets. It also encourages flexible product designs involving configurability, modularity, and open standards.

In accordance with complexity theory, we also find evidence for the development of hierarchies during periods of stability. For instance, in stable industries the dominant agents, such as companies and workers, tend to form new, higher-level agents. These include industry associations, trades unions, and professional institutions.

Once these hierarchies develop, the agents at one level will interact reflexively with agents at all other levels, and these multiple tiers of interactions substantially increase the complexity. This goes some way to explain the multitude of possible evolutionary paths in a CAS, and why accurate predictions are so elusive.

Incidentally, complexity theory informs us that when, in the very near future, AI systems begin communicating reflexively with one another, they too will combine to form hierarchies with new, higher-level agents. We should be alert to this possibility, which could have startling implications.

Emergence

According to complexity theory, we would also expect to see some form of emergence within the technological realm. An emergent quality is a unique feature arising from interactions between the agents in a system. What emerges will differ significantly from 'the sum of the parts'.

At the level of individual technologies or products, the emergent quality, arising from the interactions among components, could be what we call *functionality*. Although some of these emergent qualities yield immediate benefits to stakeholders, others may be slower to emerge, or even detrimental.[47] It could be argued that acid rain and concrete cancer are both examples of emergent effects from the complex interaction of agents.

It might also be claimed that emergent properties provide the fuel for invention and innovation. In his book *The Nature of Technology* (2010), W.B. Arthur describes technology as being *autopoietic*, a term introduced by biologists Francisco Varela and Humberto Maturana. An autopoietic system is self-producing or self-generating:

> … slowly over time, many technologies form from an initial few, and more complex ones form using simpler ones as components. The overall collection of technologies bootstraps itself upward from the few to the many and from the simple to the complex. We can say that technology creates itself out of itself.[48]

In other words, the technological realm at time T1 has an emergent property of new technological possibilities. Some of these possibilities materialise as inventions and innovations, thereby creating a modified technological realm at time T2. This modified realm now offers further technological possibilities, and so the cycle continues, *ad infinitum*. From this perspective, the person we call an inventor is someone who perceives these emergent qualities. In other words, they *perceive* a product or technology where currently there is none.

Path dependency

Complexity theory explains our 'path dependent' world. In complex, multi-agent environments each starting point leads down an unknown future path. We can therefore view both success and failure as systemic outcomes based on these unique historical paths.

It is misleading to link substantial events or trends to the isolated actions of particular individuals or teams.[49] Just as contemporary historians tend to dismiss the traditional 'great men of history' view of global political change, so we should also be wary of viewing successful 'tipping point' entrepreneurs as historically significant figures. They're not 'great men of technology' (or great women of technology, for that matter). They're simply hard-working incrementalists who just happened to be in the right place (or context) at the right time. To call them geniuses is a form of myth-making. They're not that special.

Box 5.3   STRATEGIC AND TACTICAL MOVES

"Instrument everything"

Data management is one of the great challenges of our time. Perhaps we already have too much data. Alternatively, it may be argued that we have too little.

Three senior consultants at Cognizant, Malcolm Frank, Paul Roehrig, and Ben Pring, wrote about the long-term prospects for data in their book, *What to Do When Machines Do Everything* (2017). Their broad conclusion was that future organisational success requires the capture of as much relevant data as possible. Value will then be generated from the analysis of this data, particularly with the help of artificial intelligence (AI).

Capturing data in technical environments often involves the use of sensors – typically small devices for monitoring, measuring, and recording. Sensors can detect pressure, temperature, acceleration, vibration, position, humidity, strain, proximity, gas, radiation, sound, light, colour, smoke, moisture, and much, much more. They sense using a variety of techniques, such as the piezoelectric effect and the Hall effect. Many sensors are mass-produced and inexpensive.

Sensor technologies are central to the functioning of the so-called Internet of Things (IoT). By feeding their data into AI solutions, sensors present an opportunity for ambitious organisations to improve performance and compete more effectively.

To benefit from the IoT and its world of data abundance, we must first integrate sensors within our products and operational processes. The advice from the Cognizant team is simple: "to know everything about everything, you need to instrument everything."[50] They note that a typical Airbus A350 has approximately 6,000 sensors generating 2.5 terabytes of data per day.[51] *Ingenia* magazine also reports on a recently constructed office building at 22 Bishopsgate in London (UK) with half a million sensors feeding an ICONICS building management system.[52]

What might the data from these sensors reveal? Could they pre-empt failures, or replace ponderous human decision making with decisive sub-second responses? Could hidden relationships between components or events be identified through the application of AI?

In order to develop an effective technology strategy you will need to extract critical insights from your data. Do you have all the data you need? If not, what opportunities do you have to capture more? Are you making the most of sensor technologies?

Things fall apart

All technologists and engineers are conscious of the fragility of the systems or products they build and manage. Without vigilance, in the form of monitoring and maintenance, most technologies rapidly lose performance, efficiency and functionality. Even with the benefit of constant attention weaknesses eventually emerge, leading to failure. We could say that, in the technological realm, *time has a deleterious effect*. But why does this happen?

As argued in Chapter 2, all technologies have a physical, material dimension. Most materials lose their integrity over time as a result of natural chemical, biological and physical processes. For example, rubber perishes through exposure to light and air, inducing chemical changes in the polyisoprene, and Perspex becomes brittle and discoloured because of UV effects upon the plastic, degrading it into other carbon molecules.[53] Polypropylene has a 'glass transition temperature' (Tg) of between zero degrees and minus 20°C, meaning that in cold weather it will lose its molecular mobility and become shatter-prone.[54] Meanwhile, metals are subject to a host of corrosive effects, the most familiar being oxidation (rust). All of the above are examples of chemical or electrochemical processes.

Metals are also prone to heat expansion (and subsequent contraction). If these changes breach designed tolerances, shearing and other forms of rupture or buckling will follow. Fatigue is another process to which many materials are susceptible. It is caused by cyclic stress, leading to the emergence of cracks, and eventually to breaks. Another important degradation process is erosion, particularly from wind and water friction. Spalling, on the other hand, is the freeze-thaw action on solids, causing the disintegration of brick and stone.

Many forms of degradation and subsequent uncertainty can be directly attributed to living organisms, such as fungi, rodents and insects. These were discussed in the previous chapter. Meanwhile, all products and systems are susceptible to destruction by probabilistic mechanisms; let's call them 'accidents'. For example, if a typical road vehicle is wrecked in a crash, on average, every 800,000 km of driving, then we might say that every vehicle, if driven indefinitely, will end its functional life in an accident. Of course, what normally happens is that, before the collision occurs, one of the aforementioned processes of disintegration will have consigned the vehicle to the scrapyard.

We can therefore be confident that most physical materials and engineered products have a finite useful life. In short, everything falls apart. It's what I call *disintegrity*, one of the 18 'origins of uncertainty' described in the next chapter.

Beyond the material aspects of technology, we also see degradation affecting logical components, such as knowledge, or product architectures. The loss of knowledge or expertise, for instance, is often caused by the departure of skilled personnel or by inadequate documentation. Software is particularly prone to this degradation. It increases both the total number of bugs and the average length of time that software remains offline while less knowledgeable personnel are learning to fix broken code.

These deficits in knowledge and their impact on system integrity contribute to the system's *technical debt*. A small debt may be manageable, but larger technical debts undermine quality and hinder progress. The 'interest' on the debt must be paid in the future, in the form of additional work. Attempts to rectify weaknesses often incur further debts, as fixes or patches are hurriedly applied without accompanying documentation. This only reinforces the debt cycle. Technical debts increase uncertainty and are rarely fully repaid. Under the weight of this debt, systems become inefficient and eventually 'fall apart' through decommissioning and replacement.

The growth of technical debt in coding environments is sometimes called *software entropy*, because it resembles the scientific definition of *entropy* – a measure of systemic disorder.[55] To physicists this disorder leads inexorably towards the disintegration of all things within the Universe – entropy being a feature of the second law of thermodynamics.

Entropy is therefore a useful analogy for describing decay in technological environments. For instance, we might say that entropy increases in proportion to the technical debt. To counter these effects, skilled and diligent professionals are needed. Eben Hewitt, the author of *Technology Strategy Patterns* (2018), is an enterprise solutions architect. He explains the role of such architects within large organisations:

> The architect defines standards, conventions, and toolsets for teams to use...As application or solution architects, they help within a system, within an ecosystem, and across an organization to create a common set of practices for developers that help things both go quicker and be more understandable and maintainable. This is a form of containing entropy.[56]

One of the world's leading thinkers on technical safety, James Reason, argues for constant vigilance because risk can never be entirely eliminated from technological environments. He writes, "Safety is a guerrilla war that you will probably lose (since entropy gets us all in the end), but you can still do the best you can."[57] And in their book *Embracing Complexity* (2015), Boulton *et al.* refer to entropy, implying that it could be analogous with complex adaptive systems (CAS), because the reflexive behaviour of agents leads to ever more unpredictable behaviour,[58] i.e. to systemic disorder. This apparent relationship between technological environments, complexity theory, and entropy's inexorable progress towards disorder is unnerving.

Perhaps we have another new risk category: *entropic technical risk*.

A DEFINITION FOR *ENTROPIC TECHNICAL RISK*

The likelihood and impact of disruption arising from entropic processes of disintegrity within products, systems, and organisations.

We can acknowledge these processes of disintegration, while simultaneously taking steps to control their effects. For example, although physical components are susceptible to failure, as outlined earlier, it may be possible to equalise these susceptibilities among components of the same type. This reduces the degree of randomisation in the incidence of failure. NASA provides a good historical example. Historian T. Heppenheimer describes testimony given to the US Congress by NASA's Charles Feltz. It reveals the organisation's diligence during the Apollo program. One of the reasons for the high cost of NASA's engineering was this 'war' against entropy. Even the simplest of bolts required scrupulous attention:

> ... the iron ore for those fasteners came from a particular section in a specific open-pit mine in the Mesabi Range, near Duluth, Minnesota. The bolts then took eleven steps to manufacture, and the product had to be certified at every step, through meticulous tests. This certification applied to the ingot smelted from the ore, the billet forged from the ingot, and the steel rod extracted from the billet, as well as the bolts themselves that were milled from the rod. The fasteners that resulted were some fifty times more costly than the ones that Feltz might buy in a hardware store, but this was what it took to send astronauts to the moon.[59]

It might be argued that NASA gradually lost this obsession, in part due to the stupendous costs involved. The deaths of 14 astronauts in subsequent decades only affirmed James Reason's observation that "entropy gets us all in the end".

That concludes the second of my three-chapter survey of techno-logical uncertainty. For the benefit of practitioners, many of the ideas presented in Chapters 4 and 5 are condensed into a checklist of the so-called 'origins of uncertainty'. These are 'the root causes of the root causes', and will be described in the next chapter.

Glossary for this chapter (Items in bold are also defined in the same table)

agent	An actor within a **complex adaptive system** (CAS). The agent adapts **reflexively** to both the actions of other agents and the **emergent** environment.
analytical risk	A commonly occurring, but rarely acknowledged, category of risk. It concerns the likelihood and severity of erroneous outputs arising from poorly selected, badly designed or improperly used analytical tools.
CAS	See **complex adaptive system**.
complex adaptive system (CAS)	An environment consisting of multiple entities, known as **agents**, interacting **reflexively** with one another and in response to other environmental changes. A typical CAS is characterised by periods of stability tipping occasionally into periods of instability, and *vice versa*. The technological realm may be said to resemble a CAS.
complexity	A generic term for the phenomena associated with **complex adaptive systems**.
complexity science	The academic study of **complex adaptive systems**.
complexity theory	A series of descriptions and explanations for the characteristic behaviours exhibited by **complex adaptive systems**.
emergence	A distinguishing characteristic of all **complex adaptive systems**. It is a quality which cannot be explained by an examination of the individual system parts, but which emerges from their **reflexive** behaviour.
entropic technical risk	The likelihood and impact of disruption arising from **entropic** processes of disintegrity within products, systems and organisations.
entropy	A measure of systemic disorder – from the second law of thermodynamics. To physicists this disorder leads inexorably towards the disintegration of all things within the Universe.
incommensurability	A term introduced by Thomas Kuhn to describe the principle that two competing scientific **paradigms** cannot occupy the same intellectual space. In relation to technological paradigms, the same principle may be applied to operational or physical space.

(Continued)

knowledge management	A package of solutions aimed at rectifying the inaccessibility of high-value information within organisations. It aims to get the right knowledge to the right people at the right time.
Leavitt's Diamond	A diamond-shaped visual tool which emphasises the fact that within organisations **reflexive** relationships exist between four entities: the organisational structures; the work to be performed (the tasks); the people who do the work; and the technologies used to perform or support the work.
lifecycle analysis	A useful method for analysing any type of entity undergoing transitions from 'birth' through to 'death'.
near-miss reporting	A mechanism for capturing the details (including root causes) of events which might have had more serious consequences. Typically it will involve self-reporting, which requires honest disclosure by all parties and a subsequent sharing of lessons learned. See **no-blame culture**.
no-blame culture	A workplace or industry-wide culture aimed at discovering the causes of errors and failures. Honesty is encouraged by means of a guarantee that no blame will attach to those who participate. See **near-miss reporting**.
paradigm	A definitive model or pattern.
paradigm risk	The likely impact, positive or negative, arising from the real-time emergence of a new scientific or technological **paradigm**.
paradigm shift	The switch from one scientific or technological **paradigm** to another.
path dependency	In a **complex adaptive system**, different starting points result in different pathways, each producing a uniquely different outcome, all other things being equal.
reflexivity	The characteristic behaviour of **agents** within a **complex adaptive system**, responding both to other agents and to their environment.
Rumsfeld Matrix	A simple 2 x 2 matrix enabling analysis, within a given context, of all four paired permutations of 'known' and 'unknown'.
scale effects	Significant changes in the behaviour of entities, such as products or systems, as they increase or decrease in scale.
tipping point	The environmental conditions which coincide with, or precipitate, a transition from stability to instability (or *vice versa*) in a **complex adaptive system**. Also known as *pivot points* and *lever points*.

Notes

1 Kahneman, D. (2011) *Thinking, Fast and Slow*. London: Penguin. 251.
2 Westwick, P. (2020) *Stealth: The Secret Contest to Invent Invisible Aircraft*. New York: OUP. 162–164.
3 Davies, B. (2014) 'Robots in Theatre'. *Ingenia*, Issue 58, 33–39.
4 Afuah, A. (2003) *Innovation Management*. New York: OUP. 123–126.
5 Faulkner, P., Feduzi, A. and Runde, J. (2017) 'Unknowns, Black Swans and the Risk/Uncertainty Distinction'. *Cambridge Journal of Economics*, 41 (5), 1279–1302.
6 Joyeux, D. (2019) 'A New Contender for Energy Storage'. *Ingenia*, Issue 78, 30–35.
7 Chang, H. (2011) 'When Water Does Not Boil at the Boiling Point'. *Philosophy of Engineering*, Vol.2. Royal Academy of Engineering, London, October 2011. Available at: https://www.raeng.org.uk/publications/reports/philosophy-of-engineering-vol-2, 14–20.
8 Petroski, H. (1994) *Design Paradigms: Case Histories of Error and Judgment in Engineering*. New York: CUP. 93.
9 Frank, M., Roehrig, P. and Pring, B. (2017) *What to Do When Machines Do Everything*. Hoboken: Wiley. 170.
10 Furuya, S. *et al.* (2018) 'Global Asbestos Disaster'. *International Journal of Environmental Research and Public Health*. Available at: https://doi.org/10.3390/ijerph15051000 (Accessed: 25 October 2022).
11 Sloan, J. (2020) *Learning to Think Strategically*. Abingdon: Routledge. 188.
12 Kahneman, *Thinking, Fast and Slow*. 207–208.
13 Braun, E. (1998) *Technology in Context*. London: Routledge. 120.
14 Braun, *Technology in Context*. 122.
15 Boulton, J.G., Allen, P.M. and Bowman, C. (2015) *Embracing Complexity*. Oxford: OUP. 10–11.
16 Boulton, Allen and Bowman, *Embracing Complexity*. 83.
17 Madhavan, G. (2016) *Think Like an Engineer*. London: Oneworld. 41–42.
18 Braun. 111.
19 Boulton, Allen and Bowman. 73.
20 Boulton, Allen and Bowman. 72.
21 Kuhn, T.S. (1996) *The Structure of Scientific Revolutions*. Chicago: University of Chicago Press.
22 Lipton, P. (2010) 'Engineering and Truth'. *Philosophy of Engineering*, Vol.1. Royal Academy of Engineering, London, June 2010. Available at: https://www.raeng.org.uk/publications/reports/philosophy-of-engineering-volume-1, 7–13.
23 McDougall, W.A. (1997) *The Heavens and the Earth*. Baltimore: Johns Hopkins University Press. 18–19.
24 Feynman, R.P. (2001) *The Pleasure of Finding Things Out*. London: Penguin. 112.
25 Dosi, G. (1982) 'Technological paradigms and technological trajectories'. *Research Policy*, Vol. 11, Issue 3, 147–162.
26 Afuah, *Innovation Management*. 34–35.
27 Arthur, W.B. (2010) *The Nature of Technology*. London: Penguin. 157–158.
28 Shane, S.A. (2009) *Technology Strategy for Managers and Entrepreneurs*. Pearson Prentice-Hall. 20–21.
29 Botsman, R. (2017) *Who Can You Trust?* London, UK: Penguin. 244–245.
30 Petroski, *Design Paradigms*. 30–80.

31 Petroski. 42.
32 Petroski, H. (2006) *Success Through Failure: The Paradox of Design.* Princeton: PUP. 184.
33 Howarth, S. (1997) *A Century in Oil: the "Shell" Transport and Trading Company 1897–1997.* London: Weidenfeld & Nicolson. 294.
34 Dyer, K. and Greaves, P. (2017) 'Futureproofing the Next Generation of Wind Turbine Blades'. *Ingenia,* Issue 70, 31–35.
35 Buchanan, A. (2006) *Brunel.* London: Continuum. 113–123.
36 Kenward, M. (2016) 'Taking Engineering to Industry'. *Ingenia,* Issue 69, 42–46.
37 INCOSE (2023) Systems Engineering Handbook (Fifth Edition). Hoboken: Wiley. 15.
38 Boulton, Allen and Bowman. 21.
39 Holland, J.H. (2014) *Complexity: A Very Short Introduction.* Oxford: OUP. 32.
40 Holland, *Complexity.* 2.
41 Tiwana, A. (2017) *IT Strategy for Non-IT Managers: Becoming an Engaged Contributor to Corporate IT Decisions.* Cambridge, MA: The MIT Press. 165.
42 Franssen, M. (2010) 'Roles and Rules and the Modelling of Socio-Technical Systems'. *Philosophy of Engineering,* Vol.1. Royal Academy of Engineering, London, June 2010. Available at: https://www.raeng.org.uk/publications/reports/philosophy-of-engineering-volume-1, 45–53.
43 Headrick, D.R. (2009) *Technology: A World History.* New York: OUP. 144.
44 Boulton, Allen and Bowman. 151.
45 Cadle, J., Paul, D. and Turner P. (2014) *Business Analysis Techniques.* Swindon: BCS. 20–23.
46 Rumelt, R. (2017) *Good Strategy, Bad Strategy.* London: Profile Books. 191–193.
47 Pyster, A., Hutchison, N. and Henry, D. (2018) *The Paradoxical Mindset of Systems Engineers.* Hoboken: Wiley. 92.
48 Arthur, *The Nature of Technology.* 21.
49 Boulton, Allen and Bowman. 158–159.
50 Frank, Roehrig and Pring, *What to Do When Machines Do Everything.* 71.
51 Frank, Roehrig and Pring. 66.
52 Ferguson, H. (2019) 'A Square Peg in a Round Hole'. *Ingenia,* Issue 80, 12–17.
53 Institute of Making, 'Materials'. Available at: https://www.instituteofmaking.org.uk/materials-library (Accessed: 28 June 2022).
54 MIT School of Engineering, '*Why Do Plastics Get Brittle When They Get Cold?*' Available at: https://engineering.mit.edu/engage/ask-an-engineer/why-do-plastics-get-brittle-when-they-get-cold/ (Accessed: 28 June 2022).
55 Mannan, U. *et al.* (undated) *The Evolution of Software Entropy in Open Source Projects: An Empirical Study,* available at https://ir.library.oregonstate.edu/downloads/z029pc12x?locale=en (Accessed: 29 June 2022).
56 Hewitt, E. (2018) *Technology Strategy Patterns.* Sebastapol, CA: O'Reilly. 11–12.
57 Reason, J. (2008) *The Human Contribution.* Farnham: Ashgate. 287–288.
58 Boulton, Allen and Bowman. 60.
59 Heppenheimer, T.A. (1997) *Countdown: A History of Spaceflight.* New York: Wiley. 264–265.

6 The origins of uncertainty

Eighteen sources of shock and surprise

This chapter presents

- A description of "the root causes of the root causes" underlying all technological uncertainty.

This chapter establishes

- New concepts and terminology associated with causation.

Our interest in uncertainty relates to the fact that strategy is concerned exclusively with the future. If the future were more certain, we could simply plan a sequence of actions. Instead we must strategise, or navigate through the uncertainty. This imposes an intellectual burden on strategists who need to be capable of identifying the sources of uncertainty in their technological environments.

Recent chapters have examined the concept of uncertainty as experienced throughout the technological realm. Chapter 4 focused on the intrinsic and extrinsic causes of uncertainty for both products and organisations. Chapter 5 explored uncertainty from the perspective of lifecycles, knowledge, analytics, paradigms, complexity, and the processes of disintegration.

Given the above, we ought to be in a better position to understand the origins of technological uncertainty. Understanding 'the root causes of the root causes' has been a quest of mine for many years, and I wish to share my findings here. Having carefully cross-referenced all of the research undertaken for this book, I now conclude that there are 18 distinct (though not mutually exclusive) origins of uncertainty in technological and engineering environments. Each of these will be described below.

These origins differ from conventional 'root causes', because the latter are always case-specific. There are tens of thousands of root causes for unexpected events, and new types of root causes are emerging all the time as technology evolves. So we must go deeper – to the origins of the roots.

DOI: 10.4324/9781003472919-7

The following 18 origins are applicable to almost any context within the technological realm and may be used as a checklist when making critical decisions. Each origin has been given a short, meaningful title.

1. Innovation

An innovation is more than a mere idea or invention. It is the practical realisation of original thinking. This results in a new or improved value-adding process or product. Most innovations are simply incremental improvements, but some are more radical in nature.[1] These are sometimes described as being 'disruptive'.

The emergence of new technologies can either complement or undermine pre-existing technologies. Some innovations compete directly, while others create substitutes. Innovations often cause demand for older technologies to decline. From an organisational perspective, some innovations will be 'competence enhancing', others 'competence destroying'.[2] Both imply unforeseen change.

Innovations often introduce novel safety risks. We were reminded of this by Paul Virilio's remark in Chapter 4: "When you invent the ship, you also invent the shipwreck". **In general, it is the timing and potential impact of innovations that cause uncertainty.** (Chapter 10 will look at innovation in much greater depth.)

2. Compatibility

In Chapter 2, Box 2.3 *Exploiting compatibility* explains the importance of this concept within technological environments. Products, systems and processes may either be compatible or incompatible with other products, systems and processes. Three types of formal compatibility were described: *backward*, *forward* and *horizontal*. However, compatibility has wider implications than this, because sometimes two or more entities will be combined in a single device or system despite the fact that their degree of compatibility is poorly understood. For example, adverse biological or chemical reactions are possible, as happened with the discovery of 'concrete cancer' (see Chapter 5). There can also be more subtle compatibility challenges, such as those involving the optimisation of components. An example from aircraft design is provided by Pyster *et al.*:

> ... an aeronautical engineer working on avionics will intuitively know that placing a piece of heavy electronic equipment inside the aircraft could move its center of gravity unfavorably. An

electronics engineer doing the same task may not recognize this as readily.[3]

People are also components with whom systems need to be compatible. When Donald Norman investigated the 1979 nuclear accident at Three Mile Island, his committee found that "the plant's control rooms were so poorly designed that error was inevitable: design was at fault, not the operators."[4] The study of ergonomics seeks to improve this type of compatibility.

Fortunately, compatibility can also be associated with more positive outcomes, e.g. where people or teams are working particularly well together. As these examples show, it's possible to use a fairly broad interpretation of compatibility without diluting its meaning.

The uncertainty associated with compatibility relates to the unforeseen consequences of new technology configurations or component combinations.

3. Complementarity

Technologies don't function in isolation. They exist within a wider socio-technical environment consisting of people, processes, goods and services. If these external entities reinforce or support the technology in some way, we describe them as being *complementary*. Economists say that entities are complementary if a change in the demand for one corresponds with a change in demand for the other. For instance, washing machines and detergents are complementary products, as are domestic freezers and frozen foods, or satellite dishes and TV broadcasts. There is a mutual dependency. It therefore follows that a weakening or loss of complementarity within the wider environment could undermine a technology's prospects.

The technology owner often has limited control over complementarity, unless directly involved in the production of complementary products. For example, in General Electric's early years the company took the strategic decision to be involved in both electricity generation and the production of complementary consumer products, such as lamps.[5]

We should also consider the relationship between complementarity and compatibility. Almost without exception, where technical compatibility exists between two products, they will also be complementary with one another.

It is the availability and quality of complementary goods and services, especially those from third parties, which introduces uncertainty about the prospects for a technology's longevity or further development.

Box 6.1   ANALYTICAL TOOLS AND TECHNIQUES

Failure modes and effects analysis (FMEA)

A broad strategic focus upon improving operations may require analytical tools for enhancing the quality of products and managing product risks.

Failure modes and effects analysis (more commonly known as FMEA) is one such tool. Most experienced technologists and engineers will be familiar with FMEA. Originating in the US, it has been widely used for decades.

The American Society of Quality (ASQ) describes FMEA as "a step-by-step approach for identifying all possible failures in a design, a manufacturing assembly process, or a product or service." It may be used "during the earliest conceptual stages of design and continues throughout the life of the product or service."

The tool's name is explained in two parts: "failure modes", or the ways that something might fail, and "effects analysis", which means studying the consequences of failures.[6]

The safety engineering consultants, Risktec Solutions, explain that an FMEA may be performed as a desktop exercise or within a multi-disciplinary workshop environment, and this should ideally be done early in the design process when it is still possible to make inexpensive changes. Risktec lists the basic steps as follows:

- Identify individual system components and their function within the system.
- Deduce credible failure modes for each component.
- Determine failure causes for each component failure mode.
- Establish failure effects for each failure mode at a local and system level.
- Identify available failure detection means and safeguards for each failure mode.

As with all analytical tools, FMEA has some limitations, such as its focus on one component at a time, thereby omitting more complex failures.[7]

FMEA is the subject of an international standard: IEC 60812. Examples of FMEA worksheets are easily found online, e.g. at the ASQ website.

4. Analytics

Thomas Chermack, a specialist in 'organisational learning, performance and change' at Colorado State University, writes that:

> Strategic problems or dilemmas are complex and ambiguous, with unknown solutions. These issues can become frustrating to work on without a sound set of tools for analyzing and understanding them.[8]

However, as we saw in the previous chapter, many analytical methods, both quantitative and qualitative, are unreliable. For instance, not only is data often flawed, but so are the analysts who work on the data. The tools we use may be inappropriate for the task, or incapable of addressing complexity. Our assumptions may be poorly framed, or simply incorrect.

Of course, if most analysis is imperfect, then so must be the synthesis which we subsequently use to create our solutions. **Uncertainty is therefore directly related to our confidence in analytical outputs and the decisions which they inform.**

5. Conversion

Technical work involves many types of conversion activity. In all cases, inconsistencies or errors can arise. For instance, measurements may be converted between imperial and metric units, and languages may be translated to enable publication of technical documentation in other countries. Even if we assume that these conversions have been handled with care and integrity, uncertainty will remain. Converted quantities are only as precise as the chosen number of decimal places or the accuracy of instruments, so absolute values will differ. The translation of words between languages is subject to an even greater loss of fidelity. Indeed some words or phrases have no equivalents in other languages.

Perfection, or near-perfection, is rarely essential to the satisfactory performance of a technology, so in most instances small conversion errors should not cause concern. Occasionally, though, egregious errors do arise. In 1998 the Mars Climate Orbiter was lost due to a failed imperial/metric conversion affecting navigation.[9] In order to be pragmatic about this type of uncertainty, our concerns should be risk-oriented. **In other words, the greater the potential for loss or harm, the more we should be scrutinising conversions of all kinds.**

6. Precision

Absolute precision is only achievable in mathematics and logic. In the less rarefied world of professional practice, imprecision is the norm. The accuracy of measurement data, for instance, will be dependent on the tools chosen, their calibration, and the way that readings are captured. A micrometer is clearly more precise than a tape measure, but neither delivers absolute precision.

Numerical precision is clearly of fundamental importance to engineers, but so is the precision of language. Misleading terminology or phrasing can lead to failures in communication. The written specifications produced at the commencement of a project will often feature imprecise requirements. If these cannot be identified and rectified early, weaknesses will become embedded in the project. Linguistic imprecision is a significant 'human factor' in socio-technical systems, such as the written and spoken words within aircraft cockpits.

A different type of imprecision was described in the previous chapter, where manufacturing processes were unable to produce *identical* units of output. Systems of all kinds can fail due to imprecision in component manufacturing.

In most circumstances, however, minor imprecision will be inconsequential. Former McKinsey consultants, Ethan Rasiel and Paul Friga, note that an obsession with precision introduces the law of diminishing returns. It's pointless to expend resources pursuing greater precision than is necessary for the task.[10] Rather than obsessing over detail, it is more important to optimise in order to get things done. However, in tightly integrated systems, multiple instances of imprecision may, in particular circumstances, compound into a significant threat. **Precision, or rather imprecision, is a source of uncertainty in the performance of technological products and systems.**

7. Tolerance

A broadly accepted technical or scientific definition of tolerance would be "The ability of enduring" or an "allowable deviation".[11] Of interest here is the tolerance of technologies, systems and organisations to changes occurring within their environment?

At the component level, engineers will often be confident in their understanding of tolerance, which can sometimes be established in controlled laboratory conditions. However, in the context of a technology strategy, we have much broader concerns. All technologies and systems, as well as the organisations which use them, possess an attribute we call *architecture* – the particular arrangement of parts. An architecture is usually designed or structured with the aim of optimising performance.

Technological environments change continuously. Some architectures may struggle to adjust and adapt. In other words, architectures can be inflexible or *intolerant* of change, and the degree of tolerance remains a source of uncertainty until tested in real-world conditions. We might therefore describe tolerance, more generically, as *the capacity for logical and physical structures to accommodate change.*

One of the reasons why some technologies are 'disruptive' is because established products and systems cannot be re-architected, either for compatibility or complementarity, and because the organisations which use them are unwilling to lose the value of their strategic assets, including their hard-earned capabilities, skills, and know-how. This intolerance for change is often self-destructive, as we saw with the DEC case in Chapter 4.

It was noted in Chapter 3's Box 3.3 *Co-location or Cloistering?* how IBM's PC development site in Florida was created in order to evade the anticipated intolerance of people within its parent organisation. The implementation of a technology strategy could face the same challenges, as reflected in this observation of complex human behaviour by Boulton *et al.*:

> An executive can announce a new strategy, but even if this message is received by all staff we cannot know how they interpreted the strategy, much less know the extent to which they would want to comply with it. Expecting a strategy, as an organizational artefact, to impact on an organization in a predictable fashion is about as effective as pushing on a string.[12]

Tolerance is an origin of uncertainty because we lack confidence in the capacity for technologies, systems, and organisations to adjust, absorb, and retain their integrity under untested conditions, especially while experiencing environmental change.

8. Communications

By communications I'm referring particularly to the *verbal* delivery of instructions, explanations, technical requirements and, of course, strategies. (Verbal = language in both spoken and written form.) It was noted earlier that the translation and precision of communications can be a source of uncertainty in technical environments, but beyond this there are many more things to consider.

All words can be a source of uncertainty. For example, even the most exact communicator cannot control the way that words are understood by recipients. Have they processed the message correctly? Perhaps the recipient speaks the same language, but nuance is lost due to cultural differences. The recipient might not even be human, but an AI solution. How will that technology choose to interpret the words?

In another example, if a single communication is received by multiple stakeholders, each capable of comprehending it differently, there could be a discordant response.

Sometimes communications are passed through a hierarchy of gatekeepers. If each tier of this hierarchy introduces a small probability of error, how might these errors compound over multiple stages? (Think of the children's game involving the relay of a whisper between participants in a circle.)

In other circumstances, lengthy communications may be presented in shorter, edited versions. Editing implies exclusion, so what could be missing? Also, have the communicators, the editors, or the language interpreters imposed any personal or ideological 'agendas' on the message? For instance, the writers of a business case for a future project are likely to want the project approved. Similarly, for internal political reasons, messaging by technical leaders does not always reflect operational reality.

All forms of verbal communication are therefore a source of uncertainty.

Box 6.2   STRATEGIC AND TACTICAL MOVES

Choosing vanilla

The classic flavour of ice cream is vanilla. It's delicious, but unfussy. No swirls, nuts or unrecognisable bits. With vanilla you know exactly what you're getting.

This is why technical folk often refer to products as being *vanilla*, meaning unadulterated and implicitly trusted. A vanilla product is more likely to have been exhaustively tested by its supplier. It is probably produced in large quantities, so most errors or faults will have been rectified. More importantly, nobody has customised or reconfigured it. We sometimes describe it as being straight 'off the shelf' or 'out of the box'. In situations where reliability and trust are important attributes, the wisest course is often to use a vanilla product. However, this doesn't always happen – for two reasons in particular:

1 Technical people often prefer to design and build their own solutions. This activity is more professionally satisfying than making a purchase, and the end result should, in theory, meet all requirements *exactly* (whereas vanilla meets some, but not all, requirements).
2 Even in situations where a product, tool, or component has been purchased off the shelf, there is often a desire to make alterations (e.g. customisations, 'tweaks', configuration changes), again in order to satisfy all requirements.

Customisation, though, leads to additional product complexity and to challenges associated with both knowledge sharing and 'ownership' of the solution. Have the changes been documented? Will additional training be needed? Whose job will it now be to maintain the customised version of the product? Who will be accountable for any failures? Furthermore, it often takes considerably longer to create and test a customised version than to simply implement a vanilla solution. So, is it wise to shun vanilla?

The Pareto Principle teaches us that approximately 80% of the value in any solution may be attributed to just 20% of the effort expended in creating it. So, vanilla will give you 80% of what you need for 20% of the cost of a near-perfect solution.

Another formulation of this principle states that, in order to squeeze perfection from a product, the final 20% of value requires an additional 80% of effort. This expensive pursuit of perfection is sometimes called the *nirvana fallacy*.[13] Unsurprisingly, the classic dichotomy of 'make or buy' usually favours buy, unless a bespoke product will be vital to success, in which case the investment in designing and building something may be justified.

The vanilla argument is often used in relation to software. In Grant and Jordan's *Foundations of Strategy* (2015), they note that Singapore Airlines, "unlike some of its rivals ... has not developed highly customized and sophisticated yield management and other back-office software, preferring instead to buy tried-and-tested applications."[14] In another example, Oxford City Council's published technology strategy includes a set of "Technology Principles", notably "Out-of-the-box by Default".[15]

It's generally wise to choose vanilla, because the alternatives are often *Raspberry* and *Rocky Road*.

9. Knowledge

In the previous chapter we looked at knowledge. This introduced the Rumsfeld Matrix, in which the "known knowns" implied greater certainty, but all the other combinations included an "unknown" component. In reality, even the known knowns must be doubtful, because there is no such thing as perfect knowledge about anything. The deeper you dig, the more you learn. However, despite our relative ignorance, decisions still need to be made. Strategies must be devised in an uncertain environment that never stands still. That's the reality and we have to get on with it.

It's often tempting to make decisions based on knowledge of what has worked well in the past, but as Petroski reminds us, "Past successes, no matter how numerous and universal, are no guarantee of future performance in a new context."[16] This resembles the so-called 'path dependency' characteristic of complex adaptive systems, i.e. historical circumstances cannot be recreated. Historical knowledge may have less value than we think.

Organisations use technical due diligence in order to gather intelligence about acquisition targets and potential partners. Due diligence practitioners must base their recommendations (i.e. whether or not to complete the deal) on the limited amount of information they have been able to acquire. Those decisions are often incorrect, as evidenced by the frequent failures of mergers and acquisitions (described in Chapter 4).

The quantity and quality of knowledge available to support decision making will always be a source of uncertainty.

10. Pioneering

We can't progress technically without crossing boundaries. Experimentation, exploration, entrepreneurship and innovation all involve ventures into the unknown. Here we find both risks and opportunities. If a technology, product, or process is unique or untried, there will be little or no historical data with which to make forecasts or judgements. The same will apply if a technology is well-known, but used in a new context. 'Pushing the envelope' has always been a great way to learn ... and a great way to burn. Do you feel lucky?

Sometimes it's impossible to fully prototype a solution. For instance, new ship designs or tunnelling methods require full-scale builds in order to establish performance characteristics under real-world conditions. As we saw in Chapter 5, this may also cross a boundary into new paradigms, e.g. via the scale effect. Pioneering failures befell the Hubble Space Telescope (Chapter 4) and the first Shell supertankers (Chapter 5).

In general, pioneering implies uncertainty of both performance and outcomes.

11. Complex adaptation

The theory of complex adaptive systems (CAS) was explained in Chapter 5. Our engineered systems and technological environments are characterised by myriad interdependencies and reflexive behaviour by multiple agents. The evolution of a CAS cannot be predicted in detail beyond the present moment. Many different paths may be followed into the future, so a range of possible outcomes must be anticipated. For example, one of the challenges facing analysts who attempt to model future developments is that some of the factors that will determine outcomes **do not yet exist.**

Not only will they emerge during the time period addressed by the model, but having emerged they will then become reflexive agents, further influencing the direction of progress.[17]

An economy is one of the best examples of a CAS, and we cannot divorce technology from economics. A 2021 analysis of developments in the fusion energy sector, performed by the Institution of Mechanical Engineers (IMechE) and Assystem, highlighted the impossibility of forecasting the cost of constructing fusion reactors, particularly over a time horizon spanning multiple decades. There are simply too many economic and other variables: "Labour costs, supply chain readiness and experience, borrowing costs, labour productivity and project know-how, safety and technical regulation all have an impact on capital cost."[18]

If there is only one truth, it is this: Complexity implies uncertainty.

12. Finity

The technological realm is subject to multiple constraints. Some of these are rooted in nature, such as the speed of light. Other constraints are resource-based, or enshrined in standards and protocols. A professional technologist or engineer is expected to understand these constraints – the limitations imposed upon their own products, systems, and projects.

For simplicity, let's assume that the constraints established by science are fixed (although as Thomas Kuhn pointed out in the previous chapter, 'facts' can be overturned through scientific revolutions). But other constraints, such as those associated with resourcing, standards, and protocols are different. They're relatively fluid. What is initially perceived to be limited, or bounded, is often found to be more flexible. For example, consider the resource constraints on a project, particularly the so-called 'iron triangle' of *time*, *money*, and *quality*. Are these ever fixed on a project? Such constraints can often be re-negotiated.

Let's consider the performance envelope for an aircraft? What happens if the certified maximum take-off weight of 250,000 kg is exceeded by just one kg? Nothing. By ten kg? Nothing again. It still flies. So what is the maximum take-off weight? Where is the limit? Nobody really knows, because it varies with context. Indeed, there are probably circumstances where the aircraft will fail to leave the runway despite being *under* weight (e.g. due to a rare combination of meteorological or atmospheric conditions). Limits are perplexing and enigmatic.

In Chapter 5 we saw how scale-effects emerge when unknown thresholds are passed. This caused the collapse of the Quebec Bridge in 1907 and the sinking of the *Marpessa*. These scale thresholds are an unknown limit in new technologies and new product designs.

In modelling exercises involving extrapolation, erroneous results may arise from a failure to account for limits arising within a complex system, such as saturation and substitution effects among the variables.[19] The growth of one variable will cease when saturation has been reached, while another may be halted by the emergence of a substitute, or it might grow even faster as it becomes the substitute for another variable. Can these constraints be reliably incorporated in extrapolation models, especially in complex adaptive systems? No, they can't.

So, although there are technical limits or transition points in most scenarios, we don't truly know where they are. There is, however, a difference between a *de facto* limit, one which exists as fact, but which can only be discovered empirically, and a *de jure* limit, one laid down as a rule by an authority, such as a regulator. We cannot place too much trust in *de jure* limits, because the conditions under which they were established (e.g. by the rule-making institution) may not resemble our current operating environment. Rules-based limits are founded on multiple assumptions, and these must be fully understood before pushing any technology close to its mandated boundary.

It's likely that when the OceanGate submersible was lost over the *Titanic* wreck in June 2023, one of its components reached a physical limit. Water pressure was clearly a factor in the loss, but the limit reached might have been the number of dive cycles causing material fatigue in the hull, rather than its particular depth at the time.

So, in any scenario finity threatens our assumptions and decisions? **Finity** **is the category of uncertainty we associate with the mercurial nature of limits.**

13. Disintegrity

In Chapter 5 I referred to "the deleterious effects of time". Without continual monitoring and maintenance, all things have a natural tendency to fall apart. This applies to products, systems, and organisations. The causes may be chemical, biological, physical, and even psychological. Sometimes we use non-technical terms to refer to these processes, including 'ageing', and 'wear and tear', but the outcomes are just the same.

Entropy is a useful analogy, borrowed from thermodynamics. But beyond the analogy, real entropic effects are also one of the factors at work in the natural disintegration of everything. The passage of time leads to increasing disorder.

Disintegrity is an origin of uncertainty associated with entropic effects, whether directly or by analogy.

14. Vitacausa

"We can't ignore the fact that the greatest source of uncertainty in the technological realm is life itself: everything from bacteria to blue whales." I made this assertion in Chapter 4, and I stand by it. Living organisms, such as rats (which like to chew), birds (which jet engines dislike to chew), fungi (which cause rot), and bacteria (which cause sickness), are frequent sources of uncertainty in both products and organisations. Missing from that list, of course, are humans (which never cease to surprise us).

Consequently, there is immense diversity in this topic and too much to summarise here. However, a few examples of human-induced uncertainties should be sufficient to make the point. Many are perceived as positive, such as the surprises associated with creativity, invention, and great decision making. But there are others which cause concern, such as sickness, keyboard errors, scope creep, fraud, sabotage, fatigue, and 'pushing the envelope'. In fact, in many technical environments up to 80% of accidents can be attributed to the actions of just one species: humans.[20]

It's important to remember, though, that human operators (users) are not always the ones at fault when things go wrong. Root causes are often traced back to designers or poor management decisions. Either way, they're all 'human factors'.

So, given that living organisms are one of the principal causes of uncertainty, we need to assign a suitably generic, yet meaningful label to this classification. Unable to source an appropriate word, I have turned to Latin, combining *vita*, meaning life, with *causa*, meaning cause. So the label *vitacausa* simply translates as 'causes from lifeforms'. **Vitacausa encapsulates all the origins of uncertainty associated with living organisms.**

This is such a broad category of uncertainty that it appears to include some of the origins already described, notably *Communications*, *Knowledge*, and *Pioneering* (numbers 8, 9, and 10, respectively). However, these cannot be subsumed within vitacausa for two reasons. Firstly, their importance is such that they benefit greatly from the higher profile of being listed separately; secondly, artificial intelligence is already engaged with each of these origins of uncertainty, often in ways indistinguishable from human behaviour. But vitacausa does **not**, by implication, include AI. Therefore those three origins cannot be sub-categories of vitacausa.

15. Terracausa

The living realm may be our greatest source of uncertainty, but the non-living realm is hardly a paragon of dependability. Here, I'm referring to all non-living components of what we know as 'the Earth'. The Earth is often viewed as a system consisting of land, water, atmosphere, and everything gravitationally dependent upon the planet, such as the Moon.

Earth's uncertainties range from the frequency of desert rains to the abundance of rare metals and the intensity of earthquakes. Falling space debris, lightning strikes, and reversals in the Earth's magnetic field are other rarer, but no less valid, considerations.

The upsides of Earth's uncertainty are often welcomed, including bountiful harvests, calm seas, and tail winds. But the downsides may be existential: volcanoes, tsunamis, and droughts, for instance.

Again, in the absence of a suitable collective name for these phenomena I have devised the term *terracausa*, or 'causes from the Earth'. **Terracausa encapsulates all the origins of uncertainty associated with non-living entities in the Earth system, which includes the land, seas, atmosphere, and the Moon.**

Box 6.3   STRATEGIC DICHOTOMIES

Disrupt and cannibalise OR Protect and suppress?

Richard N. Foster of McKinsey & Company wrote that "A change in technology may not be the number-one corporate killer, but it certainly is among the leading causes of corporate ill-health."[21] He was referring not to minor technological changes, but to the disruptions wrought by new technologies – those once-in-a-generation events that re-shape industries. Some historical moments of disruptive innovation have already been noted, such as the emergence of steam power, colour film, the jet engine, and the smartphone.

This raises an interesting question. If new technologies present so many risks to organisations, why would any corporate strategist promote or support the introduction of a technology which has the potential to disrupt its own operations? What incentive is there for a company to develop any technology capable of undermining the status quo? What happens if a corporation's over-enthusiastic R&D lab discovers or invents such a technology? What should the strategic response be?

One of the main concerns is that the innovation would require substantial new capital investment whilst simultaneously 'cannibalising' the company's existing range of products. Core competences (skills, experience and know-how) would be instantly devalued. Meanwhile, it's uncertain how the market will respond. The innovation, though exciting and impressive, could re-shape the industry, altering customer preferences and re-structuring supply chains. A company's status and future integrity could be threatened.

For risk averse organisations, the logical strategic response is to protect the status quo by suppressing the new technology. There are various ways to do this including:

- Secure as many associated patents as possible, then do nothing with the IP. If necessary, buy the patents from other inventors, or buy their companies in order to acquire and suppress the technology.[22,23]
- Require employees to sign restrictive covenants preventing the leakage of the new proprietary knowledge.[24]

If you have ever wondered why it took the world so long to adopt electric cars, or why battery technologies have evolved at such slow rates for decades, some answers *may* be found above.[25,26]

16. Cosmicausa

In the world of risk management, threats or opportunities from beyond the Earth system are generally dismissed. For example, although it's accepted that an asteroid collision could have catastrophic effects, the likelihood of this event is deemed so low that the classic formula of **Risk = Probability × Impact** produces a result too small to justify further consideration.

From the perspective of professional practice this indifference to extra-terrestrial causes is understandable, but for the purposes of identifying *all* origins of uncertainty, which is the purpose of this chapter, the known unknowns of outer space clearly need to be acknowledged. So we require a collective term encapsulating such phenomena as solar storms, UV damage to materials, comets, asteroids, meteors, even black holes. (Should you be wondering, the possibility of an alien invasion is already covered by *vitacausa*, see above.)

Unfortunately, there are few upsides in this category. As for the downsides, a severe solar storm (an event likely to cause widespread electrical disruption on Earth over many days) would probably attract the greatest risk score given its relatively high likelihood.

These 'causes from the Universe' are here known collectively as *cosmicausa*. **Cosmicausa encapsulates all the origins of uncertainty associated with non-living entities in the extra-terrestrial environment.**

17. The execution gap

During the time between a strategic or tactical decision and its execution or delivery, the operating environment will change. Consequently, the context in which the decision was originally made will no longer exist, and some (or all) of the supporting evidence may have gone. The decision inevitably loses value. It depreciates.

For instance, most large and medium-sized organisations choose, from time to time, to build their own bespoke software. However, during the course of software development, as Amrit Tiwana explains, "business needs might change, competitors might alter their strategies, technologies can evolve, or regulatory agencies may impose new rules."[27] In other words, the goalposts will almost certainly move.

More generally, it follows that the greater the lapse in time between a decision and its execution, the greater the likelihood that the outcome of the decision will be sub-optimal. Chermack makes a similar argument in a critique of traditional corporate planning:

> The illusion is that planning can function like a machine, that the steps of organizational planning need only be carried out. The basis of that illusion is an assumption that things more or less stay the same.[28]

Let's consider the value of decisions to start large capital projects. Major investments in ships, refineries, and power plants, for example, are pursued in parallel with the uncontrollable evolution of their technical, economic, natural, and political environments. Meanwhile, management and personnel at all levels will be subject to the usual revolving doors of promotions, secondments, redundancies, and so on. It is therefore unsurprising when new technical requirements emerge mid-project, causing costly re-work and contractual disputes. Uncertainty in the outcomes of a project will increase with every day that passes.

The solution is to deliver projects more quickly, but experienced project managers know how difficult it is to speed up, even with an injection of additional resources. Doubling the size of a development team doesn't double the speed of execution. It can even slow progress down.

Paul Stevens, Editor of *Strategic Positioning in the Oil Industry* (1998), explains how multiple 'oil shocks', beginning in the 1960s, resulted in major investment decisions failing to keep up with events.[29] For example, when the Suez Canal was closed indefinitely in 1967, oil companies concluded that their tankers should be built substantially larger in order to benefit from economies of scale, rather than be limited in size to squeeze through the Canal. (Note: In Chapter 3 we saw how Shell began this trend after the first closure of the Canal ten years earlier, in 1957.) Yet by the time hundreds of supertankers had been designed, built and launched within a relatively short period, the world economic recession of the 1970s meant that demand for their cargoes was already in decline. Furthermore, the Canal had been reopened. Gradually the demand for oil came back, but by the 1990s many supertankers of a similar age were ready for simultaneous decommissioning, and there was limited enthusiasm to undertake another round of costly and lengthy shipbuilding to replace them.

If ever there was an argument against unnecessarily large and lengthy projects, or in favour of prompt and decisive action by management, it is the problem of the execution gap. In their book *How Big Things Get Done* (2023), Professor Bent Flyvbjerg (Oxford University) and Dan Gardner emphasise and reiterate the dictum, "Think slow, act fast."[30] Take care to make the right decision, then execute at the earliest opportunity. Dithering is not delivering.

The execution gap is a key source of uncertainty, and the degree of uncertainty grows in proportion to the length of the gap.

18. Unknown unknowns

Thus far, I have named 17 origins of uncertainty. All should be familiar to technologists and engineers. However, this begs a question: Is it possible that we will encounter new types of uncertainty in the future? If so, these could only originate from sources, concepts or paradigms unforeseeable today. On a Rumsfeld Matrix, these would be classified as "unknown unknowns".

Although we don't know what they're going to be, we should at least acknowledge the potential for unknown unknowns, so that if (or when) they emerge we will be able to say that we anticipated them.

This anticipation, however, doesn't convert them into 'known unknowns', because we have no evidence, or reason to believe, that they exist today, or ever will exist in the future. In other words, there is a subtle difference between a known unknown (such as next week's weather) and **the knowledge that unknown unknowns are a permanent and indescribable threat to all technological environments.**

For ease of reference, all 18 origins are summarised in Table 6.1.

It's possible that my analysis has failed to identify some origins. Perhaps there should be 19 or even 20. If so, I apologise. Any new discoveries will be included in future editions of the book.

Table 6.1 The 18 origins of uncertainty in the technological realm

Origin		Description
1	Innovation	Uncertainty arises from the timing and impact of innovations, especially those that compete with, or complement, existing technologies.
2	Compatibility	Uncertainty associated with the consequences for compatibility arising from new technology configurations or component combinations within a product or system.
3	Complementarity	Uncertainty in the availability and quality of complementary goods and services, over which technology owners and operators have little or no control.
4	Analytics	The absence of absolute confidence in analytical outputs, leading to uncertainty in the subsequent decisions they inform.
5	Conversion	Uncertainties associated with the integrity of converted quantities and language translations.
6	Precision	In complex products or systems, the uncertainty of precision is baked in via multiple components and tools. Absolute precision is achieved only in mathematical logic.
7	Tolerance	Uncertainty in the capacity for any technology, system or organisation to retain its integrity under untested conditions, or while experiencing change.
8	Communication	Uncertainty arising from the probability that there will be errors of comprehension whilst transmitting and receiving written or spoken information.
9	Knowledge	The absence of confidence in the knowledge and data used to support strategic decisions introduces uncertainty. It's not what we know, but what we don't know.
10	Pioneering	Uncertainty in the performance of technological products, systems and processes that are unique or untried within a particular context.

(Continued)

Table 6.1 (Continued)

Origin		Description
11	Complex adaptation	Uncertainty in the future direction and behaviour of a complex adaptive system (CAS) consisting of multiple reflexive agents.
12	Finity	The existence of *de facto* limits throughout the technological realm. The quantity and position of these limits remain unknown until empirically discovered.
13	Disintegrity	The literal and metaphorical intrusion of entropic effects (such as ageing, erosion, and chemical transitions) leading inexorably towards 'disorder'.
14	Vitacausa	All uncertainties associated with the actions of living organisms. Throughout the technological realm human beings are the predominant source of unexpected outcomes.
15	Terracausa	All uncertainties associated with non-living entities within the terrestrial environment of land, water, atmosphere, and satellites (i.e. the Earth 'system').
16	Cosmicausa	All uncertainties associated with non-living entities in the extra-terrestrial environment, such as solar flares, UV light, and asteroids.
17	The execution gap	Unexpected outcomes arising from environmental and contextual changes during the elapsed time between a decision and its execution. Uncertainty grows in proportion to the length of this gap.
18	Unknown unknowns	Causes of uncertainty originating from sources, concepts or paradigms hitherto unknown or unforeseeable.

Concluding remarks

All decisions in technological environments are tinged with uncertainty, but this shouldn't prevent progress from being made. Success is attainable, despite the fact that uncertainty obeys an exponential relationship with time. Let me explain.

We know that technological activity takes place within a complex adaptive system, constantly evolving via multiple reflexive relationships. One consequence of this reflexivity is that similar starting points produce highly differentiated outcomes. Paths easily diverge. We know from experience that it's considerably easier to predict near-term events than those with longer time horizons.

The phrase 'trumpet of uncertainty' is used to describe the shape of possible outcomes, relative to time.[31,32] This trumpet is a useful metaphor and worthy of visualisation (see Figure 6.1).

Over the longest timescales, only the most robust physical or logical entities, such as core infrastructures and scientific knowledge, are likely (though never certain) to remain intact. We can therefore anchor some of our forward thinking to these more reliable entities. Like stepping stones, they help us to hop from one year to the next without getting our feet wet. Occasionally a hitherto sturdy rock will wobble, and we brace ourselves for a soaking. These unexpected and unwanted events happen to all of us, and to all organisations. They include the paradigm shifts discussed in the previous chapter.

This near-exponential relationship with expected outcomes should inform our strategy development work, particularly in relation to goal-setting and action planning. We must ask some

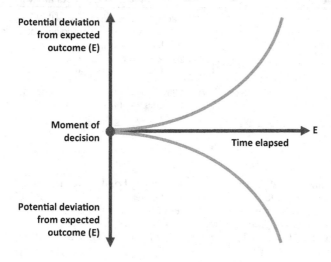

Figure 6.1 The trumpet of uncertainty

important questions. What sort of time horizons can we realistically use when setting targets, initiating projects, and allocating funds? How often should we review and revise our strategies?

In a later chapter, the work of managing and navigating through this uncertainty will be explored and numerous solutions offered. In the next chapter, however, we will look at the strategic mindset and the characteristics of good and bad decision makers.

Glossary for this chapter (Items in bold are also defined in the same table)

competence	The combination of experience, skills and know-how that enables individuals and organisations to participate and perform successfully.
complementarity	The attribute of supporting a technology economically, yet indirectly. In general, a change in the demand for a technology will correspond with a change in the demand for its complementary products. For example, domestic satellite dishes are complemented by the production of television programmes.
disruptive technology	An **innovation** that radically undermines the market strength of established technologies. It does this either by competing directly or creating substitutes.
failure modes and effects analysis (FMEA)	A tool for improving product quality and managing product risks. The American Society of Quality (ASQ) describes FMEA as "a step-by-step approach for identifying all possible failures in a design, a manufacturing assembly process, or a product or service."
FMEA	See **failure modes and effects analysis**.
innovation	The practical realisation of original thinking, resulting in a new or improved value-adding process or product. Most innovations are incremental improvements, but some are more radical, known as **disruptive technologies.**
trumpet of uncertainty	A graphical visualisation of uncertainty in complex environments, illustrating the variation in possible outcomes.

Notes

1 Braun, E. (1998) *Technology in Context*. London: Routledge. 18.
2 Afuah, A. (2003) *Innovation Management*. New York: OUP. 143.
3 Pyster, A., Hutchison, N. and Henry, D. (2018) *The Paradoxical Mindset of Systems Engineers*. Hoboken: Wiley. 207.
4 Norman, D.A. (2013) *The Design of Everyday Things*. Cambridge (MA): MIT Press. 7.

5 Rothschild, W.E. (2007) *The Secret to GE's Success*. New York: McGraw-Hill. 182.

6 American Society for Quality, 'Failure Mode and Effects Analysis (FMEA)'. Available at: https://asq.org/quality-resources/fmea (Accessed: 23 July 2022).

7 TÜV Rheinland Risktec Solutions, *'What Is Failure Modes and Effects Analysis?'* Available at: What is Failure Modes and Effects Analysis? | Risktec (tuv.com) (Accessed: 23 July 2022).

8 Chermack, T.J. (2011) *Scenario Planning in Organizations*. San Francisco: BerreATT-Koehler. 245–246.

9 NASA, *'Mars Climate Orbiter'*. Available at: https://solarsystem.nasa.gov/missions/mars-climate-orbiter/in-depth/ (Accessed: 3 July 2022).

10 Rasiel, E.M. and Friga, P.N. (2001) *The McKinsey Mind*. New York: McGraw-Hill. 39.

11 *McGraw-Hill Dictionary of Scientific and Technical Terms* (2003). Sixth Edition. USA: McGraw-Hill. 2159.

12 Boulton, J.G., Allen, P.M. and Bowman, C. (2015) *Embracing Complexity*. Oxford: OUP. 159.

13 Madhavan, G. (2016) *Think Like an Engineer*. London: Oneworld. 86.

14 Grant, R.M. and Jordan, J. (2015) *Foundations of Strategy*. Chichester: Wiley. 122.

15 Oxford City Council (2018) *Customer, Digital and Technology Strategy 2019-2021, First Working Draft – 11 December 2018*, available at https://www.slideshare.net/OxfordCityCouncil/draft-customerdigitaltechnology-strategy (Accessed: 23 March 2019).

16 Petroski, H. (2006) *Success Through Failure: The Paradox of Design*. Princeton: PUP. 3.

17 Boulton, Allen and Bowman, *Embracing Complexity*. 83.

18 Institution of Mechanical Engineers and Assystem (2021) *Fusion Energy: A Global Effort – A UK Opportunity*, available at https://www.imeche.org/policy-and-press/reports/detail/fusion-energy-a-global-effort-a-uk-opportunity (Accessed: 14 November 2021).

19 Braun, *Technology in Context*. 111.

20 Flin, R., O'Connor, P. and Crichton, M. (2008) *Safety at the Sharp End: A Guide to Non-Technical Skills*. Farnham: Ashgate. 1.

21 Quoted in: Utterback, J.M. (1994) *Mastering the Dynamics of Innovation*. Harvard: HBS Press. 162.

22 Afuah, *Innovation Management*. 313.

23 Basalla, G. (1988) *The Evolution of Technology*. Cambridge (UK): CUP. 127.

24 Basalla, *The Evolution of Technology*. 86.

25 Cross, N. (2008) *Engineering Design Methods: Strategies for Product Design*. Chichester: Wiley. 211.

26 LeVine, S. (2016) *The Powerhouse*. New York: Penguin. 118.

27 Tiwana, A. (2017) *IT Strategy for Non-IT Managers: Becoming an Engaged Contributor to Corporate IT Decisions*. Cambridge, MA: The MIT Press. 168.

28 Chermack, *Scenario Planning in Organizations*. 1.

29 Stevens, P. (ed.) (1998) *Strategic Positioning in the Oil Industry*. Abu Dhabi: ECSSR. 4–5.

30 Flyvbjerg, B. and Gardner, D. (2023) *How Big Things Get Done*. London: Macmillan. 18.

31 Cunningham, S. and Kwakkel, J.H. (2016) 'Technological Forecasting' in van der Duin, P. (ed.) (2016) *Foresight in Organizations*. Abingdon: Routledge. 106–107.
32 The origins of the concept and phrase 'trumpet of uncertainty' remain unclear. The author wishes to thank Jonathan Rosenhead (Emeritus Professor of Operational Research at the London School of Economics) for his help in identifying a source. Additional contributions came from Geoff Royston, former Head of Strategic Analysis and Operational Research in the Department of Health for England. One suggestion for the originator of the expression is John Weeks (1921-2005), an architect best known for hospital designs.

7 Strategy in mind
How our thoughts shape decisions

This chapter presents

- An examination of the strategic and decision making mindset.

This chapter establishes

- Some desirable personal attributes and characteristics.
- Some 'red flag' attributes and characteristics.

All evidence points to the fact that strategy-making is an activity of both high risk and high value. It's also inexpensive. The investment in time and energy to develop a formal technology strategy is low relative to the costs associated with asset purchases, major projects, workforce changes, and so on. In fact, strategic thinking costs little more than time, yet can be powerfully transformative.

In Chapter 1 we heard from Colin Gray, a writer on military strategy. He uses one of the key lessons from World War II to illustrate the high value of strategic thinking relative to strategic assets:

> An uncontroversial point about that conflict is that superior technology could not rescue the great German adventure … from the consequences of its own political folly. With near-embarrassing comprehensiveness German military equipment was by far the best on the battlefield.[1]

In other words, **you can't compensate for poor strategy with great technology, but it's conceivable that great strategy can compensate for poor technology.**

Moving away from the military context, one wonders how many failed projects and wasted opportunities there have been where, in spite of exceptional technologies, poor decision making brought little more than rust and ruin? For example, we have already looked at the collapse of DEC, a manufacturer of high-end computers, and most technology historians are familiar with the

DOI: 10.4324/9781003472919-8

Betamax story, in which Sony's superb compact video recorder was outsmarted by the clunky VHS format. Here we could also add the Anglo-French Concorde, which was technologically brilliant – ahead of its time. However, a product that's ahead of its time is also a product at the wrong time. In economic terms, Concorde flew like a lead balloon.

This is why we need to examine the art of strategic thinking. What sort of knowledge, experience, or psychological traits would we expect to find in a great technology strategist? Who can we trust to make the right decisions at the right time in complex environments?

We know that technologists and engineers have superb minds, combining self-discipline with creativity and an eye for detail, but do they always have a strategic mindset? In the pages that follow, this mindset will be explored from various perspectives.

We shall be looking at two sets of personal attributes: those associated with good strategic thinking and, by way of contrast, the 'red flags' associated with poor decision making. The distinction between strategic thinking at the organisational level and that for individual technologies or products will also be explored.

Ahead for strategy

In the Preface, I described Matthew Boulton as "the first great technology strategist of the modern era." A master of both men *and* machines, his contemporary James Boswell called him "an *iron chieftain*".[2] What can we learn from Boulton's methods and management style?

Even before his recruitment of the young James Watt, Boulton had built an impressive and efficient manufacturing operation at Soho in Birmingham, producing decorative metal goods and coinage in substantial volumes. A culture of innovation was evident at the plant, impressing many who saw it, including Watt on his first visit in 1767.[3]

The biographers of both Boulton and Watt have noted the latter's absence of what Gray calls "strategic sense".[4] James Watt was a pure technical engineer with little entrepreneurial or strategic flair. It was therefore incumbent upon Boulton to counter Watt's yin with his more dynamic yang. Boulton, having foreseen the commercial value of Watt's prototype rotative engines, gave his inventive partner enough time, space, and confidence to deliver his finest work.

Another example of Boulton's management style involved a generous challenge to one of his senior engineers, John Southern, an event described by Boulton's biographers:

Southern … persuaded him to adopt an entirely new method of conveying power to the coining presses. Boulton encouraged Southern to construct the mechanism and, if it worked, undertook to pay him £500 for the idea, making him superintendent of the mint machinery. It did, and Boulton paid up.[5]

Southern's bonus would today buy an extremely fine house.

By 1788 Boulton's Soho works had become the world's first factory to employ a powered continuous flow operation, each machine positioned such that the output from one supplied input to the next.[6] The Boulton and Watt company began to manufacture Watt's state-of-the-art steam engines, selling them to factories around the world. Neither man could have achieved this without the other, yet it was Boulton's strategic sense that ensured success, kick-starting a global industrial revolution.

In general, history tends to remember the winners while forgetting the losers. More than a century after Boulton and Watt, the brilliant Scot, John Logie Baird, was outsmarted by his arch rival, Guglielmo Marconi, in the race to develop broadcast television. Baird had already given the first-ever public demonstration of a wireless video transmission in 1926, but in a high-stakes competition to supply the newly formed BBC, Marconi emerged victorious. Generously, Baird remarked upon his rival's competence as a strategist:

Marconi was a man for whom in some respects I had a great admiration; he played every card with such consummate skill and ability. Every advantage was grasped and consolidated. All rivals were asked into the fold or crushed. Alliances were formed with those too big to be roped in and too powerful to crush … Nevertheless although the invention of no single device of fundamental importance can be attributed to Marconi, it was he who ventured forth like Christopher Columbus and forced upon the attention of the world the existence of a new means of communication.[7]

Real-world tales from engineering history are both instructive and a pleasure to discover. However, to thoroughly examine strategic thinking we'll need to consider more contemporary insights.

This way or that way?

Julia Sloan, the management consultant and teacher of business strategy at Columbia University, addresses the characteristics of strategic decision makers in her book *Learning to Think Strategically* (2020). Sloan takes the view that strategic responsibilities are distributed *throughout* an organisation and that key decision-making skills can be taught: "Strategic thinking is not the by-product of position, precedence, or status. It is not an elitist function. It is learnable."[8]

One of Sloan's distinctive contributions to the subject is her assertion that "Dealing with natural contradictions, paradoxes, and polarities is a central part of strategic thinking".[9] In other words, strategic decision makers must grapple with the reconciliation or resolution of extreme positions:

> Our business world is a paradoxical network of ... fragmentation *and* globalization, heterogeneity *and* uniformity, passive consumption *and* active customization, individualism *and* tribalism, and the old *and* the new.

She calls these "AND polarities", arguing that they lead to successful strategies and innovations because the desire to reconcile the polarity "forces two opposing or contradictory ideas or opinions into a single new thought or novel concept".[10] I was struck by the similarity between Sloan's "AND polarities" and my "strategic dichotomies", which are described throughout this book (and listed in Appendix 4). **Generally, we might conclude that it's the ability of decision makers to resolve or reconcile dichotomies that marks them out as effective strategic thinkers.**

Trusting intuition

Another insightful area of Sloan's research involves *intuition*, a concept most of us are familiar with. However, rationalists are likely to doubt its validity in serious decision making. Sloan argues that intuition is a form of experience-based pattern recognition, where a pattern is "any repeatable concept, thought, or image whose repetitions together make up an approach to a problem, a way of looking at things."[11] Therefore, intuition "draws from a vast reservoir of knowledge in our subconscious and is rooted in past experience – by no means is it an irrational process."[12] James Dyson, an engineer best known for his innovative and globally successful vacuum cleaners, makes an oblique reference to intuition when describing his own business acumen: "you never really know how you do it, you just do it. It's like asking a horse how it walks."[13]

Sloan argues that intuition can be especially powerful if used alongside formal analysis.[14] A similar suggestion is made by E. Rasiel and P. Friga based on their experiences of working for McKinsey & Company. Fact-based analytical solutions lie at the heart of their consulting methodology, but they make it clear that "we believe intuition and data complement each other. You need at least some of each to have a solid basis for your decisions."[15] In some respects, this tension between intuition and rationality is analogous to that between qualitative and quantitative analysis. They support one another by acting as a form of 'sanity check'. When contradictions arise between them, this should signal the need for a deeper dive into the circumstances surrounding the contradiction. However, when intuition and rationality are broadly aligned, confidence levels should be high.

If intuition supports strategic thinking, then it seems clear that the type and extent of personal experiences, gained over a lifetime, will determine the quality of strategic decisions. Perhaps Henry Mintzberg is expressing a similar view when he says, "Most people would agree that strategic thinking means seeing ahead. But we can't see ahead unless we see behind, because any good vision of the future has to be rooted in an understanding of the past."[16]

Sloan examines the significance of personal experience at some length. She is particularly interested in "informal learning", that which is "predominantly unstructured, unplanned, experiential, non-institutional, and non-routine". This type of learning can take place "at work, at play or elsewhere."[17] Much of it comes from day-to-day business interactions. She quotes from one American technology executive:

> It's just what I have to do – reading and going to places to hear other people, and I talk to a lot of people to see what they're thinking and learning. I think a big part of being able to make really good strategy is to constantly know what's going on all over the world.[18]

Other executives gained strategic skills from living and working in other countries.[19] Sloan writes:

> The experience of travel offers us an environment in which to challenge our own and others' assumptions, to rattle our core belief systems, to expand our perspectives, to test and to imagine new possibilities. When we travel, we see new connections and different relationships between and among objects, people, and values. Sometimes, we are forced to break our comfortable habits and use new patterns ... The very success of our travel depends on other people and things we cannot control.[20]

She argues that it isn't necessarily the details of these experiences that we need to draw upon, it is the metaphors and analogies that emerge from them. She quotes from a banker who says, "I knew strategy making! I'd say probably better than just about anybody, and it came from my farming background. I'd been doing it for years – so I knew it."[21] One can easily translate the challenges facing a farmer (seasonal cycles, uncertain weather, crop and animal diseases, error-prone machinery) to modern technology management.

The arts are also singled out for their relevance. Amongst other things, the arts implicitly teach us that there are virtually no limits to what can be achieved. Consider Picasso's mould-breaking representations of the real world, or Henry Moore's abstract sculptures. Beyond their creative challenges, theatre and film are also substantial managerial undertakings. Sloan argues that an appreciation of the theatre encourages systems thinking due to the complex relationships between multiple components – the writers, performers, audience, technicians, and so on.[22] While immersed in a film or sitting in a theatre, one can't help but wonder at the coordination and cooperation involved. The stream of credits after a movie attest to this fact.

Informal learning of a similar nature is also available from hobbies such as gardening and sport. Both involve the pursuit of goals in relatively uncontrolled, dynamic environments. Team sports also involve the priceless mix of people management and the pursuit of excellence, while simultaneously out-guessing opponents in a zero-sum, real-time contest. What better training for strategic thinking could there be? **Hence, to be involved with the arts or sport is more than self-indulgence. These are mind-shaping experiences which impact intuitively upon our decision making.**

It's a people thing

Sony's founder, Akio Morita, wrote that "We learn a lot by listening to our employees ... wisdom is not the exclusive possession of management."[23] We might therefore find evidence that the smartest strategists choose to employ and consult with other smart people. Perhaps the collective mind is greater than the sum of its parts.

We have already seen how Matthew Boulton recruited and utilised the talents of both James Watt and John Southern to maximum effect. Sixty years later, in 1833, the Great Western Railway company (GWR) invested its faith in a brilliant young engineer to undertake the design and construction of its new route from London to the South West of England. Isambard Kingdom Brunel was only 27 years old.[24] Brunel's exploits have since become legendary, but equally remarkable was his response, a few years later, to a letter from an ambitious young engineer called Daniel Gooch.

At just 20 years old, Gooch was keen to join Brunel's enormous, state-of-the-art rail project. At their first meeting, which presumably took the form of an interview, Brunel must have realised that he had someone very special before him. Gooch was immediately appointed the project's Chief Locomotive Assistant – an extraordinarily senior position.[25] Railways were an exciting new technology, so perhaps they belonged naturally to the younger generation. Within three years Gooch was designing and building the finest, fastest, and most reliable steam locomotives in the world. He went on to become the Chair of GWR, while also serving as a Member of Parliament and entrepreneur, laying the first telegraph cables across the Atlantic. Gooch later wrote, "I was very young to be entrusted with the management of the locomotive department of so large a railway; but I felt no fear, and the result has been a success."[26] His 21st-century equivalents could be Wernher von Braun or Steve Wozniak. With such talented people on board, it follows that strategy is made easier both to develop and execute.

Another contribution to this debate comes in the form of Sydney Finkelstein's book *Superbosses* (2016), in which he argues that something special happens when great bosses recruit and mentor talented young managers. Many of these go on to achieve remarkable things themselves. Among his various case studies, Finkelstein describes the influence of Larry Ellison, the founder of Oracle Corporation. In one ten-year period, nine of Ellison's closest associates progressed in their careers to become the CEOs, chairs, or COOs of other tech companies, including Salesforce, EMC, and Veritas.[27] Finkelstein's thesis lacks a theoretical foundation, but the premise is convincing enough; these superbosses create a hot-house environment in which leadership and strategic skills thrive.

Box 7.1   STRATEGIC DICHOTOMIES

Locate in a cluster OR Locate independently?

Economists use the term *agglomeration* to describe how a geographical region becomes associated with a particular industry or technology. Historical examples include textile manufacturing in Manchester (UK), automotive manufacturing in Detroit, and watchmaking in Switzerland. Some contemporary examples include nuclear energy in North West England, biotechnology in Massachusetts, and software development in Bengaluru.

According to economist W.B. Arthur, "once a region – or a country for that matter – gets ahead in an advanced body of technology, it tends to get further ahead. Success brings success, so that there are positive feedbacks or increasing returns to regional concentrations of technology."[28]

These so-called 'clusters' host both public and private sector organisations. Sometimes a university will catalyse the effect. For example, the universities of Cambridge and MIT are focal points for regional digital and biotech clusters. Alternatively clusters may grow around transport hubs such as ports or 'special economic zones', the latter set up by governments to stimulate regional economies.

There are good reasons to locate within a cluster, and equally good reasons to avoid them!

Advantages: Access to a pool of labour with valued skills and experience. There will be dedicated investors in the area, plus opportunities to engage in partnerships and collaborative projects with other local firms. Knowledgeable suppliers are also attracted to locate within the cluster. Networking and information sharing, both formal and informal, will be much easier. A cluster location sometimes enhances a company brand.

Disadvantages: In successful clusters the costs of land, buildings and salaries are typically high, and employees are more easily poached by competitors.[29] Also, the act of moving to a cluster will initially be disruptive, perhaps incurring redundancies.

Alternatives: It is possible to benefit from clusters without having to relocate. For example, your company could partner with, or acquire, a business already within the cluster. Or you could make an outsourcing arrangement with a specialist already based there. Moving *closer*, but not *into*, the cluster might be a more viable option.

In order to create these organisations of insightful decision makers, much depends upon the recruitment process. It is relatively easy for technologists and engineers to employ people with similar social and educational backgrounds, but such people may be unable to offer anything new. Contemporary management thinking highlights the intrinsic value of ensuring genuinely diverse skillsets and experience among decision making groups, particularly company boards. Sloan argues for "Surrounding ourselves with people who can and will challenge, test, and engage in meaningful critical dialogue", thereby avoiding the problem of only hearing from "people who reinforce our perspectives and echo our opinions." Decision makers should be "suspending judgment and acknowledging that there are other credible and legitimate perspectives that weigh upon a strategic issue."[30] This helps, for instance, to ensure that alternative interpretations of data will be presented.[31]

In the field of *scenario development* (a structured method for analysing alternative organisational futures) one of the most successful early practitioners, Frenchman Pierre Wack, insisted upon bringing so-called "remarkable people" into scenario conversations. T. Chermack, a specialist in scenario development, describes these as "people with a completely different outlook or mental model ... known for their ability to think unconventionally."[32] The fundamental argument here is that strategists should avoid the groupthink of echo chambers, aiming instead for new insights and game-changing ideas from people who may be 'remarkably' different.

This notion, that the competence of the people who surround the strategists is just as significant as the competence of the strategists themselves, can be extended to include the wider geographical community. The strategic dichotomy in Box 7.1 *Locate in a cluster OR Locate independently?* explains how the siting of an organisation can improve its workforce profile. Peter Westwick's excellent history of the secret US programme to develop stealth aircraft examines the curious fact that southern California was home to an extraordinary number of creative engineers, many of whom moved between such local industries as theme parks and aircraft manufacturing. There is "a regional culture of expansive imagination and entrepreneurialism. Southern California had long attracted iconoclasts, visionaries, and dreamers, nourishing a culture of risk-taking and boundary-pushing." According to Westwick, the abiding philosophy of local engineers is that "if you believe it, you can make it", an attitude essential to the development of radar-invisible aircraft.[33] It may therefore be argued that **when a diverse and talented group of people work in close proximity to one another a process of osmosis is at work, each person absorbing the insights and creativity of their colleagues.** It becomes a reinforcing cycle. This osmosis theory could help to explain the performance, and underperformance, of many organisations.

Bridging the divide

Another of the attributes we would expect to find in effective technology strategists is, of course, deep knowledge of the organisation and its business operations. However, for too long a divide has existed between the technology/engineering functions and those associated with running the business, e.g. accounts, operations, marketing, and sales. Surely the most effective strategists are those determined to take a more holistic view of technology's role within, and influence upon, the wider organisation.

Now, more than ever before, technologists and engineers should aim to complement their technical skills with deep organisational knowledge. Eben Hewitt, author of *Technology Strategy Patterns*, offers advice from his own experience:

> To gain support for your strategy, you must have alignment from only three groups of people: The people who will pay for it ... The people who will execute it ... The people who will ignore or undermine it if their views, aspirations, and concerns aren't represented (your peers). Therefore, you must have a 360-degree view of the organization.[34]

He also advises that it's helpful to understand an organisation's 'origins' – its history, culture, people, and the evolutionary reasons for its internal policies and processes. Hewitt believes that multi-skilled, multi-disciplinary business-technologists "will be highly effective, and highly prized, because maintaining that distinction is increasingly a barrier to progress, creativity, and innovation."[35]

Writing in the *MIT Sloan Management Review*, Gerald Kane *et al.* make the equally valid point that there is also an obligation on business managers to become better acquainted with technological capabilities:

> Although leaders don't need to be technology wizards, they must understand what can be accomplished at the intersection of business and technology. They should also be prepared to lead the way in conceptualizing how technology can transform the business.[36]

The former McKinsey consultants, Rasiel and Friga, advise all strategists to remain focused on organisational capabilities because, quite simply, "The most brilliant strategy in the world won't help if your organization can't implement it."[37] The conclusion must be that insular and purely technical people will struggle to produce effective strategies for their organisations. **To become effective strategists, technologists need to interact with all levels of the organisation, firstly in order to understand its needs and concerns, and secondly to proffer high value technical advice, particularly to business leaders.**

Box 7.2   STRATEGIC AND TACTICAL MOVES

Exchanging knowledge

One of the intangible sources of value in organisations is intellectual capital. This consists of employee knowledge and skills, trade secrets, intellectual property (IP), specialised working practices, and the network of internal and external relationships. Without this capital an organisation cannot function.

In most workplaces the value of employee knowledge can be multiplied through sharing. The most useful knowledge often resides in the heads of the more experienced staff. Meanwhile, other valuable information is recorded in documents or databases, frequently inaccessible to the people who need them. Formal attempts to rectify these challenges are sometimes referred to as *knowledge management* (KM).

The aim of KM is to get the right knowledge to the right people at the right time. It sounds easy, but it's not. For example, there are many reasons people may be reluctant to share the knowledge they have, or perhaps they simply don't have enough spare time to properly record it. Sometimes there simply isn't a suitable mechanism available.

Larger organisations, especially those which are geographically dispersed, face particular challenges. Not only do employees have fewer opportunities to interact, but knowledge repositories may be technically and physically isolated. Gaining access to this information and making sense of it may require special permissions or advanced IT skills.

These barriers are costly. How much better would your products or customer service be if staff had access to all of this un-shared knowledge? Instead, they are forced to either 'reinvent the wheel', scale back, or abandon the particular task they are trying to perform.

A few years ago I helped in the construction of a KM framework at an international engineering consultancy. With professional staff in 14 countries across three continents, it was vital that a mechanism existed for knowledge sharing. We collaborated with a university to help in the research and selection of tools. There was no silver bullet, so a multi-faceted approach was taken. Our solution consisted of:

- A default browser home page with colour-coded links to all key knowledge repositories.
- Subject-specific discussion forums, accessible to all staff.
- A directory of personnel, listing their key areas of expertise, certifications, language skills, etc.
- Opportunities for sharing knowledge with colleagues in short lunchtime teaching sessions.

Other KM tools you may wish to explore include staff secondments and mentoring programmes.

KM is **not** a 'nice-to-have' capability. It's a serious, value-adding endeavour. However, there is often scepticism (and resistance) from the most experienced employees. For this reason, **a KM framework is likely to fail without the visible backing and leadership of senior personnel**.

Step up, speak up

Among the key personal attributes we should be looking for in technology strategists are those associated with effective communications. Writing in the *HBR Guide to Thinking Strategically* (2019) Roger Martin observes that "Strategic choice-making cascades down the entire organization, from top to bottom ... every person in the company has a key role to play". Therefore, an effective strategist has the skills to communicate internally – down, across, and up.

Any technologist or engineer with supervisory responsibilities must, first and foremost, ask the basic question posed by Martin: "How can I communicate the logic of my strategy choices to those who report to me?"[38] If we can't communicate down then tactical effectiveness will be lost. Communicating across, on the other hand, involves dealing with fellow team members and internal customers. Lisa Lai, writing in the *HBR Guide*, argues that if you believe that your team or project is failing to align with the organisation's strategy, "you have a responsibility to challenge the value of doing that work."[39] Be prepared to speak up. In a similar vein, Sloan refers to the need for strategists to have the confidence to challenge experts within their own work group.[40]

Most technologists and engineers will also be familiar with the situation where a customer appears to want something that they don't really need, or perhaps their wishes don't align with the current technology strategy. There are two ways to handle this: an easy way and a hard way. The former involves capitulation to the client. A good strategist, however, would take the latter approach, which involves a commitment to honesty and pragmatic negotiation. (See Box 9.3 *Satisfying client wants OR Satisfying client needs?* in Chapter 9.)

Finally, we must consider the challenge of communicating upwards, especially to CIOs, COOs, CTOs, and CEOs. People high on status, but low on technical skills will often need to be coached, guided, and persuaded. In these circumstances, a good strategist should be respectful but firm. Hewitt tells it straight:

> ...speak truth to power. Tell powerful people what they need to hear, not what they want to hear. You'll be seen as (and actually be) honest, forthright, forthcoming, objective, strong, confident, and smart. These are cherished, and rare, qualities.[41]

Apparently, in spite of his relative youth, I.K. Brunel was not afraid to give the directors of the future GWR a piece of his mind. His biographer, Angus Buchanan, quotes Brunel rebuking the directors for their cost-centric tendering process:

You are holding out a premium to the man who will make you the most flattering promises, and it is quite obvious that he who has the least reputation at stake, or the most to gain by temporary success, and the least to lose by the consequent disappointment, must be the winner in such a race.[42]

His opinion was forthright and unwavering, advocating for a quality solution rather than short-term investor returns. This was an especially brave statement given that Brunel had not, at this stage, secured the role of Chief Engineer. Hewitt's advice could almost have been written for Brunel because, by 'speaking truth to power' he succeeded in winning the contract. Brunel's insistence upon quality, and the Board's apparent acquiescence, resulted in one of the most remarkable achievements in engineering history. The GWR's physical infrastructure – Brunel's bridges, tunnels and stations – remain in daily use today, nearly 200 years later.

So it is clearly established that strong communication skills are a key attribute for technology strategists. **Writing and talking should be confident, succinct, clear, and persuasive.**

When the going gets tough

Strategic thinking is only the precursor to action. Getting things done is much harder. The execution of strategy rarely goes smoothly and often leads to failure. Even great strategists must learn to live with setbacks.

For this reason, it might help to view individual strategies as being part of a higher-level *grand strategy*, a concept introduced in Chapter 1. We might say that a grand strategy resembles a *portfolio* of separately managed strategies, not all of which will be successful.

This portfolio idea brings to mind the working practices of venture capitalists and other investors. The portfolio concept consists of diversified commitments, the majority of which are expected to bring low returns or even losses. However, it's the small number of highly successful investments that raise a portfolio's average returns to desirable levels. Kane *et al.* quote John Halamka, the CIO of an American health care provider, who accepts that, when managing multiple technology initiatives, "Failure is a valid outcome".[43]

All portfolios are built on this philosophy, you win some and you lose some, with the intention that the former compensates for the latter. I would therefore argue that a similar portfolio mindset is a key attribute for every strategist. It's about having the resilience and doggedness to keep going in the face of tactical setbacks.

Around the same time that Brunel was completing the Great Western Railway (while simultaneously building the world's largest ships and experimenting with novel screw propellers), his work hit the buffers with an ill-fated project called the South Devon Railway (SDR). Unlike the GWR, the SDR was designed to be powered, not by Daniel Gooch's locomotives, but by atmospheric pressure. Utterly radical in conception, the vacuum-propelled trains would be free of smoke, lightweight and therefore better able to tackle gradients. Yet the technology was unreliable, proving particularly difficult to maintain. The enterprise failed soon after the start of passenger operations.[44] In spite of this high-profile embarrassment, Brunel simply moved on to other things and his reputation remained intact. We might speculate that Brunel's own portfolio, his personal grand strategy, was to pursue a career of multiple, parallel and often unrelated projects, not all of which could be expected to prove successful. The net outcome, however, was positive for his legacy and reputation.

Nearly two centuries later, the body managing Britain's railway infrastructure, Network Rail, wrote in its own *Technical Strategy* document, "Being more ambitious means taking more risks. We need to be prepared for some of our ideas to fail during development."[45] It's an enlightened attitude to technology management which more leaders should openly adopt.

At the beginning of the 20th century the Wright brothers were indomitable in their quest to discover the secrets of powered flight, despite widespread public scepticism. After the conspicuous failure of their prominent rival, Samuel Langley of the Smithsonian Institution, the Chicago Tribune mocked the many amateur inventors seeking to conquer the air. On 10 December 1903, they wrote:

> Nature has fitted us with appliances for getting short distances through the water, also with appliances for getting over the ground short and long distances, but no trace of a wing can be found or anything that indicates nature intended us to navigate the air. There is little possibility of that until we become angels.[46]

Seven days later, at Kitty Hawk, the brothers became angels.

When Henry Mintzberg wrote that thinkers and organisations must be able to "see it through" he was emphasising this attribute of resilience.[47] **So here's the question: As a technology strategist would you, like the Wright brothers, have the necessary resilience to 'see it through'?**

It's systemic

Writing in the *HBR Guide*, Liane Davey observes that "Strategic people create connections between ideas, plans, and people that others fail to see."[48] Therefore, an attribute we might value is the ability to see technical environments as a panoply of interacting entities and systems. This idea combines the systems thinking introduced in Chapter 2 and the complex systems of Chapter 5. Guru Madhavan of the US National Academy of Engineering says that a systems-level thinker recognises that "nothing is stationary, and everything is linked. The relationships among the modules of a system give rise to a whole that cannot be understood by analyzing its constituent parts."[49]

One engineer noted for his systemic approach was the 18th-century French artillery officer, Jean-Baptiste Vaquette de Gribeauval. He revolutionised both the technology and organisation of artillery units by examining the overall efficiency of the transportation, assembly and firing of guns. His innovations ranged from the interchangeability of parts to the design of horse harnesses and the organisation of personnel.[50]

However, the systems mindset involves more than merely recognising the existence of systems and their component parts. It must also take account of the whole systems lifecycle, beginning with the strategic identification of needs and ending with disposal. The very best systems thinkers, such as systems engineers, will take time to contemplate end-of-life tasks, even during the design and development phases, because the retirement or disposal of an engineered solution could influence its assembly methods and the choice of materials.

Great technology strategists will also be comfortable analysing every level of a technical environment. The low level incorporates such details as component design and materials selection. Higher levels enable the study of interacting systems and their stakeholders.

A founder of Harvard's *Advanced Leadership Initiative*, Rosabeth M. Kanter, wrote that "Effective leaders zoom in and zoom out."[51] All too often, however, technologists and engineers zoom in, only to become transfixed (if not mesmerised) by the internal complexities of their systems.

The technical architect, Eben Hewitt, knows only too well how easy it is for the minutiae of day-to-day operational challenges to undermine the big picture thinking which most technological environments require:

Solving local problems is an important part of our jobs, and needs to be done. But architects and leaders who too frequently focus on too fine-grained matters, on small issues with few branches, can actually perpetuate and worsen the organizational dysfunction that they purport to address...Because we do not raise our visor to the horizon of context, we do not scale as well as we might, either in our own roles or in helping the organization to do so.[52]

This need for both depth and breadth of analysis is echoed by E. Braun's comment that "The twin enemies of successful strategic thinking are myopia and tunnel vision."[53]

Lift your head. Look up. Look around. There is more to successful technology management than localised responsibilities. Your own system is probably either a sub-system or part of a greater system of systems, and all of these systems have a before-and-after lifecycle. **Strategic thinkers know this, because they are also systems thinkers. It sets them apart.**

Piece by piece

This 'zooming in and zooming out' complements another of our desired attributes: the need to analyse and synthesise. The processes of analysis and synthesis involve deconstructing a problem, device, system, or idea, thereby gaining an understanding of its composition, before re-assembling the parts, perhaps in a novel way. In Matthew Syed's *Black Box Thinking* (2015) he explains how the careful analysis of seemingly efficient, well-designed, fully functional systems will always reveal opportunities for further small improvements or "marginal gains". This leads to substantial improvements over the medium to longer term.[54] The theory of marginal gains is a million miles away from the glamour of game-changing inventions, but its effect on technological progress is probably just as great. The *Black Box* in the book's title is a reference to the flight data recorders which, when analysed after an accident, enable incremental improvements to aviation technologies, to the training of pilots, air traffic controllers and aeronautical engineers. Compare aviation safety today with its record in the 20th century. The accumulation of marginal gains has been transformative.

Syed's most compelling case study is that of Great Britain's Olympic cycling team, led by Dave Brailsford, who applied marginal gains theory to rider training and the design of bicycles. Within a few years the GB team had begun to dominate Olympic cycling, winning countless gold medals. Brailsford then moved on to professional team cycling, resulting in three different riders winning the *Tour de France* every year for seven years, from 2012 to 2018. This type of analysis and synthesis resembles the methods adopted by the Wright brothers in their Ohio workshop:

> They broke a job into its parts and proceeded one part at a time. They practiced each small task until they mastered it, then moved on. It didn't sound like much, but it avoided discouragement and led to success. And it kept them uninjured and alive.[55]

All of this effort and energy is indicative of highly motivated individuals with clear strategic goals in mind. Ambitious technologists and engineers must expect to labour for extended periods, analysing and synthesising, without any guarantee of success. **We have already established the need for resilience in the strategic mindset, but patience is another essential attribute.**

Seeing is believing

Another positive attribute is visionary thinking. This may sound rather nebulous, but there is clear evidence that great strategists know how to "see beyond", as Mintzberg frames it.[56]

In 1830, an excited 24-year-old engineer bought a ticket to ride the world's first passenger railway, the 31-mile (50 km) Liverpool to Manchester line. It had only recently opened and was crude in operation, with roofless carriages and burning embers drifting through the smoke. The inspired young engineer immediately wrote, "the time is not far off when we shall be able to take our coffee and write while going, noiseless and smoothly, at 45 miles per hour – let me try."[57] His name was, of course, Isambard Kingdom Brunel, and within a few decades his trains would be transporting high profile guests, including European heads of state, in comfortable carriages over long distances at speeds averaging 60 mph (97 km/h).[58] Coffee, however, was probably not available until some years later.

In 1961 the US President, John F. Kennedy, gave a speech to a joint session of Congress in which he ignited the booster under America's Apollo spaceflight project.

> I believe that this nation should commit itself to achieving the goal, before this decade is out, of landing a man on the moon and returning him safely to earth.[59]

It was the sort of challenge that engineers adore: an opportunity to combine technical creativity with generous financial resources, yet without detailed specifications for *how* it should be done. Today we might call this 'management by outcomes', in contrast to the more prescriptive 'management by process'. Technical people generally prefer the former. This focus on objectives ensured that America's goal was achieved five months ahead of Kennedy's arbitrary deadline.

Sony co-founder, Akio Morita, notes the power of Kennedy's speech in his autobiography, *Made in Japan* (1987).[60] Later he tells the story of his Sony co-founder Masaru Ibuka's original vision for creating a domestic TV recorder. In the 1970s video recording devices, used only in TV studios, were large, cumbersome and very expensive. However, Ibuka found inspiration in a book:

> ... nobody knew exactly where we were headed until he tossed that paperback book onto the conference table and said that was the target, a videocassette the size of the book that could hold at least one hour of color program. That focused all the development. It wasn't just a matter of making a small cassette – a whole new concept of recording and reading the tape had to be devised.[61]

The Betamax recording system became admired for its quality and compact design. Although it subsequently lost the 'format war' to VHS, one can only admire the genius and ultimate success of Ibuka's vision.

Visionary thinking is about conceiving outcomes and objectives that are ambitious, yet achievable. The best strategists are able to convey a vision and inspire colleagues to achieve it.

Levelling with the stakeholders

At the start of this book I briefly noted the difference between technology strategies at the organisational level and those at the product level. They make different demands.

At the organisational level, technology strategists are largely focused upon broad technological domains, managing systems, and forming teams to deliver solutions. The best performers will be politically adept, assertive and confident, with perhaps a T-skills profile. In other words, they may have one area of deep specialisation, the vertical stalk of the T, plus a broad range of high level technical and managerial skills.

By contrast, the best product strategists will be suited to working within smaller teams, and may be less gregarious individuals. They will know their technology specialism in great depth, along with complementary and competing technologies. They must understand the market for which their technology is destined, and the very best product strategists will also be exploring designs and innovating configurations tailored to new markets. However, most product strategists will probably need some encouragement to 'zoom out' for the bigger organisational picture described above.

One thing is clear, though. **All strategists need to be disciplined and passionate about generating long-term benefits for their stakeholders. An awareness of who those stakeholders are, and how best to serve them, is vital.**

Table 7.1 Some of the attributes associated with effective strategic thinking and decision making

Attribute	Description
Comfortable resolving polarities and dichotomies	Not deterred by the apparent irreconcilability of contradictions or paradoxes. Believing that a resolution exists and being able to find it.
Intuition from experience	Able to convert historical patterns of activity, mainly derived from personal experience, into metaphors or analogies, facilitating insights and action.
Thriving amongst talent	Seeking the company of "remarkable people" in order to benefit from their insights and produce better strategies.
Organisational knowledge	Possessing a broad, multi-level understanding of the organisation – its history, its people, its processes, its business model and, above all, its capabilities.
Communication skills and confidence	Able to deal with people at all levels and equipped with an array of persuasive communication and negotiation skills.
A portfolio mindset	Accepting that a good strategy can withstand occasional tactical failures, especially if these are viewed within the context of a portfolio of initiatives.
Resilience	Remaining undeterred by technical setbacks, personal criticism or by opposition from doubters and competitors. Taking the long view.
Systems thinking	Recognising that the whole is greater than the sum of the parts. Observing and analysing the interactions and interdependencies between components, products, people and wider systems, including the environment and the economy.
Zooming in and out	Comfortable switching between complex technical details and the higher level observations of systemic relationships with stakeholders and the wider world.
Analysis and synthesis	Skilled at patiently breaking down entities into their component parts, then generating value by re-assembling those parts into new and better forms.
Visionary thinking	Conceiving of outcomes and objectives that are ambitious, yet achievable. Conveying the vision and inspiring colleagues to take on the challenge.
Stakeholder focus	Identifying and managing the key stakeholders, according to the level at which strategy is being developed.

Red flags

The first part of this chapter explored the personal attributes associated with good strategic thinking and decision making. However, the reality is that many technologists and engineers will never develop a strong strategic mindset, while others will have days when they are simply in the wrong frame of mind to make good decisions. So what personality traits and suspect behaviours should we look out for? What are the red flags?

All about you

Let's begin with *self-interest*. As a personality trait it's regarded as acceptable within many social, political and organisational cultures. However, technology strategists have an obligation to act, not in their own self interest, but in the interests of their employer or client. For most professionals, these mental gymnastics are easily learned and competently executed, but some fail to recognise the need for such integrity. These people can do a lot of damage, both to their stakeholders and themselves.

This is sometimes known as the *agency problem*, or the *principal-agent problem*. It arises when we delegate responsibility to someone, assuming that they will act in *our* interests, not theirs. Unfortunately, some decision makers act in ways that put their own interests ahead of their principals. Often this self-interest is concerned with personal reputation or the pursuit of wealth. For a small minority it can even manifest itself in criminal behaviour, such as soliciting bribes from suppliers.

These are the types of psychological challenges that fascinate Daniel Kahneman, the behavioural scientist and winner of the Nobel Prize in Economics. In his influential book, *Thinking, Fast and Slow*, he recounts a story from another leading economist, Richard Thaler, who had been in conversation with 25 divisional managers of a large company:

> He asked them to consider a risky option in which, with equal probabilities, they could lose a large amount of the capital they controlled or earn double that amount. None of the executives was willing to take such a dangerous gamble. Thaler then turned to the CEO of the company, who was also present, and asked for his opinion. Without hesitation, the CEO answered, "I would like all of them to accept their risks." In the context of that conversation, it was natural for the CEO to adopt a broad frame that encompassed all 25 bets.[62]

The 'agents' (in this case the managers) were thinking of their own reputations, whereas the 'principal' (here represented by the CEO) was adopting the shareholders' perspective. Framed in this way, as a series of bets, we can see that the CEO was adopting the portfolio approach to long-term gains, discussed earlier. He was willing to accept some failed investments, but individual managers weren't.

Let's take another more familiar example. In Thomas Heppenheimer's *Countdown: A History of Spaceflight*, the principal-agent problem emerges in relation to the funding of NASA projects.[63] NASA's business case for the Space Shuttle stated that its re-usability would make it more affordable. It should therefore appeal to taxpayers and their political representatives in Washington. However, some observers noted that the shuttles were a relatively small proportion of overall costs. Most expenditure would be associated with shuttle crews. This is because human spaceflight is always a substantially more complex, riskier, and therefore more costly activity than un-crewed missions. Technically, the Shuttle didn't need astronauts. It could have been designed to operate largely autonomously, taking instructions from ground control. But this was anathema to NASA, an organisation still basking in past glories of men on the Moon. Furthermore, a significant institution within NASA was Houston's Manned Spacecraft Center (now the Johnson Space Center). Houston's existence would be under threat if the Shuttle were designed to fly without the need for a pressurised cabin, potable water, oxygen, liquidised food, and a vacuum toilet. On the basis of this persuasive and self-interested lobbying by NASA, the Shuttle programme got the financial support it needed. The ultimate cost of this immense undertaking, both in dollars and human lives, was eye-watering. On this occasion, the agent had successfully hoodwinked the principals.

Keep digging?

This need to keep an institution 'busy' with new projects resembles the dilemma faced by many organisations today, which struggle to provide their teams of software developers with a steady pipeline of relevant, high-value work. Inactive software developers are viewed as a financial liability, but rather than scale back the team, small projects are found 'to keep them busy'; hence the all-too-familiar accumulation of over-engineered internal applications (e.g. for staff development or expenses control) and nice-to-have features in core applications which, apart from using high-value developer time, must then be maintained for an indefinite period by the same precious developers.

If you're in a deep hole and someone throws you a spade, what should you do? Do you cut out some steps, or dig deeper?

There are parallels with the so-called *sunk costs fallacy*, which discourages decision makers from abandoning activities, especially large projects, into which substantial amounts of money have already been sunk.[64] The fallacy's 'logic' goes like this: "We may be over budget, but we're nearly there. If we stop now, all of that investment will be lost. The fact that the business case is now weaker should not derail us. We need to take pride in finishing it. It will only cost a million dollars more. Let's keep going." This is similar to the gambling mentality of chasing bets. It's the attempt to recover losses by laying further stakes, despite knowing that the odds favour the casino. **Sometimes it's better to be transparent about failures, mismanagement, or over-resourcing. Fess up. Stop digging down. Dig out, and move on.** Kahneman puts it into context with a military analogy:

> This is where businesses that are losing ground to a superior technology waste their remaining assets in futile attempts to catch up. Because defeat is so difficult to accept, the losing side in wars often fights long past the point at which the victory of the other side is certain, and only a matter of time.[65]

This book's earlier case studies involving DEC and Kodak come to mind. Faced with the option of a manageable medium-term failure or an irreversible commercial disaster, it surely makes sense to opt for the former?

Getting attached

Another of Kahneman's research interests is the *endowment effect*, which causes people to over-value something they own or in which they have invested significant psychological resources.[66] It manifests itself as an emotional personal attachment. This attachment could be to a favoured but now ageing technology, for instance, or to an impressive but inefficient production process. Such defensiveness will be viewed by others as irrational.

In order to create radar-invisible aircraft, one of the challenges facing managers at Lockheed was encouraging its Skunk Works engineers to re-think aircraft design and construction methods from the bottom up. Westwick explains that, "Like generals fighting the last war, Skunk Works veterans wanted to keep doing what had worked for them in the past. In essence, they wanted to make a stealthier SR-71." The SR-71 spy plane was truly a triumph of engineering, but it had been designed in the late 1950s. Clinging to these old ideas simply would not result in a groundbreaking stealth design. This endowment effect was implicitly acknowledged by a Lockheed program manager, who noted that "Nothing fails like success."[67]

You might believe that such irrationality will never affect *your* decision making, but it's worth remembering that it could affect some of your competitors, suppliers and customers. Therefore, from a strategic perspective, the endowment effect, and all the other red flags highlighted in this chapter, deserve to be better understood because they enable us to recognise these behaviours within our wider operating environment.

Fallacious optimism

Another insight is the *planning fallacy*, which affects people producing plans or forecasts. According to Kahneman it causes those forecasts to be "unrealistically close to best-case scenarios".[68] All technologists know from bitter experience that best-case scenarios never materialise. The previous chapters on uncertainty should help to explain this.

There are many reasons over-optimistic plans are made with such regularity. In some cases they are clearly fraudulent attempts to gain favour or funding. However, the planning fallacy may also be attributed to an innocent enthusiasm by those supporting an idea or proposal. This exuberance is known as *optimism bias*. Kahneman explains.

> When forecasting the outcomes of risky projects, executives too easily fall victim to the planning fallacy. In its grip, they make decisions based on delusional optimism rather than on a rational weighting of gains, losses, and probabilities. They overestimate benefits and underestimate costs. They spin scenarios of success while overlooking the potential for mistakes and miscalculations. As a result, they pursue initiatives that are unlikely to come in on budget or on time or to deliver the expected returns – or even to be completed.[69]

Kahneman also refers to a study by Flyvbjerg *et al.* which looked at rail projects undertaken worldwide between 1969 and 1998. It found that in more than 90% of cases, the number of passengers expected to use the system was overestimated. The average overestimate was 106%, more than double, and the average cost overrun 45%.[70] Fortunately there are various ways to mitigate the damage caused by these behaviours, including *reference class forecasting* (explained in Box 7.3). It is even possible to deliver training aimed at overcoming optimism bias. Apparently this was effective at Royal Dutch Shell where geologists had acquired a reputation for over-estimating the likelihood of successful drilling operations.[71]

Box 7.3 ANALYTICAL TOOLS AND TECHNIQUES

Reference class forecasting (RCF)

We are all familiar with the long and notorious history of major projects exceeding their original budgets and delivery dates. So is it possible to improve the accuracy of estimated project lengths and costs?

One proposed method, based on the Nobel Prize winning work of D. Kahneman and A. Tversky, is called Reference Class Forecasting (RCF).

It is noted that under-estimates of project length and costs are often caused by *optimism bias* – the adoption of best-case scenarios during project planning. RCF attempts to quantify this bias in order to improve the information available to policy makers, project sponsors and programme managers.

The RCF method uses proprietary databases of historical project data. This includes original cost and time estimates, plus the actual costs and delivery dates. Much of this work is attributed to Professor Bent Flyvbjerg of Oxford University.

RCF can be used at the commencement of any major project in order to understand how similar projects, i.e. those within the same 'reference class', performed in the past. In many cases the data will show, with a high degree of statistical confidence, the expected final cost and delivery time.

One of the main challenges with RCF involves the so-called 'reference class problem', which requires the analyst to choose the correct reference class for comparison. For example, when planning to construct a cruise ship, which class of similar projects should we examine in order to estimate the likelihood of the build being completed on budget and on time? Compare these three possible reference classes:

1 All ships of similar scale (cargo, passenger, and military) built in the same country in the past five years.
2 All cruise ships built worldwide (including smaller and larger vessels) in the last ten years.
3 All ships (of any type) built within the same yard in the last three years.

A recent analysis, using data from UK and US public infrastructure projects, concluded that cost overruns were reduced from an average of 38% to 5% when RCF was used at the planning stage.[72]

The management of expectations is particularly important in *all* business environments, so we owe it to ourselves, our colleagues, and our clients to neutralise the effects of the planning fallacy and optimism bias. When managing teams in the financial services industry, my response to the potential for optimism bias among technical staff was always to **double** their estimates for the time required to complete a task. This 'rule of thumb' was rarely reflected back to the individuals concerned, nor was it mentioned when communicating upwards, but it was always adopted (and usually right). The engineer might say, "that's a five day job". Rather than try to explain optimism bias to the engineer (which would lead to lengthy debates about complexity, 'known un-knowns', and so on), I would simply report to stakeholders that the job will take ten working days. It would of course be finished on the ninth or tenth day. All expectations having been met, everyone was happy, and life went on.

If pushed, I might have reduced the margin to 50%. This was the approach taken by Major General John Medaris of the US Army. On learning that the Soviet Union had beaten the United States into space with the launch of Sputnik 1, the lead US engineer, Wernher von Braun, excitedly promised an immediate response to the American Secretary of Defense, Neil McElroy: "We have the hardware on the shelf. For God's sake turn us loose and let us do something. We can put up a satellite in sixty days, Mr McElroy." Overhearing this, Medaris, who was von Braun's immediate superior, stepped in. "No, Wernher, ninety days."[73] In fact, it was 119 days before Vanguard 1 followed Sputnik into orbit. This outcome vindicates my own rule: always double the estimate.

This is where I stand (for now)

The *affect heuristic* is a very different phenomenon.[74] Put simply, humans tend to allow their current emotions to shape their current beliefs. In other words, our opinions can swing wildly in response to how we feel at the time, regardless of the evidence available.

Kahneman describes the work of Paul Slovic and his colleagues. They looked at individual attitudes towards controversial technol-ogies, such as water fluoridation, chemical plants, and food preservatives. The research found that strongly held positions could be reversed relatively easily by introducing new and emotionally engaging information. He quotes from psychologist Jonathan Haidt, who says, "The emotional tail wags the rational dog."

The affect heuristic is perhaps analogous with the old adage that *where I sit is where I stand*. In other words, a person only needs to move between 'seats' (i.e. roles) within an organisation to undergo an instantaneous change of opinion on issues of substance.

The implication for technologists is that both the support for a strategy, and opposition to it, can be surprisingly fickle. **A single unexpected event, a well-made argument, or the emergence of self-interest could profoundly shift attitudes … including your own.**

Techno-ideologies

Two more factors known to influence behaviour are *technological optimism* and *technological determinism*.

Technological optimism (not to be confused with *optimism bias*, described earlier) is the belief that technology is generally good and should be encouraged. An educational technologist and researcher, Mark Webster, studied the views of technology directors and instructors in the US education sector.[75] Technological optimism inclined decision makers to be advocates for new applications of technology. New kit or new features were intrinsically desirable.

Technological determinism, on the other hand, is a belief in the inevitability of technological development or evolution. Advocates argue that 'progress' should not, indeed cannot, be prevented. Webster's research uncovered what he describes as "cognitive dissonance", because some educational practitioners appeared to believe both that technologies should be responsive to educational needs, and also that educational practice needed to "keep up" with technology, or be left behind. In other words, rather than being selective in their adoption of educational technologies, they felt compelled to use whatever the market was presenting. One interviewee, clearly a determinist, said, "Not all technology is good, but it's an unstoppable force, and it has to be used and harnessed properly." Another argued that "Technological change is inevitable and we should not resist it. That is my philosophy!"

The positions of optimists and determinists are clearly ideological, and the combination of optimism and determinism can be powerful. Each ideology appears to imbue the technological realm with a higher purpose or mission – like a primitive form of religion.

However, neither optimism nor determinism is compatible with rational or evidence-based decision making, because when viewed objectively and dispassionately, technology offers neither grounds for optimism nor pessimism. Nor is progress inevitable. A dislikeable technology can simply be ignored, or we can halt its development by removing financial support. One of Webster's subjects explained, "I'm not a fan of technology for its own sake, and as a decision maker I like to see reasons for implementing technology."

There should be no inevitability when making technological choices. Evidence, logic and reason offer the best guides to decision makers.

So, what's the story?

Another cognitive flaw is known as the *narrative fallacy*. It sees the past and the future as two halves of a continuum, like the narrative of a story. Imagine you're reading the middle pages of a novel. You know everything that has happened thus far, and all the characters in the plot. Naturally you assume that the same characters from the first half will continue to appear, and that the events in the first half will somehow shape those in the second.

But in the real world there is no such narrative. The future is not a linear continuum of the past. It is permanently shrouded in fog and peppered with hazards. Consequently, the narrative fallacy distorts strategic thinking. Hewitt describes how it may, for example, lead to inaction:

> Maintaining the status quo – the Do Nothing strategy – is far and away the dominant strategy of people and corporations ... People assume the future will look like the past.[76]

Kahneman describes a similar phenomenon called *hindsight bias*:

> Everything makes sense in hindsight, a fact that financial pundits exploit every evening as they offer convincing accounts of the day's events. And we cannot suppress the powerful intuition that what makes sense in hindsight today was predictable yesterday. The illusion that we understand the past fosters overconfidence in our ability to predict the future.[77]

The key message here, which was examined in earlier chapters, is that the past and the future are disconnected and that any attempts to extrapolate from the former to the latter are fraught with danger.

Blissful ignorance

Often our thinking is hindered by the constraints we place on ourselves. For example, there is a disposition known by the German term *Einstellung*, which refers to a person's preference for relying upon familiar ways of doing things.[78] *Einstellung* is the comfortable and convenient way to make decisions. It implicitly rejects creativity or innovation.

Sloan argues that this mindset is harmful for strategists, who must always be willing to embrace change. "An adaptive strategist is able to respond rapidly and effectively to unexpected events, and can quickly shift from a planned sequence of actions to an alternative that is more appropriate." Hence, "An over-reliance on detailed plans and regimented procedures crowds out adaptive potential."[79]

Kahneman introduces something similar to *Einstellung* in his phrase "what you see is all there is" (or WYSIATI). In his words, "A mind that follows WYSIATI will achieve high confidence much too easily by ignoring what it does not know."[80]

Another related phenomenon is the *availability heuristic*, which causes us to make high-confidence decisions based only upon the information readily available to us.[81] However, this will usually be small relative to the amount that could be revealed by research. The potential for flawed decisions due to this constraint should be obvious.

Clearly *Einstellung*, WYSIATI and the availability heuristic are all self-imposed limitations on our capacities to make good, or at least better, decisions. The purpose of listing them here is so that we can start to address our own decision making limitations. In order to consciously correct them we must expand our horizons by embracing new information and ideas.

A litany of weaknesses

Sloan offers yet more examples of what she calls "detrimental manifestations of our habits of mind."[82] She warns us to be wary of people who may be too satisfied, too conformist, too proud, or too expert.

The first group, the "satisfieds", are comfortable with the status quo and therefore have no desire to see changes. Are they, perhaps, afflicted by *Einstellung*? Their strategies should be treated with suspicion. The "conformists", on the other hand, display a type of "club" mentality. This may be the result of a management training programme intended to develop a cadre of future leaders. Conformists will "fail to adopt a habit of challenging the corporate frames and remain unclear about their strategic role: is it to maintain existing frames, or is it to truly shatter and reframe?"[83] Her third 'detrimental manifestation' is pride. This may cause a reluctance to acknowledge the uncertainty inherent in all strategies and decisions, expressions of which could be perceived as a sign of weakness. Given that strategy and uncertainty are inseparable, this excess of personal pride is surely incompatible with the role of a strategist for whom, as John Halamka reminded us earlier, failure should be accepted as "a valid outcome" within a portfolio of initiatives.

Fourthly we come to experts. Why does Sloan think that exceptionally knowledgeable and skilled individuals will struggle with strategic decision making?

> Sometimes, highly expert people make up their minds so quickly that they overlook critical flaws in the process because of their deep knowledge, successful experience, and acquired and trusted intuition.[84]

She's not alone. Kahneman takes a similar view. He refers to Philip Tetlock's famous 20-year research programme on expert judgement, later described in his book *Superforecasting* (2016). Tetlock made some surprising discoveries about the inability of experts to understand how the future would unfurl. Kahneman explains that "people who spend their time, and earn their living, studying a particular topic produce poorer predictions than dart-throwing monkeys who would have distributed their choices evenly over the options."[85]

This warning about experts might imply that the best strategic thinker is someone who does not have extensive experience of the technology under consideration. At least the decision would then be based upon objective analysis from first principles, rather than a near-instantaneous judgement based on expert intuition. In fact, a generalist lacking any domain-specific expertise may prove to be a highly effective technology strategist.

It was noted earlier that a strategist needs the ability to 'zoom out' in order to analyse the wider environment, which can include multiple systems-of-systems and complex socio-technical relationships. It seems reasonable to argue that experts are less predisposed to do this because it weakens their expertise, removing them from the comfort zone of their technical specialism.

In the final chapter of this book I will recommend ways to identify people with an appropriate balance of skills, and other attributes, to perform strategic roles.

Control is illusory

One of my personal red flags is the 'uncontested genius', the sort of technologist or engineer who has earned the respect, not only of colleagues, but also of journalists, politicians and business leaders. It may be wise not to name any current examples, but dozens have gone before. The likes of Marconi, Benz, Brunel, or Westinghouse might easily, were they alive this century, have acquired a similar fawning devotion, perhaps with their own YouTube channels, podcasts, and ghost-written tales of derring-do.

Today's leading technical entrepreneurs often benefit from being able to speak without serious challenge, either from the media or politicians. Yet, their impressive careers do not necessarily endow them with special powers of foresight, nor the ability to offer advice beyond their immediate technical domains.

Too many of our best-seller lists and bookshelves are filled with publications describing the achievements of such people, despite the fact that it's often easy to show how luck played a significant role in their success. In complex systems *path dependency* always ensures uniqueness. **Hence, there is no template for building a highly profitable technology business, because it is not a reproducible activity.**

Entrepreneurial success emerges from countless events, many of which are random. Furthermore, the context is always unique, i.e. a particular geographical location, at a particular time, within a particular cultural milieu. If these events are not reproducible, what is there to learn from these people, beyond a string of historical facts? "I thought this" and "I did that", then "such and such happened". It's all very interesting, but not much use to us *today*, in *this* place, in *this* cultural context.

Kahneman has little time for the authors: "These stories induce and maintain an illusion of understanding, imparting lessons of little enduring value to readers who are all too eager to believe them."[86] He calls this belief that entrepreneurs have a proven and repeatable formula for success, and that luck is not a factor, the "illusion of control".[87] If you want something to read on a long flight, then go ahead, pick up a billionaire's autobiography, but read it with a very critical eye (then place it in the washroom where a fellow passenger may find a use for it).

One of history's favourite engineers was Nikola Tesla, the man who gave us AC electricity, and much else besides. Imagine being a business owner in 1900, listening to Tesla imparting his wisdom:

> ... there can be no doubt that, at a time not very distant, iron, in many of its now uncontested domains, will have to pass the scepter to another: the coming age will be the age of aluminium...The absolutely unavoidable consequence of the advance of the aluminium industry will be the annihilation of the copper industry. They cannot exist and prosper together, and the latter is doomed beyond any hope of recovery. Even now it is cheaper to convey an electric current through aluminium wires than through copper wires: aluminium castings cost less, and in many domestic and other uses copper has no chance of successfully competing.[88]

What sort of strategic decisions would be made after hearing this? There isn't a single genius on Earth who can penetrate the fog of a complex future.

Uncontested 'expert' opinions are unhealthy, and everyone involved in strategy development, regardless of rank or experience, should be open to challenge.

Fortune favours the bold

Another personal attribute of concern is *low self-confidence*. An effective strategist needs the ability to deal with people at all levels of the organisation, whether presenting a new way forward to the Board, facilitating workshops, or issuing instructions to colleagues.

An absence of confidence may go some way towards explaining the strategic weaknesses, particularly in business affairs, of many technologists. Boulton and Watt were successful partners because Boulton combined his strategic insights and self-confidence with Watt's quiet technical intelligence. Watt could never have done it alone. His biographer, David Miller, talks of "Boulton's wildness and Watt's timidity."[89] At an earlier stage of his career, before meeting Boulton, Watt wrote to a friend that, "I would rather face a loaded cannon than settle an account or make a bargain. In short I find myself out of my sphere when I have anything to do with mankind."[90] Like Watt, Tesla also struggled with the entrepreneurial and strategic side of his work. Compare Watt's feelings (above) with Tesla's memories of his own youth: "My bashfulness was such that I would rather have faced a roaring lion than one of the city dudes who strolled about."[91] Perhaps Tesla would have achieved more with a Boulton-like figure beside him.

In order to master today's complex socio-technical environments, strategists need to be as comfortable with the *socio* as with the *technical*.

It is possible to develop greater self-confidence through age and experience, but for some aspiring technology strategists this attribute will prove elusive. Arguably this is more important when strategising at the organisational level than at the product level, which is perhaps where more introverted technologists and engineers should focus their career ambitions.

Nature or nurture?

In this chapter we have explored the relatively abstract concept of strategic thinking. All strategies begin in the mind, so strategic thinking is directly linked to the technology strategies pursued by organisations. We could have simply relied upon the findings of earlier researchers, such as Nuntamanop *et al.* in 2013. Their study of business leaders concluded with seven strategic thinking competencies: conceptual thinking, visionary thinking, creativity, analytical thinking, learning ability, synthesizing ability, and objectivity.[92] These findings are obviously of interest, but our concern here is with technologists and engineers, not general business leaders. There might be a significant difference between business strategists and technology strategists, so this chapter offered an opportunity to deliver a more targeted presentation of ideas.

How are the best characteristics and behaviours developed? Is it through nature or nurture? Upon reviewing the contents of this chapter, it seems evident that many attributes of a good technology strategist can be nurtured, i.e. learned. For instance, we can teach the portfolio method for achieving net gains, and encourage learning about the organisation and its history.

However, some attributes may be more difficult to acquire. We can't all be endowed with the assertiveness and self-confidence needed to deal with powerful people, and some psychological traits, such as the endowment effect or the sunk costs fallacy could prove difficult to overcome. It may be that nature predominates.

Table 7.2 Some of the attributes associated with ineffective strategic thinking and decision making

Attribute	Description
Excessive self-interest	A manifestation of the principal-agent problem. The strategist's decisions may favour personal interests, such as earnings or career prospects.
Sunk costs fallacy	An unwillingness to terminate a failing project or operational activity into which large and irrecoverable investments have been made.
Endowment effect	An over-valuation or psychological attachment to something owned or emotionally invested in, including favoured projects and technologies.
The planning fallacy and optimism bias	The deliberate or subconscious use of unrealistic best-case scenarios to forecast costs, future performance, project completion times, or the likelihood of failure.
The affect heuristic	An emotional and immediate (though shallow) response to information, influencing a decision maker's opinion. Contrary information can easily reverse that opinion.

(Continued)

Table 7.2 (Continued)

Attribute	Description
Technological optimism	A belief that technological solutions are generally positive and should be promoted, even if non-technological solutions are more appropriate for the circumstances.
Technological determinism	A belief that the growth, evolution and propagation of technology is inevitable; hence it is pointless to resist.
The narrative fallacy and hindsight bias	A perception that technological change is a continuum, in which the past is foreseeably connected to the future, and the future derived from the past.
Einstellung	The condition affecting someone who has become comfortable with long-established ways of working, and who is therefore unwilling to change/adapt.
The availability heuristic and WYSIATI	Making decisions with undue confidence based upon the limited amount of information available at the time; hence, "what you see is all there is" (WYSIATI).
Satisfieds	Decision makers who are comfortable with the status quo and therefore unlikely to propose anything that might undermine it.
Conformists	Decision makers who, subconsciously or otherwise, choose to design solutions within a limited framework of organisational norms.
Excessive pride	This causes a failure to acknowledge the presence of significant uncertainty in expected outcomes, leading to raised expectations and damaging surprises.
Out-of-depth experts and uncontested geniuses	Too much credence can be given to the pronouncements of apparently talented technologists, particularly when they venture outside their specialist field.
Low self-confidence	The necessity for social networking, and also for dealing with difficult colleagues or senior personnel, places a premium on self-confidence and the ability to speak out.

For example, we might assume that James Watt's son would have inherited some of his father's reticence and lack of strategic sense. James Watt junior joined the Boulton and Watt company in 1794. Would Watt junior, like his father, also "rather face a loaded cannon than settle an account or make a bargain", or would he, by osmosis, have absorbed some of Matthew Boulton's strategic genius?

In 1802 a rival industrialist, Matthew Murray of Leeds, had attracted the attention of the Boulton and Watt company. Not only was Murray close to infringing upon their intellectual property, but his newly constructed Round Foundry was producing better quality castings. Watt junior took the initiative. He travelled up to Leeds and secretly surveyed Murray's site. The adjacent land was then purchased, preventing Murray's thriving business from expanding any further.[93] It was a smart move and straight from the Boulton playbook. It's not known what his father thought of James junior's Machiavellian streak, but it certainly gives support to the osmosis theory.

It may therefore be the case that, in developing a strategic mindset, nurture trumps nature. If so, this book might succeed in its goal of nourishing strategic thinking in technologists and engineers.

Glossary for this chapter (Items in bold are also defined in the same table)

agglomeration	The process by which a geographical region attracts public and private organisations associated with a particular industry or technological domain. This creates a **cluster**.
cluster	See **agglomeration**.
non-compete clause	A feature of many employment contracts, the clause seeks to contain the leakage of intellectual property, know-how and skills. Typically it will forbid former employees from transferring to competitors within a specified number of years.
principal-agent problem	An ownership or management challenge, caused by delegating responsibility to agents, such as employees and contractors. It is assumed that agents will act in the principal's interests, rather than their own. This problem arises when they don't.
RCF	See **reference class forecasting**.
reference class forecasting (RCF)	A tool for improving the accuracy of estimated project lengths and costs. RCF uses proprietary databases of historical project information. This data includes the original cost and time estimates, plus the actual costs and project durations.
T-skills profile	An attribute of personnel with one area of deep specialisation, represented by the vertical stalk of the T, plus a broad 'horizontal' range of higher level skills and experience.

Notes

1 Gray, C.S. (2018) *Theory of Strategy*. Oxford: OUP. 104.
2 Tann, J. and Burton, A. (2013) *Matthew Boulton: Industry's Great Innovator*. Stroud: History Press. 175.
3 Miller, D.P. (2019) *The Life and Legend of James Watt*. Pittsburgh: University of Pittsburgh Press. 63.
4 Gray, *Theory of Strategy*. 22.
5 Tann and Burton, *Matthew Boulton*. 152.
6 Tann and Burton. 150.
7 Baird, J.L. (2004) *Television and Me*. Edinburgh: Mercat. 104.
8 Sloan, J. (2020) *Learning to Think Strategically*. Abingdon: Routledge. 54.
9 Sloan, *Learning to Think Strategically*. 25.
10 Sloan. 248–249.
11 Sloan. 173.
12 Sloan. 168.
13 Dyson, J. (2011) *Against the Odds: An Autobiography*. Andover: Cengage Learning. 256.
14 Sloan. 168–174.
15 Rasiel, E.M. and Friga, P.N. (2001) *The McKinsey Mind*. New York: McGraw-Hill. 32–35.
16 Mintzberg, H. (2018) 'Strategic Thinking as "Seeing"'. *Manage Magazine* [online]. Available at https://managemagazine.com/article-bank/strategic-management-article-bank/henry-mintzberg-strategic-thinking-seeing/ (Accessed: 9 September 2020).
17 Sloan. 56.
18 Sloan. 80.
19 Sloan. 219–220.
20 Sloan. 63.
21 Sloan. 85.
22 Sloan. 242.
23 Morita, A. (1987) *Made in Japan*. London: Collins. 145.
24 Buchanan, A. (2006) *Brunel*. London: Continuum. 63.
25 Buchanan, *Brunel*. 70.
26 *The Diaries of Sir Daniel Gooch*. (2006) First published 1892. Stroud: Nonsuch. 232–233.
27 Finkelstein, S. (2016) 'Secrets of the Superbosses'. *Harvard Business Review: Talent Management*. Available at https://hbr.org/2016/01/secrets-of-the-superbosses (Accessed: 22 March 2022)
28 Arthur, W.B. (2010) *The Nature of Technology*. London: Penguin. 161.
29 Kerr, W.R. and Robert-Nicoud, F. (2020) 'Tech Clusters'. Harvard Business School Working Paper 20-063. Available at https://www.hbs.edu/ris/Publication%20Files/20-063_97e5ef89-c027-4e95-a462-21238104e0c8.pdf (Accessed: 28 March 2022)
30 Sloan. 151–163.
31 Sloan. 179.
32 Chermack, T.J. (2011) *Scenario Planning in Organizations*. San Francisco: Berrett-Koehler. 93.
33 Westwick, P. (2020) *Stealth: The Secret Contest to Invent Invisible Aircraft*. New York: OUP. 14–21.
34 Hewitt, E. (2018) *Technology Strategy Patterns*. Sebastapol, CA: O'Reilly. 102–103.
35 Hewitt, *Technology Strategy Patterns*. xviii.

36 Kane, G.C. *et al.* (2015) 'Strategy, not Technology, Drives Digital Transformation'. *MIT Sloan Management Review, Research Report*, Summer 2015. Available at https://www2.deloitte.com/content/dam/Deloitte/fr/Documents/strategy/dup_strategy-not-technology-drives-digital-transformation.pdf (Accessed: 28 August 2019).

37 Rasiel and Friga, *The McKinsey Mind*. 97.

38 Martin, R.L. (2019) 'Strategy Isn't What You Say, It's What You Do' in *HBR Guide to Thinking Strategically*. Boston (MA): HBR Press. 52–53.

39 Lai, L. (2019) 'To Be a Strategic Leader, Ask the Right Questions' in *HBR Guide to Thinking Strategically*. Boston (MA): HBR Press. 175.

40 Sloan. 110.

41 Hewitt. 166.

42 Buchanan. 63–64.

43 Kane *et al*, *MIT Sloan Management Review, Research Report*.

44 Buchanan. 110–111.

45 Network Rail (2013) *Network Rail Technical Strategy (NRTS)*, available at https://www.networkrail.co.uk/industry-and-commercial/research-development-and-technology/our-strategy-for-research-development-and-technology-rdt/ (Accessed: 17 February 2019).

46 Tobin, J. (2003) *To Conquer the Air*. New York: Free Press. 199–200.

47 Mintzberg, *Manage Magazine*.

48 Davey, L. (2019) 'Reflect on Your Actions and Choices' in *HBR Guide to Thinking Strategically*. Boston (MA): HBR Press. 110.

49 Madhavan, G. (2016) *Think Like an Engineer*. London: Oneworld. 21.

50 Madhavan, *Think Like an Engineer*. 17–21.

51 Kanter, R.M. (2019) 'Zoom In, Zoom Out' in *HBR Guide to Thinking Strategically*. Boston (MA): HBR Press. 92.

52 Hewitt. 185–186.

53 Braun, E. (1998) *Technology in Context*. London: Routledge. 54.

54 Syed, M. (2015) *Black Box Thinking*. London: John Murray.

55 Tobin, *To Conquer the Air*. 156.

56 Mintzberg.

57 Buchanan. 36.

58 Platt, A. (1987) *The Life and Times of Daniel Gooch*. Gloucester: Alan Sutton Publishing.

59 Heppenheimer, T.A. (1997) *Countdown: A History of Spaceflight*. New York: Wiley. 196.

60 Morita, *Made in Japan*. 165.

61 Morita. 167.

62 Kahneman, D. (2011) *Thinking, Fast and Slow*. London: Penguin. 340–341.

63 Heppenheimer, *Countdown*. 250–260.

64 Kahneman, *Thinking, Fast and Slow*. 345–346.

65 Kahneman. 318–319.

66 Kahneman. 289–299.

67 Westwick, *Stealth*. 51.

68 Kahneman. 250.

69 Kahneman. 252.

70 Kahneman. 250.

71 Kahneman. 264.

72 Park, J.E. (2021) 'Curbing Cost Overruns in Infrastructure Investment: Has Reference Class Forecasting Delivered Its Promised Success?'. *The European Journal of Transport and Infrastructure Research (EJTIR)*, Vol. 21, Issue 2, 120–136.

73 Heppenheimer. 123.
74 Kahneman. 138–140.
75 Webster, M.D. (2017) 'Philosophy of Technology Assumptions in Educational Technology Leadership'. *Educational Technology & Society*, Vol. 20, Issue 1, 25–36.
76 Hewitt. 77.
77 Kahneman. 218.
78 Madhavan. 155.
79 Sloan. 262
80 Kahneman. 239
81 Kahneman. 129–136.
82 Sloan. 108–111.
83 Sloan. 182.
84 Sloan. 108.
85 Kahneman. 219.
86 Kahneman. 207–208.
87 Kahneman. 259.
88 Tesla, N. (2011) *My Inventions and Other Writings*. New York: Penguin. 134–135.
89 Miller, *The Life and Legend of James Watt*. 67.
90 Muirhead, J.P. (1854) *The Origin and Progress of the Mechanical Inventions of James Watt, Vol II*. London: John Murray. 34.
91 Tesla, *My Inventions and Other Writings*. 26.
92 Goldman, E. and Scott, A.R. (2016) 'Competency Models for Assessing Strategic Thinking'. *Journal of Strategy and Management*, Vol. 9, Issue 3, 258–280.
93 Tann and Burton. 170.

Part II

Strategy in practice

In Part I, technology strategy was introduced in a relatively abstract and theoretical way. The core components of this book and its key themes were explored, including systems, technology, engineering, design, uncertainty, risk, and strategic thinking. Their purpose was to lay foundations for the remainder of the book.

We have now reached the point where abstraction begins its transformation into action. We can turn our focus to the so-called 'real world', where practitioners are faced with multiple and competing stakeholders, moral dilemmas, and internal demands for innovation. A chapter will therefore be dedicated to each of these topics.

The final chapter in this section presents some practical solutions for navigating technological uncertainty.

DOI: 10.4324/9781003472919-9

8 A stake in the strategy

Understanding the parties that matter

This chapter presents

- A comprehensive analysis of stakeholders in the technological realm.

This chapter establishes

- A distinction between direct and indirect stakeholders.
- The strategic nature of stakeholder management.

Sir Sidney Camm, the military aircraft designer, famously remarked that "All modern aircraft have four dimensions: span, length, height and politics."[1] He was acknowledging a universal truth about the importance of stakeholders in the development and management of engineering solutions.

In addition to the political interest in technologies, there may also be complex relationships with suppliers, investors, the media, and regulators. And perhaps the most important stakeholders of all are the buyers and users of technology. Altogether, 15 different types of technology stakeholders are identified and described below.

Defining and categorising

So, what is a stakeholder? Most definitions refer to parties which "can affect" or be "affected by",[2] or which have "an interest or concern in something".[3] An ISO vocabulary guide even recommends that parties who merely *perceive* themselves to be affected should be considered stakeholders.[4]

It's easy to assume that all stakeholders must be people, but this is misleading. For instance, it is commonplace to view the natural environment as a stakeholder (e.g. of industrial processes). We can also do the same for the sources of technology inputs and the destinations of technology outputs. In other words, machines and production processes hold 'stakes' in the machines and

DOI: 10.4324/9781003472919-10

processes with which they interact. For example, in a continuous flow manufacturing operation, such as a foundry, the rolling mill is surely a stakeholder of the furnace, and *vice versa*. This is a much more systemic interpretation of what we mean by 'stakeholder'.

In order to settle upon a working definition, it seems appropriate to focus on the key phrase 'affecting or affected by' (see above). It isn't always possible to discern precisely who is affected by a technology, so the ISO's reference to *perception* may also be important. We surely have an obligation to acknowledge people or organisations who perceive some form of benefit or harm from our technological activities, so the mere act of acknowledging them transforms those parties into stakeholders.

DEFINITION FOR *STAKEHOLDER*

A technology stakeholder is any entity with the capacity for affecting, being affected by, or perceiving an effect from, a technology.

There are many suggestions for types or categories of stakeholders. For instance, business analysts may refer to *primary* and *secondary* stakeholders. According to Robert Freeman *et al.* in *Managing for Stakeholders* (2007), primary stakeholders shape the business and its operations; they include investors and suppliers. Secondary stakeholders, however, are more distant and less influential, so governments and competitors may fall into this category. They point out that the identification of primary and secondary stakeholders varies according to context.[5] For instance, a competitor's status will change if it collaborates in a joint venture.

Another approach is to classify stakeholders according to their value-relationships with each technology. Some stakeholders, such as suppliers, investors, complementors, and users, are more likely to experience a benefit, or value-gain, from a technology. This benefit could be financial or merely some form of psychological satisfaction. Other stakeholders, such as failing competitors or a polluted river, will be experiencing a value-loss. There is also a value-neutral group, neither gaining nor losing from a technology, such as regulators and standards organisations. Again, these are dynamic categories, because membership will vary according to time and context. A stakeholder could be a value-gainer today, but a value-loser tomorrow.

In the 1990s Colin Eden and Fran Ackerman mapped the 'power' and 'interest' of stakeholders into a simple matrix, in order to

Table 8.1 The power-interest matrix

High interest	Subjects	Players	Potential responses to the stakeholders in each quadrant:
Low interest	Crowd	Context setters	**Subjects** – We should keep these individuals or groups informed.
	Low power	High power	**Players** – We must manage these relationships carefully. **Crowd** – These only need to be monitored. **Context setters** – It is necessary to ensure their satisfaction.

differentiate between them.[6,7] Table 8.1 illustrates their power-interest matrix and explains the four types of stakeholder that emerge.

However, my preference is to differentiate between stakeholders based on the directness and formality of their relationship with a technology. For example, many employees have a direct, formal relationship with the technologies they manage, as do suppliers, buyers, and investors. This formality may be contractual in nature. By contrast, the media, local communities, or the makers of complementary products have an indirect, informal, non-contractual relationship. In this chapter I will describe many of the stakeholder types, placing each into one of these two broad categories: *direct* and *indirect*.

In Figure 8.1, a dotted line is used to separate the direct, formal stakeholders from the indirect, informal ones. The illustration also

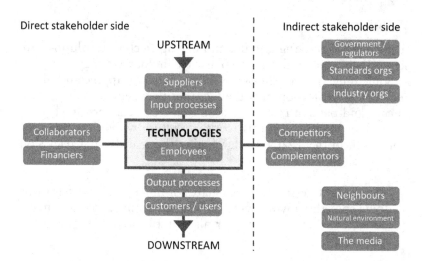

Figure 8.1 Two types of technology stakeholders: 1) Direct stakeholders, both horizontal and vertical; 2) Indirect stakeholders, some horizontal, but generally more independent and detached

distinguishes between stakeholders located 'upstream' of a technology (e.g. suppliers) from those located 'downstream' (e.g. users). Upstream and downstream stakeholders are often described as being in a 'vertical' relationship with an organisation, which explains their orientation in the model. Other stakeholders are operating at the same level, and so have a 'horizontal' relationship. The remaining stakeholders are more detached. These include governments, industry bodies, and the media.

Direct stakeholders

Imagine the world from the perspective of a business-critical technology. There are stakeholders in all directions. At the centre will be employees, the people responsible for your design, construction, and operation. The parties upstream are relying upon you to receive their outputs as your inputs. Those downstream are awaiting your outputs. Turn to the side and you will find various stakeholders with financial interests, and perhaps organisations collaborating as partners.

We might say that each of these stakeholders has a formal, direct relationship with you. This relationship could be a contractual obligation to supply inputs or to be employed as an operator. There could also be contractual arrangements with collaborating universities, or with joint venture partners sharing the costs of development. Let's take a closer look at the strategic importance of these direct stakeholders.

Employees

The people who design, build, and manage technical solutions are key stakeholders and central to any technology strategy.

Something which outsiders often fail to appreciate about technology professionals is the fact that they generally possess an energy and passion rarely found in non-technical personnel. John Logie Baird epitomised this working culture while describing his approach, in the 1920s, to developing the world's first television transmissions:

> I was not interested either in shares or money ... but I felt I was doing something worthwhile. It was interesting enough to make me willingly work night after night until three and four in the morning.[8]

Fifty years later another engineer, Mark Miodownik, was disappointed by the workplace culture he experienced at the start of his career:

I just wasn't enthused because it was 9am to 5pm office work, and people left on the dot of 5pm. I was left wondering where the engineering passion was in the company.[9]

Miodownik went on to develop a stellar research career. This motivation and self-discipline have important implications for the way that technology professionals should be managed.

Sometimes it's necessary for these instincts to be reined in so that they become focused upon organisational goals. Julia King, the former Head of Materials at Rolls-Royce aero engines, has described how "the company's materials people loved the idea of developing futuristic new alloys." Her challenge was "to get people from being most excited by their subject to being excited about delivering new products and making money."[10] It's necessary to gain a psychological understanding of technical professionals. Akio Morita, Sony's co-founder, explains in his autobiography that it isn't sufficient merely to supply engineers with the finest equipment and laboratories. What they need is inspirational challenges.[11]

In short, technical people need little supervision in order to deliver high quality, high value work, providing their tasks are both inspiring and strategically directed.

This capacity for hard work with minimal supervision is conducive to successful strategy execution, because implementation always requires the engagement and support of frontline workers. It is their responsibility to understand the current strategy and to devise appropriate tactical responses to the changes arising within their working environments (see Chapter 5). The authors of *Embracing Complexity* (2015), Jean Boulton *et al.*, argue that "If strategy is to have any effect it has to influence the day-to-day activities of the people inside the organization."[12] So, technologists need to be enthused, challenged, and tactically empowered.

This combination of drive, commitment, and empowerment may be used to good effect in the innovation process. Under Akio Morita, Sony gave technical professionals ownership of their own product innovations as each idea progressed through the various corporate functions, from design through to marketing.[13] The equally innovative 3M Corporation has also been recognised for granting employees generous allocations of both time and money in order to pursue their ideas.[14,15]

It should therefore be clear that a comprehensive technology strategy will need to address employee management practices, particularly empowerment and the freedom to innovate. But there is also the difficult question of who is best suited to manage technology professionals.

It is often observed, and it's certainly my own observation, that few engineers enjoy taking on management roles. The transition from hands-on, solution-oriented work to the deskbound nature of management, is not easy. It's the prospect of dealing with difficult people, controlling finances, and navigating internal bureaucracy that deters many superbly talented technical professionals from stepping up. Wilbur Wright spoke for many when he wrote that, "it is always easier to deal with things than with men".[16]

Richard Rumelt, author of *Good Strategy, Bad Strategy*, defines the role of an engineer in a way that helps to explain this reluctance: "An engineer starts with complexity and crafts certainty."[17] Unfortunately, management starts with complexity ... and stays that way. For this reason, there may be a logic to recruiting professional managers with no engineering background into technical environments. Professional managers are skilled at delegating, facilitating meetings, inspirational speaking, and financial management, but can this compensate for an absence of engineering expertise? The answer is that it *might*, but suspicions will always remain. Akio Morita viewed the prospect of non-technical professional managers as "dangerous".[18] The obvious compromise is to seek out those few engineers who also possess a natural gift for management. Give them all the support they need (e.g. a capable personal assistant and finance administrator), and sit them atop a flat structure of empowered fellow professionals. Arguably this solution would suit everyone involved.

At a higher level than local management, there is often a tension in the relationship between engineering functions and other business teams, such as finance, operations, and marketing. This tension was explained in Chapter 3 (Box 3.3 *Co-location OR Cloistering?*), where arguments were presented for either integrating or physically isolating the engineering teams. Objectively, it's hard to disagree with the notion that engineering personnel need to mix and share spaces with their non-technical colleagues, because this enables technical challenges to be better understood. It's also likely to foster a more commercially-focused mindset among engineers. Nigel Cross writes that, during engineering design processes, "production and marketing development must proceed in parallel and with mutual interaction".[19] Similarly, at James Dyson's vacuum cleaner business, he consciously created the conditions for cross-functional relationships:

> The graphics and engineering people are in the geographical centre of the office, and that reflects the centrality of design and engineering to the whole operation. But there are no department boundaries or borders or walls ... freedom of movement and of expression is total.

Dyson sought to blend his engineering and business cultures by insisting that every new employee, "from the lowliest member of staff to a non-executive director", builds a vacuum cleaner on their first day of work.[20] Morita also describes how similar ideas of functional mixing and cross-fertilisation were instilled at Sony.[21]

Sometimes specific roles are created with the intention of spanning this divide. Peter High's book, *Implementing World Class IT Strategy* (2014) mentions job titles such as Business Technology Officer (BTO) and Business Information Officer (BIO). The latter is described as having "knowledge of the strategy, plans, needs, opportunities, and issues of the division to which he or she is aligned but equal knowledge of IT's capabilities, skills, and strategy".[22] The traditional Business Analyst role is not dissimilar.[23] The importance of these bridging roles, which bind engineering expertise with core business activities, cannot be underestimated.

Eben Hewitt, author of *Technology Strategy Patterns*, believes that IT should now be transitioning from a "subservient order-taking" role to a more proactive position of "co-leadership" in the development of organisational strategies,[24] and Peter High argues that IT "should and can become a center for promoting a coordinated, well-thought-out program of strategies for the company as a whole".[25] These ideas are symptomatic of a movement, now well under way, towards the emergence of engineers as influential business strategists and future organisational leaders, such as CEOs.

Strategies are also concerned with decisions about the geographical location, size, and composition of engineering teams. Co-location solutions, in which technologists share their spaces with other business functions, were discussed earlier, but there are many other strategic considerations for the siting of teams. For example, 'follow the Sun' support arrangements, involve three or four groups of employees, each performing the same function, but split across multiple time zones. A very different type of siting strategy involves the establishment of 'captive centres' thousands of kilometres from the corporate HQ. Their purpose is to benefit from geographical clusters of knowledge and expertise, perhaps in order to serve a regional market, or (more likely) with the aim of reducing operating costs. Boeing, Microsoft, Apple, and Google all employ large numbers of personnel in captive centres around the globe.[26] Locating operations in a thriving 'technology cluster' is another option. This offers various advantages, but also significant disadvantages, as described in Chapter 7 (Box 7.1 *Locate in a cluster OR Locate independently?*).

Strategies should also address the attributes expected of employees. Skills and experience may be optimised through strategic investments in training and changes to recruitment practices. In preparing for the future, strategists must ensure that personnel possess the right technical and non-technical skills.

The latter are sometimes known as 'complementary' or 'soft' skills. For example, Jo da Silva of the Arup Group values "the ability to define problems, to ask the right questions, and to assemble information and think creatively".[27] Similar arguments for complementary skills are made by Flin *et al.*, whose research focuses mainly upon the competences associated with safe engineering environments. In their view soft skills "are as critical as the 'hard' technical skills and, in fact, are essential when competent technical people do technical things in technical work settings."[28] For example, they cite the improvements in aviation safety resulting from 'crew resource management' training (or CRM), which focuses upon verbal communication and working relationships within the cockpit. The range of complementary skills useful to technologists and engineers is long and undoubtedly has strategic implications in certain sectors.

Skills requirements vary over time, especially in maturing industries. As a new technology sector evolves, the rate of product innovation will tend to decrease, while the rate of process innovation increases. This is a consequence of the need to improve productivity and efficiency as firms compete to sell broadly similar products. Consequently, the general profile of employees shifts from being well-paid, multi-skilled, creative individuals towards lower-paid staff with commodity skills, executing tasks that are less demanding, often repetitive, and semi-automated. This change of employee profile is well-documented by researchers.[29,30] Technology strategies for organisations in maturing sectors must address these inevitable changes to employee profiles before productivity and efficiency begin to be impacted.

Another topic which often arises in discussions of employee attributes is *diversity*, a word that means different things to different people. Fundamentally, though, there is a clear logic to the necessity for diverse skillsets and experience within technical environments. Let's look at some examples.

A contemporary debate within engineering concerns the innate bias within some AI tools caused by the data used to 'train' them. Clearly, if you pull data mainly from American or European sources, one cannot expect the 'intelligence' to have a global perspective. Many of its decisions will be geographically and culturally biased. The result is a poor-quality product. It has always been too easy for designers (usually well-educated, able-bodied, middle-class, culturally 'western' men) to overlook the needs of dissimilar users. The evidence for this is undeniable. For instance, the ethicist Deborah Johnson notes that "For decades, engineers designed buildings with entrances at the top of steps and sidewalks too narrow for wheelchairs."[31]

Many of these examples are now being rectified, although the transition to better designs has been too slow for many observers.

Dervilla Mitchell, a senior civil engineer with Arup, notes that, from a corporate or team perspective, "If you have a wide range of skills and a wide range of perspectives, you're much more likely to develop successful solutions".[32] In relation to gender diversity, and greater opportunities for women in technology, Miodownik argues that it "will change what engineering is and how it is done. It will change which problems are chosen and how they are solved."[33] Beyond gender, we should also be concerned with diversity of ethnicity and culture, age and life experience, personality types, even socioeconomic background.

One particularly strong justification for diverse engineering teams emerges from the complexity of technological environments. Organisations struggle to navigate these complex adaptive systems (CAS), as explained in Chapter 5. In particular, management foresight is limited due to the non-linear characteristics of CAS environments, in which cause and effect relationships become blurred. The authors of *Embracing Complexity*, Boulton *et al.*, explain how organisations can improve their probability of success within a CAS:

> To enhance this capability the organization will likely need to extend the diversity of its knowledge resources, to encourage experimentation, and to enhance the ability of people with different skills and experience to interact with each other and find novel solutions.[34]

This argument ties the diversity debate to the immense challenges associated with our complex, socio-technical, and highly systematised world.

The examples above demonstrate that diversity is an issue of strategic significance because, where it is taken seriously, it helps to eliminate, or at least mitigate, a host of undesirable outcomes. Consequently, Grant and Jordan advise that, when recruiting, managers "must resist the temptation to clone".[35] And former McKinsey consultants, Rasiel and Friga, argue that "It's not enough to be open to candidates with varying backgrounds ... you have to seek them out".[36]

One type of employee really stands apart: that rare individual we view as a very special talent. Their positive impact upon organisational performance tends to be out of all proportion to their physical presence. It's vital, from a strategic perspective, that such individuals are not only recognised and employed, but retained for as long as possible.

One such talent was Daniel Gooch, the engineering genius recruited by I.K. Brunel to design and build locomotives for the Great Western Railway. His story was told in Chapter 7. Another was Charles Steinmetz who, in the 1890s, General Electric wanted to employ for his mastery of electrical engineering. GE vigorously pursued Steinmetz, offering various inducements. They finally resorted to buying the company which employed him, thereby acquiring both his services and his many patents.[37] By contrast, in the early 1980s, the Disney Corporation was already employing John Lasseter, a pioneer in computer animation. However, there was little appreciation within Disney for Lasseter's disruptive digital techniques, so he was asked to leave. Within a few years, Lasseter was leading Pixar to global success. Meanwhile, Disney was struggling to compete with Pixar's creativity and technological superiority, so they acquired Pixar in 2006. As a consequence, Lasseter returned as Disney's head of animation.[38] Sweet irony.

Therefore, talent management has strategic implications. The smartest individuals must be allowed to flourish, because they have the potential to contribute to the organisation in unforeseen ways. What do these special employees know, perhaps intuitively, that we don't? What innovations will they deliver that would otherwise be missed? There is no guarantee that there will be a return on this investment, but such rare individuals present a unique opportunity for their employers.

Technology strategies, once developed, must be explained to employees. This action has consequences, because there will often be difficult decisions about retraining, reassignment, and redundancy. Furthermore, there are likely to be some personnel who will fundamentally disagree with the strategic direction chosen. Digital strategist, Eben Hewitt, recommends tackling these situations head on:

> Not everyone will make it through the journey ... You will need to sort out the audience into roughly thirds: who is on board, gets it from the beginning, and is a believer and an ally; who will need to change their ways but can be retrained or nurtured if you spend the time to help the audience, and who is not on board and can't or won't make the journey ... you need to give those people a nice severance package and help them find the door.[39]

Strategy implementation is often brutal, and this example raises interesting questions. Should a strategy be compromised in order to mollify its more vocal objectors? And if so, is a compromised strategy likely to be an effective strategy? The first question involves internal politics – only you and your colleagues can answer that. The second question, however, is central to this book.

Any strategy is better than no strategy, and all employees have a tactical role in its execution. So it's the responsibility of technologists and engineers to ensure that even a weakened strategy is implemented with energy and purpose.

Box 8.1   ANALYTICAL TOOLS AND TECHNIQUES

The skills matrix

Forward looking organisations must ensure that the skills of professional staff match strategic ambitions.

A simple but effective tool for managing the competences of personnel, and the teams they belong to, is the skills matrix (Table 8.2).

Table 8.2 A skills matrix

	Skill 1	Skill 2	Skill 3	Person score
Person 1	1	0	2	3
Person 2	3	2	3	8
Person 3	3	0	1	4
Skill totals	7	2	6	Team score 15
Experts	2	0	1	

The scoring system should be simple, e.g. 0 = No knowledge/ experience, 1 = Some knowledge or experience, 2 = Good knowledge/experience, and 3 = Expert.

The matrix should only include business-critical skills, such as Project Management, Business Analysis, Product Design, Team Leadership, Systems Analysis, and specific programming languages or software applications. A reasonable limit on the number of skills is around 20 to 25.

Benefits: Areas of expertise and current deficiencies are clarified, enabling training and recruitment plans to be developed with confidence. If a matrix is shared internally, any member of staff can quickly locate a colleague with appropriate skills. It also enables the setting of improvement targets for individuals and entire teams.

Administration: It's vital to include any skills that are likely to be needed in the future, but when a skill is no longer valued by the organisation, the column must be removed. Optionally, skills can be weighted to indicate importance. In order to minimise the administration involved, each person can be asked to self-assess by completing their own row of the matrix.

There is no incentive to either over-state or under-state one's own competences, partly because colleagues can peer review each other's self-assessment.

The matrix is an effective, low-cost tool for synchronising skills with the current strategy.

Suppliers

Upstream of every technology we find its suppliers. We mostly associate the concept of supply with external providers of goods and services, such as raw materials, manufactured commodities, data, even people (e.g. consultants). To perform at maximum efficiency, most technologies require a predictable supply of inputs above a minimum quality standard, and this imperative imposes a premium on the skilful management of supplier relationships.

Harvard's Michael Porter has made many important contributions to the academic study of strategy. In his *value chain analysis*, described in Chapter 1, suppliers constitute the first link in the value chain. He refers to this stage as 'inbound logistics'. However, Porter's most significant contribution was probably his *Five Forces* analysis, in which he describes the 'bargaining power' of suppliers as one of the forces most likely to influence corporate strategy.[40] This power manifests itself in various ways, notably in the form of prices and the reliability of supply.

We may, therefore, have concerns relating to a supplier's market dominance. This could be due to its possession of important intellectual property or its adoption of the most advanced production techniques. Suppliers like these, with few if any competitors, pose a clear threat because they can choose to take their services elsewhere, perhaps favouring a competitor, or they may simply raise prices beyond levels of commercial viability.

Developing the capacity to switch suppliers, perhaps by adopting more widely available components and raw materials, rebalances the relationship in favour of the technology owner. A technology strategy may therefore need to propose re-designing critical products and processes in order to de-risk the sources of components and materials.

One of the key phrases associated with the strategic management of suppliers is 'make or buy'. The essence of this dichotomy is whether it is preferable to have total control over the supply of resources (including their design and production) or to rely instead upon purely contractual arrangements (e.g. purchasing and leasing). Technology owners often lack consistency in their approach to this dichotomy, so let's examine it further.

When we look objectively at an organisation, the make or buy debate reveals much about its internal priorities and even more about the competence of its decision makers. Here are some hypothetical make or buy decisions, presented as questions. Should a manufacturer produce every single component needed for its product range, or only those components which it can't acquire at a fair price on the open market? Should an organisation 'make' its own competence by training employees to perform specialist tasks, or should it simply recruit (buy in) people with the necessary skills and experience? Is it wise to deploy an internal software team, currently responsible for building and maintaining core business applications, to create a new payroll system for the HR Department, or should the HR Department go to a third-party supplier?

These examples demonstrate the breadth of the make or buy debate. It raises questions about risk, opportunity, priorities, necessity, competence, time, money, ambition, scale, and, in many cases, common sense. Make or buy helps to define an organisation's sense of purpose. It is therefore a question of immense strategic importance.

The make or buy dichotomy goes beyond the purchasing of resources. It can also involve acquisition of the suppliers themselves. 'Vertical integration' is the acquisition of third parties in either an upstream or downstream direction (see Figure 8.1). We will look at downstream integration later in this chapter, but when the acquisition target is a supplier the buyer is said to be expanding upstream.

One of the main benefits of supplier integration is the elimination of costs associated with managing the supplier relationship. Following acquisition, the supplier's outputs are now originating internally, meaning that they've become non-transactional internal transfers between two stages of the production process. 'Buy' has therefore become 'make'. Powerful corporations, particularly in the software sector, make a habit of acquiring small, specialist suppliers. This has the additional benefit of denying competitors the opportunity to purchase services from them or even to acquire them using the same make or buy logic. The desire to gain exclusive control over a supplier is a common motive for vertical integration.

Upstream vertical integration is far from new. In the late 19th century Thomas Edison's General Electric business sought to acquire many specialist producers in the new electricity distribution industry. GE therefore became a manufacturer of the dynamos, motors, and conductors needed for its core business.[41] This organisational culture of acquisitions contributed to GE's transformation into one of the world's largest companies.

Some years later Pirelli, the Italian tyre manufacturer, acquired plantations in Asia to secure rubber supplies and avoid market price instability. This internalisation of rubber production was maintained until the 1950s, at which point Pirelli sold its plantations while simultaneously researching the development of synthetic rubber. Ironically, the transition to synthetic products never materialised, so the company was required to obtain its rubber on the open market, with all the uncertainty that entails.[42]

One of the disadvantages of upstream integration, however, is the dependence which a technology then has on a single internal supplier. There may be an administrative obligation to use this internal source of components and materials, even when third parties are offering better quality or a more responsive service. Dependence upon a monopoly supplier is always a significant business risk, and General Motors (GM) learned this the hard way during a strike at one of its brake manufacturing sites in 1998. As a consequence, vehicle production was halted in 24 assembly plants across the United States.[43]

Upstream integration is sometimes called insourcing, the inverse of which is outsourcing (also known as sub-contracting, or contracting out). In its simplest form, outsourcing involves swapping an internal service or supply function for an external one. This may involve a physical transfer of people and other assets, or it could be a straight switch to an external supplier combined with the dismantling of the internal function.

Much has been written about outsourcing, mainly due to its widespread use by both public and private sector organisations, and also because of the controversies associated with it, notably redundancies and the transfer of work to low-wage economies. Three variations of the outsourcing model are described in Box 8.2 *Offshoring OR Nearshoring OR Onshoring?*

Box 8.2   STRATEGIC DICHOTOMIES

Offshoring OR Nearshoring OR Onshoring?

If a decision is made to outsource work functions, a dilemma will immediately arise concerning the location of outsourced teams.

Technically, this is a *trichotomy*, because there are broadly three options. The contractors can be based in the same country, or in a nearby country (within the same continent), or thousands of kilometres away on a different continent (where labour costs may be substantially lower). These three locations are known respectively as 'onshore', 'nearshore', and 'offshore'.

While working in the London financial services industry I experienced all three outsourcing models, with my infrastructure teams based in the UK (onshore), Ireland and Hungary (near-shore), and India (offshore).

Although costs generally underlie many outsourcing decisions, there are other drivers. Table 8.3 captures some of the key advantages and disadvantages of each option.

Table 8.3 Table of advantages and disadvantages when locating teams offshore, nearshore, and onshore

	Advantages	Disadvantages
Offshoring	• Large cost reductions. • Choice of providers and technologies. • You are treated as a customer by the staff. • Replaces complex people management with easier contract management. • Consistent productivity (fewer absences).	• Necessity to research tax and legal implications. • Zero informal contact with contract staff. • Expensive travel for face-to-face meetings. • Significant cultural differences. • Time zone difference. • Staff are loyal to the contracting firm, not to you. • Less internal innovation and 'going the extra mile'. • Trade secrets/know-how is shared with outsiders.
Nearshoring	• Some cost reductions. • Choice of providers and technologies. • You are treated as a customer by the staff. • Replaces complex people management with easier contract management. • Consistent productivity (fewer absences).	• Necessity to research tax and legal implications. • Limited informal contact with contract staff. • Significant costs of travel for face-to-face meetings. • Some cultural differences. • Possible time zone difference. • Staff are loyal to the contracting firm, not to you. • Less internal innovation and 'going the extra mile'. • Trade secrets/know-how is shared with outsiders.
Onshoring	• Uncomplicated tax and legal implications. • Frequent contact with contract staff. • Limited cultural differences. • No time zone differences. • Choice of providers and technologies. • You are treated as a customer by the staff. • Replaces complex people management with easier contract management. • Consistent productivity (fewer absences).	• No cost benefits relative to employing staff. • Staff are loyal to the contracting firm, not to you. • Less internal innovation and 'going the extra mile'. • Trade secrets/know-how is shared with outsiders.

Where outsourcing is pursued vigorously, the core organisation controls a network of sub-contracted suppliers. It is therefore acting as a 'system integrator'. This became the policy at NASA under its first Administrator, T. Keith Glennan.[44] NASA's major sub-contractors, such as Rocketdyne, Lockheed, Boeing, and Grumman, delivered most of the familiar, iconic hardware. More recently, Boeing adopted similar practices in the design and development of the 787 Dreamliner. However, their role as system integrator was tested to its limits by a string of widely reported technical challenges.[45] Whether these would have plagued an internally developed 787, we'll never know.

In conclusion, supplier relationships take many forms. Ties may be strong or loose. The supplier may be internal or external. Its people may be sitting in the same room, or 5,000 miles away. Relationships may be friendly or fractious. But the questions to ask are these: What's best for the technology, and what's best for the organisation as a whole? Your answers should help to cut through the myriad options for securing the supplies you need.

Customers

We can disaggregate a technology's customers into three groups: buyers, users, and beneficiaries. Buyers make acquisition decisions. Users consume the technology's output, often directly controlling the technology itself. Beneficiaries merely gain the value derived from the technology's use. As technologists, we need to be concerned with each of these groups, although some will be more strategically important than others.

We usually associate customers with people. However, as mentioned elsewhere in this book, it's entirely feasible for both users and beneficiaries to be non-human entities, such as machines and animals. It's also likely that we will increasingly see intelligent machines becoming technology buyers.

Some stakeholders combine all three roles. This is especially true in the world of consumer products. For example, many players of computer games and riders of bicycles will not only have bought their products, but they will also be the sole user and the only beneficiary.

In the first instance, buyers need to be persuaded of a technology's benefits. Therefore, issues of design, quality, reliability, and efficiency are likely to shape the technologist/buyer relationship. However, most buying decisions are guided by the technology's future users and beneficiaries. Hence, during design and development activities, it is the users who are typically the primary concern, rather than its buyers, assuming these are different people.

Let's take a brief look at two topics related to the technologist/customer relationship: firstly technology design, then technology networks.

Technology strategies need to address design. For example, a strategy can specify a new design methodology, or outsource/insource the design function. One might assume that designers have always been focused upon the real needs of technology users, but this is not strictly true. An interesting case is described by Ibo van de Poel and Lambèr Royakkers, who report on a controversial herbicide (branded 2,4,5-T) which was sold widely in the UK during the 1970s. Agricultural workers expressed concerns about its apparent health effects, but a government advisory committee used laboratory studies to dismiss their fears. They argued that the herbicide was harmless "provided that the product is used as directed". But in the real-world the product was being used in challenging outdoor farming environments. It wasn't right to assume that the containers were always in good condition and clearly labelled, or that workers had the right solvents, pressure valves, spray nozzles, and safety clothing.[46] The product's designers had simply not given enough thought to the real needs of its users.

This focus upon user needs and experiences is taken more seriously today. Indeed the professionalism of design practice and the quality of technological products has improved immensely since the 1970s. This may be attributed, in part, to the emergence of new user-centred methodologies. The perspective of the user is now encapsulated in terms such as *human-centred design, universal design,* and *inclusive design.* These more enlightened approaches to design have been integrated within mainstream education. They are even captured in an ISO standard (ISO 9241-210:2019) entitled *Ergonomics of Human-System Interaction.*[47]

Some of the benefits emerging from these contemporary design methodologies include more enthusiastic user 'buy-in' for product changes; generally safer devices and working practices; improved functionality, with unnecessary features removed; cultural inclusivity (e.g. for different language groups); ergonomic improvements; and greater accessibility for users with physical or sensory impairments. Here are two good examples of user-centric design:

1 A leading thinker on this topic, Donald Norman, praises the use of date and time in Microsoft's products:

Here, it is possible to specify dates any way you like: "November 23, 2015," "23 Nov. 15," or "11.23.15." … . As long as the program can decipher the date, time, or telephone number into a legal format, it is accepted. I hope the team that worked on this got bonuses and promotions.[48]

2 In 2020 *Ingenia* magazine reported on the development of an all-electric mini-digger by JCB. The company's Chief Innovation Officer, Tim Burnhope, explained how the new design was calibrated for customer acceptance:

It uses the same bodywork, but we designed it so the diesel engine could be replaced with the battery and motor. It's the same weight, so you can tow it on the same trailer. All the access points on the bodywork are identical, with a charging point where you normally put the diesel fuel in. To a customer it feels the same, and the only real difference to the operator is that the fuel gauge has been replaced with a battery level gauge.[49]

Two contemporary trends involve the design of so-called 'personalisation' and 'relationalisation' features. As described by Ming-Hui Huang and Roland Rust,[50] these approaches are now common practice within digital services. The authors define personalisation as "the process that uses a customer's information to provide an adaptive service offering". This can be offered either to individuals or to entire market segments. Some technologies feature so-called adaptive personalisation, involving dynamic, real-time adjustments in response to user behaviour. A personalisation strategy can only deliver benefits where users are heterogeneous. For homogenous market segments, standardisation is more appropriate.

Huang and Rust describe relationalisation as a design strategy for establishing deeper, longer-term relationships with users. Organisations, especially in the private sector, are increasingly interested in the development of "deep psychological connections with customers."[51] These more fulfilling and rewarding relationships are contrasted with conventional, short duration, transactional customer interactions. The business case for relational technologies may be evaluated against customer lifetime value (or CLV), a tool for quantifying the benefits of 'loyal', returning users.

The internet of things (IoT) and AI, combined with data science, are playing increasingly important roles in the emergence of both personalised and relational products. The so-called Fourth Industrial Revolution, or IR4.0, which includes the ability to mass-customise products, is associated with both of these concepts.

One of the most successful tools devised by engineers for conquering markets is the network. As a business concept, technological networks have been around for a long time. Railway and telephone networks were all thriving before 1900. In fact, any device (whether digital or non-digital) which is designed to be compatible with other devices is participating in a form of network, especially if communication or movement is facilitated between them.

Networks are highly successful generators of value. The reason for this success is explained by Metcalfe's Law, which describes how every member of a network values their membership more highly with the addition of each new member.[52] Imagine having the option of subscribing to one of two independent and technically isolated mobile networks; the first has one million subscribers and the second has two million. Which would be more valuable to you as a customer? Presumably the latter. Furthermore, having chosen to join the larger network, you now have an incentive to encourage others to join the same one, because their membership makes your network larger and even more useful to you. You would also welcome an opportunity for your network to integrate with the smaller network, partly because this adds even more users to your own, and also because it greatly simplifies the process of communicating with *all* mobile network subscribers through a single interface, i.e. your phone.

The key takeaway from Metcalfe's Law is that both the network controllers and the network users desire to grow the network, with the aim of overwhelming or absorbing all other networks. We saw in Chapter 4 how Great Western Railway (GWR), despite its superior broad gauge technology, was forced into adopting the rival 'standard gauge', following a Government edict aimed at maximising the benefits to passengers and freight carriers.[53] Some years later, telephone networks were also being formed into state-run monopolies, partly to reduce the power of private operators, but also to unify systems for the benefit of all users. The recent phenomenon of digital social networks is yet another manifestation of Metcalfe's Law in action.

In a network race, there can only be one ultimate winner. Although this is a desirable objective, many ambitious businesses have discovered, to their cost, that it's extremely difficult to build a dominant network. It generally involves substantial up-front investment in platform development while racing against competitors to capture most of the market. Once a tipping point has been reached, the users are expected to prefer consolidation onto the winning platform.

However, structural flaws in a network platform can prove insurmountable. It's interesting to note, for instance, that when a raft of sophisticated gaming platforms emerged around the year 2000, including PlayStation, Nintendo, and Xbox, none managed to dominate the sector. MIT's Michael Cusumano explains how the manufacturers kept the console prices relatively low in order to drive sales, hoping to generate revenues from complementary products (mainly games). But some buyers simply acquired multiple consoles due to their low prices. Furthermore, many of the popular games were available on more than one console, thereby breaking the proprietary hold of the manufacturers.[54] Two decades later, these brands continue to compete for customers, although online gaming communities (another type of network) offer new possibilities for capturing market share. We still await the emergence of a gaming monopoly in which most users choose to be on the largest platform in order to share the same experiences.

So, the relationship between technologies and their customers may be reinforced by a strategic focus upon product design, and the exploitation of network effects. In both cases, clever technical solutions may be needed in order to facilitate them. This presents opportunities for technologists and engineers to demonstrate their capacity for making high value, creative contributions to organisational success.

The strategic importance of customers, especially product or service users, can never be over-stated.

Box 8.3   STRATEGIC AND TACTICAL MOVES

Weakening the hold of monopolists

Some stakeholders are 'monopolists'. They acquire an unfair advantage due to an absence of competition. It's important to think strategically about managing your organisation's relationship with these monopoly stakeholders.

For example, a company controlling 90% of a particular raw material will have a monopoly over supply, and the owner of a proprietary technology platform, which you need to use, is in a similar position. Such suppliers present a substantial risk to the quality, consistency, and cost of resources.

Another type of monopolist is the holder of a patent underpinning a vital technology. They have the power to withhold access, or to set unreasonable licensing fees.

A customer can also be a monopolist. If your company is dependent upon a single or dominant buyer, they can abuse that position by making unfair demands upon you. For example, they may demand continued support for ageing designs[55] or the inclusion of specific functionality. Nevertheless, the loss of that customer would be commercially damaging.

It's also possible for employees to exercise monopoly powers. Trade unions and professional associations are a manifestation of this. A type of geographical monopoly can occur when particular skills are concentrated in one locality.

Technology strategies may be used to counter these stakeholder monopolies.

Diversification is one solution for mitigating the risks associated with concentrations of power. For example, suppliers are more easily diversified if standard components are used, or by selecting materials available from multiple sources.

The diversification of customers is primarily a marketing challenge, i.e. attracting additional customers or finding new markets. This should be covered by the business strategy, but technologists can proactively propose and design new products that meet the needs of alternative markets.

Employee monopolies can be mitigated by geographical diversification (i.e. using multiple sites), and pre-empting trade union formation by listening and responding to employee needs before relations deteriorate. Ensuring that rare skills are acquired by more personnel (via knowledge management, Box 7.2) also helps to reduce dependency upon a few key individuals. Outsourcing is a relatively blunt instrument to achieve the same result.

Patent and copyright monopolies (e.g. in software) can sometimes be avoided, although this may require substantial investment in R&D. One low-cost alternative is *open-source* solutions.

Overcoming monopolies involves a trade-off between the additional costs involved and the subsequent mitigation of risk. However, this may not always be true, as evidenced by the current popularity of low-cost, high-quality open-source products.

Collaborators

Organisations often collaborate in order to maximise the value to be gained from shared technology projects. These temporary collaborations are sometimes called an alliance, a consortium, or joint venture. The latter is perhaps the most formal arrangement, typically involving shared equity in a new firm.

The collaborating organisations will be some combination of two or more companies or public institutions. Such alliances may be formed at any stage of the technology lifecycle, from conception and design through to manufacturing, marketing, and even decommissioning. The particular purposes or advantages of a collaboration can include: sharing risks, such as those involving expensive research; establishing a set of shared industry standards; exchanging ideas and information; accessing specialist resources (e.g. tools, expertise) belonging to partners; and gaining detailed knowledge of another organisation prior to acquisition or merger.[56]

In order to illustrate the diversity of collaborative arrangements, let's look briefly at some examples. We've already seen (in Chapter 4) how JVC built an alliance of partners in order to launch the VHS recording system, ultimately triumphing over Sony's superior Betamax product. Sony's failed go-it-alone strategy contrasts with their much more successful, multi-decade R&D relationship with Philips, which began in the 1950s. This collaboration produced many impressive innovations, from audio cassettes to laser discs.[57]

Mobile telephony standards are the product of a multi-decade collaboration under the auspices of the European Telecomm-unications Standards Institute (ETSI). This has resulted in compre-hensive agreements leading to the deployment of four generations of mobile/cellular telephony: GSM, 3G, 4G, and 5G. Writing for *Ingenia* magazine, the UK's ETSI representative, Professor Stephen Temple, explains the four stages of cooperation leading to each new standard: 1) aligning the research goals; 2) aligning the technical standard; 3) harmonising the spectrum bands; 4) syn-chronising the network deployment. After stage 4) the collabora-tors break away in order to compete for customers. Temple explains that the collaboration addresses "a particular innovation market failure, where nothing can happen unless an entire industrial ecosystem acts together."[58]

Sometimes collaboration activities lead to such close working relationships between organisations that one party decides to acquire the other. This happened following many years of coopera-tion between Lockheed Martin and the General Dynamics' aircraft division, as they jointly pursued a US Government contract to build the F-22 Raptor. Having won the contract, Lockheed then acquired the GD aircraft division. Military researcher, David R. King, explained the context for this event:

> Changing levels of uncertainty impact how firms are organized. The experience of Lockheed ... demonstrates that under high uncertainty firms are likely to collaborate to lower risk. However, decreased uncertainty and maturing technology build pressures for firms to consolidate ... to internalize key resources within a single firm.[59]

In other words, in order to deliver the contract, Lockheed needed to create a unified operating unit, which inevitably required the absorption of its collaborator.

More recently, Rolls-Royce in the UK has assembled an engi-neering consortium with the aim of building a fleet of small modular reactors, or SMRs. The group consists of stakeholders from the private and public sectors, such as Atkins, Laing O'Rourke, Jacobs,

The National Nuclear Laboratory, and the Nuclear Advanced Manufacturing Research Centre. The novelty underpinning SMRs is their construction from factory-built components. These modules, comprising 90% of the plant, can be tested in the factory before transportation to site.[60] This new construction method involves substantial risk, partly because no single organisation possesses all the necessary expertise. Collaboration is therefore the only viable option. Perhaps, if the SMR programme proves successful, we will see mergers or acquisitions among the consortium members, as happened with the F-22 programme.

The pharmaceutical industry has become particularly synonymous with collaborations. By the early 21st century, the sector was struggling with the costs and uncertainties associated with lengthy drug development programmes (typically ten years or more). However, the emergence of personalised medicine and a host of ambitious biotech startups caused a re-think.[61] It was clear that the larger and more established companies needed access to the innovative R&D resources of smaller specialists. In return, the pharma giants could offer their commercialisation knowledge acquired over decades in the sector. Today, industry news bulletins are filled with stories of alliances between companies new and old, large and small, often joined by public research institutes or universities. The COVID-19 pandemic between 2020 and 2022 highlighted the effectiveness of bringing such organisations together in pursuit of high-priority goals.

Collaborations sometimes raise concerns. Internally, these might include the wisdom of sharing IP with third parties or the additional relationship management workload on senior staff.[62] Externally, it may be feared that relationships will evolve into illegal forms of collusion, such as price-fixing.

Nevertheless, the ability to foresee the need for collaboration, and to build an effective alliance for mutual benefit, has become a key strategic skill for technology leaders.

Financiers

The relationship between financial stakeholders and technologies is more nuanced and multi-faceted than one might imagine. There are many actors within this category of stakeholder including owners, taxpayers, and investors. In addition to these stakeholders, we also need to consider some of the financial mechanisms underpinning their behaviour.

Regardless of an organisation's size, its owners or funders will usually have some interest in the technologies associated with its products and processes. In smaller organisations, especially private companies, this interest is likely to be particularly strong, with the technologists and owners in daily contact. Sometimes the technologists will be the owners of the company. Contrast this situation with large corporations and major infrastructure projects, where the financiers will be geographically distant from the engineering activities and may have little personal interest in technologies. Grant and Jordan contrast the situation at Apple in its early days, where Steve Jobs and Steve Wozniak could agree strategies between them, with the situation in more mature companies where multiple layers of bureaucracy lie between owners and technology decision makers.[63]

Financiers are in a 'principal-agent' relationship (explained in Chapter 7), where the financiers are principals and the technology managers are agents. In the public sector, we might argue that taxpayers are the principals supplying the funds, whereas their agents are the leaders of major technology or engineering projects. In both the public and private sectors, the development of technology strategies is typically delegated to the agents, who report back to the principals in the form of published strategies (similar to those reviewed in Chapter 1).

Private sector owners have one overriding goal: obtaining a healthy return on investments. They therefore take a medium to long-term view on the contribution which technologies can make to the bottom line. This should, at least in theory, result in a constructive, forward-thinking, and patient relationship between technologists and owners.

The public sector, however, is often characterised by a form of short-termism attributed to the merry-go-round of politicians and policy changes. In democracies, these are often linked to electoral cycles of between four and six years. Technology is often perceived as the solution to society's problems, so new policies, such as those relating to de-carbonisation, public health, and transport infrastructure will often, to the delight of engineers, bring substantial investments in development projects. However, some activities, such as military procurement and government IT systems, are particularly susceptible to interference, scope creep, and sudden cancellations. Hence, the methods for procuring and delivering engineered solutions in the private and public sectors differ significantly. These differences run deep, and they undoubtedly influence the mindset of technology strategists in each sector.

Another relationship is that between speculative investment in the private sector and major technology transitions. For instance, during the so-called 'railway mania' of the mid-19th century, Brunel and his fellow engineers benefited greatly from the frenzy of fevered investing.[64] Similarly, in the 1990s software developers thrived during the 'dot com boom'. Today's investing frenzies support AI, blockchain developments, and digital currencies. Although speculative investing is often irrational and disreputable, it's probably true to say that investors seeking rapid and abnormally high returns are always the technologist's friend.

Financiers often adopt methodologies that can influence technology strategy. For example, portfolio investing (described in Chapter 7) encourages technologists to pursue novel ideas in search of substantial returns. Project failures are viewed as an occupational hazard for such investors. However, this freedom to take risks is often extinguished when investors and business leaders use Net Present Value (NPV) as their guide to decision making. NPV uses discounted cash flow analysis to quantify the expected future outcomes from major investment projects. According to MIT's James Utterback, discounting is "a method that favours modest near-term rewards of high probability to extravagant long-term possibilities of high uncertainty." In other words, a focus upon NPV favours safer investments with more reliable outcomes, in contrast with the more speculative investments associated with portfolio management. The NPV mindset predominates in publicly listed companies because of shareholder demands for a steady flow of favourable earnings.[65]

It's reasonable to assume, therefore, that technology strategies are of great interest to all financial stakeholders. However, as I found during my search for published strategy documents (in Chapter 1), very few are available for scrutiny, and most of these are issued by non-profit organisations. For investors in the private sector, information about current strategic thinking is very limited.

One exception was a Toshiba presentation from 2018. This document gave a surprising amount of detail about R&D and product development intentions for the next five-year period.[66] It was information that would clearly be of interest to competitors, so why was it shared online? Could this openness about Toshiba's technological future have been aimed at informing and enthusing private investors? That seems the most likely explanation. Perhaps other companies should take note.

Indirect stakeholders

Many stakeholders have a less formal, non-contractual relationship with technologies and products. In Figure 8.1, these are shown to be a mixture of public and private organisations, along with some less clearly defined entities, such as neighbours, the natural environment, and the media. Let's briefly look at the significance of these indirect stakeholders for technology strategists.

Governments and regulators

Governments clearly 'affect', and are 'affected by', the technology strategies of organisations within their jurisdictions. Governments affect strategy by the following means: legislation and the use of regulations; industrial and research policies; the commissioning of major projects; the promotion of international trade; plus various forms of financial support, including innovation grants and favourable loans. Some of these topics have already been addressed. For instance, taxpayer financing was mentioned earlier, and Chapter 3 discussed the nature of industrial policy.

Governments are affected by the technology strategies of organisations in various ways, but especially by the taxes generated via commercial success. It's for these reasons that governments feel obliged to support, protect, and regulate the more profitable industries. Van der Poel and Royakkers of TU Delft describe a regulation as:

> A legal tool that can forbid the development, production, or use of certain technological products, but more often it formulates a set of the boundary conditions for the design, production, and use of technologies.[67]

In fact, the strong performance of the UK pharmaceutical sector has been attributed to a history of successful regulatory oversight, including the country's approval regime for new drugs.[68]

Therefore, technology strategists should not only monitor government behaviour closely, but also engage with its representatives in order to lobby for favourable actions and policies.

It's worth noting that lobbying contributed to the birth of the Industrial Revolution. The successful partnership between Matthew Boulton and James Watt was only made possible by Watt's personal lobbying of Parliament, in 1775, in order to prevent his steam engine patent from expiring before it could be commercialised. He was granted another 25 years.[69] Had Watt failed, that particular episode in history would have taken a very different path.

Standards organisations

Today, it's difficult to perform any technological task without encountering a set of industry-wide, national, or international standards – project management standards, electrical standards, metrology standards, safety standards, and so on.

Responsibility for defining these usually rests with independent standards organisations. We encountered a set of international standards earlier, in relation to the mobile telephony agreements for 4G, 5G, etc. Meanwhile, the International Organization for Standardization (or ISO, based in Switzerland) is responsible for thousands more that are globally recognised.

So what exactly is a standard? According to Grant and Jordan, a technical standard is "a format, an interface or a system that allows interoperability."[70] But apart from ensuring interoperability (i.e. compatibility), standards also establish minimum levels of quality in design, functionality, and performance. Standards help to build confidence and trust among parties.

Apart from certain government regulations relating, for example, to road safety and construction quality, most standards are not enforceable in law. However, it is possible to face opposition from industry rivals, particularly when attempting to create a favourable standard. Indeed, one of the advantages to being a 'first mover' or early leader in any sector is the ability to determine proprietary standards which others must then follow for compatibility. Examples include the Sony/Philips CD-ROM, ARM Holdings' microprocessor architecture, and the Adobe Portable Document Format (PDF).[71]

It is usually possible to engage directly with independent standards organisations, and this might be a sensible course of action. Participation in the development of standards enhances an organisation's ability to shape the environment it is operating within. Indeed, a failure to influence standards could have detrimental long-term consequences.

Within most organisations, there is probably an acceptance that applicable standards should always be adhered to. However, when a decision is made to lead the development of a new standard, or to deliberately ignore an existing standard, that choice is clearly of strategic significance.

Industry organisations

Of the many indirect stakeholders, perhaps the least strategically important are the industrial and professional bodies which represent particular sectors. Some of these institutions also oversee standards for the sector, but most are established for the purposes of sharing ideas, agreeing industry-wide policies, assisting with sector recruitment, promoting values, and lobbying political decision makers.

Industry associations are typically organised at a national level. There are thousands of examples worldwide. Picking one at random, the Canadian Association of Recycling Industries (CARI) engages in a broad range of activities on behalf of its eponymous sector. As with most trade and industry associations, CARI's work is funded largely through membership fees.[72]

A small number of industry organisations adopt an international profile. For instance, founded in 1987 and based in Frankfurt, the International Federation of Robotics (IFR) brings together engineering firms, research institutes, and other interested parties with the aim of sharing data, fostering partnerships, influencing policy makers, and so on.[73] It seems likely that we will see a growth of these international associations as the world becomes 'smaller' through globalisation.

Membership of a trade association is unlikely to deliver any short-term strategic gains. However, engagement in a cross-sector alliance, while aiming to strengthen the broader operational environment, should prove beneficial in the longer-term.

Competitors

There is no doubt that companies can *affect, or be affected by*, their competitors. Perhaps surprisingly, this means that our competitors are also our stakeholders.

For example, there might be circumstances when we want to establish a working relationship with one or more of our rivals. We saw earlier how standards institutions, such as ETSI, rely upon the participation of competing telecoms companies in order to develop new generations of mobile telephony. We have also noted the work of industrial organisations and trade associations – informal networks of competitors seeking to promote their own sectors.

Another form of loose cooperation occurs when competitors within a single industry cluster together geographically. These 'agglomerations' (as economists call them) usually emerge without any formal planning. Each of the competitors within a cluster clearly expects to gain something from the informal arrangement. This is how Westwick explains the concentration of aircraft manufacturers in southern California after WW2, including Douglas, Lockheed, Northrop, Hughes, and others:

> The firms in the area could tap a network of close tolerance machine shops, electronics fabricators, and other specialized suppliers, along with a specialized, skilled workforce. Engineers could bounce from firm to firm, accumulating experience and spreading ideas.[74]

Today, most developed nations have one or more significant industrial or technology clusters, from Finland's "pharmacluster"[75] to the hugely influential Silicon Valley. See Chapter 7 for a brief analysis of this topic in Box 7.1 *Locate in a cluster OR Locate independently?*

The former Chair of Royal Dutch Shell, Henri Deterding, believed in the importance of maintaining cordial working relationships with competitors. He wrote in his memoirs that, "To crush a rival is to make an enemy."[76] It's always worth remembering that those you meet on the way up, you may have to pass on the way down. It feels counterintuitive, but it really is possible to hug your competitors while embracing competition.

Complementors

In Chapter 6 we saw that technologies or products may be described as complementary if a change in the demand for one correlates with a change in demand for the other. Examples of complementary products include AA batteries and portable electronic gadgets, or domestic freezers and frozen food. There is a mutual dependence based on positive reinforcement. It therefore follows that a weakening or loss of complementarity could undermine a technology's prospects.

The technology owner often has limited control over complementarity, because complementary goods and services are typically the responsibility of independent producers. These complementors must therefore be regarded as important stakeholders.

Thomas Edison recognised the importance of complementary products when developing his electricity distribution networks in the late 19th century. He wanted to be involved with most components of the electrical ecosystem, including cabling, light fittings, and bulbs, often resorting to acquisition of the complementors.[77]

However, although it's desirable to have a thriving complementary ecosystem, it isn't always necessary to take ownership of the complementors. For example, smartphone apps complement smartphones, but Apple has no desire to own the app producers. There's a healthy and highly competitive market in app development, for which Apple merely acts as the quality controller and gatekeeper.

There are many ways for a producer to encourage and support its complementors. For instance, if technical compatibility is important, the specifications for doing this will need to be published. These guidelines must not be overly complex, otherwise potential complementors might prefer to support a competitor.

Backward compatibility will also be important, especially if complementors have invested in products compatible with older versions of your technology. For example, in the 1980s when portable stereo 'boom boxes' were being re-designed to support the emerging compact disc technology, new models often retained the older cassette tape functionality. They offered both a tape drive *and* a CD drive. This may be explained, in part, because many CD producers were still heavily invested in the supply of taped music, so relationships would have been strained if manufacturers (such as Hitachi and Sony) had immediately abandoned tape drives. Although the addition of CD players caused sound systems to become bulkier and more expensive, all parties, including buyers, had something to gain from this compromise.

Another way to support complementors and the wider technology ecosystem is to publish product roadmaps. These simple tools illustrate the planned longevity of existing product versions and provide advance notification of forthcoming versions or even new products. In Chapter 1, the technology strategies of 14 organisations were reviewed. Of these, three contained roadmaps. Patrick van der Duin's book, *Foresight in Organizations* (2016), contains a useful analysis of roadmaps by Ben Römgens.[78]

Given the symbiotic nature of complementarity, successful complementors should probably be invited to participate in the development of your organisation's technology strategy. This would enable a constructive exchange of information, insights, and ideas for future product development. It's likely that many corporations already do this.

Do you have complementors? If so, do you know who they are? Do you talk to them?

Neighbours

It's easy to forget that the people who live and work in adjacent buildings and nearby communities are stakeholders with considerable influence over the success of an organisation and its technologies.

Local communities are home to most of its workers, and they ensure that basic infrastructure, such as access roads and waste removal services are functioning well. Neighbours run the local authorities and councils, they often have a vote, and they can support or object to planning applications. Neighbours can be your friends or your enemies. Don't ignore them.

There are many good reasons for ensuring that community relations are strong and mutually supportive. Consider, for a moment, some of the common sources of discord. Does your site pollute water sources, emit noise, or smell? Does it devalue neighbouring properties? Do vehicle movements damage road surfaces? Are your buildings and other facilities an eyesore? Do employees spend the company's money in local businesses, or is everything trucked in?

You may remember the description of boundary-less socio-technical systems in Chapter 2. These required decision makers to use more inclusive 'systems thinking'. Community impact is one aspect of this.

There are many ways to ensure satisfactory community relations; too many to mention here. However, a simple set of rules or policies may not be enough, especially for multi-site or international operations. Chemical engineer John Turnbull writes, "Good engineers know that what works in Japan will not be the same as what works in Arizona and respond accordingly."[79]

These ideas aren't new. Shell's historian, Stephen Howarth, has described various ways that the Anglo-Dutch corporation engaged with local communities during a century of operations. In the 1930s, waste methane from a Shell plant in Venezuela was piped free of charge to residents in Maracaibo for heating and lighting,[80] and more recently, waste heat from Shell refineries in France and Sweden has been used for neighbourhood domestic heating schemes.[81]

For a contemporary example of successful community engagement, *Ingenia* magazine describes the development of a large sewage treatment facility at Peacehaven, on England's south coast. The developer, Southern Water and partners, have successfully navigated their way through various technical, social, and political challenges, including engaging with opposition groups and satisfying local planners. Some of the mitigations involved careful architecting and landscaping of the site, educational and archaeological initiatives, and the employment of apprentices.[82]

Technologists and engineers are well placed to advise their leadership teams on the strategic benefits of community engagement, because they understand both the impacts of their work and the potential mitigations. Engineers can propose innovative solutions for ensuring that neighbours become friends and constructive collaborators.

The natural environment

We often think of stakeholders as people or organisations, but an argument can be made for including non-sentient entities. For example, the natural environment both *affects and is affected by* technology. It supplies inputs of all kinds to technological systems and receives outputs in various forms, including pollution. The natural environment is therefore a stakeholder.

The authors of *Ethics, Technology and Engineering* (2011), van der Poel and Royakkers, contrast the so-called *anthropocentric* perspective of the natural environment, in which nature is subservient to human needs, with the *biocentric* view, which sees an "intrinsic value" in nature.[83] The contemporary popularity of biocentrism has resulted in nature being granted 'legal personality' in certain circumstances. In other words, the law has obligations to protect the environment.

Some readers may be sceptical towards biocentrism, but it would be unwise to ignore its implications for technology strategy. Many organisations are now responding proactively.

Mark Fletcher, head of Arup's Global Water Business, offers some advice for engineers: "Design needs to embrace a greater understanding of our natural systems, natural processes, and their interdependencies with other systems" including transport, energy, and food. It's important to "design with nature" and adopt the systemic perspective of regenerative design, enabling a circular economy.[84]

Martin Massey, a climate change leader in the UK's Institute for Risk Management, has written about corporate environmental policies in the context of enterprise risk. One area of concern is staff recruitment and retention, because some companies are failing to align with the values of current and future employees. Younger people are often attracted to environmentally-friendly operations, and expect to see full compliance with environmental regulations.[85]

Massey provides a list of actions which organisations can take today in order to mitigate the enterprise risks associated with climate change. These include:

- Reducing energy consumption (e.g. more efficient machinery, LED lighting).
- Reducing material waste in production processes (e.g. better use of by-products).
- Minimising packaging.
- Contracting with renewable energy suppliers.
- Introducing electric vehicle (EV) fleets.
- Encouraging EV use by personnel (e.g. by offering charging points).
- Encouraging working from home.[86]

In some respects, the natural environment is the largest and most complex of all organisational stakeholders, and some expertise is required to manage this relationship effectively. For those companies that get it wrong, there could be repercussions from neighbours, regulators, employees, customers, investors, and, above all, from competitors with a head start.

The media

There is one more stakeholder group to be considered. The 'media' are mass-market communicators who reach their audiences via TV, radio, publishing, and the internet. Your organisation's technologies, products, and projects will occasionally invite their attention. The consequences of this will depend upon how other stakeholders choose to react.

As a source of ideas and information, the media are invaluable to us. How else would we learn about innovations in faraway places, political involvement in regulatory frameworks, or ground-breaking research results and discoveries?

Let's also consider how our technology strategies are communicated. As we saw in Chapter 1, documented strategies are rarely made publicly available. This is unfortunate, because transparency would be helpful for many stakeholders, notably investors, collaborators, complementors, and future employees. Do we need to be so shy about sharing our strategies? If not, and we choose to publish, the media are there to help us.

Stakeholder partnerships

The way we choose to draw our 'system' boundaries will determine which entities become our stakeholders and the nature of our relationships with them.

We must not forget the lessons from Chapter 5, which viewed the operating environment as a complex adaptive system (CAS). Each actor within our stakeholder network is adapting to the actions of other actors. Moreover, each stakeholder has independent motives, and these influence its own strategies.

The key to navigating this complexity is via proactive stakeholder relations, recognising that each of our stakeholders is a potential partner in the business of generating and sharing value. So, when developing technology strategies, it's vital to know: 1) who those stakeholders are; 2) how they can help us; and 3) how we can help them.

Glossary for this chapter (Items in bold are also defined in the same table)

beneficiary	The recipient of a technology's value, e.g. the **user**, or an investor.
buyer	Typically a person or organisation that purchases access to a technology, e.g. by owning or leasing.

(Continued)

(Continued)

captive centre	A workplace, established in a distant location but staffed mainly by **employees**, aiming to capture value from a regional cluster of knowledge or expertise.
collaborator	Any organisation participating in a cooperative arrangement, e.g. an alliance, consortium, or joint venture.
competitor	A rival operator, typically producing similar or substitute products. There may be circumstances when it is rational to cooperate with competitors.
complementor	An independent organisation responsible for the production of complementary goods and services.
customer	A **downstream** recipient of technology outputs. Customers may be **buyers** or **users** and can include machines or animals.
diversification	A risk mitigation tactic involving the deliberate introduction of variation and choice among **suppliers** and **customers**. Product ranges can also be diversified in order to appeal to new market segments. Contrast with **diversity**.
diversity	A recruitment policy aimed at capturing a broader range of life experiences, economic backgrounds, and cultural knowledge. Contrast with **diversification**.
downstream	Any later step in the value chain.
employees	Workers directly contracted to an organisation. These are the most influential of all **stakeholder** groups, mainly because of their involvement in every stage of the technology lifecycle. Contrast employees with **outsourced** workers, who are **suppliers**.
financier	An investor, owner, or provider of funds, such as grants and subsidies.
government	The executive arm of the state. The government is a **stakeholder** in technologies due to its role in legislation and **regulatory** action. It also receives taxation revenues derived from technological goods and services.
industry organisation	An institution associated with a specific industrial sector, established for the purposes of sharing ideas, agreeing sector-wide policies, promoting recruitment, defining values, and lobbying **governments**. Sometimes called a trade association.
integration	The process of acquiring and merging an external **stakeholder**. Vertical integration involves the acquisition and absorption of **suppliers** or **customers**. Horizontal integration merges organisations at the same stage of production, e.g. **competitors** or **complementors**.
make or buy?	A classic decision-making dilemma concerning the most appropriate way to gain access to an asset or resource. Do we a) design and build it internally, or b) purchase it?

(Continued)

media	Mass-market communicators who reach their audiences via TV, radio, publishing, and the internet. The media can be both friend and foe. Most **stakeholders** are influenced by it.
Metcalfe's Law	The value of a **network** grows in proportion to the square of the number of participants. It explains the tendency towards exponential network growth.
monopolist	A **stakeholder** dominating control over key resources or markets. Monopolists may be **suppliers**, **employees**, or **customers**.
natural environment	All non-artificial contents of the Earth, both above and below the surface.
nearshoring	The use of **outsourced** teams based on the same continent, but in a different country, often to save costs.
neighbours	People and organisations in geographical proximity to an engineering activity. The local community.
network	Three or more interconnected nodes facilitating communication or movement between them. Many networks grow exponentially according to **Metcalfe's Law**.
offshoring	The use of **outsourced** teams based on a different continent, often to save costs.
onshoring	The use of **outsourced** teams based in the same country.
outsourcing	Swapping an internal service or function for an external one. This swap may involve a physical transfer of people and other assets, or it could be a straight switch to an external **supplier** combined with a dismantling of the internal function.
regulator	An arm of **government** that, according to van der Poel and Royakkers, "formulates a set of the boundary conditions for the design, production, and use of technologies." These conditions are known as regulations.
skills matrix	A tool for recording and managing the competences of **employees** and their work groups.
stakeholder	A technology stakeholder is any entity with the capacity for affecting, being affected by, or perceiving an effect from, the existence of a technology.
standard	According to Grant and Jordan, a technical standard is "a format, an interface or a system that allows interoperability." Standards also establish minimum levels of quality in design, functionality, and performance. They help to build confidence and trust among interested parties. Examples: electrical standards, metrology standards.
standards organisation	An independent body responsible for defining either industry-wide, national, or international technology **standards.**
supplier	An **upstream** provider of technology inputs. Suppliers may be independent organisations or internal support functions.

(Continued)

(Continued)

systems integrator	An organisation that creates value by coordinating and managing independent **stakeholders**, especially **suppliers**. NASA is a good example of a systems integrator, because it **outsources** the production of most of its key resources.
trade association	See **industry organisation**.
upstream	Any earlier step in the value chain.
user	The entity, typically a person, who directly operates or interacts with a technology.
user-centred design	A design methodology focusing upon the **user** experience. Sometimes called human-centred design, inclusive design, or universal design.

Notes

1 'Sir Frederick Page' [obituary], *Daily Telegraph*, 7 June 2005. Available at https://www.telegraph.co.uk/news/obituaries/1491503/Sir-Frederick-Page.html (Accessed: 13 November 2019).
2 Cuppen, E. (2016) 'Stakeholder Analysis' in van der Duin, P. (ed.) *Foresight in Organizations*. Abingdon: Routledge. 208.
3 *Concise Oxford English Dictionary*. 10th edn. (2002). Oxford: OUP. 1397.
4 Massey, M. (2022) *Climate Change Enterprise Risk Management*. London (UK): Kogan Page. 109.
5 Freeman, R.E., Harrison, J.S. and Wicks, A.C. (2007) *Managing for Stakeholders*. New Haven: Yale University Press. 6–8.
6 Grant, R.M. and Jordan, J. (2015) *Foundations of Strategy*. Chichester: Wiley. 19–20.
7 Cuppen, *Foresight in Organizations*. 211–212.
8 Baird, J.L. (2004) *Television and Me*. Edinburgh: Mercat. 91.
9 Kenward, M. (2014) 'His Marvellous Materials'. *Ingenia*, Issue 61, 43–47.
10 Kenward, M. (2017) 'Forging Links Between Academia and Industry'. *Ingenia*, Issue 70, 40–44.
11 Morita, A. (1987) *Made in Japan*. London: Collins. 166.
12 Boulton, J.G., Allen, P.M. and Bowman, C. (2015) *Embracing Complexity*. Oxford: OUP. 161.
13 Morita, *Made in Japan*. 170.
14 Afuah, A. (2003) *Innovation Management*. New York: OUP. 104.
15 Grant and Jordan, *Foundations of Strategy*. 219.
16 Tobin, J. (2003) *To Conquer the Air*. New York: Free Press. 362.
17 Rumelt, R. (2017) *Good Strategy, Bad Strategy*. London: Profile Books. 242.
18 Morita. 169.
19 Cross, N. (2008) *Engineering Design Methods: Strategies for Product Design*. Chichester: Wiley. 206.
20 Dyson, J. (2011) *Against the Odds: An Autobiography*. Andover: Cengage Learning. 256–257.
21 Morita. 185–186.
22 High, P.A. (2014) *Implementing World Class IT Strategy*. San Francisco: Wiley. 94–95.

23 Cadle, J., Paul, D. and Turner P. (2014) *Business Analysis Techniques*. Swindon: BCS. 1.
24 Hewitt, E. (2018) *Technology Strategy Patterns*. Sebastopol, CA: O'Reilly. 11.
25 High, *Implementing World Class IT Strategy*. 18.
26 Tiwana, A. (2017) *IT Strategy for Non-IT Managers: Becoming an Engaged Contributor to Corporate IT Decisions*. Cambridge, MA: The MIT Press. 185.
27 Kenward, M. (2019) 'Structures for a Sustainable Society'. *Ingenia*, Issue 80, 38–42.
28 Flin, R., O'Connor, P. and Crichton, M. (2008) *Safety at the Sharp End: A Guide to Non-Technical Skills*. Farnham: Ashgate. 10.
29 Utterback, J.M. (1994) *Mastering the Dynamics of Innovation*. Harvard: HBS Press. 82–91.
30 Grant and Jordan, *Foundations of Strategy*. 318–319.
31 Johnson, D. (2020) *Engineering Ethics*. New Haven: YUP. 173.
32 Kenward, M. (2020) 'Teams that count'. *Ingenia*, Issue 84, 38–42.
33 Kenward, M. (2014) 'His Marvellous Materials'. *Ingenia*, Issue 61, 43–47.
34 Boulton, Allen and Bowman, *Embracing Complexity*. 150.
35 Grant and Jordan. 216.
36 Rasiel, E.M. and Friga, P.N. (2001) *The McKinsey Mind*. New York: McGraw-Hill. 136.
37 Rothschild, W.E. (2007) *The Secret to GE's Success*. New York: McGraw-Hill. 24–25.
38 Grant and Jordan. 217.
39 Hewitt, *Technology Strategy Patterns*. 210.
40 Cadle, Paul and Turner, *Business Analysis Techniques*. 6–8.
41 Rothschild, *The Secret to GE's Success*. 6–7.
42 Pellegrini, C.B. (2017) *Pirelli Technology and Passion 1872-2017*. London: Third Millenium. 42–54.
43 Grant and Jordan. 252.
44 McDougall, W.A. (1997) *The Heavens and the Earth*. Baltimore: Johns Hopkins University Press. 196.
45 Grant and Jordan. 256.
46 van de Poel, I. and Royakkers, L. (2011) *Ethics, Technology and Engineering: An Introduction*. Chichester: Wiley. 174–175.
47 International Organization for Standardization, 'ISO 9241-210:2019 *Ergonomics of human-system interaction – Part 210: Human-centred design for interactive systems*'. Available at: https://www.iso.org/standard/77520.html (Accessed: 11 January 2023).
48 Norman, D.A. (2013) *The Design of Everyday Things*. Cambridge (MA): MIT Press.
49 Cumins, N. (2020) 'Groundbreaking digging'. *Ingenia*, Issue 84, 14–18.
50 Huang, M. and Rust, R.T. (2017) 'Technology-Driven Service Strategy'. *Journal of the Academy of Marketing Science*, Vol. 45, Issue 6, 906–924.
51 Huang and Rust, *Journal of the Academy of Marketing Science*.
52 Ries, E. (2011) *The Lean Startup*. London, UK: Penguin. 39.
53 Buchanan, A. (2006) *Brunel*. London: Continuum. 78.
54 Cusumano, M. (2010) 'Technology Strategy and Management: The Evolution of Platform Thinking'. *Communications of the ACM*, Vol. 53, Issue 1, 32–34. Available at https://mitsloan.mit.edu/shared/ods/documents?PublicationDocumentID=5976 (Accessed: 01 February 2023).
55 Utterback, *Mastering the Dynamics of Innovation*. 196–197.
56 King, D.R. (2006) 'Implications of Uncertainty on Firm Outsourcing Decisions'. *Human Systems Management*, Vol. 25, 115–125.

57 Morita. 67.
58 Temple, S. (2021) 'How to Make a Mobile Technology Revolution'. *Ingenia*, Issue 87, 30–33.
59 King, 'Implications of Uncertainty on Firm Outsourcing Decisions'.
60 Macfarlane-Smith, S. and Stein, P. (2021) 'Nuclear Designs on a Low-Carbon Future'. *Ingenia*, Issue 87, 10–14.
61 National Centre for Universities and Business (NCUB) (2012) *Enhancing Collaboration, Creating Value: Business Interaction with the UK Research Base in Four Sectors*, available at https://www.ncub.co.uk/insight/enhancing-collaboration-creating-value-business-interaction-with-the-uk-research-base-in-four-sectors/ (Accessed: 05 October 2022).
62 Braun, E. (1998) *Technology in Context*. London: Routledge. 19.
63 Grant and Jordan. 314.
64 Basalla, G. (1988) *The Evolution of Technology*. Cambridge (UK): CUP. 177–181.
65 Utterback. 226.
66 Toshiba Corporation (2018) *Toshiba's Technology Strategy*, available at https://www.toshiba.co.jp/about/ir/en/pr/pdf/tpr20181122e_1.pdf (Accessed: 01 August 2019).
67 van de Poel and Royakkers, *Ethics, Technology and Engineering*. 259.
68 Afuah, *Innovation Management*. 319–320.
69 Derry, T.K. and Williams, T.I. (1961) *A Short History of Technology*. London (UK): OUP. 322–323.
70 Grant and Jordan. 211.
71 Grant and Jordan. 210.
72 Canadian Association of Recycling Industries (CARI) Available at https://cari-acir.org/ (Accessed: 19 January 2023).
73 International Federation of Robotics (IFR). Available at https://ifr.org/ (Accessed: 19 January 2023).
74 Westwick, P. (2020) *Stealth: The Secret Contest to Invent Invisible Aircraft*. New York: OUP. 14.
75 Brännback, M. and Renko, M. (2002) 'Technological and Strategic Change in the Finnish Pharmaceutical Industry: The Emergence of a Cluster'. *Pharmaceuticals Policy and Law*, Vol. 5, 27–40.
76 Howarth, S. (1997) *A Century in Oil: the "Shell" Transport and Trading Company 1897–1997*. London: Weidenfeld & Nicolson. 77.
77 Rothschild. 6–7.
78 Römgens, B. (2016) 'Roadmapping' in van der Duin, P. (ed.) *Foresight in Organizations*. Abingdon: Routledge. 145–168.
79 Turnbull, J. (2010) 'The Context and Nature of Engineering Design'. *Philosophy of Engineering*, Vol. 1. Royal Academy of Engineering, London, June 2010. Available at: https://www.raeng.org.uk/publications/reports/philosophy-of-engineering-volume-1, 30–34.
80 Howarth, *A Century in Oil*. 170.
81 Howarth. 339.
82 Kenward, M. (2014) 'Bringing Cleaner Seas to Sussex'. *Ingenia*, Issue 60, 38–42.
83 van de Poel and Royakkers. 280.
84 Fletcher, M. (2021) 'Rethinking the Future through Design'. *Ingenia*, Issue 87, 8–9.
85 Massey, *Climate Change Enterprise Risk Management*. 112.
86 Massey. 152 and 349.

9 Do it right!

Conflicting values in a complex world

This chapter presents

- An exploration of the ethics underlying many strategic decisions.

This chapter establishes

- The key differences between major ethical frameworks.
- A practical method for 'processing' and resolving ethical dilemmas.

There's a right way and a wrong way to engineer. The right way usually leads to satisfied clients, success, and recognition. The wrong way leads to failure, unpaid invoices, and sometimes death.

In professional engineering, being 'right' requires training, diligence, and hard-work. Indeed, these three attributes might be viewed as the cornerstones of professionalism. Surely, by committing to these principles an engineer can do no wrong.

Is that true? After a moment's reflection, this interpretation of 'right' and 'wrong' in engineering appears to be missing something, and that 'something' is of fundamental importance.

In the 1990s I lived a short walk from Staveley Road in Chiswick, west London. It's a quiet residential street of neat, modest homes, built around 1930. Like many west London streets, it's lined with trees. Those on Staveley Road are noticeably smaller and less aged. Outside number five Staveley Road is a small monument. It commemorates an event in September 1944 when a pioneering example of high-quality engineering arrived at its destination after a record-breaking 320-kilometre journey through near-space, across the North Sea. The rocket, a V2, had been launched from The Hague in the direction of London. Without warning or sound it arrived outside number five, killing and injuring dozens of local residents, including three-year-old Rosemary Clarke.[1]

The development team of V2 engineers would have been thrilled at the success of their multi-year, ground-breaking project to build machines capable of reaching space and delivering payloads to

DOI: 10.4324/9781003472919-11

their destinations using advanced navigation. One of those celebrating, team leader Werner von Braun, would later become a household name as lead engineer for the Apollo Moon missions.

The question we might ask is this: Did the end justify the means? Was it necessary for the residents of Staveley Road to be sacrificed in order that humanity could 'slip the surly bonds of earth', walk on the Moon, explore the Solar System, and, most recently, discover exoplanets bearing chemical signs of life?

Can we also make the argument that von Braun and his team were justified in using their engineering education in a way that prevented Rosemary Clarke from ever becoming an engineer herself? Were they duty-bound to use their professionalism for more constructive purposes? Was the responsibility of the engineering team limited to the technology itself, or did they share responsibility with military strategists for the *indiscriminate* way that the rockets were eventually used? In other words, should we judge engineers purely by the virtues of their professional skills, or should we also judge them by the consequences of their work?

These are just a sample of the many fundamental questions raised by the subject of this chapter: engineering ethics. At this stage, it's important not to be too judgemental. Establishing the rights and wrongs of professional behaviour requires careful consideration of facts, contexts, motives, awareness, and much, much more.

Ethics and strategy

Professional technologists and engineers will (one hopes) always want to choose the right way over the wrong way, but how can they know which is which? They need guidance, and the source of this guidance is called *ethics*.

There is a popular misconception that ethics is simply shorthand for things like generosity of spirit, abiding by the law, non-violence, and so on, but that's not strictly correct. **Ethics is the discipline of determining actions that are morally right from those that are morally wrong in any given context.** Consequently, it's possible to conceive of situations in which the ethically 'right' thing to do in a particular context might involve the withdrawal of generosity, flouting the law, or even an act of violence.

For example, among criminals, there are ethical codes involving the sharing of spoils, proportional punishment, and respect for territory. A well-known criminal ethic is the refusal to 'squeal' on fellow criminals. You don't have to be nice to be ethical. An intelligent gangster is probably more ethically reflective than the average nurse or monk.

Similarly, in business, there are many ethical judgements about right and wrong which have no basis in formal codes of conduct, religious commandments, or the law. For instance, it might be viewed as unethical for a large company to make egregious demands upon a small supplier, or for invoice payments to be delayed without good reason.

Whichever context we choose to examine, ethics will intrude upon decision making. So, how might ethics influence technology strategy?

Box 9.1 What is morality?

Morality is one of those concepts which we might claim to understand, but then struggle to define. Indeed it seems that many writers are content to discuss "morals" and "morality" without attempting to explain the meaning of those terms. There is good reason for that, because it's not easy to do.

Morality is generally associated with principles and opinions. For example, the Concise Oxford English Dictionary defines morality as "principles concerning the distinction between right and wrong or good and bad behaviour."[2]

The authors of Ethics, Technology and Engineering (2011), Ibo van de Poel and Lambèr Royakkers, refer instead to opinions. They explain that morality is "The totality of opinions, decisions, and actions with which people express, individually or collectively, what they think is good or right."[3] Accordingly, "Moral values help us determine which goals or states of affairs are worth striving for in life, to lead a good life or to realize a just society."[4]

Hence, the concept we know as ethics is, in the view of van de Poel and Royakkers, "The systematic reflection on morality."[5]

The key word here is "systematic". So, whereas morality is a relatively intangible concept based on principles and opinions, ethics is more akin to processes, frameworks, and mechanisms. We might say that ethics is morality engineered.

Let's begin with some hypothetical events. Would you disapprove of the actions taken in these examples?

The truth, but not the whole truth: An engineering team is drafting a formal proposal in support of an exciting infrastructure project. It contains only objective facts, but they choose to exclude any 'inconvenient' data which might undermine the case for funding it.

Employment practices: Engineering vacancies are being filled. It has been decided to use this as an opportunity to redress imbalances within the workforce, including the under-representation of particular demographic groups. In some cases, more experienced or better qualified people will be overlooked.

Design limitations: A development team has been asked to deliver a quick prototype. In order to achieve this, zero time is devoted to ensuring accessibility for users with physical impairments.

Product choices: In selecting machinery for a new plant, the buyers focus only upon price and reliability. They ignore information about the toxicity of by-products and the design of safety features.

De-regulation: A company has been vehemently opposed, over many years, to the introduction of a new technical regulation. It is now legally enforceable. In defiance, the management decides to ignore the regulation and accept any fines that might subsequently be imposed.

Medical progress: A pharmaceutical R&D department has discovered a low-cost 'wonder drug' capable of rapidly suppressing a common disease with few side-effects. However, this would cannibalise a recently introduced and highly profitable product, requiring daily medication for life. A decision is made to suppress knowledge of the new discovery, but only until the older product has repaid its original development costs.

Within the law: A new manufacturing process consumes large volumes of water and creates very unpleasant odours. A planning application has been rejected. A site is then chosen in a poorly developed country where the government has promised not to enforce environmental controls in return for the economic benefits, which include the creation of many jobs, thereby alleviating poverty in local communities.

Intelligent machines: An autonomous truck is being 'trained' for different accident scenarios. It is smart enough to understand the nature of its load. When transporting crates of rare 17th-century Chinese porcelain to an exhibition, a pedestrian falls into the road. Avoiding the pedestrian will cause the vehicle to strike a concrete pillar, likely destroying its cargo. It is decided that, in this scenario, the truck should not deviate from its path.

When exploring ethics through the use of hypotheticals, there are usually no unequivocally right or wrong decisions. Various supporting arguments can be constructed, though often hotly contested. However, it's *impossible* to avoid making decisions. This is because **a decision to postpone a decision is still a decision.** All actions and inactions have consequences.

In situations like these, we need some form of ethical framework to help us. The most important characteristic of such a framework is that it produces guidance, or even answers, which we will feel comfortable supporting and implementing. At the end of this chapter, a methodology for confident ethical decision making will be presented.

Box 9.2 STRATEGIC AND TACTICAL MOVES

Ethical by design, ethical by default

Article 25 of the European Union's *General Data Protection Regulation* (GDPR) mandates data privacy "by design and by default".

The EU wants digital products to be designed with privacy built-in. These features must also be 'turned on' by default. 'By design and by default' removes the burden upon buyers of having to understand and configure complex digital products *before* using them.

'By design and by default' is a versatile phrase, adaptable to many product development policies. A commitment to ethical development 'by design and by default' builds trust with clients and communicates a clear message to technical staff. Let's consider how this might work, with some examples:

Inclusion and accessibility: Arguably goods and services should aim to maximise the number of customers able to use them. They can be designed for inclusion and accessibility, and these features should not require 'turning on' through adaptation, customisation, or configuration.

Safety: Much can be done at the design stage to create safer products, systems, and services. Many supporting methodologies are available for design teams, including the Hazard and Operability Study (or HAZOP) and the Bowtie Method (both featured in Chapter 11). Safe configurations and working practices must be ready by default, i.e. on 'day one', and not *after* the first major incident.

Longevity: Should physical products be designed to last as long as possible? If your organisation supports this policy, designers could focus upon the durability of materials, modularity, repairability, and forward compatibility (see Chapter 2). Machine performance can also be pre-configured to optimise longevity.

It's possible for clear ethical positions to be baked into a product's design and 'turned on' by default. This removes risk, fear, and frustration for users. *Ethical by design and ethical by default* is, therefore, a sensible design strategy.

Levels of analysis

The challenge of engineering ethics should now be evident. It's not as simple as merely concluding that indiscriminate V2 rockets are bad, but peaceful Moon rockets, their successors, are good. There is much more nuance involved.

For example, is it right to conflate a technology (rocketry) with its individual artefacts (the V2, the Saturn) and their subsequent uses (violence, exploration)? It can reasonably be argued that we should separate these three levels of analysis – technologies, artefacts, and their uses – from one another.[6] There may also be a fourth level of analysis, known as *mediation*.

The concept of mediation is described by van de Poel and Royakkers as "The phenomenon that when technologies fulfil their functions, they also help to shape the actions and perceptions of their users."[7] In other words, the use of a technology induces a type of second-order effect entirely separate from the artefact and its application. They give the example of obstetric ultrasound machines, which produce live moving images of the foetus in the womb. Ultrasound reveals potential 'abnormalities' in unborn children. This information will clearly have an impact on the parents-to-be. Consequently, widespread use of the technology could become responsible for changing the wider culture of pregnancy and parental choices.

Let me introduce some of my own examples of technological mediation. The invention of the railway resulted in ribbon developments of commuter suburbs, with homes clustered around railway stations, whereas the car, with its point-to-point capabilities, created concentric urban growth, or 'sprawl'. Therefore these transportation technologies display second-order effects in the shaping of cities. Is this also the concept that Marshall McLuhan was referring to, when discussing the technologies of mass communication, which spawned his famous phrase, "the medium is the message"? One of the determinants of the television news agenda, for example, is the existence of accompanying video. If an event is not captured on video, it may not be regarded as 'news'. We might also consider the idea of 'moral hazard', the undesirable changes in human behaviour caused by particular technologies. For example, it is sometimes said that the moral hazard of introducing safety features to machinery is an increase in operator carelessness. More generally, perhaps the moral hazard of modern health care is an inducement for people to lead increasingly unhealthy lives. This idea of mediation is clearly a very different way of looking at the ethics of technology. It therefore seems clear to me that mediation corresponds to a fourth level of analysis.

Here are those four levels again:

1 Technology ethics
2 Artefact ethics
3 Application ethics
4 Mediation ethics.

The reader is encouraged to keep these four levels of analysis in mind as we briefly examine some real-world cases.

Classic case studies

Every experienced technologist or engineer can, with a little prompting, recall at least one occasion when they faced an ethical decision related to their job. For this reason, we could easily compile thousands of case studies, some more dramatic than others. In general, the literature on this subject uses a relatively small number of high-profile cases. Some of these are summarised below.

Mistakes in Manhattan: The structural engineer, William Le Messurier, designed New York's Citicorp Center, completed in 1977. Due to plot constraints, the design was particularly challenging for Le Messurier's company, but it complied with all necessary building regulations. During construction, the builders deviated from Le Messurier's preferred methods. He was unaware of this, although their work remained technically and legally acceptable. It was also approved, without Le Messurier's knowledge, by one of his employees. Within a few months of the building's opening, a group of university researchers concluded that it was potentially unstable in storm-force winds. Rather than attempt to defend his work against the accusations, Le Messurier immediately reviewed the project. He concluded that the combination of his design and the construction methods was flawed. Opting for transparency, he notified all relevant parties and supervised the costly repairs. His own reputation and that of his company had clearly been jeopardised, but his prompt response to a complex set of circumstances, prioritising public safety over personal pride, brought him widespread praise.[8]

Too many hands: The *Herald of Free Enterprise* was a roll-on/roll-off ferry operating daily between the UK and Belgium. In 1987 the ship capsized outside Zeebrugge harbour with many fatalities. Numerous causes were attributed to the disaster, not least the ingress of water through bow doors which were left open as the ship departed. The closing of bow doors had been entrusted to a single employee on the vehicle deck, but he had fallen asleep. There was no indicator on the ship's bridge to confirm the status of the bow doors. Next, due to the absence of internal bulkheads, the presence of water on the vehicle deck exacerbated the ship's instability. Bulkheads are excluded from this type of ship because their presence hinders vehicle movements and reduces capacity. After the incident, blame was attached to many individuals and organisations, ranging from the ship's marine architects to individual crew members, including the Captain who was directly responsible for the integrity of the vessel. The original designers of the safety systems, and of course the ferry's owners, Townsend Thoresen, were also implicated. In the field of ethics, attributing blame in this type of situation is known as 'the problem of many hands'.[9] No single individual could be held personally liable for the whole sequence of events, although there was undoubtedly a collective responsibility for the disaster.

Spar fight: The Brent Spar oil storage platform had been operational in the North Sea for 15 years when its owners, Shell and Esso, agreed to decommission it in the early 1990s. The Spar was a massive cylindrical tank, anchored and floating vertically, with the bulk of its structure beneath the surface. As the main operator, Shell commissioned studies to determine the most suitable method of disposal, concluding that the Spar should be emptied, then towed to one of the deepest parts of the Atlantic and sunk. According to Shell, onshore disposal was a more hazardous operation. Approval for sinking the platform was granted by the UK government. However, this soon met opposition from environmental activists, notably Greenpeace, who occupied the platform. The Brent Spar decommissioning project became an international incident as people across Europe, particularly in Germany, agitated against the sinking. Later, the plan was reversed and the platform towed to Norway for dismantling. Much of the debate over Brent Spar involved the use of contentious data presented by the opposing parties.[10] The engineering logic, which favoured sinking, was focused on short-term outcomes. This was defeated by public opinion with its longer-term view of how best to treat the natural environment. In other words, disposal by sinking could have set an unwanted precedent.

Defeat device: In 2015 a major engineering scandal emerged, capturing worldwide attention. It concerned the use of 'defeat devices' on Volkswagen diesel vehicles. The engine management software had been designed to detect when a vehicle was undergoing a government mandated emissions test. The software would then change the operation of the engine to minimise harmful emissions restricted under environmental regulations. When not in test mode, under normal driving conditions, the emissions would greatly exceed permitted levels. It therefore alleged that customers, believing they had bought 'clean' vehicles, had been defrauded. Subsequent investigations focused on both Volkswagen's management culture, and also on the engineers who knowingly wrote the illegal code. Curiously, these engineers received no personal gain from their illegal work, other than impressing their managers with their ability to produce apparently clean engines. It remains unclear whether managers were aware of the deceit perpetrated by the engineers. At least one software developer, James Liang, who produced a US version of the code, went to jail.[11]

Super pipes: In 1990 UK customs officials halted the export of some steel 'pipes' which had been manufactured to a very high specification. It was immediately suspected that these were *supergun* components. The supergun concept, invented by Canadian engineer Gerald Bull, was being funded and developed by the Government of Iraq.[12] It would feature a 156-metre barrel capable of either putting small satellites into orbit or, more likely, firing 600 kg shells over 1,000 km. A British company, Sheffield Forgemasters, had received the lucrative contract to make these 'pipes' and it remains unclear whether they genuinely understood their purpose. However, given the unusually high specifications involved, we might question whether, as specialist steel fabricators and engineers, they had a duty to find out. They could have advised their client that pipes don't, under normal circumstances, need such high specifications, and that their price would therefore be higher than necessary. Without challenging the client, how could they guarantee that the manufactured product would be fit for purpose?

Lethal design: One of the most notorious cases in engineering ethics involves the Ford Pinto, a car manufactured for the US market in the 1970s. In an attempt to compete with increasingly popular smaller vehicles being imported from Europe and Japan, Ford hurried the new Pinto design into production. The smaller scale of the vehicle resulted in a dangerous compromise with the fuel tank's position. It became more susceptible to puncture in rear end collisions. However, the vehicle was compliant with extant safety regulations. Many Pinto customers and their passengers died in subsequent post-collision fires. Ford engineers were quick to highlight the flaw to management, but in a subsequent legal case, Ford used a cost-benefit argument (including the cost of human life) to justify the design and their subsequent refusal to fund corrective work to existing vehicles.[13]

Challenging the management: It's likely that more has been written about the 1986 *Challenger* disaster than any other case in the field of engineering ethics. The debate has focused mainly upon organisational cultures and hierarchical relationships involving engineers and their business managers. It was already known that the rubber O-rings on the solid rocket boosters (produced by Morton Thiokol) were susceptible to rupture in low temperatures and that a rupture would jeopardise the integrity of the entire Shuttle vehicle. However, when a high-profile launch was scheduled for a freezing January day, the manufacturer's concerned engineers were unable to persuade their managers, and NASA's administrators, to postpone until temperatures improved. Beyond the lives of astronauts, there was much more at stake. The mission had attracted national media and political attention, largely because a school teacher would be on board. Furthermore, Morton Thiokol's hopes of renewed NASA contracts clearly depended upon the delivery of good news rather than bad. Consequently, the company's management over-ruled their own engineers, advising NASA that they had no further objections to the launch.[14]

It should now be evident that moral or ethical dilemmas are ever-present in engineering practice and technology management. It follows, therefore, that strategy development will sometimes require the analysis and resolution of ethical challenges. When these situations arise, how should we respond?

Ethical frameworks

People have been studying ethical dilemmas for thousands of years. Greek philosophers were among the first recorded ethicists, so they're often associated with the origins of the discipline. However, we can be certain that, long before the advent of civilisations, people were debating ethical matters. As a species, we have a natural inclination to differentiate between right and wrong.

Since the Renaissance, philosophers have provided countless suggestions for ethical decision-making frameworks. However, writers on the ethics of engineering and technology generally focus on a small number of these. Three of the most discussed frameworks are examined below.

Apart from philosophers, we can also draw upon the ethical guidance issued by employers and professional institutions. These will also be discussed.

Consequentialism and utilitarianism

Van de Poel and Royakkers define *consequentialism* as "The class of ethical theories which hold that the consequences of actions are central to the moral judgement of those actions."[15] A consequentialist is interested primarily in 'ends' rather than 'means'. In some formulations, almost any means may be used to achieve a desired outcome.

Like many established philosophies, consequentialism has ancient roots, but we now generally associate it with the 19th-century philosophy of *utilitarianism*. The British philosopher Jeremy Bentham devised utilitarianism as a guide to ethical decision making which, he argued, should always aim to maximise net utility. Deborah Johnson, author of *Engineering Ethics* (2020), explains that "The sum total of happiness in the world is what is at issue. Thus, when you evaluate your alternatives, you have to ask about their effects on the happiness of everyone."[16] This is sometimes referred to as 'the greatest happiness for the greatest number'.

Consequentialism or utilitarianism could be perceived as outward-looking with a long-term, societal focus. It pays limited attention to low-level activities, short-term impacts, or local needs. What matters is the bigger picture or the 'greater good'. However, would a Board of Directors accept an employee's argument that society's interest should be placed ahead of the organisation's?

For a technology strategist, a consequentialist approach would aim for the achievement of overall net satisfaction at the organisational level, though this could have dire consequences for external stakeholders, e.g. in the form of pollution.

Deontology and Kantianism

According to Johnson, *deontology* translates from ancient Greek as the 'science of duty'. It encapsulates the idea that "actions that are done from a sense of duty are morally worthy, and those done for self-interest or simply out of habit are not."[17] Deontology contrasts with utilitarianism because it involves acting on principles rather than being guided by consequences.[18]

This ethical framework is sometimes known as Kantianism, due to its association with the 18th-century German philosopher, Immanuel Kant. His single most influential idea was probably the *categorical imperative*, which equates individual actions with universal rules. In other words, a deontologist would ask: "Would it be right for everyone to act this way?" An action is only morally acceptable if it could be adopted as a universal rule. Therefore, it's immoral to take an action if its wider adoption would be broadly unsustainable.

Is it, for instance, acceptable to break a promise made to a colleague if you don't want colleagues to break promises made to you? Or, to take a more strategic example, is it acceptable to manipulate engineering data in order to gain project approval from the management? Presumably not, because you wouldn't want colleagues to manipulate the data they present to you. Deontology is therefore about acting according to mutually beneficial and sustainable principles or rules. It's the duty of doing things the right way. The consequences are of less significance.

Virtue ethics

Rather than passing judgement upon the individual decisions that people take, we might instead focus upon the qualities, or *virtues*, possessed by the people themselves.[19] The implication is that a person of virtue is able to consistently make the right judgement and act appropriately in any given situation.

The writings of Aristotle, over 2000 years ago, contain some of the earliest descriptions of virtue ethics.[20] One could argue that Aristotle's ideas are also associated with contemporary professional practice, as we will see.

Virtue ethics is a relatively efficient decision-making framework, because it only requires agreement upon the characteristics of virtuous decision makers. Once these criteria have been established, the behaviour of people who possess these characteristics requires little scrutiny. Their decisions should, by default, be ethically robust.

It follows from this that decisions made by any person (or indeed any thing) can be regarded as morally acceptable if, upon reflection, they would have been made by a virtuous person.[21] In a technological context we can ask: "What would a good or virtuous engineer have done in these circumstances?"

So what are the attributes of a virtuous technologist or engineer? This makes for an interesting debate, and could also be quite contentious. Johnson refers to the work of Charles Harris, a professor of engineering ethics at Texas A&M University, who has been prominent in this field for many years:

> He distinguishes two kinds of virtues in engineering, the technical and the nontechnical. In discussing the technical excellences of being an engineer, he mentions the obvious importance of mastery of mathematics and physics, engineering science, and design as an important virtue, but he also mentions sensitivity to risk and sensitivity to tight coupling or complex

interactions as technical virtues. For the nontechnical virtues, he discusses the importance of techno-social sensitivity, respect for nature, and commitment to public good.[22]

In their 1987 article for the journal *Engineering Ethics*, Heinz Luegenbiehl and Don Dekker provided a list of 50 "professional values". These included courtesy, curiosity, decisiveness, leadership, patience, perseverance, problem-solving ability, rationality, selflessness, and tolerance.[23] I would add two more to their fifty. Firstly *courage* to respectfully disagree with clients and managers, and occasionally to deliver bad news. And secondly, the possession of *an ethical mindset*, in order to give appropriate attention to ethical matters (as we are doing here).

These virtues are not necessarily innate or inherited. They may require education, training, mentoring, and other forms of personal development. However, once these virtues are acquired, a technologist or engineer can be trusted always to make ethically robust decisions. At least, that's the theory.

Employer guidance

A more familiar form of ethical guidance is the type provided by employers. Many large organisations choose to capture their values and principles in writing, often accompanied by advice. They then use training and regular reminders to staff in order to achieve a degree of ethical conformity.

One excellent example, of which I had first-hand experience, was the *Integrity Policy* of General Electric (GE). At the time I worked there, the corporation had over 300,000 employees worldwide, all of whom were expected to adhere closely to the tenets of the Policy. One only had to say the word "Integrity" and colleagues would know precisely what you were referring to. After their induction training on the Policy, employees were required to perform annual refreshers, reading through the Integrity Policy and signing against each of its provisions.

Today the Policy is available in 17 languages and may be viewed on the GE website.[24] Altogether there are 19 ethical categories under which approximately 100 instructions are listed. These include the following:

- Do not misrepresent or falsify quality, safety, or productivity metrics for internal or external reporting.
- Report any issues or concerns you observe related to suppliers' facilities, treatment of workers, sub-suppliers, and business practices.

- Stop any work which seems improper, unsafe, or about which you are uncertain.

GE explain that their code of conduct is intended:

> to hold our employees to a higher standard above and beyond simply following the letter of the law. We expect our employees and our Board of Directors to comply with the spirit of these policies and our company values.[25]

When I worked there, an important feature of GE's Integrity Policy was the provision of a hotline through which employees could report internal breaches. The Policy was, and remains, impressive.

In terms of the philosophical frameworks described earlier, this type of guidance resembles most closely the deontological or Kantian approach, because it consists of duties and rules related to ethical best practice. It might also be argued that these are universal rules, because both GE and its employees would expect other organisations and their employees to adopt the same behaviours.

Does your organisation offer a similar form of guidance? Is there a strategic benefit in doing so?

Professional codes

In a similar vein, most professional bodies develop and publish a code of ethics. Sometimes these codes offer decision-making guidance. However, in many cases, their primary purpose is to reinforce the integrity of the profession by communicating its values and virtues. As Johnson explains, "codes of ethics help to define what it means to be an engineer and what it means to hire an engineer."[26]

According to Van de Poel and Royakkers, these codes have three functions: 1) conducting a profession with integrity and honesty; 2) obligations towards employers and clients; and 3) responsibility towards the public and society.[27]

Let's look at two professional bodies selected at random. The first, Engineers Australia, has a *Code of Ethics and Guidelines on Professional Conduct*, which includes:

- Maintain and develop knowledge and skills.
- Uphold the reputation and trustworthiness of the practice of engineering.
- Practise engineering to foster the health, safety, and wellbeing of the community and the environment.[28]

The Indian Institute of Chemical Engineers has a *Code of Ethics for Members*, written in a very different style. It includes the following:

- To him that has engaged my services, as employer and client, I will give the sincerest of my performance, integrity, and fidelity.
- I dedicate myself to the dissemination of engineering knowledge, and, especially to the instructions of younger members of my profession in all its arts, ethos, and traditions.
- I will work with others to make the world a better place for future generations.[29]

There is clearly a virtuous dimension to some of these statements. Indeed, referring back to the philosophical frameworks earlier, we might say that they blend virtue ethics with duty ethics.

This could be an opportune moment to read the ethics of your own professional association. Can you identify traces of consequentialism, deontology, and/or virtue ethics? How does your own behaviour, and that of your colleagues, match up to the code?

Laws and regulations

Like many inventors and entrepreneurs, John Logie Baird liked to 'push the envelope', both technically and ethically. In 1923, while experimenting in his laboratory, which happened to be above a shop in a busy arcade, he was electrocuted and nearly killed with an explosive 2000-volt shock. This was followed, unsurprisingly, by lurid newspaper headlines and a request from the landlord to vacate the building.[30] On another occasion, he chose to demonstrate his new invention, television, by broadcasting moving pictures from south-east London to a theatre in the West End. In his own words, "This transmission was by wireless and to a public audience and, strictly speaking, illegal, but no objection was raised."[31]

The siting of Baird's dangerous laboratory was probably unwise, and the broadcast was a clear breach of the law. Was it acceptable for Baird to commit an offence in order to develop his invention? Did he have a duty, at least in a democratic society, to observe the law at all times? If we believe that he did, then we are implicitly adopting a Kantian or deontological position. Alternatively, we might conclude that Baird's technically brilliant work produced such outstanding results that his means of delivering those benefits should be forgiven. This would be a utilitarian argument. Or thirdly, as a person with tremendous intelligence, creativity, energy, and bravery we might say that Baird had all the virtues of a great engineer and that his actions were, therefore, above criticism.

There is clearly a correlation between laws and social morality. It is public opinion that often drives the implementation of new laws and regulations. However, the law is unable to formalise the *entire* breadth and depth of public morality. That would involve too much work for politicians and the legislature. Consequently, *the law is an incomplete representation of public morality.* The converse is also true, because some laws cannot easily be traced back to social values and principles. They may, for instance, be the result of political compromises. We might conclude from this that the law is both a proxy for, but only an approximation of, the morality and ethics of society. Is this approximation sufficient for us to perceive the law as a type of ethical framework? I would argue that it is, and hence its inclusion here.

Individual technical regulations, such as those breached by Baird governing wireless broadcasting, may be too specialised to reflect public opinion. They will, however, be founded upon some easily understood principles, such as the need to prevent two broadcasters from transmitting over the same wavelength, or the need to prevent seditious or anti-democratic forces from using the airwaves to organise and communicate.

In addition to those laws and regulations that do exist, we should also be concerned for those that do not. This happens because the implementation of laws typically lags behind the ethical concerns they're designed to address.[32] It can take many years for an emerging public concern to be codified in a law or set of regulations. Therefore, we often observe a legal vacuum during which technologists and engineers have free rein to experiment and deliver ethically questionable products. This absence of effective laws or regulations is an ongoing debate in the fields of artificial intelligence, autonomous vehicles, robotics, biotechnology, and many other rapidly developing sectors.

Does this legal vacuum absolve us from our responsibilities to make ethical judgements about right and wrong? Given that our knowledge of an emerging technology is likely to be more extensive than that of the general public and their legislators, is it reasonable to argue that we have an obligation to anticipate where future lines are likely to be drawn, and voluntarily remain within them? This, of course, is a hypothetical question, and like so many similar philosophical enquiries, there is no definitive answer.

Ethical decision tools

We've established that engineering presents an immense variety of ethical dilemmas. Therefore, what we need is a simple tool to help us analyse ethical challenges before resolving them. There's only one problem. No such tool exists. What we do have, however, are various mechanisms for identifying salient issues, clarifying arguments, and narrowing down options. Four of these are described below.

Cost-benefit analysis

The first and perhaps best-known decision-making tool is *cost-benefit analysis*, or CBA. We generally associate the CBA with quantitative commercial decisions involving planned expenditures and anticipated revenues, but it's much more versatile than that. For instance, when analysing the viability of novel power sources, such as nuclear fusion, all forms of energy inputs (costs) must exceed the usable energy outputs (benefits). In fact, we probably use CBA more often than we realise.

It's clear from the description of consequentialism (above) that if 'ends' are more important than 'means', then benefits must exceed costs. This lies at the heart of Bentham's utilitarianism, which aims to achieve 'the greatest happiness for the greatest number'. In order to do that it's necessary to quantify net happiness, which means calculating the happiness value, then deducting any unhappiness (or pain) caused by our actions. In its crudest form, X amount of pain may be justified by >X amount of pleasure. It's easy to understand why some commentators dislike the application of utilitarian methods; they can be used to justify causing limited harm to some groups in order that greater pleasure can be delivered to others.

Most large-scale civil engineering projects involve this type of decision making. For example, dams and reservoirs are constructed in rural areas for the purpose of dispatching electricity and water to distant urban populations. This frequently results in the evacuation and flooding of villages located within river valleys. This utilitarian solution causes immense distress to the communities involved, despite the financial compensation they presumably receive.[33]

In its most sophisticated form, CBA involves accounting for both quantitative (tangible) and qualitative (intangible) values. Intangibles may include factors such as cultural impact, organisational reputation, environmental effects, and so on. The greatest challenge when using CBA is establishing effective measures and agreed weightings for these intangibles. It is because of this innate difficulty that intuition will often be called upon to make the final judgement after completing a CBA. (The nature of intuition was discussed in Chapter 7.)

Box 9.3   STRATEGIC DICHOTOMIES

Satisfying client wants OR Satisfying client needs?

For technologists and engineers who work with clients, a familiar dilemma involves the translation of customer 'wants' into a solution satisfactory to all parties.

The solution designer (an engineer, architect, or systems analyst) may feel inclined to 'push back' for various reasons, leading to tensions in the relationship. The fact that an engineer is often financially dependent upon the client presents a professional challenge, but the most successful engineers become skilled at holding these 'difficult conversations'. Nevertheless, there might be an unspoken or implicit 'red line' beyond which the designer will withdraw from a potentially lucrative project. This red line could be technical or even ethical.

These situations can arise from the fact that engineers often know what a client needs, despite a client's insistence to the contrary! This is why a well-executed design process will involve, in its earliest stages, a drill-down into underlying client motivations, leading to discoveries and revelations which change the original requirements. The Double Diamond Design Process Model (explained in Chapter 2) addresses this activity in the first diamond: *Discover* and *Define*. With the adept use of diplomatic language, a client's ***real*** needs can be discussed and agreed prior to the second diamond: *Develop* and *Deliver*.

A designer must be careful not to impose personal beliefs, values, or principles upon the client's needs. However, there is a professional obligation to point out the impact which the client's original preferences will have upon stakeholders (including the client).

Sometimes the design process will function as a type of ethical education for the client, and many professional codes of ethics address this dichotomy. One example is provision No.6 of Engineering New Zealand's *Code of Ethical Conduct*:

6 Inform others of consequences of not following advice

> If you become aware that your professional advice may not be followed, and consider that a failure to observe that advice may have adverse consequences, you must inform the recipient of the advice of those adverse consequences.[34]

A competent strategic thinker will find the compromises, and the words, necessary for satisfying all parties. From both the technical and ethical perspectives, it's important that what a client needs, the client also wants.

The ethical Delphi

The Delphi method is a forecasting technique, developed in the 1950s by the RAND corporation. Its original purpose was to guide military leaders on the likely direction of particular technological advances. However, it was later adopted more widely for describing broader technological futures.[35]

The method involves a novel technique for eliciting expert opinion. Instead of bringing a group of subject matter experts (SMEs) together for round-table discussions, Delphi uses anonymous written submissions. These are collected, summarised, and redistributed among the participants. A new round of opinions is then solicited. After two or three rounds of submissions and redistributions, a final summary statement is issued. This, it is hoped, represents a consensus opinion.

One of the strengths of the Delphi method is that the anonymity prevents hierarchy or status from intruding on the open expression of ideas. Furthermore, the method provides ample time for contemplation and informed responses.

Payam Moula and Per Sandin (2017) explain how the Delphi method has, on occasions, been adapted for the elicitation of ethical insights. The SMEs involved in an 'ethical Delphi' undertake a similar process of submissions and redistributions, coordinated by an administrator. However, according to Moula and Sandin, "the ethical Delphi is not focused on reaching consensus but rather highlights where consensus and disagreement exist."[36]

Although resource-heavy and relatively slow (typically requiring many weeks to complete), an ethical Delphi should help decision makers make better-informed ethical judgements.

Consensus conference

A different form of collective judgement is the *consensus conference*. This idea originated with the Danish Board of Technology. It involves a large number of citizens (typically more than 30), interrogating a panel of experts before reaching a consensus view. The first event in 1987 was entitled "Gene technology in industry and agriculture".

Firstly, the citizen panel is given an educational introduction to the subject under debate. This enables them to submit challenging and well-informed questions to a panel of experts. Later, at the main conference event, these experts will present their responses to the original citizen panel. Finally, the citizens debate among themselves before collectively issuing a conclusion and some recommendations. It's a very democratic and transparent approach to the process of differentiating between right and wrong in contentious ethical matters. A conference aims to bridge the gap between experts and non-experts, enabling new knowledge or ideas to emerge from the process.

Many organisations have published guidance on how to plan and deliver consensus conferences, including the state government of Tasmania (Australia)[37] and the United States Environmental Protection Agency (EPA).[38] This guidance emphasises the significant amount of time required to organise a conference. It also advises on the number of people needed to administer the process, and the relatively high costs involved. The *Consensus Conference Manual* (2006), by Annika Nielsen *et al.*, provides a thorough introduction to the method.[39] Although it's difficult to imagine private companies going to these lengths, one can see why public institutions are interested in the concept, especially if they have the time and money to organise conference proceedings.

Where does this take us?

Why is this topic strategically significant, and why should we allow ethics to intrude on the important work of simply getting things done? A leading Arup engineer, Jo da Silva, explains:

> Engineering used to be only about technical parameters ... It has increasingly become about environmental parameters and more and more it is becoming about social parameters. We are realising that how humans interact with what we create and design is part of the overall performance of the system.[40]

Technology can do great things. That's a fact. But sometimes it delivers the worst imaginable outcomes. As long ago as 1855, during his inaugural lecture as the UK's first Professor of Technology, George Wilson explored the subject's darker side, emphasising safety:

> The preventable human suffering, and the needless loss of human life, which are occasioned by our industrial doings, are in amount altogether appalling. There is not a public building, I suppose, which is not sprinkled with the blood of slain workmen. Every railway is inaugurated, as if we were pagans, by the sacrifice of human victims. Our ships bury every year in the sea thousands whose lives are not half spent ...[41]

A century of targeted legislation has seen improvements in the safety and reliability of engineering solutions beyond anything Professor Wilson could have imagined.

More recently, Professor Levent Orman of Cornell University reminded us that "Technology is not like a gentle rain that falls on all equally ... It is more like a thunderstorm that benefits some but devastates others."[42]

That's why we need to study ethics and establish a satisfactory way of incorporating it within strategic thinking. So, what *should* a technologist or engineer do when faced with an intractable ethical dilemma?

The superficial attraction of consequentialism, described earlier, with its maximisation of net benefits, is soon undermined by the harms delivered to those who stand in the way of 'progress', especially the natural environment and, of course, people. It's true that arguments can be constructed to defend even the most uncomfortable utilitarian actions (such as the flooding of communities to make reservoirs), but those arguments count for nothing. This is because consequentialism harbours an even greater flaw which destroys its credibility as a guide to decision making.

In Chapters 4, 5, and 6 I emphasised the role of uncertainty. A major theme was the ubiquity of complex adaptive systems (CAS). Complexity explains the impossibility of making even moderately accurate forecasts of technological, economic, and social futures. The agents in CAS environments react and adapt in ways too numerous for us to analyse and predict. We only need to recall some of the unintended consequences of technological decisions described in those chapters - a long list of historical shocks and surprises, some of which we called 'unknown unknowns'.

Given our knowledge of uncertainty, we can therefore safely conclude that, when reaching a technological or managerial decision, there is no quantitative means of calculating 'the greatest benefit for the greatest number'. We simply can't know all of the possible outcomes. It's a futile activity. Complexity scuppers consequentialism.

So now, with consequentialism debunked we must, at the very least, consider adopting the duty ethics of deontology. Professor Roland Clift, a Fellow of the Royal Academy of Engineering, is more convinced by this line of thinking:

> If we have to abandon the pseudo-certainty of utilitarianism, that says to me that our ethical code as engineers needs to be deontological. We need to be guided by principles of conduct, not by expectations of outcome.[43]

There are good reasons to agree with Clift's position. The universal rule of Immanuel Kant's 'categorical imperative' offers a symmetry which probably appeals to most engineers. An action is morally defensible if it ought to be adopted as a universal rule. We simply ask, "Would it be right for everyone to act this way?" The categorical imperative exposes the hypocrisy of forcing experiences upon others that we would not wish upon ourselves. We therefore have a moral obligation to abide by the imperative in our professional duties as technologists and engineers. Occasionally, we might believe that negative consequences could arise from our decision. But we also know that the operating environment is so complex, and in such continuous flux, that the future is mostly unforeseeable over the medium term.

Using the same argument, the emergence of unexpectedly negative outcomes should never be used to criticise a decision made according to duty. The decision was made in the right way. That's what matters.

Kant's deontology is not incompatible with Aristotle's virtue ethics. The idea that virtuous engineers (i.e. those with problem-solving skills, courage, creativity, and so on) will always make good decisions is clearly appealing. This is why we see it reflected in so many professional codes of ethics. We might also say that one of the virtues of a professional technologist is a 'sense of duty'. This leads us towards a hybrid of Kantian ethics and virtue ethics. It combines the morality of duty (Professor Clift's "principles of conduct") with traditional professional virtues. This combination feels reassuring and robust.

I recognise that the subject of engineering ethics is considerably more nuanced than it has been possible to convey in this chapter. Academic ethicists and professional philosophers may choose to find fault in my reasoning. However, **as professional decision makers, we are all amateur ethicists, and we can do no more than make the most of our current levels of knowledge and understanding. Decisions simply have to be made. They cannot wait for us to consult philosophers.**

We could, however, process our decisions in a more structured and transparent manner, thereby demonstrating our desire to design and deliver things the right way. I will now propose a technique for doing that.

Box 9.4   ANALYTICAL TOOLS AND TECHNIQUES

The RACI matrix (of ethical obligations)

A tool familiar to many readers will be the RACI matrix, which captures the relationships between people and a particular activity. The RACI acronym consists of **R** for responsible, **A** for accountable, **C** for consulted, and **I** for informed (Table 9.1).

Table 9.1 An RACI matrix of ethical obligations

	Person or role 1	Person or role 2	Person or role 3	Person or role 4
Task 1	C,I	I	I	R
Task 2	C	-	A,C	-
Task 3	A	I	R	C
Task 4	-	R,A	I	-

The example shown includes some people performing multiple functions, e.g. Person 1 in Task 1. Meanwhile, some tasks are missing key assignees; no one has been made *accountable* for Task 1, while Task 2 is missing the *responsible* person necessary for delivering it.

The ethics of participation: One interesting feature of a RACI matrix is its representation of ethical obligations. For example, the **responsible** person is aware of the task they have been assigned to, but this person may simply be 'following orders'. Does that absolve them from the ethics of the action? The **accountable** person may not have given the original instructions, but they have the authority to ensure that the task is completed correctly. The accountable person ought to know the nature of the work and its ethical implications. Arguably, their obligations are greater than those of the *responsible* implementor. Any person **consulted** will be aware of the task and probably has an opportunity to influence the way it will be performed. They could indicate their ethical concerns and suggest a more acceptable method. Finally, the people **informed** are likely to be aware of the task, and possibly its ethical implications, but they may not receive this information until after its completion. They will, however, be in a position to raise retrospective concerns. Indeed it may be unethical for them not to do so.

Therefore, a RACI matrix could be interpreted as an *ethical obligations matrix*.

Ethical Due Process

Ethical dilemmas will occasionally arise while developing technology strategies. Consider the possible ethical implications of the following: product design policies, decommissioning methods, the development of personnel, safety management systems, changing suppliers, and so on. We need to establish a practical approach to resolving ethical dilemmas as they emerge. Sometimes intuition will suffice, but for the more difficult challenges, something more rigorous and procedural is required.

Perhaps we need to 'design' our decisions. Deborah Johnson, who is a former professor of ethics in the Department of Engineering and Society at the University of Virginia, explains this approach:

> Ethical decision-making often requires a form of creativity. Instead of deducing the correct answer from a theory, one must synthesize many elements, make trade-offs, and design a solution.

> ... viewing ethical problems as design problems is closer to the real-world experiences of engineers as they try to balance many factors and consider the uncertainties that go with each step that they take.[44]

Familiar design methods, such as the *Double Diamond Design Process* (Chapter 2, Box 2.1), can be adapted to assist with an ethical decision. The first diamond defines the precise nature of the problem. The second diamond then explores all options before converging upon an answer.

It may be argued that the Double Diamond method lacks the rigour or direction needed to assist with philosophical enquiries. Perhaps we require something more prescriptive, such as a step-by-step guide. One method for doing this, known as the "ethical cycle", is proposed by van de Poel and Royakkers. It has five stages, or "phases" as follows:

Phase 1: A statement of the moral problem
Phase 2: Analysis of the problem
Phase 3: Options for action
Phase 4: Evaluation of the ethics
Phase 5: Critical reflection before arriving at a morally accept-
    able action.[45]

Full details of the ethical cycle are provided in their book, *Ethics, Technology and Engineering* (2011). Similar methods have been proposed elsewhere. For example, both the National Institute for Engineering Ethics (NIEE)[46] and Chris MacDonald, a professional ethicist at Toronto Metropolitan University,[47] have published step-by-step guides.

I have chosen to draw upon all of these ideas in order to create a composite decision-making technique called *Ethical Due Process*. Its name is a reference to the concept of legal due process, a series of administrative steps designed to maximise the likelihood of delivering justice. In most legal systems, if due process is not followed, justice is deemed to have failed.

Table 9.2 The nine steps of Ethical Due Process

ETHICAL DUE PROCESS		
Action step		**Advice**
1	**Define the ethical problem**	Aim to produce a statement of the ethical problem in two or three sentences. What values or principles are in conflict?
2	**Determine the facts**	Objectivity is critical when gathering information to support the decision.
3	**Identify stakeholders**	A stakeholder is any entity likely to affect, or be affected by, the decision. Consider organisations, people, and the natural environment. Stakeholders were discussed in Chapter 8.
4	**Analyse stakeholder positions**	What are their motivations or goals? How much power or influence do they have? How could they be impacted? Do they have responsibilities or obligations?
5	**List the decision options**	It's likely that there will be more than one way to resolve the problem. Refer to the leading ethical theories and frameworks.
6	**Evaluate each option**	Use available analytical tools (see above). Consider relevant laws, regulations, and codes. Look for similar cases or precedents. Use your experience and judgement.
7	**Discuss options with stakeholders**	It may be important to gain some form of stakeholder approval or consensus for the final decision. What is their response to your proposal?
8	**Select the most ethically responsible course of action**	This may emerge unequivocally from work undertaken in the previous steps. However, it's more likely that personal judgement (perhaps even intuition) will be needed to make the final call.
9	**Sanity check**	Ask yourself: Am I comfortable with this decision? Will my decision stand up to public scrutiny? Would I have difficulty explaining this to a reporter, or a judge, or to my colleagues, or even my own family?

Ethical Due Process contains nine actions which ought to be within the capabilities of any professional technologist. Table 9.2 lists the actions and offers advice for completing them.

The phrase 'due process' is significant. If someone has made a contentious ethical decision, being able to demonstrate adherence to a 'best practice' process should help to protect them against criticism. What's more, a documentary trail will exist as evidence that due process had been followed.

We might speculate upon the impact that this process would have had on Werner von Braun, as he contemplated the development of non-discriminating lethal technologies, such as the V2 rockets. He would probably have constructed a clever argument to defend his actions. In ethics, a "clever argument" is often all that's needed.

However, I'd like to believe that scientists, technologists, and engineers fortunate enough to receive an ethical education would only take controversial courses of action which they could support with evidence of due process. Ethical Due Process therefore acts as a safety net for their reputations.

Technology strategy can be analysed from many angles. The two most recent chapters adopted the perspectives of *stakeholders* and *ethics*. Next, we will analyse *innovation*, one of the most frequently discussed of all topics in the strategy literature.

Glossary for this chapter (Items in bold are also defined in the same table)

categorical imperative	A feature of Kantian ethics, or **Kantianism**. The imperative mandates that a decision or action is unethical if its wider adoption could not be sustained as a universal rule, applicable to all.
citizen panel	A gathering of non-experts, consulted for their opinions during research. See **consensus conference**.
consensus conference	A method for discovering the **ethical** stance of non-experts (i.e. the public). Conference participants are firstly educated in the subject matter before submitting questions to experts. After receiving answers, they debate among themselves before making recommendations.
consequentialism	A philosophical position which holds that the effects of actions are central to the **ethical** judgement of those actions. An important branch of consequentialism is **utilitarianism**.
cost-benefit analysis	A decision-making tool for calculating net benefits, sometimes associated with **consequentialism**.
defeat device	A product feature engineered to evade regulations, such as environmental controls.
Delphi method	A technique for eliciting knowledge, ideas, and conclusions from anonymous subject matter experts. The participants engage in multiple rounds of written exchanges, coordinated by administrators. One variation is the so-called **ethical Delphi**.

(Continued)

deontology	The philosophical belief that decisions and actions should be informed by a sense of **duty**. Deontology is often associated with the philosophy of Immanuel Kant (hence **Kantianism).**
duty	Within **deontology**, the principal basis for **ethical** decisions.
ethical Delphi	A method for eliciting knowledge and ideas from anonymous subject matter experts. The aim is to inform an **ethical** debate, rather than to reach a conclusion. It's a variation of the **Delphi method**.
Ethical Due Process	A step-by-step technique for reaching decisions on contentious **ethical** issues. A documented 'due process' offers a form of protection against criticism.
ethics	The philosophical discipline of differentiating, in any given context, between actions that are **morally** right from those that are morally wrong.
Kantianism	The branch of **deontology** associated with philosopher Immanuel Kant.
mediation	The observable phenomenon that when technologies perform their functions, they also influence (or mediate) the actions and perceptions of users. This induces second-order effects, e.g. moral hazard.
morality	The totality of opinions, decisions, and actions with which people express what they think is good or right.
problem of many hands	An ethical and legal dilemma involving the attribution of blame in circumstances where many parties have contributed independently to an undesirable state of affairs.
professional code	**Ethical** guidance produced by organisations to assist their employees or members.
utilitarianism	A branch of **consequentialism** developed by Jeremy Bentham in the 19th century. It aims to quantify the net benefits of a proposed action.
virtue	A desirable attribute or characteristic of an individual which, according to the philosophy of **virtue ethics**, contributes to morally correct behaviour. The virtues of a professional engineer, for instance, may include rationality and leadership.
virtue ethics	The philosophical belief that people of **virtue** are, by implication, **ethically** responsible actors.

Notes

1 Brentford & Chiswick Local History Society, 'Commemorating the Chiswick V2'. Available at: https://bit.ly/3YuqSJY (Accessed: 06 February 2023).
2 Concise Oxford English Dictionary. 10th edn. (2002). Oxford: OUP. 925.
3 van de Poel, I. and Royakkers, L. (2011) Ethics, Technology and Engineering: An Introduction. Chichester: Wiley. 71.
4 van de Poel and Royakkers, Ethics, Technology and Engineering. 75.

5 van de Poel and Royakkers. 71.
6 Brey, P. (2017) 'Ethics of Emerging Technology' in Hansson, S.O. (ed.) *The Ethics of Technology*. London: Rowman & Littlefield. 188–189.
7 van de Poel and Royakkers. 201.
8 van de Poel and Royakkers. 100–101.
9 van de Poel and Royakkers. 250–253.
10 Howarth, S. (1997) *A Century in Oil: the "Shell" Transport and Trading Company 1897–1997*. London: Weidenfeld & Nicolson. 318–23 and 381–383.
11 Johnson, D. (2020) *Engineering Ethics*. New Haven: YUP. 131–134.
12 Park, W. (2016) '*The tragic tale of Saddam Hussein's 'supergun*'. Available at: https://www.bbc.com/future/article/20160317-the-man-who-tried-to-make-a-supergun-for-saddam-hussein (Accessed: 14 February 2023).
13 van de Poel and Royakkers. 67–70.
14 Heppenheimer, T.A. (1997) *Countdown: A History of Spaceflight*. New York: Wiley. 323–326.
15 van de Poel and Royakkers. 78.
16 Johnson, *Engineering Ethics*. 55.
17 Johnson. 59.
18 Clift, R. (2011) 'Children of Martha: On Being an Engineer in the Environment'. *Philosophy of Engineering*, Vol. 2. Royal Academy of Engineering, London, October 2011. Available at: https://www.raeng.org.uk/publications/reports/philosophy-of-engineering-vol-2, 48–55.
19 van de Poel and Royakkers. 95–101.
20 Johnson. 63.
21 van de Poel and Royakkers. 126.
22 Johnson. 65–66.
23 Morse, L.C. and Babcock, D.L. (2010) *Managing Engineering and Technology*. Upper Saddle River, NJ: Pearson. 394.
24 General Electric Company, '*Open reporting is a cornerstone of GE's commitment to integrity*'. Available at: https://www.ge.com/sustainability/reports-hub#integrity (Accessed: 16 February 2023).
25 General Electric Company, '*Integrity is critical in everything we do*'. Available at: https://www.ge.com/sustainability/ourculture (Accessed: 16 February 2023).
26 Johnson. 37–38.
27 van de Poel and Royakkers. 38.
28 Engineers Australia (2022), '*Code of Ethics and Guidelines on Professional Conduct*', available at https://www.engineersaustralia.org.au/sites/default/files/2022-08/code-ethics-guidelines-professional-conduct-2022.pdf (Accessed: 16 February 2023).
29 Indian Institute of Chemical Engineers, '*Code of Ethics for Members*'. Available at: https://www.iiche.org.in/code_ethics.php (Accessed: 16 February 2023).
30 Baird, J.L. (2004) *Television and Me*. Edinburgh: Mercat. 48.
31 Baird, *Television and Me*. 125.
32 van de Poel and Royakkers. 41 and 260.
33 BBC, 'Tryweryn: *The man who bombed a dam to save a village*'. Available at: https://www.bbc.co.uk/news/uk-wales-64560239 (Accessed: 18 February 2023).
34 Engineering New Zealand, 'Ethical Code of Conduct'. Available at: https://www.engineeringnz.org/engineer-tools/ethics-rules-standards/ (Accessed: 03 March 2023).

35 Marchau, V. and van de Linde, E. (2016) 'The Delphi Method' in van der Duin, P. (ed.) *Foresight in Organizations*. Abingdon: Routledge. 59–79.

36 Moula, P. and Sandin, P. (2017) 'Ethical Tools' in Hansson, S.O. (ed.) *The Ethics of Technology*. London: Rowman & Littlefield. 119.

37 Tasmanian Government Department of Health and Human Services (undated), *Consensus Conference*, available at https://doh.health.tas. gov.au/__data/assets/pdf_file/0009/85095/Consensus_Conference.pdf (Accessed: 17 August 2023).

38 United States Environmental Protection Agency, 'Public Participation Guide: Consensus Workshops'. Available at: Public Participation Guide: Consensus Workshops | US EPA (Accessed: 20 February 2023).

39 Nielsen, A. *et al.* (2006) 'Consensus Conference Manual'. Available at https://estframe.net/uploads/qyEJ2dPN/et4_manual_cc_binnenwerk_40p. pdf (Accessed: 20 February 2023).

40 Kenward, M. (2019) 'Structures for a Sustainable Society'. *Ingenia*, Issue 80, 38–42.

41 Wilson, G. (2017) *What is Technology?* Online: CreateSpace Publishing.

42 Madhavan, G. (2016) *Think Like an Engineer*. London: Oneworld. 177.

43 Clift, *Philosophy of Engineering*, Vol.2., 48–55.

44 Johnson. 67–68.

45 van de Poel and Royakkers. 133–160.

46 Morse and Babcock, *Managing Engineering and Technology*. 397.

47 MacDonald, C. (2010) 'A Guide to Moral Decision Making'. Available at http://www.ethicsweb.ca/guide/ (Accessed: 24 February 2023).

10 What's new?

Succeed by innovating and by not innovating

This chapter presents

- An examination of the role that innovation plays in technology strategies.
- Descriptions of innovation types and innovation tools.

This chapter establishes

- The difference between proactive, reactive, and inactive innovation strategies.
- The fact that innovation is a low strategic priority for most organisations.

How important is innovation? Much has been written about this topic in recent years – probably too much. For this reason, only one chapter of this book is dedicated to innovation. Furthermore, I'll present an unfashionable argument: that **innovation is rarely of fundamental importance to a technology strategy**.

However, it can't be denied that this is a fascinating subject. New products and processes can be thrilling to learn about, and even more thrilling to experience for the first time. The leading edge of technology is guaranteed to make headlines. From re-usable spacecraft to the latest surgical techniques, we applaud the inspirational work of inventors, pioneers, and entrepreneurs. But let's be realistic. In most organisations, for most of the time, success does not depend upon the implementation of bold new ideas. For the majority of managers and technologists, the overriding focus is simply on getting things done effectively, efficiently, safely, and (in the private sector) profitably. For an organisation to survive and grow, consistency, quality, and wise leadership are often more important than the creation of innovative products and processes.

Of the 14 real-world technology strategies reviewed in Chapter 1, very few mentioned innovation, and those only briefly. It clearly wasn't central to their strategic thinking. This can be explained in

DOI: 10.4324/9781003472919-12

part because most of the documents were published by non-profit organisations, for whom innovation is probably less critical. It's the private sector that generally takes the greatest interest in being either the first or the best.

Profitability is undoubtedly a major innovation driver. Grant and Jordan, in *Foundations of Strategy* (2015), argue that "Innovation forms the key link between technology and competitive advantage"[1] and in *Mastering the Dynamics of Innovation* (1994), MIT Professor James Utterback warned that "Failure to innovate is a prime source of business failure."[2] These arguments support the view that, at least for businesses built on technology, standing still equates to going backwards. For such organisations, the mantra is often 'innovate or die'.

Yet, we should not be distracted by this theory of success. There is overwhelming evidence that innovation is neither necessary nor sufficient for making healthy profits. Indeed a rejection of innovation can be the fast-track to success, as will be explained later. This chapter will therefore be keeping innovation firmly in perspective.

It will firstly examine the difference between invention and innovation. Eight different types of innovation will then be described. The sources of innovation, including some specialised tools will also be presented. And the chapter will conclude by analysing three different types of familiar innovation strategy.

Invention and innovation

The concepts of invention and innovation are easily confused, not helped by their similarities in spelling. However, it's important to understand the difference.

We associate inventions with original ideas leading to patentable artifacts. According to the UK Government, an invention may be granted a patent if it is an entirely new idea "that can be made and used, a technical process, or a method of doing something".[3] These patenting rules are broadly similar in other countries.

Patenting has a long history, but it came to prominence during the Industrial Revolution. Governments saw that it was economically beneficial to give inventors a monopoly over the commercial exploitation of their ideas for a limited time period. This, it was believed, would act as a stimulus to inventive research. Abraham Lincoln is reported to have said that the patent system "added the fuel of interest to the fire of genius".[4] Worldwide, many millions of inventions have subsequently been patented.

However, many 'inventive ideas' are never formally recognised by the authorities. They may go unpatented due to a shortage of funds to pay for the legal process, or because the idea has already

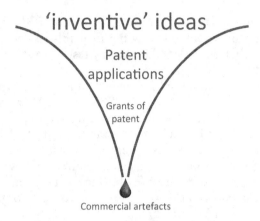

'inventive' ideas

Patent
applications

Grants of
patent

Commercial artefacts

Figure 10.1 The invention funnel

entered the public domain prior to registration, or simply because the patent office is unconvinced of the claim's novelty. Far more patents are requested than granted by the authorities. Only a small proportion of these are developed into commercially viable products.

This process of funnelling 'inventive' ideas into usable artefacts is visualised in Figure 10.1. It corresponds with the observation of historian George Basalla, that "there is an excess of technological novelty and consequently not a close fit between invention and wants or needs".[5]

By contrast, an innovation is much less formal than an invention. An innovation can be *any* type of original, value-adding product or process that undergoes the transition from a simple idea to real-world implementation.

Whereas inventions tend to be broadly recognised and legally protected, innovations may be more localised and informal. In other words, it's not important whether an innovation is truly original from a global perspective. It merely needs to be the right creative solution, at the right time in a particular context.

Figure 10.2 illustrates how creative thinking may lead to both inventions and innovations. Some ideas that are claimed as inventions will be granted patents, but most of these add zero value because they are not developed, and many of those that are developed go on to fail. However, innovations, by definition, always deliver real value.

When developing technology strategies, it is often more helpful to think about innovations than inventions, because the former are often more directly relevant to organisational progress and success.

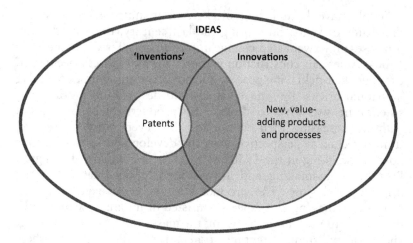

Figure 10.2 The relationship between ideas, inventions, and innovations

Types of innovation

This chapter looks at the role of innovation within technology strategies. It will describe eight types of innovation, presented in four pairs: product and process; radical and incremental; proprietary and open; organisation and system.

Product and process

Product innovation is a familiar concept. Over tens of thousands of years, it has brought us millions of new or improved goods and services. Without product innovation there would be no hammers or GPS navigation, no heart transplants or mobile apps, no watch batteries or submarines. Innovative products are emerging all the time, in every corner of the world. Some will be transformational and historic, like concrete, diesel engines, and gene editing. However, most will go unnoticed, and many will disappear almost as quickly as they emerged.

Products take the form of both physical artefacts and processes. However, we need to distinguish between products delivered in the form of processes (such as heart transplants) and the processes which *enable* products to exist. These production processes are less visible than the products they support, but they may be just as significant to the organisations that develop and exploit them. *Process innovation* is concerned with improvements to these production processes. Some examples will help to clarify this distinction between product innovation and process innovation.

People have been laying bricks and manufacturing glass for thousands of years, but during the last century, these production processes underwent step-change improvements. Firstly, in the early 1900s, American construction engineer Frank Gilbreth decided to examine the bricklaying process, including the ergonomics of laying individual bricks. By improving scaffold designs and mortar consistency he was able to double the productivity of bricklayers without increasing their workload.[6] But even more impressive, from a technical perspective, was the development of continuous flow glassmaking in the 1950s by the British company, Pilkington Brothers. Glassmaking had always been labour-intensive, batch oriented, and slow. The product was therefore expensive. The process for making glass sheets consisted of mixing raw materials, melting them in a furnace, casting the glass, annealing it, grinding, and finally polishing. After much trial and error, Pilkington Brothers innovated a continuous flow production technique, which involved floating liquid glass along a trough of molten tin. The glass cooled as it travelled, emerging as thin sheets and perfectly smooth, ready for cutting. The output from this remarkable, high-speed process became known as 'float glass'. It was 50% more energy efficient, and labour costs were reduced by 80%. The trial and error of development had wasted 100,000 tons of glass (although fortunately this could be recycled).[7] It was a classic process innovation. Significantly, the end product was more or less unchanged. Today almost every new building in the world contains inexpensive glass manufactured by the Pilkington process.

Boeing developed the 777 airliner in the 1990s by re-thinking the traditional aircraft development process. They created more than 200 small 'design-build teams' (DBTs). These worked independently, but were networked together on IBM mainframes. Each DBT combined the skills and experiences of multiple process roles. There would be a combination of design engineers, manufacturing specialists, financial analysts, and sometimes customer representatives.[8] What had previously been a serial process of handovers between specialists was now more real-time and parallel.

Researchers James Utterback and William Abernathy found that between 1880 and 1920 the number of process steps in the manufacture of light bulbs fell from 200 to just 30. The bulbs were originally made by skilled labour using standard tools, but this gave way to specialised equipment operated by less skilled workers. Production rates gradually increased as the laborious manufacture of individual bulbs evolved into batch processing. Eventually, this became a near-continuous process.[9] These improvements were the result of multiple, independent process innovations.

Over many decades we have heard predictions that the world is destined to run out of oil. However, various process improvements have enabled not only new discoveries, but a remarkable virtuosity in extracting oil from known, but hard-to-reach, reserves. Process innovations have included directional drilling, slim-hole drilling, and measurement-while-drilling (MWD).[10]

In order to streamline construction of the massive nuclear power plant at Hinkley Point (south-west England), the main contractor, Laing O'Rourke, has introduced industrial manufacturing processes. In contrast with traditional construction techniques for nuclear plants, which involve much open-air welding and concrete-pouring, at Hinkley Point many of the larger "components" are being delivered installation-ready from a purpose-built fabrication facility nearby.[11] This 'design for manufacture and assembly' (or DfMA) minimises the impact on schedules caused by inclement weather. It also improves product quality, reduces waste, and provides better working conditions.

In recent decades, information technology has played a major role in process innovation. In his book *IT Strategy for Non-IT Managers* (2017), Amrit Tiwana explains the role of digital assets in transforming organisations, both internally and externally. For example, IT has a "disintermediating" effect, eliminating third-party intermediaries, such as brokers, agents, and miscellaneous 'middlemen'.[12] One very simple but visible example arose during the COVID pandemic. Instead of chauffering interviewees to their TV studios, broadcasters simply invited guest to join 'video calls' from their homes. This practice appears to have become permanent. By excluding the limo and taxi companies, who added zero value to the process of making TV programmes, studio costs have been reduced.

IT also enables greater coordination throughout the value chain (see Box 1.3 *Value chain analysis*, in Chapter 1). For example, enterprise resource planning (ERP) software, such as Oracle and SAP, delivers this type of process innovation in a single package. With a fully deployed ERP, internal teams are able to share information in real-time, not only with each other, but also with upstream suppliers and downstream buyers. The impact of this innovation can be transformative. When the Italian tyre manufacturer, Pirelli, chose to implement SAP in the early 1990s, the company's CEO, Tronchetti Provera declared, "Unlike our competitors, we have the means to compete on a global scale. It is called SAP."[13]

ERP implementations are fairly rare due to the cost and complexity of their configuration. However, in most organisations small, locally developed software solutions are commonplace. These bespoke applications are often created in order to gain a competitive advantage through process innovation. One former telecommunications consultant told me about the desire by a phone company to vary charges according to the way that customers wanted to use their phones, e.g. infrequent phone users preferred lower rental charges and higher call charges, while frequent users preferred the reverse. Standard billing systems were unable to offer this form of differentiation, so a decision was made to create a proprietary solution. The client's subsequent ability to offer variable pricing led to the capture of substantial market share.[14] Here, the process innovation did not involve disintermediating the value chain. Instead, it was used to increase the value of a single, critical process step (i.e. billing).

If we consider the overall technology or product lifecycle, it is sometimes said that there are two main phases of innovation: firstly product-focused, and later process-focused. Initially, the emphasis is upon design. When technologies are new, buyer preferences are uncertain, and there will be few, if any, standards to constrain the creativity of entrepreneurs and designers. They want to experiment with ideas and test the market. However, this type of product design innovation slows down as the so-called *dominant design* emerges (see Chapter 4). At this later stage in the technology lifecycle, product innovation is de-prioritised in favour of process innovation. During this second phase, producers are seeking ways to compete more effectively against similar products. This shifts the innovation focus onto internal processes likely to affect costs, quality, and reliability. Therefore, product innovation gives way to process innovation.

Hopefully, the distinction between products and their production processes is now clear, along with the distinction between product innovation and process innovation. Beyond products and processes, there are other ways of categorising innovations. For instance, we could say that some are 'radical' in nature, while others are 'incremental'. Let's examine this perspective.

Radical and incremental

Radical innovations are typically rare, but of great significance. They do more than disrupt existing technologies and industries, they also enable a stream of further innovations. An innovation can also be described as economically radical if it causes existing product types (or entire industries) to lose their competitive strengths. Many analysts associate radical innovations with Joseph Schumpeter's theory of creative destruction, which explains how one industry emerges to replace another.[15] For example, the motor vehicle dismantled the equine economy, and digital cameras destroyed chemical-based photography. Hence, the motor vehicle and the digital camera were both radical innovations.

Referring back to the discussion around product innovation and process innovation, it is somewhat easier to find examples of radical products than radical processes, but there are examples of the latter. For instance, the impact of Pilkington's float glass manufacturing process (clearly radical) has already been described, and there's no doubt that Henry Ford's moving assembly lines changed the face of industry in the 20th century. More recently, within the software sector, Agile methodologies (e.g. Scrum) have radically transformed the development processes of coding, testing, and releasing.

However, innovations can be 'radical' without being particularly disruptive. James Dyson's bagless 'dual cyclone' vacuum cleaner only affected a single product category, and most rival companies minimised the impact with counter-innovations and strong marketing. Similarly, the jet engine may have supplanted some piston engine manufacturing, but it also precipitated a boom in air travel which supported many established aviation businesses. Indeed, propeller-driven short-haul airliners are still being built today. Neither the Dyson cleaner nor the jet engine were economically radical in the Schumpeterian sense.

Now let's turn to *incremental innovation*. The principal contrast between radical and incremental innovation is that the latter builds upon established knowledge and existing features in a constructive way. An incremental innovation improves products and processes by, for example, reducing costs, automating features, or increasing reliability. Let's consider some examples.

As rocketry evolved in the early post-war era, one of the most important incremental product innovations was the directional, gimballed engine. Until that time, rudder vanes had absorbed around 17% of propulsion energy, so the gimbal contributed greatly to overall performance, enabling the design of technically more ambitious rockets through the 1950s and beyond.[16]

The fantastically successful Sony Walkman, which enabled users to hear recorded music while on the move, is sometimes described as a revolutionary product. The Walkman was a scaled-down tape cassette player with headphones.[17] Hence, from a technical perspective it was an incremental rather than radical innovation.

A substantial leap in this product category did occur, many years later, with the advent of the Apple iPod. The iPod dispensed with physical recordings, utilising the new MP3 file format stored in flash memory. It was a radical innovation due to its destruction of the market in physical storage media, such as tapes and CDs, and its transformative impact on commercial music distribution.

Turning our attention from products to processes, we might observe that most process innovation is incremental, rather than radical. Processes typically evolve via changes to a single step in the value chain, or perhaps by less visible improvements, such as greater energy efficiency, or enhanced data management. These individual process innovations rarely make headlines, but can be significant when aggregated over the longer term.

We have seen how both products and processes evolve through innovations, and how these innovations may be radical or incremental in nature. We can also categorise each innovation according to 'ownership'. Who is responsible for the innovation? Who takes the credit? Who should reap the rewards? This leads us to a comparison of 'proprietary' and 'open' innovation.

Box 10.1   ANALYTICAL TOOLS AND TECHNIQUES

Product innovation and the Ansoff Matrix

The Ansoff Matrix is a tool familiar to business leaders and marketing professionals. It was introduced in the 1950s by the scientist and corporate strategist, Igor Ansoff.

The matrix assists firms with their product-market analysis and strategy development. Companies may deploy resources to achieve four possible aims: 1) to further penetrate existing markets with existing products; 2) to develop new products for existing markets; 3) to launch existing products in new markets; 4) to diversify by devising new products for new markets (Figure 10.3).

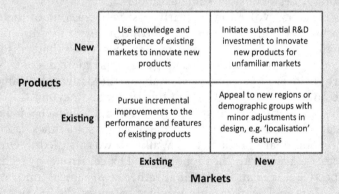

	Existing	New
New (Products)	Use knowledge and experience of existing markets to innovate new products	Initiate substantial R&D investment to innovate new products for unfamiliar markets
Existing	Pursue incremental improvements to the performance and features of existing products	Appeal to new regions or demographic groups with minor adjustments in design, e.g. 'localisation' features

Markets

Figure 10.3 Product innovation and the Ansoff Matrix

The diagram above is structured like a conventional Ansoff Matrix. However, each of the four quadrants describes the innovation implications for the product-market combination.

Engineers ought to be proactive in suggesting directions for further product development using their knowledge of the latest discoveries, materials, and manufacturing techniques.

Proprietary and open

Innovations are typically 'owned' by their creators. Often their details are protected by non-disclosure agreements or intellectual property (IP) rights, such as patents. The aim is to maximise the commercial benefits of an innovation before equivalent knowledge and skills are developed elsewhere, or before legal protection expires. This protective ownership of new ideas is known as *proprietary innovation*

A perfect example of proprietary innovation is the wide range of highly original, legally secured product designs from Apple Inc., including their distinctive computers, peripherals, smartphones, and music players.

Proprietary innovation can be difficult and costly to pursue. Firstly, it relies heavily upon R&D investment and creative employees as the source of innovative ideas. This can be a significant economic constraint, especially for smaller organisations. Secondly, there is no guarantee that viable ideas will emerge with sufficient frequency (if they emerge at all). Thirdly, IP lawyers are expensive, so attempts to deter and lockout competitors using legal protection are often costly. Consequently, a non-proprietary approach is attractive to many organisations.

Innovation that occurs in less acquisitive, more collaborative, and transparent environments is sometimes called *open innovation*. Here, ideas emerge in shared or public domains, and ownership rights are treated with less reverence.

Open innovation delivers numerous benefits. It enables commercially viable ideas to be generated and adopted at relatively low cost. It also encourages other participating organisations to form an 'ecosystem' of complementary or compatible goods and services. In this type of open environment, the originators of ideas have fewer opportunities to gain financially from their innovations, but the benefits of openness are perceived to outweigh the costs.

One such open innovation environment is the Moodle learning platform which, since the early 2000s, has enroled millions of users onto online training and education courses.[18] Although Moodle is a private organisation, its learning management system (LMS) is available free-of-charge, while software features and fixes are developed by a global community of enthusiasts. It's one of the many successful examples of open innovation in the software sector.

Another familiar example of open innovation was described in Chapter 8. There, we saw how the collaborative efforts of telecoms companies, facilitated by the European Telecommunications Standards Institute (ETSI), have enabled successive iterations of the mobile telephony standards, now approaching their sixth generation (or 6G).

Table 10.1 Types of technological innovation, with one example from each category

	Proprietary		Open	
	Radical	Incremental	Radical	Incremental
Product	Diesel engine	Sony Walkman	The World Wide Web	Mobile telecommunications, such as 4G, 5G, 6G
Process	Pilkington float glass method	Phone billing according to the type of voice call	Agile software development methods, e.g. Scrum	Design-build teams (DBTs)

However, proprietary innovation and open innovation are not mutually exclusive. There are hybrid solutions which combine the best of both approaches. For example, companies can collaborate in research, development, and market testing without necessarily sharing their innovations in the public domain. Also, businesses sometimes use open competitions, encouraging customers and suppliers to submit ideas for new products. One scheme, Procter & Gamble's 'Connect and Develop', was introduced with the aim of acquiring more ideas from external sources. This initiative increased the productivity of P&G's research division by 60% over five years, and more than a third of new products originated from outside the organisation.[19,20]

Although these hybrid approaches are classified as open innovation, they fall some way short of the transparency and community engagement associated with Moodle, for instance. Nevertheless, there is a clear difference of philosophy between the secretive nature of proprietary innovation and open innovation's willingness to share.

Table 10.1 should help to clarify the relationships between proprietary and open innovation, along with the four other types of innovation already discussed.

Organisation and system

Some of the most dramatic technological innovations are those which add value by improving the shape or structure of organisations. When this occurs in the private sector, it is often known as business model innovation. Some well-known examples of new business models enabled by technological changes are: renting movies (made famous by Blockbuster); online social networks (i.e. users supply the content, advertisers supply the revenue); power-by-the-hour and real-time engine monitoring (pioneered by Rolls-Royce).[21]

Under normal circumstances business models are the responsibility of business strategists, rather than technology strategists. However, business leaders often rely upon engineers to highlight the innovation potential offered by technologies. It then becomes the responsibility of technology strategists to propose mechanisms for implementing the changes requested by the business.

Similarly, large technical systems can also be innovated and re-engineered. Where a system consists of multiple integrated technologies, it isn't necessary for any one technology to be innovative in order for the whole system to be regarded as novel. For instance, when I.K. Brunel was building his ships, *Great Britain* and *Great Eastern*, he brought together the pre-existing technologies of metal hull construction, steam power, and the screw propeller to create a type of system never seen before – the modern ocean liner. Similarly, when the Shinkansen rail network was built, its designers (led by engineer Hideo Shima) carefully integrated all the elements of an idealised railway: dedicated tracks devoid of tight curves, junctions, or road crossings; express-only trains; the latest propulsion systems; streamlined designs; and dedicated staff. The engineers had a clear vision for creating the finest railway in the world. This they achieved with extraordinary levels of punctuality and not a single passenger fatality since 1964.[22] The Shinkansen was a true system innovation.

Enabling and encouraging innovation

Innovations emerge from human ingenuity. It is therefore the job of organisational leaders and their technology strategists to create the conditions in which innovation thrives. This assumes, of course, that the organisation wishes to evolve and improve through the power of innovation. Sometimes it's not a high priority, and this will be explained later in the chapter.

However, for the moment let's assume that there is a desire to innovate. Professor Nigel Cross of the Open University, in his book *Engineering Design Methods* (2008), suggests some of the innovation outcomes we might want to achieve:

- Enhancing performance, e.g. capacity, power, speed, accuracy, versatility.
- Increasing reliability.
- Using less expensive materials or manufacturing methods.
- Reducing customisation costs by standardising or modularising.
- Eliminating low-value functions/components.
- Simplifying assembly sequences.
- Improving ease of use and ease of maintenance.
- Ensuring better safety/security.

- Achieving greater longevity.
- Minimising by-product waste and pollution.

Most of these items fall into two broad categories: 1) controlling costs and 2) creating or adding value. Cross warns designers that it's pointless to innovate cost reductions if customer perceptions of value are simultaneously undermined.[23] The key skill is achieving one without damaging the other.

Managers must create the internal conditions under which these promising ideas will emerge. Some external factors are also likely to support innovation efforts. I will briefly explore these internal conditions and external factors, grouped under five headings: The workplace; Direction; Shaping solutions; Tools; and The 'real world'.

The workplace

The place of work is an important factor in shaping innovation cultures. For example, we've already noted the impact of locating within technology clusters, especially those benefiting from proximity to universities. And Chapter 8 extolled the virtues of empowered workforces, especially those with a broad range of skills and life experiences. It was argued that these may be particularly effective at devising novel solutions relative to less empowered, more homogenous workgroups.

In Chapter 3, the challenges associated with combining technical and non-technical teams in the same workplace were discussed. A case was made for giving engineers a separate space (a 'cloister') in which to concentrate on their work and innovate without interruptions. Some evidence was presented to support this view, including the success of Lockheed's Skunk Works.

James Watt recounted how, in 1765, while taking a solitary walk around a park (Glasgow Green), he had the idea for adding a separate condenser to steam engines. This single innovation transformed the economics of steam power and led to a revolution in industrial productivity.[24] A century later, Nikola Tesla invented the AC motor during a walk in a Budapest park while simultaneously reciting poetry.[25] It's often said that some of the best ideas come in the shower (or the bath), so there is plenty of anecdotal evidence to support the notion that engineers benefit from periods of uninterrupted thinking time. In 1908 Wilbur Wright sent some great advice to Orville in a letter:

> Do not let yourself be forced into doing anything before you are ready. Be very cautious and proceed slowly ... Let it be known

that you ... intend to do it in your own way. Do not let people talk to you all day and all night. It will wear you out before you are ready for real business. Courtesy has limits. If necessary appoint some hour in the day time and refuse absolutely to receive visitors even for a minute at other times.[26]

Managers should acknowledge and facilitate these requirements. Many years ago I remember being told about a workplace where engineers wore a distinctive hat if they did not wish to be disturbed. Not a bad idea.

Another way to get the best from technical people is to set tough, yet feasible, challenges. In Chapter 7, we learned how Sony's co-founder, Masaru Ibuka, threw a paperback book on the table and challenged engineers to create a cassette tape no larger than the book, but capable of storing one hour of colour TV output. It had the required effect, and Betamax was born. In 2019, the Director of Product Engineering at Jaguar Land Rover, Nick Rogers, said in an interview that "If somebody says something can't be done, to most engineers that just provokes them into proving that it can be."[27]

Sometimes the sources of new innovations are literally at our fingertips. In other words, we need to make better use of the assets, or potential assets, we already have, even if we don't yet recognise them as such. For example, there are many stories of commercial waste being turned into new products or adding value in other ways. Today, one of the most valuable waste by-products is data. In their book, *What To Do When Machines Do Everything* (2017), Malcolm Frank *et al.* argue that many organisations could use data science to exploit their huge volumes of accumulated data. Senior Vice President at LexisNexis, Flavio Villanustre, is quoted as saying, "By adding a data set to another data set, you can potentially make a completely new thing."[28] Many organisations remain ignorant of these possibilities.

In-house business incubators can be another source of workplace innovation. These incubators provide basic resources, such as free desk space and power to entrepreneurs with promising ideas. Apart from current and former employees, outsiders may also be invited to participate. An interesting recent example is the *Abbey Road Red* incubator, based at the famous Abbey Road recording studios in London. Here, promising startups working with music technologies are invited to incubate their businesses. Abbey Road Studios takes a 2% equity stake in each startup. They also hope to achieve technological gains from the exchange of ideas and knowledge between their own staff and the entrepreneurs.[29] Red's first major success was reported in 2022, when Apple acquired the startup, AI Music.[30]

Direction

Innovation should be easier when the 'direction' of technology is known, or where it follows some predictable logic. This logic might include the 'stick and carrot' of incentives. Let's briefly examine three influences upon the direction of innovation.

Firstly, it's common for governments to incentivise or encourage innovation in particular sectors and for particular purposes. Often there is an economic imperative, perhaps reflected in a government's industrial policy (see Chapter 3), but in a small number of countries, notably the USA, military and other defence requirements fuel a significant amount of technological creativity. In 2023, for instance, DARPA, one of the main sources of funds for US defence innovation, consumed a budget of $4 billion. This money is disbursed among hundreds of innovation projects in order to maintain America's leadership in military technology.

Further direction is offered by so-called foresight analysis. Foresight techniques are used by specialist consultants to advise organisations on the likely evolution of significant factors influencing technological development, such as the economy and social trends. The methods used in foresight analysis include horizon scanning, citizen panels, trend analysis, the Delphi method (described in the previous chapter), and scenario development. Patrick van der Duin's *Foresight in Organizations* (2016) offers many useful insights. There will be much more on foresight in Chapter 11.

Thirdly, there is a type of innovation that involves building incrementally upon current technological capabilities. According to Rumelt, this type of innovation is so fundamental that it almost constitutes common sense:

> Build on your strengths. The idea that some corporate resources can be put to good use in other products or markets is possibly the most basic in corporate strategy.

In other words, in order to innovate successfully, it isn't necessary to take a bold leap into the unknown. Just take one step forward using the capabilities already acquired. This 'path of least resistance' often opens doors to new opportunities. For example, DuPont, a manufacturer of explosives in WW1, used its acquired chemical expertise to subsequently produce cellulose, synthetic rubber, and paints. Later, this work in synthetics led to such innovations as Lucite, Teflon, nylon, Mylar, Dacron, Lycra, and so on.[31] In Italy, Pirelli progressed from rubber tyres to rubber cabling for electric railways and telephone networks. This led to wider interests in telecommunications, and by the 1980s Pirelli was investing heavily in fibre optics, the technology replacing traditional cables.[32]

Shaping solutions

An overused expression, often applied to innovation activities, is 'thinking outside the box'. It relates to the absence of constraints upon thought processes and design. Technologists like nothing more than a blank slate on which to devise and shape their engineering solutions.

For example, magnetic resonance imaging (MRI) technologies have been evolving incrementally for decades. However, incrementalism has constrained the rate at which the technology has progressed. Consequently, when the firm Siemens Magnet Technology (SMT) chose to design a new MRI scanner from the ground up, they achieved a step-change improvement. Whereas most scanners operate in the range of 1.5 to 3 Tesla (which determines image resolution), the new 7 Tesla system achieved by SMT enables sharp enough images to view the vascularity of the brain. It is also half the weight of rival machines and can be installed more quickly by pre-cooling the magnets prior to despatch.[33] There is a case to be made for all mature technologies and product types to be re-designed with a blank slate, from the ground up, in order to 'write off' the technical debt embedded within old designs. This re-shaping can liberate a technology's innate potential.

Another type of innovation-shaping involves the use of *biomimicry* to produce solutions inspired by the natural world. Engineers (both amateur and professional) have been doing this for thousands of years. However, one famous example from the early 19th century involved Marc Brunel, I.K. Brunel's father. Many years before his son's astonishing achievements, Marc Brunel had built a reputation for his tunnel engineering skills. One of his innovations was inspired by the physiology of a burrowing 'ship worm', *teredo navalis*, which features a hardened, protective shield over its head.[34] Brunel invented the method of tunnelling within a moving shield. Not only did tunnelling work become much safer, it also delivered more reliable rates of progress underground.

Innovations are also shaped by *convergence*, i.e. the seamless integration of two or more products or processes. One of the most significant examples in recent decades has been the convergence of personal computers, cameras, music players, and mobile telephones into the ubiquitous 'smartphone'. In truth, these devices are not really 'phones' at all, but sophisticated, multi-purpose digital machines, combining functions which, only 25 years ago, would have required a roomful of equipment. Other examples of convergence are the washer/dryer and 'three-in-one' printer/scanner/copiers. Product and process convergences typically achieve reductions in physical scale, material resources, and energy consumption. There are some disadvantages, of course, such as single points of failure, functional complexity, and maintenance challenges, but these are generally outweighed by the benefits.

Finally, let's consider technology domains. In Chapter 2 these were described by W.B. Arthur as "families of devices, methods, and practices". In fact there is no agreed definition of a technology domain, but we often use terms such as *electronics*, *hydraulics*, *computing*, and *biotech* to infer groups of related technologies. One way to innovate with domains is to switch a product or process from one to another. This is easier said than done, of course, but it is feasible. For example, factory owners in the early 19th century redomained their energy supplies by disconnecting water wheels in order to install Watt's rotative steam engines.[35] More recently, when aircraft flight controls changed from mechanical human inputs to fly-by-wire technologies, aviation was also redomaining. Take a close look at your own products and processes. Are there any redomaining opportunities, perhaps involving emerging or recently established technologies?

Tools

Product and process innovations may emerge through the use of tools designed to stimulate creativity. Let's examine a few of them.

One of the best-known creativity tools, at least in organisational environments, is *brainstorming*. Emerging in the 1950s from the work of Alex Osborn in the US, brainstorming generates novel ideas through the dynamics of group interaction.[36] According to the theory, a small team of committed individuals with diverse skills and experience, devoid of hierarchy or status, can be led by a facilitator to produce a host of strong ideas relatively quickly.[37] Brainstorming's key attribute is its absence of constraints. Participants are encouraged to think and speak freely. All verbal contributions are acknowledged without negative feedback. Rather than denounce 'crazy' ideas, they are instead viewed as potential triggers to new insights, perhaps leading to ground-breaking innovations.

Another tool dependent upon group inputs is *backcasting*. Originating in the 1970s, backcasting reverses the more familiar concept of forecasting.[38] The backcasting method establishes a desired future state, perhaps five years away, then determines each of the actions, in reverse order, necessary for arriving at that state. For example, a goal to reduce reliance upon a particular type of energy should stimulate both product and process innovations. It's worth noting, however, that backcasting is very susceptible to the trumpet of uncertainty associated with complexity (explained in Chapter 6).

Another group activity is the practice of *Synectics*, which uses analogies to generate creative insights. Nigel Cross defines analogical thinking as "the ability to see parallels or connections between apparently dissimilar topics."[39] Participants are asked to focus upon certain types of analogies. One example might be the analogy of living things. Marc Brunel's tunnelling technique, described above, used the analogy of 'ship worms'. Another type is the personal analogy, by which we might imagine ourselves performing the role of a machine or stepping through a process. The history of invention and innovation is replete with analogical inspirations, often reflected in technical vocabularies. For example, the 'blades' of a propeller 'cut' through the air. Or, for a strong nautical analogy, air*liners* are manoeuvred at air*ports* by vehicles called *tugs*. What more could aviation learn from maritime analogies? Conversely, what could the shipping industry learn from the aviation sector? Synectics is a useful technique.

A very different creative tool is *morphological analysis*. It focuses upon desired product features and the possible technical means for delivering them. These ideas are captured in a 'morphological chart', an example of which is shown in Table 10.2. This particular (hypothetical) chart, for an autonomous window cleaning machine, reveals a selected combination of features, which have been emboldened. Some charts feature visual designs, rather than text. There are many examples of morphological charts online.

Table 10.2 Morphological chart for a hypothetical autonomous window cleaning machine (adapted from *Engineering Design Strategies*, N. Cross, 2008)

Feature	Means				
Attachment	**Rails**	Suction	Crane cable		
Propulsion	**Driven wheels**	Crane hauled	Pedipulators		
Power	Mains electricity	Hydrogen	Petrol	Diesel	**On-board battery**
Cleaning	Spray and wipe	Spray only	Wipe only	**Air jet**	
Drying	Squeegee	Natural air drying	Hot air blow	Radiant heat	**No drying function**
Computer	On board	Wired connect	**Wi-fi connect**		

Although the innovation tools described above can be used to support the design of both products and processes, most process innovation work uses modelling. This can include basic process flowcharts or the more complex tools associated with the unified modelling language (UML) for systems design.[40]

During the design of an engineering process, there will always be opportunities for innovations, such as those relating to efficiency or safety. However, when legacy processes are being re-modelled the focus is more likely to be upon either improving or eliminating existing steps. Here, designers (or 'process re-engineers') must question every action in the process, examining such things as reliability, duplication, sourcing, value-add, time delays, opportunities for parallel working, and so on. As we saw earlier with Pilkington's redesign of glass manufacturing, the rigorous analysis and redesign of processes can reap significant rewards.

The 'real world'

A highly effective place to innovate is in the rough-and-tumble of 'real world' operating environments. For example, organisations are often encouraged to release immature versions of new products in order to receive prompt and constructive feedback from users.[41] This approach, sometimes called the minimum viable product (MVP), involves the iteration of designs using a feedback cycle, repeatedly launching, learning, improving, and launching again. Designers quickly discover the strengths and weaknesses of their ideas. This leads to a relatively stable product devoid of unwanted features.

Arguably, the greatest ever MVP was Sputnik 1, a satellite launched by the Soviet Union in 1957. Incapable of doing anything other than transmitting periodic bleeps, Sputnik survived its launch, achieved orbit, and communicated with ground receivers. Sputnik had proved the satellite concept, to the astonishment of the watching, or rather listening, world.[42] The key point is that the Soviets didn't wait until they had a satellite capable of performing tasks. There was plenty to be learned from this most basic version.

Another type of real-world technology innovation occurs in competitive sports. The natural stresses and strains of competitive behaviour are impossible to replicate in laboratory conditions. For this reason, all equipment-based professional sports are used as test-beds for the latest innovations. For example, motor racing is an extremely effective R&D environment. The drivers, who are highly incentivised to win, seek to 'push the envelopes' imposed by vehicle designers and engineers. The latest ideas undergo continuous testing and perfection, and this often leads to their adoption by mainstream vehicle manufacturers.

In general, user feedback on products and processes, especially when delivered in the form of criticisms or complaints, can act as a tremendous spur to innovation. Organisations that fail to listen and learn from their customers are probably destined to fail overall.

The five dimensions of innovation

In Chapter 2, a new theory of technology, exclusive to this book, was presented. It deconstructed every technology into five 'dimensions', denoted by the acronym PLAYS: Physical, Logical, Architectural, Yield, and Stakeholder.

This theory should prove helpful for innovators and designers, because it enables them to think creatively about their technologies, focusing upon one dimension at a time. Some examples of how this might be done are described in Table 10.3.

Table 10.3 The five dimensions of technology innovation.

Dimension	Innovation potential and examples
Physical	The choice of materials influences costs, durability, aesthetics, weight, and so on. Also, a change of material may enable a more reliable source of supply, or facilitate access to new markets.
Logical	Technologies are defined by how they work – the methods they use to yield value. These ways of working can often be improved. For example, mechanical can openers come in many forms. Some are more reliable than others. Some may be more efficient, while others are easier to use. Is there a better way of opening a can? Re-thinking this logical dimension could even lead to a change in the technology itself, because there may be alternative technologies better suited to the task.
Architectural	Architectures may be varied according to the product's physical and logical characteristics. A different architecture might deliver performance improvements, cost savings, or safer operations.
Yield	Can the technology's yield be improved? Is there some latent value waiting to be discovered which might lead to a new market for the technology? Can we improve the way that the yield is being delivered to the stakeholders? Consider psychology and perceptions.
Stakeholder	Innovations for stakeholders will require changes to one or more of the other four dimensions. Examine the technology or product from the perspective of buyers, users, and beneficiaries. Could it be made more appealing to them? How do we improve the user experience? The beneficiary stakeholders are more likely to be satisfied if the yield value can be increased.

Strategy and innovation

During the development of a technology strategy, some consideration should be given to innovation potential. The amount of time and energy expended on this topic will vary according to various factors, especially the culture of innovation within the organisation. However, the main determinant will be the contents of the primary organisational strategy – the business strategy. **A technology strategy cannot propose a focus upon innovation activities if this is incompatible with the business strategy, or if it runs contrary to the business culture of the organisation.**

Consequently, if we were to examine a large, random sample of technology strategies across all sectors, we would find that innovation sits on a spectrum. One end of the spectrum represents a total commitment to R&D and other innovation processes, e.g. organisations like Dyson, Meta, Unilever, and the US Department of Defense. The other end, however, represents total indifference to technological innovation, e.g. many public authorities, service businesses, charities, and social enterprises.

Let's divide this innovation spectrum into three parts, each reflecting a distinctive approach toward innovation strategy: 1) the proactive approach; 2) the reactive approach; and 3) the inactive approach.

The proactive approach

A great deal has been written about *proactive innovation*. It's an exciting topic that regularly makes the headlines. Many proactive innovators have already been described in this book, from individual entrepreneurs such as Matthew Boulton, Thomas Edison, and Akio Morita, to organisations including Pirelli, DuPont, and Apple. Let's briefly consider how this approach to innovation works in practice.

In 1901 the Cambridge scientist, Humphrey Jones, was asked by Shell to analyse the oil from its Borneo wells. It was possibly the first occasion on which petroleum distillate had been studied in this way. Jones extracted around 350 pure chemical substances. In other words, a host of new products could be manufactured from the same raw material.[43] The capital expenditure required to create this new type of manufacturing would be substantial, but Board member J.B.A. Kessler made the case for petrochemical refining:

> We should have confidence, energy and courage enough to develop this new part of our business, even if it does not yield profits to start with. Do not let us be frightened by some

preliminary cost calculations which show that we may not make money in the beginning. I do not expect to make money; on the contrary, I expect it will cost a good deal of money before we can actually produce on a fairly large scale.[44]

Grant and Jordan explain that this proactive approach to innovation is how organisations "create the future". This is because "competitive advantages accrue to those companies that act as leaders and initiate change."[45] Shell were (and presumably still are) proactive innovators.

It was established in Chapter 3 that technology innovation must support an organisation's business strategy, so let's consider some examples of how this particular relationship works. Two dominant business strategies for gaining competitive advantage are *differentiation* and *cost leadership*.[46] The former involves the development of new or improved products, with the aim of outgunning competitors in the battle for buyers' attention. In order to lead by differentiation, it's necessary to innovate at the product level. The producers of consumer goods, such as toys and electronic gadgets, are familiar differentiators. Yet there is a similar amount of differentiation in business-to-business markets for machinery, consumables, and consulting services. By contrast, a cost leadership strategy might encourage a reduction in R&D expenditure and limited differentiation. Improved operational efficiency can be important in controlling costs, so this would emphasise the need for process innovation.[47]

Within organisations R&D is the source of much product and process innovation, especially the former. R&D may be conceptualised as a formal allocation of resources to the internal processes of creative thinking, analysis, prototyping, and testing. The philosopher Alfred North Whitehead wrote that "The greatest invention of the nineteenth century was the invention of the method of invention." This new 'method' helps to explain the growth of R&D centres throughout the industrialised world in the late 19th century, exemplified in the US by Edison's Menlo Park facility (opened in 1865). The success of Edison's "invention factory", as Daniel Headrick calls it, encouraged other companies to create research divisions, including Standard Oil (1880), DuPont (1902), AT&T (1911), and Eastman Kodak (1913). By 1938 there were 2,200 corporate research laboratories in the US.[48]

George Basalla describes R&D as "an investment in the long-range potential of the firm."[49] At Sony, while under the leadership of its founder, Akio Morita, the level of this investment was between 6 and 10% of sales. Writing in the 1980s, Morita explained Sony's approach:

Our plan is to lead the public with new products rather than ask them what kind of products they want. The public does not know what is possible, but we do. So instead of doing a lot of market research, we refine our thinking on a product and its use and try to create a market for it by educating and communicating with the public.[50]

The company's "Sony Spirit" statement included the line, "always a seeker of the unknown."[51] It is sometimes said that innovation comes in two forms: 'demand-pull', because it responds to the market, and 'technology push', because it originates within organisations. Sony's approach was clearly the latter.

One of the constraints upon product innovation, even within proactive firms like Sony, is the fear of *cannibalisation*, a term which Allan Afuah mentions frequently in his book, *Innovation Management* (2003). The concern is that new products, or new product versions, could cannibalise (i.e. consume) the internal capabilities and other vital assets associated with existing goods and services. For example, why would a producer of fossil-fuelled vehicles voluntarily move towards hydrogen fuel cells? Why would a manufacturer of filament light bulbs seek to develop a new range of long-life LED bulbs? The answer is that there is too much to lose from doing so, including the accumulated skills and experience of personnel, and the value of specialised machinery developed over decades to manufacture high-volume products. New product types can also damage the goodwill accumulated in relationships with longstanding clients. For this reason, organisations may opt to *suppress* potentially damaging innovations. Suppression often involves burying or locking down new ideas using intellectual property rights and non-disclosure agreements (NDAs).

For companies committed to proactive innovation, this suppression of new ideas and inventions is clearly contradictory. Fortunately, there is a solution to this quandary, because IP, especially patents, can be licensed to third parties. The licensees will then bear the risks of persuading the market to adopt the product. This is attractive for the innovator, because it externalises the costs associated with further product development and marketing. Also, the royalties from licensing can help to diversify the company's income sources. If the invention becomes successful, the innovator may then choose to bring it back in-house. By deferring the transition to a new product or technology in this way, a company defers the act of cannibalising its existing products. Licensing enables the innovator to 'buy' time while retaining control.

In fact licensing is fundamental to the business and technology strategies of many innovative companies, where the licenses become the product. In his book *Technology in Context* (1998), Ernest Braun explains that one of the reasons for the rapid success of semiconductor technologies in the 1950s was the way that Bell Labs (specialists in researching, developing, and patenting) granted licenses freely to other businesses.[52] Similarly, in 2013 the specialist in sound reduction technologies, Dolby Labs, was reported to have earned 89% of its revenues from licensing. Also, many small biotech companies specialise in R&D, aiming to license their drug discoveries to established players in the pharmaceutical sector.[53]

Most recently, in the race to develop the first commercially viable fusion reactor, a prominent startup in Oxford, First Light Fusion, has declared that their strategy involves licensing their proprietary design for a fusion reactor, while retaining the rights to mass-manufacture the 'targets' containing the reactor fuel.[54] In other words, their two major products would be a license and a fuel capsule.

However, it isn't always possible to persuade third parties to acquire licenses. For instance, James Dyson travelled around the world, unsuccessfully seeking a licensor for his bagless vacuum cleaner. It was only when this search failed that he chose to become a volume manufacturer of household appliances.[55,56]

The patent system can also be used in a strategic way to block rivals by surrounding a valuable patent with similar, but unwanted patents. Indeed, this tactic has been used for centuries. James Watt, for instance, "played the patent game" in the words of one biographer, by registering claims for five different ways to smooth the motion of steam engines. Apparently, this is now known as a *patent cluster* or *patent thicket*. Only the 'sun and planet' motion was ever put to use, but Watt's rivals had been denied the chance to develop anything similar.[57] The same approach was adopted by Bell Laboratories. According to one of its presidents, the company would deliberately occupy technical fields with "a thousand and one little patents and inventions."[58] This monopolisation of an entire field delivers immense control, enabling the IP holder to determine the fate of a technology.

A proactive innovator needs to think through the full commercial implications of a new product before launching. In the 1970s EMI created the world's first computer tomography (CT) scanner. This revolutionary technology's ability to deliver 3D internal views of objects, especially the human body, should have brought long-term global success to EMI. However, the company's strength was researching and developing technologies, rather than selling and maintaining them. Critically, it had no foothold in the healthcare sector. A potential rival, General Electric, already had immense manufacturing, sales, and customer service capabilities. GE was also an established producer of medical devices. So, within a few years, it had overtaken EMI in CT scanner sales.[59,60] EMI later declined and disappeared as an organisation. Today, GE's HealthCare spin-out remains a market leader in CT scanners.

Proactive innovators also must remember that new technologies often require an ecosystem of complementary goods and services in order to succeed. It may therefore be necessary to take responsibility for their design and production. An example of this is told by Bill Nuttall in his history of the abandoned TSR2 bomber project. The TSR2 was designed for a nuclear deterrence role, so it needed to operate autonomously from remote airfields. Consequently, the British Aircraft Corporation (BAC) were required (perhaps to their surprise) to produce items such as universal lifting trolleys, test equipment trailers, and dedicated support vehicles for the aircraft and their crews.[61] The need for such complementary products is easily overlooked in the excitable rush to develop something new.

None of the above innovations would have been possible without creative people, especially engineers, whose professional instincts are to overcome challenges and design solutions. For this reason, proactive innovation requires an appropriate recruitment policy and a commitment to the development of innovation-related skills. This human resourcing angle must not be overlooked by strategists when they produce an organisation's technology strategy. For example, it might be wise to address these questions: Are the most creative engineers suitably rewarded? And do they have the time, facilities, and management support needed to innovate effectively?

Finally, let's consider the financial costs of innovation. R&D is expensive and there are substantial business risks in pursuing a policy of proactive innovation. However, as we saw in Kessler's persuasion of the Shell Board, it is often necessary to show financial courage. In the 1980s, having led Sony to worldwide success, Akio Morita reflected in his autobiography that, "If the accountant had been in charge of our little company in 1946, our company would be a small operation making parts for the giants."[62]

Does this mean that the choice is innovate or fail? No it doesn't, because alternative strategies are available. For example, rather than being proactive, an organisation might prefer to adopt a more responsive or *reactive* approach to innovation.

Box 10.2 STRATEGIC DICHOTOMIES

Concentrated solutions OR Distributed solutions?

A fundamental dichotomy associated with technologies, processes, and organisations is the degree of coupling or integration. Product designers and system architects are often faced with a range of options on the spectrum between tight integration (centralisation) and loose integration (decentralisation). These are strategic choices.

Let's compare and contrast both ends of this spectrum: (Table 10.4)

Table 10.4 The relative advantages and disadvantages of concentrated and dispersed solutions

Concentrate/Centralise/Integrate	Distribute/Decentralise/Disperse
Examples: Multi-function, tightly integrated packages, such as smartphones; mainframe computers; large power plants supplying regional electricity needs; giant main airports for 'hub and spoke' operations.	**Examples:** Loosely integrated, modularised products, such as client-server computing environments with desktop PCs; localised and modularised power generators (e.g. wind turbines, solar PV); small regional airports engaged in 'point to point' operations.
Relative advantages: Convenient single unit, often easier to manage and control. Facilitates easy data exchanges. Security is more manageable. Resource efficient, e.g. minimises the embedded energy and use of natural resources. Generally less costly than distributed solutions.	**Relative advantages:** More flexible architectures. Ease of maintenance and upgrade via swappable modules. Customisable deployments. Usually very scalable. High availability, e.g. risk is mitigated via separation and geographical dispersion.
Relative disadvantages: More inflexible architectures. Less scalable. Cannot be tailored to the needs of small sub-groups of clients. Vulnerable to single point of failure, e.g. power loss or broken component. In general, tight integration increases repair and replacement costs, often incurring temporary loss of service.	**Relative disadvantages:** Complex networks of connectivity and service. High overheads of management and control. Hard to secure. More difficult exchanges of data and knowledge management. Requires more embedded energy and natural resources.

Often we prefer a compromise between these two extremes, but sometimes there will be no hybrid available. This can forcibly (and perhaps permanently) lock us into one end of the spectrum.

For example, is there a successful hybrid option between the hub-and-spoke model of flight operations and the point-to-point model? To maximise efficiency, flight schedules, choice of aircraft, and even the types of aircraft seats must be tailored to one or other solution.

This is a complex topic which has necessarily been simplified here. However, one thing is certain. Every technologist or engineer will face this particular dichotomy at some point in their career.

The reactive approach

Many organisations perform well without proactive innovation. R&D is costly, and the introduction of innovative products and processes generates a level of risk which may run contrary to an organisation's mission, or to the prevailing management culture. *Reactive innovation* offers an alternative approach.

There are probably hundreds of thousands of organisations worldwide that succeed by reacting to, rather than instigating, major technological innovations. These reactive innovators occupy an important niche within the economy, delivering familiar products and a wide range of complementary goods and services.

In its most basic form, reactive innovation simply involves the imitation of a successful product, avoiding IP protection where it exists. This is a perfectly legitimate business activity. Another type of reactive innovation involves joining an emerging technology ecosystem. A great technology or product may struggle to gain traction if the ecosystem of ancillary goods and services (such as raw materials, components, consumables, consulting, training courses, and repair engineers) has failed to develop. A reactive innovator recognises and responds to this problem by joining and supporting the ecosystem.

Some examples may help to clarify the scope of this innovation strategy. Grant and Jordan provide two good cases from the history of personal computing. Firstly, they describe how the proactive innovators of desktop computing, notably Tandy, Commodore, and Apple, were commercially eclipsed by reactive 'second movers', e.g. IBM, Dell, Compaq, Acer, and Toshiba.[63] Interestingly, many of these PC manufacturers were less profitable than their component suppliers, which included Intel (processors), Seagate (disk storage), and of course Microsoft.[64] In fact these suppliers were often proactive innovators within their own fields, but it was PC sales that enabled their global success. So, in that sense they were reactive.

Apart from these high-profile names, many more reactive enterprises were thriving in the ecosystem of the personal computing industry, including the manufacturers of peripherals and utility software. Most of these companies were able to succeed without investing in significant R&D or launching technological innovations of their own.

To gain the most from their strategy, reactive innovators need to be nimble. For example, in 2010 Apple launched its iPad, the first commercially successful tablet computer. Apple hadn't 'invented' the tablet, because the concept was already well-known, but they got the timing and design just right. Sales of the iPad grew so quickly that it attracted the attention of reactive innovators. Just one year later there were 100 tablets on the market from 60 manufacturers.[65] Of course, these products were generally of inferior quality, but it's likely that healthy profits were still being made by many of these second movers.

Therefore, reactive innovation may be less glamorous than the exciting world of proactive R&D, but it's often a rewarding strategy. They may be perceived as unimaginative and imitative, but reactive innovators are often the smartest players in the market. As part of a formal technology strategy, the 'wait and see' approach of reactive innovation may be the most sensible strategy of all.

The inactive approach

In 1995, as a new employee within the IT department of a large insurance company, I made the error of proposing research into the use of neural nets. I explained that they could be used to make sub-second decisions on customer claims. I had read that Sun Life in North America was also looking into this. The response to my radical suggestion was a sea of blank faces. Of course, not only did the IT management have no idea what I was talking about, but the culture within the company was not conducive to innovation. Their attitude was simple: Why bother spending money on R&D when the business of selling insurance is effectively 'a licence to print money'? Looking back, I realise that I had completely misread the culture and the people.

The reader should be able to guess where this is heading. There is another category of innovator. These are the organisations that do zero (or effectively zero) technological innovation, whether proactive or reactive. However, before scoffing at these *inactive innovators*, let's not forget that they exist in large numbers and are often very successful.

Imagine walking through a large city. You pass retailers, commercial offices, industrial premises, schools and colleges, libraries, railway stations, sports stadia, and so on. How many of these organisations are proactive or reactive technological innovators? Very few. Maybe just a few percent. Of course, most of them make extensive use of technologies, including vehicles, computers, and office machinery, but the majority have no desire or capability to innovate in any substantive way. This doesn't condemn them to failure. It simply means that their business strategies can be executed without the need for product innovation or major process transformations. Let's briefly consider a few situations where inactive innovation represents the preferred or logical approach.

We've just seen an example of how some companies choose to imitate successful products; 60 businesses decided to manufacture tablets following the iPad launch. Although I've classified these producers as reactive innovators, many of them were probably very inactive in terms of R&D. How many companies can you think of that manufacture products which they have neither invented nor improved in any significant way? For example, which company made that microwave oven in your kitchen? Did they invent it? No. Did they improve it? Probably not. There are many, many companies like this which survive through imitation, careful cost control, and skilful marketing. We can choose to define them as either reactive or inactive innovators.

A more clearcut example of inactive innovation is the construction industry, particularly housebuilding, which generally has a poor record of both product and process innovation. In the UK this is blamed upon low profit margins, which tend to discourage firms from using their revenues to invest in R&D. As a consequence, builders are forced to compete on price rather than originality.[66] Most housebuilders are inactive innovators.

Knowledge-based organisations, such as insurance companies, advertisers, business consultancies, and public authorities, usually deliver their services with off-the-shelf technologies. These include desktop computers, standard industry software, telephones, vans, and so on. Although these organisations sometimes develop bespoke software to meet specific needs, their technologies are usually mundane. How often do these organisations fail for lack of technological innovation? Rarely. Are they sometimes extremely successful? Yes.

What happens if an inactive innovator, devoid of R&D capability, decides that it needs to undertake a technological leap forward? Under normal circumstances, it would take months to recruit or train a team of researchers and developers, and even longer before prototypes emerged. However, there is another way – simply obtain the technology through a formal business acquisition. For example, a company that has already developed the desired technology may (following negotiations and due diligence) be bought outright and integrated within the acquiring organisation. Suffice to say, acquiring is *not* innovating. There are hundreds of technology business acquisitions every year, and many are initiated by inactive innovators needing some form of technological enhancement.

Some organisations are proud of their limited innovation capabilities. For example, they may have chosen to differentiate their brand by rejecting technological progress. Admittedly, this is rare, but one prominent example is the motorbike manufacturer Harley Davidson. Grant and Jordan note that the company's "old-fashioned, push-rod engines and recycled designs have become central to its retro-look authenticity." Apparently, in recent years Harley has started to access more up-to-date technologies through collaborations.[67] However, it's the companies they collaborate with who are the primary innovators, not Harley themselves.

Of course, within Harley there will be many small-scale product and process innovations which we, as outsiders, are unlikely to be aware of. And that's probably true of many 'inactive' innovators, whose internal processes will regularly be scrutinised for cost reductions, or to ensure compliance with evolving standards and regulations. Although these activities will result in low level, small-scale innovations, this shouldn't be confused with a strategic innovation culture.

Interestingly, the decision to be inactive may be the precursor to a future period of successful technological innovation. This phenomenon has been described by financier Matthew Bullock (a former Master of St Edmund's College, Cambridge). In 2012, while giving evidence to the Science and Technology Select Committee of the UK's House of Commons, Bullock described what he called the "soft company model" for creating innovative technology businesses.[68] This model is based on the empirical fact that most early-stage technology companies have a low probability of commercial survival over the medium term. This poor success rate is caused by their adoption of a so-called 'hard model'. This is the traditional model for technology startups, involving the development of new products for target markets. However, most startups that attempt to do this lack experience in both the technology and the market. Hence, they quickly run out of money and fail.

Box 10.3 STRATEGIC AND TACTICAL MOVES

Invoking the precautionary principle

When new technologies emerge, so do new threats. Electricity electrocutes, radiation burns, air conditioning systems harbour Legionella bacteria, asbestos pierces the lungs, combustion gases warm the atmosphere.

Some of these effects are well known to the innovators. However, serious detrimental impacts often emerge years, decades, and even centuries later.

In response, some commentators call for wider adoption of the so-called precautionary principle. This argues for a moratorium on the implementation of novel technologies which threaten the *possibility* of serious harm, even in the absence of supporting scientific evidence.

The precautionary principle is deeply controversial, because it can be used to hold back promising technologies which appear to offer a net benefit to society. Genetically modified organisms (GMOs), for instance, have been delayed for decades by political support for the precautionary principle.

Unfortunately, evidence for the long-term effects of many technologies cannot be ascertained prior to their widespread use. For example, nanotechnologies would need to be trialled on a very large scale before the impact of nanoparticles on living organisms could be studied across a range of environments. It is therefore impossible to *prove* their safety, in advance, by scientific means.[69]

The behavioural economist and Nobel Prize winner, Daniel Kahneman, is sceptical about the precautionary principle. He quotes from the legal scholar, Cass Sunstein, who lists technologies which would have been vetoed by the principle, including aeroplanes, antibiotics, radio, and X-rays.[70]

Most technologists and engineers are culturally averse to constraints being placed upon their freedom to innovate. The precautionary principle challenges both their curiosity and their livelihoods. But we must face the fact that, just occasionally, our enthusiasm for innovating and launching new technologies will have negative repercussions.

These 'known unknowns' hang over novel technologies like the sword of Damocles. Will the thread break and the sword fall? If so, when, and who will be beneath it? Businesses selling harmful technologies could, in the future, face legal sanctions, compensation demands, and even bankruptcy.

In order to avoid these existential threats, we might choose to unilaterally invoke the precautionary principle, at least until the implications of new and complex technologies are better understood.

How many entrepreneurs and profit-hungry businesses would be prepared to impose such a self-denying ordinance? Presumably, very few, but the argument needs to be made and understood by all innovators in the technological realm.

The improved model that Bullock proposed involves making a calculated transition from a 'soft company' into a 'hard company'. This means beginning commercial operations as a 'soft' consulting or research business. If any innovations emerge, this only happens as incidental by-products of the work being performed for clients. This strategy buys time for the company to gain further skills, experience, and market knowledge. Eventually, a full-scale internal product development may be attempted, and it should have a good likelihood of success. **The soft company is therefore a non-innovating service provider, but with ambitions to become a hard company and a more proactive innovator in the future.** According to a report by the East of England Development Agency, a "classic example of a soft start company" was Cambridge Antibody, which began as a small, contract R&D outfit in the early 1990s. Over the course of 15 years, it slowly transitioned from contract work for clients to developing its own IP. This gradual 'hardening' of its business model made it an attractive prospect for acquisition by the pharmaceutical giant AstraZeneca,[71] completed around 2005.

Across the globe, there are millions of organisations using, and sometimes making, technologies. Statistically, these organisations are as likely to be private businesses as not-for-profit entities. We can reasonably make two assumptions:

1 Although many private companies are proactive innovators, most are not.
2 Most non-profit organisations are either disinterested in pro-active innovation or have insufficient resources to undertake it.

This leads to the conclusion that **for most technologists and engineers, in most organisations, innovation is not an important strategic or tactical concern.** They are more likely to be focused upon such challenges as regulatory compliance, recruitment and skills development, safe operations, system reliability, security matters, and so on.

It's important to put innovation into this wider and more realistic context. **Some organisations succeed by innovating, but most organisations survive, and often thrive, by rarely innovating at all.**

In theory, at least, all organisations should produce technology strategies, regardless of their approach to innovation. For technologists and engineers, the key strategic skill is knowing when to innovate proactively, when to respond or react to the innovations of others, and when to focus on those strategic concerns that have nothing whatsoever to do with innovation.

Glossary for this chapter (Items in bold are also defined in the same table)

Ansoff Matrix	A tool for assisting firms with their product-market analysis and associated strategy development. The matrix maps Products (existing and new) against Markets (existing and new). Therefore, each quadrant has a particular relationship with **innovation** activities.
backcasting	A reversal of forecasting. The backcasting method establishes a desired future state, perhaps five years away, then determines each of the actions, in reverse order, necessary for arriving at that state. The first step (i.e. the next step) may necessitate, or inspire, an **innovation**.
biomimicry	An **innovation** method which uses analogies from the natural world, such as organisms, animal behaviour, and biological processes. See also **Synectics**.
brainstorming	A method for generating ideas involving group interactions within a carefully facilitated environment, devoid of negative feedback and other social constraints.
cannibalisation	A pejorative term for the scenario in which a new product undermines or 'consumes' the internal capabilities associated with existing goods and services. For example, a manufacturer of electric storage heaters would be cannibalising its capabilities by developing heat pumps.
continuous flow	A type of production process that integrates the outputs and inputs of successive process steps. This results in high volumes of throughput. It is a significantly more efficient production method than batching.
convergence	An **innovation** method involving the combination of two or more established products, processes, or technologies into a new type of product, process, or technology.
cost leadership	A business strategy aimed at competing on price. It seeks to achieve cost reductions via both **product innovation** and **process innovation**.
DBT	See **design-build team**.
design-build team (DBT)	A process **innovation** involving the formation of multi-role product development teams. A large project (or programme) will have many DBTs, each consisting of, for example, a design engineer, a manufacturer, a finance specialist, and a marketeer.
differentiation	A business strategy encouraging **product innovation** in order to differentiate a company from its competitors.
disintermediation	A **process innovation** that eliminates intermediaries, e.g. agents and brokers, from within multi-stage production processes. Intermediaries often add little or no value.

(Continued)

inactive innovation	The absence of strategic **innovation** activities. Contrast with **proactive innovation**. Compare with **reactive innovation**.
incremental innovation	A type of **innovation** that significantly enhances an existing product or process. Contrast with **radical innovation**.
intellectual property (IP)	Ideas that are legally recognised for their novelty. IP is protected under law from unauthorised use. IP includes copyright, design rights, and **patents**. Protection is time-limited, e.g. a patent may be enforceable for 20 years.
invention	An original idea for something that may be made or used, or for a process of some kind. If the idea's novelty is acknowledged by a patenting authority, it may be granted **intellectual property** (IP) rights, in the form of a **patent**. It will then be protected under national and international law.
IP	See **intellectual property**.
licensing	The sale of **intellectual property** to third parties. For companies that specialise in **R&D**, licenses may be viewed as products.
minimum viable product (MVP)	An immature version of a new product, incorporating only core and unproven functionality, released early in order to receive prompt and constructive feedback from users.
morphological analysis	An engineering design method which examines the range of possible component solutions for a new product or process.
MVP	See **minimum viable product**.
open innovation	A type of **innovation** involving idea-sharing, and sometimes shared development processes. Contrast with **proprietary innovation**.
patent	A grant of legal protection by a patenting authority formalising the recognition of an **invention**.
precautionary principle	A moratorium on the implementation of novel technologies which threaten the possibility of serious harm, even in the absence of supporting scientific evidence.
proactive innovation	A strategy involving significant investment in **R&D** and other **innovation** activities. Contrast with **inactive innovation**. Compare with **reactive innovation**.
process innovation	A type of **innovation** for improving the value chain. Contrast with **product innovation**.
product innovation	A type of **innovation** resulting in new or improved outputs from a production process. Innovative products can include both goods and services. Contrast with **process innovation**.

(Continued)

(Continued)

proprietary innovation	A type of **innovation** associated with ownership and **intellectual property** rights. However, sometimes a proprietary innovation will be protected via secrecy (e.g. trade secrets) rather than IP. Contrast with **open innovation**.
R&D	See **research and development**.
radical innovation	A novel idea that disrupts existing technologies and industries. It also enables or encourages a stream of further **innovations**. Contrast with **incremental innovation**.
reactive innovation	A strategy of reacting to, rather than instigating, major technological **innovations**. Reactive innovators occupy an important niche within the economy, delivering familiar products and a wide range of complementary goods and services. Compare with **proactive innovation** and **inactive innovation**.
research and development (R&D)	An organisational process supporting **innovation** activities. It includes creative thinking, analysis, prototyping, and testing.
Synectics	An **innovation** method that uses analogies to generate creative ideas. It requires the ability to see parallels or connections between apparently dissimilar things. See also **biomimicry**.

Notes

1 Grant, R.M. and Jordan, J. (2015) *Foundations of Strategy*. Chichester: Wiley. 198.
2 Utterback, J.M. (1994) *Mastering the Dynamics of Innovation*. Harvard: HBS Press. xxiv.
3 GOV.UK, *Apply for a patent*. Available at: https://www.gov.uk/patent-your-invention (Accessed: 09 May 2023).
4 Derry, T.K. and Williams, T.I. (1961) *A Short History of Technology*. London (UK): OUP. 279.
5 Basalla, G. (1988) *The Evolution of Technology*. Cambridge (UK): CUP. 135.
6 Rumelt, R. (2017) *Good Strategy, Bad Strategy*. London: Profile Books. 170.
7 Utterback, *Mastering the Dynamics of Innovation*. 106–116.
8 Pyster, A., Hutchison, N. and Henry, D. (2018) *The Paradoxical Mindset of Systems Engineers*. Hoboken: Wiley. 119–121.
9 Utterback. 83.
10 Howarth, S. (1997) *A Century in Oil: the "Shell" Transport and Trading Company 1897–1997*. London: Weidenfeld & Nicolson. 360–363.
11 Kenward, M. (2018) 'Foundations for a Construction Revolution'. *Ingenia*, Issue 75, 38–42.
12 Tiwana, A. (2017) *IT Strategy for Non-IT Managers: Becoming an Engaged Contributor to Corporate IT Decisions*. Cambridge, MA: The MIT Press. 60–61.

13 Pellegrini, C.B. (2017) *Pirelli Technology and Passion 1872–2017*. London: Third Millenium. 130.

14 Keevil, A. (2020) Email exchanges with the author, 1–11 November 2023.

15 Ganguly, A., Nilchiani, R. and Farr, J. (2011) 'Identification, Classification, and Prioritization of Risks Associated with a Disruptive Technology Process'. *International Journal of Innovation and Technology Management*, Vol. 8, Issue 2, 273–293.

16 Heppenheimer, T.A. (1997) *Countdown: A History of Spaceflight*. New York: Wiley. 45.

17 Morita, A. (1987) *Made in Japan*. London: Collins. 80.

18 Moodle, *Making quality online education accessible for all*. Available at: https://moodle.com/about/ (Accessed: 09 May 2023).

19 Grant and Jordan, *Foundations of Strategy*. 221–222.

20 Walton, N. and Pyper, N. (2020) *Technology Strategy*. London (UK): Red Globe Press. 188.

21 Rolls-Royce, *Rolls-Royce celebrates 50th anniversary of Power-by-the-Hour*. Available at: https://www.rolls-royce.com/media/press-releases-archive/yr-2012/121030-the-hour.aspx (Accessed: 09 May 2023).

22 Pyster, Hutchison, and Henry, *The Paradoxical Mindset of Systems Engineers*. 114–118.

23 Cross, N. (2008) *Engineering Design Methods: Strategies for Product Design*. Chichester: Wiley. 177–179.

24 McKie, R. (2015) 'James Watt and the sabbath stroll that created the industrial revolution'. *The Guardian*, Friday 29 May 2015. Available at: https://www.theguardian.com/technology/2015/may/29/james-watt-sabbath-day-fossil-fuel-revolution-condenser (Accessed: 09 May 2023).

25 Tesla, N. (2011) *My Inventions and Other Writings*. New York: Penguin. 39-40.

26 Tobin, J. (2003) *To Conquer the Air*. New York: Free Press. 314.

27 Kenward, M. (2019) 'Driven to an Electrifying Future'. *Ingenia*, Issue 79, 42–46.

28 Frank, M., Roehrig, P. and Pring, B. (2017) *What To Do When Machines Do Everything*. Hoboken: Wiley. 62.

29 Gray, R. (2017) 'Music for the Masses'. *Ingenia*, Issue 72, 18–22.

30 Abbey Road Studios, *Abbey Road Red Demo Day 2023*. Available at: https://www.abbeyroad.com/news/abbey-road-red-demo-day-2023-3305 (Accessed: 09 May 2023).

31 Rumelt, *Good Strategy, Bad Strategy*. 171–172.

32 Pellegrini, *Pirelli Technology and Passion 1872–2017*. 40–89.

33 Anon (2016) 'Improving Access to the Gold Standards of MRI Scanning'. *Ingenia*, Issue 67, 35.

34 Buchanan, A. (2006) *Brunel*. London: Continuum. 22–29.

35 Arthur, W.B. (2010) *The Nature of Technology*. London: Penguin. 72–73.

36 Hartman, R. (2016) 'Foresight and Creativity' in van der Duin, P. (ed.) *Foresight in Organizations*. Abingdon: Routledge. 201.

37 Cross, *Engineering Design Methods*. 48–51.

38 Quist, J. (2016) 'Backcasting' in van der Duin, P. (ed.) *Foresight in Organizations*. Abingdon: Routledge. 125–140.

39 Cross. 51.

40 Cadle, J., Paul, D. and Turner P. (2014) *Business Analysis Techniques*. Swindon: BCS. 132–157.

41 Ries, E. (2011) *The Lean Startup*. London, UK: Penguin. 93–113.

42 McDougall, W.A. (1997) *The Heavens and the Earth*. Baltimore: Johns Hopkins University Press. 141–149.
43 Howarth, *A Century in Oil*. 143.
44 Howarth. 144.
45 Grant and Jordan. 176.
46 Grant and Jordan. 131–132.
47 Grant and Jordan. 132–136.
48 Headrick, D.R. (2009) *Technology: A World History*. New York: OUP. 117–118.
49 Basalla, *The Evolution of Technology*. 126.
50 Morita, *Made in Japan*. 79.
51 Morita. 147.
52 Braun, E. (1998) *Technology in Context*. London: Routledge. 75.
53 Grant and Jordan. 205.
54 Turrell, A. (2021) *The Star Builders*. London (UK): W & N. 157.
55 Grant and Jordan. 205.
56 Dyson, J. (2011) *Against the Odds: An Autobiography*. Andover: Cengage Learning.
57 Miller, D.P. (2019) *The Life and Legend of James Watt*. Pittsburgh: University of Pittsburgh Press. 100–102.
58 Basalla. 127.
59 Grant and Jordan. 208.
60 Goodrich, J. (2023) 'How This Record Company Engineer Invented the CT Scanner'. *IEEE Spectrum*, 12 January 2023. Available at: https://spectrum.ieee.org/invention-of-ct-scanner#toggle-gdpr (Accessed: 09 May 2023).
61 Nuttall, W.J. (2019) *Britain and the Bomb: Technology, Culture and the Cold War*. Dunbeath: Whittles. 65.
62 Morita. 168.
63 Grant and Jordan. 200.
64 Grant and Jordan. 200.
65 Grant and Jordan. 196.
66 National Centre for Universities and Business (NCUB) (2012) *Enhancing Collaboration, Creating Value: Business Interaction with the UK Research Base in Four Sectors*, available at: https://www.ncub.co.uk/insight/enhancing-collaboration-creating-value-business-interaction-with-the-uk-research-base-in-four-sectors/ (Accessed: 09 May 2023).
67 Grant and Jordan. 96.
68 Science and Technology Select Committee (2012) *Written evidence submitted by Matthew Bullock*, available at: https://publications.parliament.uk/pa/cm201213/cmselect/cmsctech/348/348we25.htm (Accessed: 09 May 2023).
69 van de Poel, I. and Royakkers, L. (2011) *Ethics, Technology and Engineering: An Introduction*. Chichester: Wiley. 239–241.
70 Kahneman, D. (2011) *Thinking, Fast and Slow*. London: Penguin. 351.
71 East of England Development Agency (on behalf of the East of England Science and Industry Council) (2010) *Exploding the Myths of UK Innovation Policy*, available at: https://www.cbr.cam.ac.uk/wp-content/uploads/2020/08/specialreport-explodingthemyths.pdf (Accessed: 09 May 2023).

11 Navigating uncertainty
Getting to where we want to go

This chapter presents

- A description of methods for mitigating uncertainty in the technological realm.

This chapter establishes

- The navigational value of design, risk management, and foresight techniques.
- Why strategies should be viewed as proposals, rather than plans.

We are now approaching the sharp end of the book. Earlier chapters have explored strategy from many angles, including strategic theory, the strategic mindset, stakeholder relationships, and innovation. The remaining two chapters will complete the scope of the book by examining practical approaches to developing better technology strategies.

We know that this endeavour presents one particularly large hurdle: *uncertainty*. This was visualised by the 'trumpet of uncertainty' (Figure 6.1, Chapter 6), illustrating how decisions made today will be increasingly jeopardised by the passage of time. Much of this uncertainty is attributed to complexity and the characteristics of complex adaptive systems (explained in Chapter 5). It is complexity that makes strategising necessary, yet difficult.

Jean Boulton *et al.*, authors of *Embracing Complexity* (2015), emphasise "the central place of chance, variation, messiness, and randomness in the evolution and emergence of the unknowable future."[1] We experience this in our perpetual cycles of shock and surprise, of failure and success, of destruction and growth. Each new technology destroys other technologies, while simultaneously planting the seeds of its own destruction. Each problem is solved, yet each solution presents new problems. There is no respite for technologists and engineers. Ditto for strategists.

A classic example of this dilemma is presented by our aversion to uncomfortably warm buildings. We solved this, intelligently,

DOI: 10.4324/9781003472919-13

with air conditioning systems. But this technology uses refrigerants, which are now known to increase atmospheric temperatures. Our instinctive response to higher temperatures was simply to install more aircon systems, thereby exacerbating the problem. In addition to the climate challenge, many aircon systems harbour Legionella bacteria, deadly to humans. But that's okay, because we can treat those systems with chemicals which suppress bacterial growth. Yet those chemicals degrade the pipework. But that's okay, because we can use corrosion inhibitors.[2] And so it goes on, *ad infinitum*. Technology begets technology. Fixes beget fixes. A complex adaptive system is a never-ending series of agent responses and adaptations to the responses and adaptations of other agents.

Similar complexity is found at the organisational level. The vagaries of economics, competitor behaviour and other 'human factors' only generate a stream of actions and reactions.

The purpose of these reminders is not to campaign for constraints upon technological progress. I am merely emphasising the challenges posed to strategists and tacticians. As we know, the engineering mindset is to seek solutions, so let's do that.

If, according to our definition of strategy (Chapter 4), one of its functions is to 'navigate uncertainty', then we will need to spend some time focusing upon *navigational methods*. What mechanisms or tools are available for looking towards the future and avoiding its pitfalls? In this chapter, three significant mechanisms are described: design, risk management, and foresight.

Design for uncertainty

Chapter 2 explained that professional technologists and engineers are, first and foremost, designers. Their primary skill involves creating solutions, optimised via trade-offs. Etymologically, engineers embody *ingenuity*.

Design also happens to be a principal weapon in the war on uncertainty, because the design of every entity in the technological realm – every product, tool, system, process, and organisation – can be optimised to mitigate for uncertainty.

From earlier chapters

We have already seen examples of how technologists design for uncertainty. In Chapter 2, for instance, the concept of forward compatibility was explained as a mechanism for ensuring product longevity within a technological ecosystem in which other products continue to evolve. Later, in Chapter 4, the idea of 'going lite' or *dennovating* a product (removing unnecessary or unwanted functionality) was proposed as one way to reduce the likelihood of technical faults and user errors. The same chapter advocated eliminating, by design, the disruptive presence of living things in technical environments, although absolute exclusion of life forms is impossible given the central role of human beings in activities such as system operations and maintenance. It was also explained how well-designed monitoring and reporting mechanisms help to predict future events. Such 'leading indicators' may be fed with data from electronic sensors designed into buildings, machinery, and other assets.

Chapter 5 discussed the analytical techniques of modelling and extrapolation. Modelling shows how systems will respond to changes in inputs and variables, enabling more robust designs, thereby influencing specifications, such as the choice of materials for improved durability. Chapter 5 also introduced the idea of entropic processes causing all things to 'fall apart'. Although entropy is a real-world physical phenomenon, it is also a convenient analogy for the processes of disintegration affecting everything, from products to organisations. The war on entropy must be fought throughout the product and organisational lifecycles, beginning with the design stage. For example, the designers of physical products can focus on quality or maintainability, while the designers of new organisational arrangements should consider their adaptability or resilience to future changes in the operating environment.

Chapter 6 briefly described 18 origins of uncertainty, many of which should be taken into consideration by designers. A widely used tool for controlling uncertainty, failure modes and effects analysis (FMEA), was also explained. When used at the design stage, FMEA helps to pre-empt anticipated faults and process errors, enabling early mitigation.

In Chapter 9 we saw how ethical challenges to products or operations can, in some circumstances, force their re-design, re-configuration or withdrawal. However, designers can use various forms of ethical analysis, such as *Ethical Due Diligence*, to pre-empt ethical objections. Although designers are typically focused on the first stage of the technology or product lifecycle, end-of-life concerns cannot be ignored. Unexpected ethical challenges sometimes emerge during decommissioning processes, as Shell discovered to their significant cost during the Brent Spar affair. Holistic end-to-end 'systems thinking' is now recognised as a key skill for all designers.

Chapter 10's focus on innovation placed a spotlight on activities associated with the design stage of the product lifecycle. For instance, the granting of formal IP protection helps to remove the uncertainty of competition, whether from similar ideas or malicious imitation. Conversely, a failure to progress technologically can create a gulf which must eventually be bridged or resolved. This may result in a disruptive upgrade project, or even acquisition by a competitor. Innovation that is incremental, rather than radical, enables products and processes to keep track with changes elsewhere in the technological domain. This mitigates the uncertainty associated with constantly evolving environments.

Chapter 10 also mentioned some of the innovative production methods associated with 'design for manufacture and assembly' (DfMA). These factory-friendly designs help to eliminate many of the uncertainties intrinsic to complex production processes, simultaneously reducing the time and costs of manufacturing, while improving the quality of output. The project to build the UK's massive Hinkley Point power station was described as benefitting from an off-site DfMA production process.

Minimum viable products (MVPs), which are related to the use of product prototypes and beta versions, were also mentioned in Chapter 10. The feedback from trialling immature products leads to rapid design improvements, reducing the market uncertainty of product launches.

Design for uncertainty is therefore a topic of considerable breadth and depth. Although there is insufficient space in this book to examine the subject in full, this chapter will consider three particularly relevant design techniques: *simplicity*, *changeability*, and the practice of *real options* analysis.

Simplicity

If there is a positive correlation between complexity and uncertainty, the converse should also be true. One might assume a correlation between simplicity and certainty. It follows that if our goal is to navigate uncertainty, simplicity can help us. In the *Guide to the Systems Engineering Body of Knowledge (SEBoK)*, a resolute assertion is made: "The first line of defense against complexity is simplicity of design."[3]

In the 1960s, at the height of the Cold War, the UK's TSR2 bomber project had become weighed down by excessive specifications and bureaucracy. Writing in 1973 (admittedly with hindsight), the aviation author Bill Gunston explained that "upon TSR.2 fell the cost burden of an entire generation of advances in structures, propulsion, systems, materials and a thousand and one other items..."[4] All the latest technological eggs had been put into one basket, and its sponsor, the UK Government, lost its grip. The project was terminated. Perhaps this was the best outcome for such a complex aircraft, for had TSR2 gone into service it would probably have been difficult to maintain, unreliable in operation, and a significant financial burden to the taxpayer.

Something similar was happening at NASA through the 1980s and beyond. The agency's operational philosophy had evolved from the rapid design and build of spacecraft, each with a specific purpose (1960s to 1970s), to producing a smaller number of highly capable machines for much more complex missions. Project lengths had ballooned from just a few months, in NASA's early years, to a decade or more by the 1990s. So many instruments were being fitted to missions that launch weights had quadrupled. Heppenheimer quotes one scientist who said that each mission "looked like the only bus out of town, so you wanted to pile everything on it." The doomed Mars Climate Orbiter spacecraft was a product of this era. Readers may remember (from Chapter 6) that this mission failed due to an incorrect imperial/metric conversion affecting navigation. NASA's white knight was its new Administrator, the reforming Daniel Goldin. Upon taking up his appointment he described the forthcoming Cassini mission as a "battleship Galactica", but it was already too late to cancel. Goldin stated his intention to "change the culture" within the agency, calling for "smaller, cheaper, faster, better".[5]

In Chapter 3 the pursuit of the latest 'cool' technologies or fashionable industry innovations was explicitly excluded from the scope of a serious technology strategy. The desire to appear technologically advanced can lead to over-complication, great expense, and dependence upon a few specialist suppliers and consultants. The University of Georgia's Professor Amrit Tiwana reminded us that "You do not need a Cadillac when a Chevy will do."[6] If we reduce the number of advanced features, we reduce the number of novel components and gain a corresponding reduction in the learning required to achieve competence. Mass production becomes easier, leading to lower costs, and sometimes better quality. Maintenance is easy.

As a concept, however, simplicity is context-specific. A screwdriver and a box of screws will hardly set an engineer's pulse racing, but show them to a person 20,000 years ago and you'll be venerated as The God of Sturdy Wooden Things. Shiny new technologies induce excitement and desirability, but there's always a drawback. That early human will need to be shown how to use the screwdriver (let's call it training), and the availability of screws will soon become a significant challenge (the problem of supply). Furthermore, if the blade snaps, it won't be possible to repair it (the need for maintenance expertise). Novelty can be extremely inconvenient.

It's often the case that older/mature technologies are more than capable of meeting current requirements. In other words, when the screwdriver breaks, or the final screw has been used, our grateful friend will probably resort to an established technique, such as binding objects with vines or other fibrous plants. There is a lesson here, articulated well by Professor Bent Flyvbjerg following his multi-year study of failed engineering and infrastructure projects. In his words, novel technologies lack "experience".[7] Adopting this analogy, would you ask a young, creative and ambitious carpenter to erect shelving for displaying your priceless collection of 18th-century scientific instruments? Probably not. An older, more experienced and conservative carpenter is preferred. So, to mitigate for uncertainty we favour technological maturity over the 'state of the art'.

Ironically, today's mature technology was yesterday's exciting innovation. Not only has it become easier to understand, it is also embedded within professional practice, and is probably more reliable. In relative terms, mature technologies, however complex they once were, are now *simple*. That's their appeal. Even the first H-bomb, or von Braun's V2 rocket, would be perceived as 'basic' by today's domain professionals. Over many decades, self-seeding ecosystems of knowledge and expertise have grown up around these technologies.

In the examples above I've tried to show that, in order to navigate uncertainty we should be favouring simpler technologies over those that are unnecessarily complex or lacking in 'experience'. It may be helpful for this policy of simplification to be imposed at the design stage.

A strategic thinker should always be weighing up the advantages and disadvantages of simpler solutions. For example, the next time you're travelling by bus or car, take a close look at the design of crossroads. Some will use traffic lights, others roundabouts (also known as rotaries, or traffic circles). The former uses electronics, consumes energy, requires periodic maintenance by skilled personnel, and is susceptible to collision damage. The latter is entirely passive and virtually maintenance free. Ask yourself these questions: Which design provides the least uncertainty for stakeholders, and which design embodies the most elegant engineering? If you remember how engineering was defined in Chapter 2, both answers should be the same.

Changeability

Technology architectures influence the options available for navigating uncertainty. Referring to corporate IT systems, Tiwana notes an important relationship between architecture and "evolvability". For example, an IT architecture can support an organisation "by doing *new* things that it was never designed to do ... This includes adding new functionality to support changed business needs and to absorb new technologies." A product or system "built for change" will inevitably remain viable for longer.[8]

This topic of system evolvability or changeability was examined by Professor Dan Hastings and his colleagues at MIT. Their pan-engineering study identified three reasons for change during the lifecycle of any system:

1 Marketplace dynamics
2 Technological evolution
3 Environmental variation.

They analysed external and internal 'change agents', arguing that external change is addressed by system flexibility, while internal change requires adaptability. Furthermore, there are three design approaches for coping with change: robustness, scalability, and modifiability.[9]

A well-known solution to the need for changeability, satisfying all three of the MIT criteria, is *modularity* – an architecture characterised by the integration of two or more semi-independent functional units, known as modules. The common interfaces between these units enable individual modular functions to combine in a component-like manner. Working together as a unified system, these modules generate value through system outputs. Typically many modules are combined to make a viable product or system. However, it isn't always necessary for every module to be active or in full working order. For instance, a few modules may be sufficient to deliver core functionality while other, less critical, modules are taken offline for repairs, upgrades, or replacement. Modularity is sometimes based upon an open standard, enabling more than one supplier of each module. This encourages competitive innovation.

One of the best-known modular products, used by billions of people worldwide, is the IBM-designed personal computer. The PC's strength lies in the freedom it gives to stakeholders (manufacturers, service engineers, users) to design, exchange, or upgrade individual modules. Consequently, a Seagate hard drive, an AMD processor, an Acer monitor, and a Logitech mouse are easily combined in the same device. Compatibility between all modules is assured.

It may be instructive to compare the traditional PC with Apple's desktop solutions. These proprietary products are more tightly integrated, non-customisable, and inaccessible to unauthorised repairers. Consequently, they're also better quality. However, this comes at a higher retail price and with greater dependence upon decision makers within Apple.

We might say that, in general, modularity helps us to navigate an uncertain future because it facilitates, amongst other things, scalability and repairability. It also enables manufacturability, which is especially useful for large, bespoke products. For instance, SMRs (or Small Modular Reactors) are believed by many observers to be the future for nuclear electricity generation. Each component of the power plant is viewed as a module. So, rather than building giant power stations in order to achieve economies of scale, one can build much smaller plants, but in larger quantities using factory production methods. This creates an 'economy of multiples', the consequence of continuous process improvement. In other words, each iteration of the product helps to drive out costs and reduce build times.[10]

Elsewhere in the energy sector, similar economies of modularisation and manufacturability are evident in the growth and success of wind and solar power. The global increase in generating capacity is now characterised by ever-shorter timescales, almost unlimited scalability, and greater resilience due to modular architectures.

Changeability is also necessary at the organisational level. In order to achieve this, it can be argued that core competences play an important role. For instance, Grant and Jordan have noted the success of such technology businesses as Honda, Canon, and 3M.[11] These companies have avoided becoming too closely associated with specific products, product ranges, sectors, or markets. They've achieved a degree of changeability by relying upon their core competences: Honda in gasoline engines, Canon in precision mechanics, microelectronics, and optics, and 3M in adhesives and material coatings. One of the 21st century's greatest corporate failures, that of Kodak, was arguably caused by a misapprehension of its own core competences. Grant and Jordan ask whether Kodak should have de-prioritised the photographic side of its business in favour of its expertise in chemicals. According to this hypothesis, Kodak might have successfully responded to the digital age by pivoting more towards chemical products, pharmaceuticals, and healthcare. (Indeed, the Kodak brand has recently been resurrected and now appears to be taking this particular path to a more promising future.)

The suggestion here is that an organisation designed, or structured, to exploit a set of core, generic competences is much more capable of dealing with the myriad sources of uncertainty. Can you list the core competences of your organisation? If not, does this make you more or less vulnerable to change?

Real options

Another way to design for uncertainty is to build future choices into engineering solutions. Grant and Jordan write that "Disruptive technologies and accelerating rates of change have meant that strategy has become less and less about plans and more about creating options for the future".[12] A methodology for doing this is known as *real options*, which uses an analogy from the financial services industry. (One explanation for the naming of real options is that it exists in the *real*-world of engineering rather than the virtual world of financial trading.)

In financial services, an option is a deferral of a purchase until some future date. The potential purchaser assumes that this deferment will be advantageous. However, in order to secure this option a fee must be paid. Cost-benefit analysis is therefore needed to estimate the probability of gaining from this arrangement.

Real options analysis is typically used in the early stages of a project with the aim of improving the lifetime value of the product being created. For example, some proportion of the project budget could be invested in technical features that are unlikely to be used in the near term, but which *may* be required in the future. Although the language and mathematics of real options is relatively new, its underlying logic (i.e. keeping options open) is as old as humanity itself.

In 2016 the application of real options theory was explored by a team of researchers from the Cambridge Centre for Smart Infrastructure and Construction. They were modelling alternative approaches to incorporating ground source heat pumps (GSHPs) within buildings. These can either be installed during construction or, if required at a later date, retrofitted at considerable expense.[13] It is, of course, preferable to install GSHPs during construction, but energy costs fluctuate and the business case for doing this may not exist at the start of a project. In the future, though, various factors may align in favour of GSHPs, e.g. government incentive schemes, rising fossil fuel prices, or falling technology costs. However, retrofitting GSHPs involves digging trenches and drilling multiple boreholes. Such work is almost inconceivable after the building has been occupied.

Three approaches were studied: 1) full installation during construction (despite the absence of an economic case to do so); 2) no preparatory work at all; 3) partial installation during construction, especially the drilling of boreholes. Method 3 might be regarded as the real options solution, because it 'buys' the option of a relatively low-cost, low-disruption GSHP installation in the future. To be successful, the price for method 3 must be acceptable to the buyers. They will need to weigh the cost of this preparatory work against the probability of a future need for GSHP.

The Cambridge team provide this succinct description of both the logic and merits of real options:

> If, at the time of conception, a designer ignores the possibility that external conditions may evolve unexpectedly over time, then a substantial risk arises that the designed object will become inadequate...[T]he most cost-effective method is not necessarily to create designs that can cope with all eventualities from the outset — in fact, it is often not feasible to do so — but to embed in the design potential options that can be called into service during the working life of the facility: a fast, easy, and economical way to adapt to changing conditions.[14]

Unsurprisingly, real options analysis involves complex probabilistic evaluations. It uses tools such as Monte Carlo analysis to ensure that the costs of embedding options will be exceeded by their likely benefits over the medium to longer term.

Here are some further examples of real options principles applied to projects:

- The 30-storey, steel and glass HCSC building in Chicago was constructed in the 1990s, after which thousands of people began working within the tower. In a smart move, the building's designers had incorporated additional strength, utilities, and elevator shafts to enable its height to be doubled should a future need arise, and it did.[15] So between 2007 and 2009 a further 27 floors were successfully added without impacting its occupants in the lower storeys.
- Writing in 1998, Paul Stevens examined the way that oil industry capacity fluctuates significantly over time. He described it as 'feast or famine', offering a convincing explanation for the feast of overcapacity:

> Because oil flows in three-dimensional space, it is subject to very large technical economies of scale. In tanks or pipes, which are the equipment of the industry, capital costs are a function of surface area while output is a function of volume. There exists an exponential relationship between the two. For example, a pipeline's capacity equals the square of its radius. Hence, large-scale projects tend to attract much lower average costs. In the oil industry, big is beautiful.[16]

Let's take a real options perspective. When building processing facilities, underestimating future demand will incur a cost in the form of lower revenues due to constrained capacity. However, as Stevens explains, it's relatively inexpensive to purchase an 'option' for future growth by installing excess capacity. So the logical outcome is over-sized facilities which might never be fully utilised. If they are needed, of course, revenues can be substantially increased with no further capital investment.

- Many highway authorities acquire more land than needed for new roads. They incorporate generous 'margins' on major routes (familiar to us as grass verges). These enable lanes to be widened if traffic levels increase. Land is of course less expensive to acquire before a road is constructed than after-wards. Using the same tactic, some firms choose to acquire land near their existing sites, thereby retaining an option to physi-cally expand operations in the future.[17]
- Grant and Jordan associate R&D investments with real options. This is because R&D enables firms to "keep abreast of new technologies that could prove promising in the future even though these technologies offer little immediate prospect of commercial development."[18] Similarly, where an industry is caught between two competing technologies, it may be sensible to develop expertise in both, until one of the technologies wins the race.[19]

Real options analysis originated at MIT's Sloan School of Management, although the technique is now studied and applied worldwide. There are plenty of materials online.

Box 11.1   Could we also have *real constraints*?

It is often illuminating to take a theoretical concept and reverse its logic. This sometimes leads to new discoveries.

So, what happens if we reverse the real options methodology? In order to do this, we would need to contemplate *removing* options embedded within engineering solutions. By implication, removing options denies future opportunities, so this action should be viewed as a self-imposed constraint.

Real options consume real resources, i.e. they incur costs. Consequently, in situations where there is a necessity to reduce costs, we could theoretically achieve this by limiting future options.

This use of *real constraints* could be justified in the interests of short-term economy. It would involve withdrawing, disabling, or abandoning the options built into a solution. For example, a budget-busting project in danger of termination could be rescued by applying real constraints to its design. The project team would need to identify any embedded options, and remove them – with great care.

> Real constraints may deliver cost reductions. However, it should be noted that if a real options analysis had already been applied to the design, the imposition of real constraints will *probably* incur additional costs over the longer term.
> Real options and real constraints are both speculative activities, but the latter involves betting against the likelihood that options will bring long term benefits. Real constraints are therefore tainted by an air of financial desperation.

The management of risk

One of the more established mechanisms for navigating uncertainty is the practice of *risk management* (RM). As a professional discipline, RM is relatively new. One of the oldest and most august professional associations, the Institute of Risk Management (IRM), was only founded in 1986. However, the basic principles of RM go back a long way.

So, what is *risk*? The IRM's *Risk Management Standard* (2002) defines risk as "the combination of the probability of an event and its consequences."[20] The meaning of that statement will soon become clearer. A more universal and concise definition is provided in the global risk management standard, ISO 31000. Here, risk is "the effect of uncertainty on objectives."[21]

The IRM embellishes its definition by noting that, "In all types of undertaking, there is the potential for events and consequences that constitute opportunities for benefit (upside) or threats to success (downside)."[22] In other words, contrary to its usage in everyday speech, the term 'risk' is not exclusively associated with bad events and bad outcomes. It can also be applied to the likelihood of achieving good outcomes.

Importantly, RM focuses upon future events that are describable and plausible, yet uncertain. Rumsfeld would have called these the "known unknowns". For example, in the technological realm a plausible, though undesirable, event might be a fire in the engine room of a ship, or the imposition of a restrictive new government regulation. Desirable events include the patenting of a new drug, or the successful extension of an asset's design life.

Methodology

It is generally accepted that the heart of the RM methodology is a four-step process. This begins with *risk identification*, *risk description*, and *risk estimation*. Then, each of the analysed risks is subject to a *risk treatment*.

Risk identification within organisations requires extensive research and acute insights. To assist with this process, many tools and techniques have been developed. These are often highly structured. Occasionally, however, they can be surprisingly informal. For instance, when undertaking a risk identification exercise, one of the best questions to ask any manager is this: "What keeps you awake at night?" Each answer identifies a potential 'event', one that could have either positive or negative outcomes. This is known as a *risk event*.

RM professionals are trained to identify all significant risk events, especially those of which managers are unaware. These can be uncovered through detailed investigations. Paul Hopkin, a Fellow of the IRM and former Head of Risk Management at the BBC, suggests four general approaches to risk identification: questionnaires and checklists; workshops and brainstorming; inspections and audits; flowcharts and dependency analysis (e.g. studying process flows to identify critical components).[23]

Throughout these activities it is vital to maintain a focus upon stakeholders and their expectations.[24] Chapter 8 listed and described many of these technology stakeholders. They can either be the victims/beneficiaries of uncertain events, or the direct causes of the events themselves. Consequently, close stakeholder engagement plays an important role in the RM methodology.

Tools

An interesting workshop tool for risk identification is called the *pre-mortem*. Its aim is to establish the possible causes of bad events in the distant future. The pre-mortem involves asking directly involved personnel to contemplate the worst possible scenario. For example, this could be the 'death' of a company, project, or product. The participants in the pre-mortem then propose explanations for the cause of the event (e.g. "The project failed because ..."). The business writer Matthew Syed calls pre-mortem "the ultimate 'fail fast' technique. The idea is to encourage people to be open about their concerns, rather than hiding them out of fear of sounding negative."[25] According to Daniel Kahneman, a pre-mortem overcomes the type of groupthink that can lead to poor decisions, and it encourages decision-makers to search for possible threats that they had not previously considered.[26]

A more structured risk identification method is the *hazard and operational study*, better known as HAZOP. Widely used in the processing industries, a HAZOP study brings together technical

Table 11.1 A sample of HAZOP parameters and guidewords[27]

Some HAZOP parameters		Some HAZOP guidewords	
Pressure	Time	No / not / none	Before / after
Temperature	Speed	More / higher	Early / late
Viscosity	Particle size	Less / lower	Faster / slower
Separation	Control	Reverse	Part of

experts, particularly engineers, in order to analyse complex processes component-by-component. The analysis is so thorough that a single HAZOP study often requires many days or even weeks to complete.

The HAZOP team, led by a skilled facilitator, analyse each activity using specified system 'parameters' and 'guidewords'. Table 11.1 lists examples:

Relevant combinations of guidewords and parameters, e.g. "lower pressure" or "before separation", are applied to each component or process step under examination. The aim is to identify all potential deviations from the design intent. These deviations are then analysed by the HAZOP team, carefully documented, and treated accordingly. Table 11.2 shows a subset of results from a hypothetical HAZOP study at a chemical plant. A completed study will typically contain hundreds of rows relating to every aspect of the plant's safety-critical and business-critical engineering processes.

Pre-mortem and HAZOP are two of the many techniques available for identifying negative/downside risks, but we can also reverse this perspective in order to search for possible *opportunities* within the technological environment. This process of identifying and analysing positive/upside risk is relatively under-developed

Table 11.2 Exemplar row and column data for a chemical processing facility HAZOP[28]

Deviation	Possible cause	Impact	Safeguard	Action
Loss of computer control	Power failure	System moves to fail safe condition	30 minute UPS power supply	Check that fail safe settings include protection of work in progress
Leak from valve	Poor quality weld	Substance pooling beneath valve and hazardous vapours	Spilled liquids run to a common sump	Update operating procedure to include routine inspection of similar valves

within the RM discipline. Historically, the profession has oriented itself towards the mitigation of unwanted events but, as the earlier definitions of risk showed, the pursuit of 'positive risk' opportunities is a logical use of RM expertise. Positive risk and negative risk are simply two sides of what should be the same professional coin.

Having identified potentially significant events, it is then necessary to estimate the scale of their associated risk. As implied by the IRM's definition of risk (see earlier), the scale of a risk emerges from the combination of probability and consequences. This introduces the classic formula, **Risk = Probability × Consequences** (or sometimes Likelihood × Impact).

The values entered into this equation may be quantitative, semi-quantitative, or qualitative. For instance, both probabilities and impacts may be described as High, Medium, or Low.[29] Alternatively they could be given numerical values, e.g. 3, 2, and 1. Some analysts choose to put financial values on the impacts, but many events lead to both tangible and intangible effects (e.g. both monetary costs and opportunity costs), so impact scores may need to be more nuanced than simple monetary values.

The output from this scoring activity is often illustrated as a *risk matrix*, which maps event probabilities against their impacts. Figure 11.1 presents two simplified risk matrices, one negative and one positive. More sophisticated versions of risk matrices, sometimes called *heat maps*, are easily found online. Once the risk events have been scored, they can be ordered and prioritised. This is often displayed in a table known as the *Risk Register*. Again, there are many examples online.

Next, the focus switches to the stage known as risk treatment. There are many ways to treat risks. For negative risks these might involve physical controls (e.g. flood barriers), new working procedures (e.g. lockout and tagout), staff training (e.g. firefighting), and

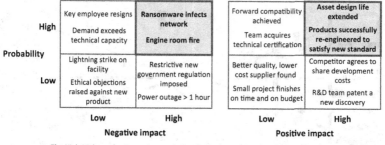

The High-High quadrants receive most attention and resources; Low-Low quadrants receive the least.

Figure 11.1 Simplified risk matrices containing examples of typical negative and positive events

so on. A common form of risk treatment is the insurance policy, as TV inventor John Logie Baird discovered in 1927:

> When the company was first formed I was the only person who could produce a picture. The technical staff consisted of half a dozen or so new men who had not attained a mastery over the many weird contrivances which I then used ... The directors were much worried over this ... So it was decided to insure me for £150,000 ... I think it was the largest life insurance policy ever taken out. Since then it has been dwarfed into complete insignificance by the Hollywood stars.[30]

The loss of a key individual, whether through death or departure, can be a major technological setback. Baird's insured value in the 1920s would be equivalent to perhaps £10 million ($13M) today.

Conversely, positive risks may reflect significant opportunities for organisations. Such risks can be treated in many ways, e.g. via project investments, influencing the drafting of international standards, the formation of joint ventures, targeted R&D, recruiting talent, and so on.

The *Bowtie Diagram* (Figure 11.2) is a popular analytical tool used by risk analysts, particularly in hazardous industries. A single diagram illustrates both the possible causes and potential effects of an unwanted event. The same diagram also shows the location of controls (sometimes called barriers). Controls on the left side are used to reduce the probability of the event occurring. Those on the right mitigate its negative effects. The purpose of these controls is to 'resist' the transition from causes into effects. The current status of each control may be illustrated by its colour. A number of software products have been developed for creating Bowtie Diagrams in workshop environments, including BowtieXP by

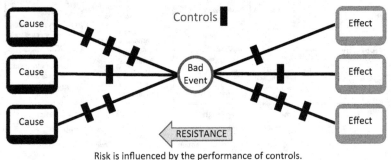

Risk is influenced by the performance of controls.

Figure 11.2 The design and components of a Bowtie Diagram

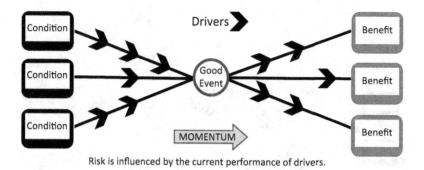

Risk is influenced by the current performance of drivers.

Figure 11.3 The design and components of a Positive Risk diagram

Wolters Kluwers. However, hand-drawn diagrams are effective for quick examinations of less complex environments.

Reversing the logic of the Bowtie Diagram creates a similar visualisation, but one potentially more valuable to strategists, because it focuses upon the upside of risk. *Positive Risk* modelling (Figure 11.3) illustrates the conditions necessary for making a desired event happen, and the potential benefits that will follow. The 'momentum' necessary for converting conditions into benefits is provided by purposeful actions, known as *drivers*.

The Positive Risk modelling method was first published by the Risk Management Institute of Australasia in 2016.[31] A real-world example is illustrated in Figure 11.4. (Note: there are currently no software tools on the market for producing Positive Risk diagrams.)

Positive Risk modelling shares features with conventional project management. Projects aim to deliver a desirable outcome, and this is equivalent to the pursuit of a 'positive risk' opportunity. Both methods identify and describe a 'Good Event', i.e. a goal or deliverable. They also define the conditions which must be satisfied in order to reach the goal, and a clear enunciation of the benefits likely to follow from the goal's attainment. **Positive Risk diagrams are, therefore, miniature project visualisations.**

Some years ago, I assisted an engineering consultancy in the development of a pioneering professional qualification. The client had already acquired a position of thought-leadership in the sector, so the strategic benefits from creating and managing the sector-leading qualification were substantial. Our goal was the qualification's satisfactory development and launch. The entire project was captured on a single Positive Risk diagram, illustrated in Figure 11.4. (Note: This diagram is only provided as a conceptual illustration, so its contents are not intended to be legible.)

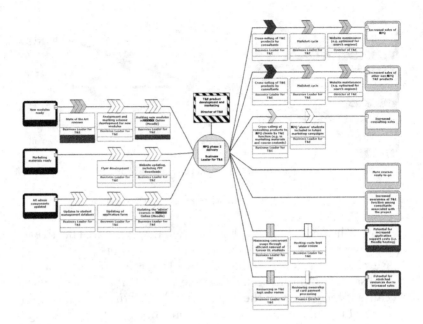

Figure 11.4 Positive Risk diagram for the launch of a new professional engineering qualification

The left side of the diagram contains the three main conditions for achieving the goal (which is located in the centre of the diagram). The right side shows the five major benefits expected to emerge after the goal. The forward arrows indicate each of the drivers, their scale, and current status. The diagram shows that two of the benefits were expected to emerge without taking any actions. In the lower right are two potentially negative effects, each requiring a couple of defensive controls.

A possible criticism of risk management is that it can appear (and feel) over-complicated. The RM profession is cloaked in esoteric language and bureaucratic processes. Fundamentally, though, risk management has just two purposes: 1) reducing the likelihood and scale of negative impact events; 2) increasing the likelihood and scale of positive impact events.

We should remember that there is always an economic imperative, because both 1 and 2 are constrained by available resources. In other words, the treatment of identified risks, both positive and negative, is hindered by the law of diminishing returns. It will always be constrained by the amount of time, money and management goodwill available. This prevents us from eliminating all of the negative risks and achieving all of the positive risks. Consequently, many *residual risks* remain. These residual risks constitute much of the uncertainty undermining the execution of technology strategies.

Box 11.2   STRATEGIC DICHOTOMIES

Risk aversion or risk taking?

People and organisations have mercurial risk appetites. Those that are *risk averse* dislike uncertainty, so they distrust complex environments, even those harbouring genuine opportunities. Those that are *risk takers*, however, embrace uncertainty. They perceive and pursue opportunities.

In decision theory, risk aversion correlates with the *maximin* strategy, which devotes resources to creating a 'safety net', maximising the minimum possible outcome. Risk taking, on the other hand, is associated with the more optimistic *maximax* strategy, which seeks to maximise the likely maximum outcome.[32]

According to the ISO, risk appetite is the "amount and type of risk that an organisation is willing to pursue or retain".[33] I would define risk appetite as reflecting *the proportion of organisational assets, including reputation, that managers are willing to expose to uncertain outcomes.*

Examples of risk aversion: Invoking the precautionary principle; a preference for reactive innovation (i.e. only responding after technologies change); the adoption of a 'zero harm' safety management culture; perceiving costs as significant threats; a policy of diversification (i.e. avoiding dependence upon dominant suppliers, buyers, or products).

Examples of risk taking: Adopting early versions of new products, such as prototypes and beta releases; engaging in R&D and proactive innovation; seeking to evade legal and regulatory hurdles; putting many eggs into one basket (e.g. commitment to a dominant supplier or customer).

Comparative appetites: Systems engineer, Arthur Pyster, contrasted his experience of risk cultures within two workplaces: the Federal Aviation Administration (FAA) and SAIC, an advanced technologies company close to Washington DC. At the risk averse FAA, "Taking longer to roll out a new system to ensure that it had very few defects when launched was highly valued across the engineering and management workforce." At SAIC, however, "A balance between quality and speed was often favored, a consequence of the values of the customers for whom SAIC worked. Many times, the customer was an intelligence agency with a hard deadline to support an operational mission. Such customers often preferred products that were 80% finished but delivered on time."[34]

Risk aversion is often associated with organisations and institutions with big reputations (and even bigger budgets). They have a lot to lose from failure. Meanwhile, we think of risk taking as the preserve of smaller, younger businesses, such as startups. But these are poor stereotypes.

In practice, risk appetite varies for each product, system, or market under consideration. According to Hopkin, questions about an organisation's risk appetite "can only be answered within the context of the strategy, project or operational activity that is being considered."[35] Similarly, Massey says that "risk appetite for specific risk types needs to be flexible and reactive".[36]

So, when it comes to developing strategies, perhaps it's not the risk appetite that shapes the strategy, but the strategy that shapes the appetite. **Over time, every organisation will flip-flop between an aversion and a hunger for risk.**

Foresight

As Chief Technology and Innovation Officer of the automotive engineering company, Ricardo, Neville Jackson said that "My job is to understand what is going on outside our business that will affect us in the future: which really important future technologies are going to have an impact on us?"[37] In other words, Jackson was interested in technology foresight.

Uncertainty and foresight are closely-coupled, with the latter being inversely proportional to the former. Better foresight leads to less uncertainty.

Decision makers hate uncertainty, so the capacity to foresee significant developments and impactful events is a highly prized skill. In the excellent book *Foresight in Organizations* (2016), its Editor, Patrick van der Duin, quotes a definition of foresight from Berkhout *et al.* (2007):

> Foresight is the ability, the skill and art of describing, explaining, exploring, predicting and/or interpreting future developments, as well as assessing their consequences for decisions and other actions in the present.[38]

In other words, foresight enables us to interpret and act upon the future. It is a skill which can, to some extent, be learned.

Our understanding of complex environments, however, suggests that foresight skills are likely to be beyond the capabilities of most strategists. Considerable caution is therefore needed when approaching this topic.

According to van der Duin, there are three categories of foresight: *predictive*, *normative* and *explorative*.[39] Predictive approaches extend from the past and the present into the future, e.g. via trend analysis, extrapolation, or evolutionary increments along a recognised direction of travel. This sounds seductively easy. However, Chapter 5 highlighted the uncertainties associated with modelling and extrapolation, while Chapter 7 warned about the dangers of treating the future as a continuation of the past – a flawed process known as 'the narrative fallacy'. In complex environments, this category of foresight is likely to be unreliable.

Normative approaches are very different. They envisage a preferred future, and then design mechanisms for getting there. Arguably, this is more about *making* the future, than foreseeing it. A familiar example of normative foresight is the technology roadmap (described in Chapter 1). Yet the world changes so quickly that many roadmaps lose their fidelity within weeks of being published. Another normative technique is *backcasting*, which simply involves establishing the desired future state, then working backwards from that position, designing each of the steps needed to get there.[40] Surely, if making the future was this easy, we'd all be doing it! Most technology startups operate on the principle that they're creating an exciting future for themselves, and yet most fail within a couple of years. Quite simply, the future cannot be made.

We might reasonably assume that large, powerful organisations are an exception to this rule. Surely they have the capacity, wealth, confidence, and influence to shape their own destinies (and the destinies of others). But does any major corporation have the dexterity to navigate successfully within complex adaptive systems? Probably not. They must also contend with countervailing forces, because their normative visions of the future will trigger responses from vested interests, financial markets, competitors, and so on. One recent example of normative hubris involved the decision by Facebook, having renamed itself Meta, to build an alternative digital universe called the Metaverse. Within a couple of years, Meta's visionary project appeared to have floundered. In that short space of time, many billions of dollars had been sunk into the flawed idea. If a company as powerful as Meta can't shape the future, nobody can.

We might therefore conclude that both predictive and normative methods are incapable of presenting confident forecasts of the future. They're unreliable because they implicitly ignore complexity and its role in uncertainty.

This leaves van der Duin's third category: explorative forecasting. As we will see, exploratory methods, such as *horizon scanning*, the *Delphi method*, and *scenario development*, take a more cerebral approach to uncertainty. Explorative forecasting accepts that there is no single, discoverable future. Instead, there are many possible futures.

Explorative foresight: horizon scanning

The activity known as horizon scanning is less complicated than its name suggests. According to the IRM, It involves looking forwards in order to identify potential threats, opportunities and emerging issues "at the margins of current thinking and planning."[41] However, they warn it is "NOT about predicting the future."[42]

Nor is horizon scanning intended only to be used by risk management professionals. In fact, it's a widely used tool for analysing and visualising possible future events on three 'horizons' – the short term, medium term, and long term.

The first stage of horizon scanning is a team-based data-gathering and filtering exercise. A wide range of sources may be used, including publications and professional websites, plus inputs from industry leaders, competitors, customers, and staff. Information of interest is then scored for likelihood of occurrence and potential impact.

After analysis this information may be presented to stake-holders in a variety of ways, one of which is the Risk Radar diagram. These are often circular, or semi-circular in shape, depending upon the purpose of the scan. The outer layer represents the most distant horizon, while the inner layers feature possible events in the medium and shorter terms. All identified risk events are marked on the diagram and numbered for reference in a table or risk register.

The example in Figure 11.5 uses a pentagon in order to present the hypothetical results of a horizon scan for a single technology.

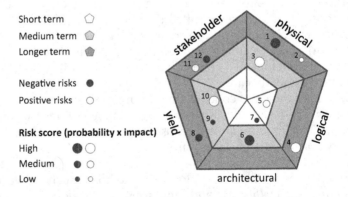

Figure 11.5 Example of a 5D Risk Radar horizon scan for a single technology

The pentagon shape reflects the fact that the five dimensions of technology (explained in Chapter 2) have been used as guidance for the scanning activity.

In 2020, the journal *Genetics and Genomics* published the results of a bioengineering horizon scan by an international team of subject matter specialists.[43] They defined bioengineering as "the application of ideas, principles and techniques to the engineering of biological systems." Participants were asked to identify issues across three time horizons: five years, five to ten years, and more than ten years. Altogether 83 issues were identified and scored for "likelihood, impact and novelty". A shortlist of 41 issues were then discussed in a workshop, resulting in a "top 20". These were grouped according to their time horizons, and listed in a table. Here are some of the results:

Five years: Crops for changing climates; State and international regulation of DNA databases.

Five to ten years: Neuronal probes expanding new sensory capabilities; Human genomics converging with computing technologies; Production of edible vaccines in plants.

More than ten years: Bio-based production of materials; Porcine bioengineered replacement organs.

The authors compared their results with a similar exercise three years prior. Substantial differences were found, attributed to a combination of the following:

- More diverse participants.
- Improved methods.
- A broader definition of bioengineering.
- Changes in the research landscape.

As this example shows, horizon scanning is not a scientifically rigorous examination of the future. It is heavily influenced by methods, timing, and participants. Nevertheless, it's capable of generating a host of insights upon which important decisions can be made.

Explorative foresight: the Delphi method

In Chapter 9 the Delphi method was introduced in the form of a so-called 'ethical Delphi'. The tool's original purpose, however, was to facilitate technology foresight for the American military.

Delphi is a structured technique for achieving consensus among experts. It is highly administrative, involving multiple rounds of anonymised consultations, idea sharing, and feedback over many weeks. Its underpinnings are described here by Ernest Braun:

> The Delphi method is based on two articles of faith. First, that experts working in a field of science or technology have a good feel of how the field might progress and when certain key results might be obtained. Second, that the consensus opinion of several experts is more reliable than the opinions of single experts.[44]

The first published Delphi exercise was organised by the RAND Corporation in 1964. Its purpose was to look ahead 50 years. Now, more than 50 years hence, the results of this exercise make for entertaining reading. Some of 1964's wilder predictions for the early 21st century included two-way communications with extra-terrestrials, gravity control, and chemical management of the ageing process.[45] Automated language translators were predicted for the early 1970s, two decades too early. More accurate, however, was its prediction for the timing of human-machine symbiosis using inter-actions between the brain and computer. Nevertheless, that first Delphi illustrates just how difficult foresight can be.

It's probably rare for Delphi to be used for time horizons as long as 50 years. Shorter horizons are certainly more easily analysed. According to L. Kemp *et al.*, Delphi has been found to outperform many other foresight methods. For example, a review of Delphi exercises in the health sector found that 14 out of 18 predictions had been accurate.[46]

Delphi's main limitations are that it's a resource-heavy exercise and relatively slow. It therefore seems unlikely that a smaller organisation would wish to use it. They might, however, make an exception for matters of great importance, such as the potential impact of a new scientific discovery on their product range or industrial processes.

Both horizon scanning and the Delphi method are good at providing limited, but thought-provoking information about possible futures. This is clearly helpful for strategy developers and decision makers, but the scope of these techniques is limited to the questions being asked. Consequently, there is a need for a broader, less prescriptive, more creative approach to foresight. This is a key characteristic of *scenario development* (below).

Explorative foresight: scenario development

In the 1960s the RAND Corporation were also responsible for developing a technique called "future-now thinking", which involved writing fictional stories about organisational futures.

Before long, major corporations including Shell, Corning, IBM, and General Motors were using the tool.[47] It later became known as *scenario development* (also *scenario planning* and *scenario analysis*).

Scenario development is based on the idea that organisations should explore more than one possible future when devising strategies, and that this activity can be supported by writing fictional scenarios based on time horizons of between 5 and 15 years.[48]

Scenario development is, like the earlier Delphi technique, a highly structured group exercise. But unlike Delphi it uses face-to-face interviews and workshops, involving a cross-section of internal personnel, along with one or two outsiders capable of challenging the group. Thomas Chermack's *Scenario Planning in Organizations* (2011) describes the method, which begins by gathering information from all of the key participants, notably their perceptions of the following:

- Future threats and general concerns.
- Future opportunities.
- Other inevitabilities and uncertainties.
- The internal and external forces driving the organisation's development.
- What the organisation should be aiming to achieve.

Indeed a wide range of information is sought, collated and analysed during the numerous workshops.

A list of relevant issues are ranked according to their potential impact on the organisation and their degree of uncertainty. Those ranked as both high impact and high uncertainty are selected for inclusion in the fictional scenarios, which are then written by team members. Typically, three or four scenarios are written, each presenting a different organisational path into the future.

According to Chermack, "scenarios must be relevant, challenging and plausible in order to be useful tools for managers." He emphasises that "plausible" means *possible*, not probable.[49] The scenario 'plots' are agreed by the team before the stories are written. Typical scenarios resemble stories, with a beginning, a middle and an end. Some common elements may be shared between the various scenarios, but each will present a very different future.

There is clearly an 'art' to the work of scenario writing, and systems thinking is important because "The ability to see interrelated forces and integrate patterns that drive events can lead to compelling presentations in the scenario stories."[50] Unsurprisingly, specialist consultants are often brought in to facilitate the work of scenario

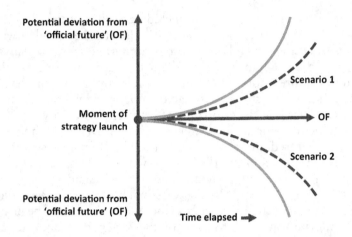

Figure 11.6 Scenario deviations from the 'official future'

development, but with sufficient commitment and resourcing, it ought to be possible for most organisations to explore this technique without requesting outside help.

Completed scenarios are sometimes compared and contrasted with the so-called "official future", the organisation's desired future path, as determined by the senior leadership. This official path to the future should be discernible from the business strategy.

We can visualise the differences between scenarios and the official future in graphical form, by superimposing them on the 'trumpet of uncertainty' (see Figure 6.1 in Chapter 6). In Figure 11.6, the official future (OF) is flanked by two scenarios, both of which remain within the boundaries of the diverging trumpet curves.

The true value of each scenario emerges when its content is tested against a proposed strategy. How resilient is the strategy to each scenario? Here, the literature refers to the so-called 'wind tunnel' analogy.[51,52] Each scenario is performing the role of a wind tunnel in which proposed strategies, like prototype aircraft, are expected to maintain stability.

However, whereas aircraft are usually able to deviate around bad weather, organisations must fly through it. Therefore the development and testing of scenarios helps to build organisational resilience. The function of wind tunnelling is visualised in Figure 11.7. Here, strategy S is shown to be compatible with both the official future (OF) and Scenario 2, but fails in Scenario 1's wind tunnel. The strategy will therefore need amending.

The oil major, Shell, were early adopters of scenario development methods. Shell's first scenarios used astonishingly long time

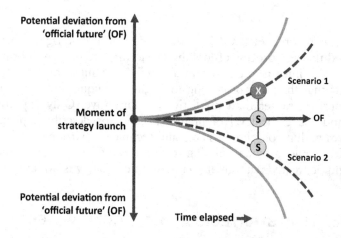

Figure 11.7 Testing a strategy in the 'wind tunnels' of scenarios 1 and 2

horizons. In the 1960s they were exploring futures through to the year 2000. This particular exercise was believed to have helped the company navigate the 1973 'oil shock' caused by the Arab-Israeli War.[53]

Shell have often used a two-tier approach to scenario development, with the first tier addressing global and industry futures. These scenarios inform the second tier, which looks at the organisation itself. Second tier scenarios might focus upon corporate regional strategies, or even the uncertainties associated with particular projects.[54] Some of Shell's most experienced scenario developers have gone on to teach the technique in leading business schools.[55]

Scenario development is expensive, and technology leaders may express doubts about its return on investment. However, the process does deliver a broad range of benefits, such as the sharing of internal information ('silo-busting'), and the personal development of participants, whose strategic acuity will improve during the process. The authors of *Technology Strategy* (2023), Nigel Walton and Neil Pyper, explain:

> By talking to each other, participants in the scenario development exercise test and challenge their own understandings of what the future might hold and the implications for what the organisation is doing in the present. A successful scenario exercise allows participants to broaden the 'mental models' they have formed, hopefully making them better able to recognise change in the external environment and adapt to this accordingly.[56]

Foresight conclusions

Strategy theorist Henry Mintzberg probably got it right when he argued that the process of looking ahead must rely upon "not much more than informed, creative intuition."[57] If Mintzberg is right, this means that the most promising foresight techniques are likely to be explorative, rather than predictive or normative. Only explorative methods have the level of nuance needed for describing plausible futures within complex business and technical environments.

Meanwhile, anyone claiming to *know* the future by other means should be treated with great scepticism. Futurology is not an 'ology'.

Box 11.3   STRATEGIC AND TACTICAL MOVES

Future-proofing

Sometimes we use an expression, but don't really know what it means. *Future-proofing* is a good example. How do we future-proof a product or system?

The first thing we discover is that maximising the longevity of an entity is not a science. It's more akin to an art.

This chapter has introduced many concepts directly relevant to future-proofing, including *changeability*, *modularity*, *scalability*, *repairability*, and the application of *real options* analysis (e.g. over-capacity by design). There were also some ancillary processes, such as *risk management* and *foresight* studies. But if our aim is to achieve indefinite longevity, what more can we do?

We might, for example, want to focus upon *quality*, aiming for component *integrity*, *reliability*, and *durability*. Another important consideration is *redundancy* – the provision of duplicated assets or features in order to reduce the probability of a total loss of functionality.

The wider socio-technical system must also be included in a future-proofing analysis. For instance, 'no-blame' reporting of near-miss incidents will reveal existing and emerging flaws, enabling timely interventions to prevent failure and loss. Furthermore, without demand from users a product or technology will die. It must remain relevant. This can be facilitated by *forward compatibility* (see Chapter 2). Another tactic is to use *extensibility*, i.e. offering new bolt-on features, perhaps assisted by third parties operating under an *open standards* framework.

Management processes will also need to be considered. The reliable supply of spares and consumables should be capable of exceeding the design life of the product or system, and good maintenance regimes are required in order to minimise the effects of 'entropic' disintegration (described in Chapter 5).

Finally, we need to consider the economics of the product/ system lifecycle. Attempts to increase longevity are challenged by the law of diminishing returns. How much time, energy and physical material should we sacrifice upon the altar of longevity?

Everything has limits, and *uncertainty* ensures that termination is often closer than we think.

Plans or proposals?

This chapter showed how strategists have a wide range of techniques at their disposal for navigating uncertainty. These were categorised under design, risk management, and foresight. There is a limit, of course, to the number of navigational approaches we can examine in a single chapter, and many others are available. See Appendix 2, *Ideas for navigating uncertainty*, for a longer list based on the contents of this book.

We must also address the 'elephant in the room'. It goes by the name of *planning* or, more specifically, *strategic planning*. According to van der Duin's categories, strategic planning is a normative foresight technique, because it's an attempt to create a chosen future. But this, as we know, implies defying complexity. As this book has shown, nothing can defy complexity over the medium to longer term.

There is a famous aphorism attributed to the Prussian general Helmuth von Moltke: "No plan survives first contact with the enemy."[58] More recently, the boxer Mike Tyson offered his own version: "Everybody has a plan until they get punched in the mouth."[59] These are the words of practitioners, not theorists.

I consider 'first contact with the enemy' and 'getting punched in the mouth' as proxies for unexpected and undesirable events. So, if a long term plan is to have any intrinsic worth it must be both robust and able to flex. However, a plan that flexes too far and too frequently ceases to be a reliable plan. It is this dichotomy that I have avoided addressing until now. Indeed, for this reason the language of planning has been deliberately excluded from the first ten chapters of the book.

The author of *Learning to Think Strategically* (2020), management consultant Julia Sloan, explains the challenge:

We tend to know intuitively that the more uncertain and unpredictable our strategic environment, the more useless our detailed plans become. Strategic thinking is not about the creation of a static plan but, rather, about setting a dynamic, sustainable thinking process in motion.[60]

Chapter 3 defined a technology strategy as "an evolving package of concerted actions within the technological realm, supporting organisational goals." Could a formal plan ever be described as an 'evolving package'? Probably not. Consequently, in Chapter 4, an assertion was made that "A strategy is not a plan. It is a proposal for navigating uncertainty."

To develop a strategy, we need to find a path towards today's objectives through the lurking shadows of tomorrow's unknowns. Superficially this may resemble 'a plan', but it must also be highly configurable from the moment of conception. To call it a plan would lead some observers to believe that it will be delivered unhindered and in full. It is surely better to call it, or at least think of it as, a *proposal*.

A well-designed technology strategy is compatible with myriad plausible futures. It must therefore combine the virtues of simplicity and changeability, with carefully controlled risks. An easy-to-follow methodology for developing this type of strategy is presented in the next chapter.

Glossary for this chapter (Items in bold are also defined in the same table)

alternative future	One of an infinite number of possible paths along which the organisation could travel, each differing in some way from the **official future**.
Bowtie diagram	A visualisation of the activities leading up to a **risk event**, and the post-event effects. Typically used to manage the activities associated with undesirable events. A variant, known as the **Positive Risk diagram**, visualises desired events.
design for uncertainty	The application of design to the challenge of anticipating the effects of uncertainty. Methods include simplicity, changeability, and **real options**.
explorative foresight	An investigative approach to foreseeing future developments, typically involving group activities. Explorative techniques include **horizon scanning**, the **Delphi method**, and **scenario development**. Compare with **predictive foresight** and **normative foresight**.
future-proofing	The art of maximising the longevity of a product or system. It can include design solutions, such as **modularity**, scalability, durability, and forward compatibility. These can be combined with management practices, e.g. maintenance scheduling and near-miss reporting,
HAZOP study	A highly structured group workshop for analysing complex industrial systems. The study aims to anticipate and mitigate every conceivable weakness.
horizon scanning	A method for capturing and visualising the likelihood and impact of short, medium, and long term events.

(Continued)

insurance	A financial solution for mitigating significant losses imposed by possible future events.
modularity	A design solution involving the integration of changeable, semi-independent functional units. It offers the benefits of upgradeability, repairability, extensibility, and so on.
normative foresight	The process of envisaging a preferred future and designing a route to get there. Arguably, this is about *making* the future, rather than foreseeing it. Familiar examples are the technology roadmap and the strategic plan. Compare with **predictive foresight** and **explorative foresight**.
official future	A phrase associated with **scenario development** techniques. It is used to describe the anticipated or desired direction in which an organisation will evolve. This will typically be reflected in the business strategy. It is highly unlikely that the official future will materialise as described. Contrast with **alternative future**.
plausible scenario	One possible future. It is the main unit of output from a **scenario development** exercise. Importantly, "plausible" does not mean "probable".
Positive Risk diagram	A variant of the traditional **Bowtie diagram**. A Positive Risk diagram visualises the activities leading up to a desired event, and its post-event effects. It may be used as a project management tool, because it illustrates a project's design and current status.
predictive foresight	An attempt to extend from the past and the present into the future, e.g. via trend analysis, extrapolation, or evolutionary increments along the current direction of travel. Compare with **normative foresight** and **explorative foresight**.
pre-mortem	A workshop tool for establishing the possible causes of undesirable future events. It involves asking personnel to contemplate the worst possible scenario (e.g. the 'death' of a company, project, or product), then to propose explanations for the cause of the event.
real constraints	A hypothetical methodology for eliminating some or all of the **real options** (and their associated costs) embedded within a technical solution.
real options	Management options, available for use in the future, can be 'purchased' and incorporated within *real* engineering designs. This involves a probabilistic analysis of future events. Contrast with **real constraints**.
risk	ISO 31000, defines risk as "the effect of uncertainty on objectives." It is often 'calculated' using the formula *Risk = Probability x Impact*.
risk appetite	According to the ISO, this is the "amount and type of **risk** that an organisation is willing to pursue or retain". It reflects the proportion of organisational assets, including reputation, that managers are willing to expose to uncertain outcomes.

(Continued)

(Continued)

risk event	A future occurrence with the potential to result in significant negative and/or positive effects.
risk management	A formal discipline for analysing and navigating uncertainty. It does this by taking carefully considered actions in advance of possible events. These events may be perceived as good or bad. Resources are deployed to either: a) reduce the likelihood and scale of negative impacts, or b) increase the likelihood and scale of positive impacts.
risk matrix	A simple two-dimensional representation of known **risks**. There are two axes, *Probability* and *Impact* (or *Likelihood* and *Consequences*). Each axis has a scale from *Low* to *High*. Impacts may be positive or negative.
risk register	A table used for evaluating the significance of known **risks**. Each risk is 'scored' by quantitative or qualitative means enabling an organisational focus upon the main threats and opportunities.
scenario development	A technique for researching and writing fictional **alternative futures** for organisations. Scenarios test the viability of current strategic thinking.

Notes

1 Boulton, J.G., Allen, P.M. and Bowman, C. (2015) *Embracing Complexity*. Oxford: OUP. 103.
2 Collier, T. (ed.) (1995) *Design, Technology and the Development Process*. London: Chapman & Hall. 49–50.
3 BKCASE (2023) 'Guide to the Systems Engineering Body of Knowledge (SEBoK), version 2.8'. Available at: https://sebokwiki.org/wiki/Guide_to_the_Systems_Engineering_Body_of_Knowledge_(SEBoK) (Accessed: 03 November 2023).
4 Nuttall, W.J. (2019) *Britain and the Bomb: Technology, Culture and the Cold War*. Dunbeath: Whittles. 132.
5 Heppenheimer, T.A. (1997) *Countdown: A History of Spaceflight*. New York: Wiley. 338–346.
6 Tiwana, A. (2017) *IT Strategy for Non-IT Managers: Becoming an Engaged Contributor to Corporate IT Decisions*. Cambridge, MA: The MIT Press. 36.
7 Flyvbjerg, B. and Gardner, D. (2023) *How Big Things Get Done*. London: Macmillan. 86–87.
8 Tiwana, *IT Strategy for Non-IT Managers*. 86.
9 Ross, A., Rhodes, D. and Hastings, D. (2008) 'Defining Changeability: Reconciling Flexibility, Adaptability, Scalability, Modifiability, and Robustness for Maintaining System Lifecycle Value'. *Systems Engineering*, Vol. 11, Issue 3, 246–262.
10 Edwards, H., Locke, A. and Jackson, A. (2016) 'Manufacturing Power Stations'. *Ingenia*, Issue 69, 30–34.
11 Grant, R.M. and Jordan, J. (2015) *Foundations of Strategy*. Chichester: Wiley. 88.

12 Grant and Jordan, *Foundations of Strategy*. 10.
13 Martani, C. *et al.* (2016) 'Design with Uncertainty: The Role of Future Options for Infrastructure Integration'. *Computer-Aided Civil and Infrastructure Engineering*, Issue 31, 733–748.
14 Martani *et al.*, *Computer-Aided Civil and Infrastructure Engineering*.
15 de Neufville, R. (201?) 'Flexibility in Engineering Design'. Available at: https://cmapspublic3.ihmc.us/rid=1MHBN740P-1HKCC2L-168D/Flexibility%20in%20Engineering%20Design-de-Neufville.pdf (Accessed: 01 September 2023).
16 Stevens, P. (ed.) (1998) *Strategic Positioning in the Oil Industry*. Abu Dhabi: ECSSR. 5.
17 Grant and Jordan. 351.
18 Grant and Jordan. 351.
19 King, D.R. (2006) 'Implications of Uncertainty on Firm Outsourcing Decisions'. *Human Systems Management,* Vol. 25, 115–125.
20 The Institute of Risk Management (2002) *A Risk Management Standard*, available at: https://www.theirm.org/media/4709/arms_2002_irm.pdf (Accessed: 17 August 2023).
21 Blunden, T. and Thirlwell, J. (2013) *Mastering Operational Risk*. Harlow (UK): Pearson. 7.
22 The Institute of Risk Management, *A Risk Management Standard*.
23 Hopkin, P. (2012) *Fundamentals of Risk Management*. London: Kogan Page. 141.
24 Hopkin, *Fundamentals of Risk Management*. 287.
25 Syed, M. (2015) *Black Box Thinking*. London: John Murray. 311.
26 Kahneman, D. (2011) *Thinking, Fast and Slow*. London: Penguin. 264–265.
27 Crawley, F., Preston, M. and Tyler, B. (2008) *HAZOP: Guide to best practice*. Rugby: IChemE. 14.
28 Adapted from Crawley, Preston and Tyler, *HAZOP*. 118–128.
29 The Institute of Risk Management.
30 Baird, J.L. (2004) *Television and Me*. Edinburgh: Mercat. 76.
31 Moar, P. (2016) 'Accentuate the Positive'. *Risk Management Institute of Australasia: Yearbook 2016*. 28–31.
32 Morse, L.C. and Babcock, D.L. (2010) *Managing Engineering and Technology*. Upper Saddle River, NJ: Pearson. 103.
33 International Organization for Standardization, *ISO Guide 73:2009(en) Risk Management – Vocabulary*. Available at: https://www.iso.org/obp/ui/#iso:std:iso:guide:73:ed-1:v1:en (Accessed: 13 September 2023).
34 Pyster, A., Hutchison, N. and Henry, D. (2018) *The Paradoxical Mindset of Systems Engineers*. Hoboken: Wiley. 168.
35 Hopkin. 149.
36 Massey, M. (2022) *Climate Change Enterprise Risk Management*. London (UK): Kogan Page. 42.
37 Kenward, M. (2017) 'Thinking About the Revolutions'. *Ingenia*, Issue 71, 42–46.
38 van der Duin, P. (ed.) (2016) *Foresight in Organizations*. Abingdon: Routledge. 7.
39 van der Duin, *Foresight in Organizations*. 2.
40 Hewitt, E. (2018) *Technology Strategy Patterns*. Sebastapol, CA: O'Reilly. 83.
41 Institute of Risk Management (2018) *Horizon Scanning: A Practitioner's Guide*, available at: https://www.theirm.org/news/horizon-scanning-a-practitioners-guide-revealed-at-irm-leaders/ (Accessed: 22 August 2023).

42 Institute of Risk Management (2018) *Horizon Scanning.*
43 Kemp, L. *et al.* (2020) 'Point of View: Bioengineering horizon scan 2020'. *Genetics and Genomics.* Available at: https://elifesciences.org/articles/54489. (Accessed: 01 September 2023).
44 Braun, E. (1998) *Technology in Context.* London: Routledge. 115.
45 Marchau, V. and van de Linde, E. (2016) 'The Delphi Method' in van der Duin, P. (ed.) (2016) *Foresight in Organizations.* Abingdon: Routledge. 66–70.
46 Kemp, L. *et al., Genetics and Genomics.*
47 Chermack, T.J. (2011) *Scenario Planning in Organizations.* San Francisco: BerreATT-Koehler. 10–13.
48 Walton, N. and Pyper, N. (2020) *Technology Strategy.* London (UK): Red Globe Press. 213.
49 Chermack, *Scenario Planning in Organizations.* 159.
50 Chermack. 162.
51 Chermack. 172.
52 Walton and Pyper, *Technology Strategy.* 214.
53 Chermack. 13.
54 Chermack. 85–86.
55 Walton and Pyper. 212.
56 Walton and Pyper. 214.
57 Mintzberg, H. (2018) 'Strategic Thinking as "Seeing"'. *Manage Magazine* [online]. Available at: https://managemagazine.com/article-bank/strategic-management-article-bank/henry-mintzberg-strategic-thinking-seeing/ (Accessed: 01 September 2023).
58 Oxford Reference, *Helmuth von Moltke 1800-91 Prussian military commander.* Available at: https://www.oxfordreference.com/display/10.1093/acref/9780191826719.001.0001/q-oro-ed4-00007547 (Accessed: 4 September 2023).
59 Smith, D. (2022) '"He's got that beast in him": the difficult legacy of Mike Tyson'. *The Guardian*, Monday 29 August 2022. Available at: https://www.theguardian.com/tv-and-radio/2022/aug/29/mike-tyson-boxing-hulu-series (Accessed: 4 September 2023).
60 Sloan, J. (2020) *Learning to Think Strategically.* Abingdon: Routledge. 264.

Part III

Something to take away

The remaining two chapters examine how technology strategies should be developed, executed, and permitted to evolve.

Firstly, Chapter 12 presents the *Five Dimensions Process* (or 5DP), a methodology for producing a formal technology strategy. The 5DP was briefly introduced in Chapter 3. In the pages that follow a more detailed step-by-step procedure is described.

The final chapter includes reflections and recommendations. It proposes an enhanced role for the growing discipline of systems engineering.

DOI: 10.4324/9781003472919-14

12 A strategy blueprint
The five dimensions process

This chapter presents

- A guide for developing formal technology and engineering strategies.

This chapter establishes

- The criteria for selecting team members and choosing when to develop or revise a strategy.
- The necessity for speed in developing strategies, and for brevity in their explanation.

Every organisation, large and small, needs a technology strategy. This is true regardless of their degree of dependence upon engineered products and systems. Indeed, even an organisation proudly eschewing technologies in favour of pre-industrial processes would, by implication, have a clear technology strategy.

Similarly, if an organisation using advanced industrial processes chooses to change nothing, to continue using the same technologies without altering either their architecture or configuration, this choice constitutes an important strategic decision. Indeed, doing nothing is sometimes more strategically significant than introducing changes.

In order to be effective, strategies need to be agreed, written and shared. However, operating without the benefit of a strategy is an experience familiar to thousands of technologists and engineers around the world. They have no formal guidance for making important tactical decisions which could affect the future prospects of their organisation. Every granular choice, from recruitment to machine configuration, from supplier selection to asset disposal, is potentially strategic in nature.

An organisation, by definition, needs to function as a unit. Each team must pull in the same direction. Without strategic guidance, the left arm won't know what the right arm is doing. Failure will come knocking. The delivery of a technology strategy must therefore be a concerted effort by all key stakeholders. This means

DOI: 10.4324/9781003472919-15

that **the contents of the strategy should be widely shared, easily
understood, persuasive, yet concise.**

It isn't enough simply to write a technology strategy.
Organisational leaders must also provide full backing and visible
support to its development. Without that commitment there is no
guarantee that the resources needed – especially money, people,
and time – will be forthcoming. Furthermore, a strategy that has
been produced without the backing of senior management will be
difficult to deliver. Personnel objecting to particular provisions will
resist, confident in the knowledge that senior leadership are not
committed to seeing the strategy implemented.

Let's assume that the need for a new technology or engineering
strategy has been recognised by the leadership and that you've just
been asked to produce that strategy. This prestigious responsibility
could help to shape your future and that of your employer or
client. So where should you begin? Who else should be involved in
the development process? What information will you need? How
will the resulting strategy be communicated, and how will it be
executed? This chapter is designed to provide the answers to these
questions.

Background

It will probably be helpful, at this juncture, to recap some of the
key evidence and assertions from earlier chapters.

Altogether, 40 real-world technology and engineering strategies
were examined during research for this book, and 14 of these were
reviewed in Chapter 1. A conclusion was reached that there is no
recognised standard approach or template for producing a technology strategy.

An important feature of this book is its theory of technology,
first presented in Chapter 2 and predicated upon the idea that
every technology possesses five necessary and sufficient 'dimensions': physical, logical, architecture, yield, and stakeholder (represented by the acronym PLAYS). This theory was used to inform
some of the content in later chapters. It also underpins the strategy
development process described below. This is why I call it the Five
Dimensions Process, or 5DP.

Chapter 3 helped to define what we mean by 'technology
strategy'. It was viewed as "an evolving package of concerted
actions within the technological realm, supporting organisational
goals." Briefly, let's unpick this definition. A strategy *evolves* in
response to the ever-changing operational environment. The actions
must be *concerted* if the organisation is to move forward in lock-step
without one group implementing changes that simultaneously

undermine the work of others. It *supports organisational goals* by helping business and technology leaders to realise their visions. Hence, an important feature of Chapter 3 was the organisation's formal business strategy, which must be the primary driver of technology-related decisions. **The technology strategy is a sub-strategy of the business strategy. What the organisation needs, the organisation must get.** Our job as technologists and engineers is to guide, advise, inspire, and propose solutions, but not to tell the organisation what to do, or to place obstructions in its path. If this critical linkage between a business strategy and its technology strategy is broken, the technological environment could become counter-productive, or even an existential threat to the organisation.

Chapter 3 also explored the idea of technological domains and their correlation with traditional engineering disciplines. Domains are 'families' of technologies, such as automotive, electronics, computing, and biotech. The hypothetical example of a shipbuilding company was used to propose the idea that domains can be used to structure the development of a technology strategy. This introduced the concept of technology sub-strategies. For instance, one important sub-strategy might be called the Digital Strategy, and this could even be divided into a lower-level suite of 'sub-sub' strategies. Using PLAYS for guidance, this might consist of a Hardware Strategy, Software Strategy, Architecture Strategy, Data Management Strategy, and User Management Strategy. Nevertheless, it should be remembered that good strategies are always "concerted". **No sub-strategy should ever be produced without reference to other approved strategies, both at the same level and above.**

Chapters 4–6 examined the challenge of uncertainty. Two important concepts were derived from this perspective: *strategy depreciation* and the *execution gap*. A strategy begins to depreciate (lose validity and value) as soon as it is produced, sometimes before it has even been communicated to stakeholders. Furthermore, individual implementation decisions are frequently undermined by changes in both the internal and external environments. These changes can occur between decisions being made and their subsequent execution. The length of this execution gap will be inversely proportional to execution success. This is illustrated in Figure 12.1.

Once produced, it is only a matter of time before your finely crafted strategy makes "first contact with the enemy" and gets "punched in the mouth" (see Chapter 11). This metaphorical opponent is *uncertainty*, and it highlights the importance of minimising the execution gap. There is a need for rapidity in the process of developing, communicating, and executing the strategy. The strategy development process must not become laboured and

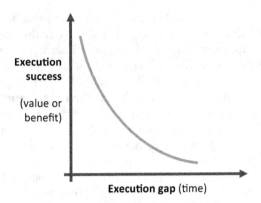

Figure 12.1 Relationship between the scale of execution success and the execution gap

bureaucratic. It should be brisk and efficient in order that execution can begin at the earliest opportunity.

Furthermore, in order to maintain the currency and validity of a strategy, it must be able to flex in response to challenges. Hence, it should be relatively short on words, because the more words we use in describing and explaining our strategy, the more words we will need to re-negotiate and re-write when uncertainty strikes. You probably won't have enough time to perform frequent revisions, so brevity is best.

In conclusion, a technology strategy should be delivered as non-detailed guidance that can be easily communicated and, when required, swiftly revised. A shorter, carefully worded strategy depreciates more slowly and will be read by more people than a document resembling a doorstop. It should be able to retain its validity for months, even years, without extensive revision.

In order to achieve this type of lean technology strategy, we must separate the more fundamental, longer-lasting strategic ideas and choices from the lower level details of how those ideas and choices will be executed. In other words, **what we call delivery or execution should not be viewed as intrinsic to the strategy. Execution is merely the mechanism by which a strategy is implemented.**

Preparations

Before developing the technology strategy you will need to establish a team. Who should be invited to join? Another consideration is timing. When should the team assemble to begin its work?

The strategy development team

What attributes are we looking for in a successful strategist? Who should be involved in the strategy development team? Chapter 7 used the work of Sloan, Kahneman and others to examine the personal attributes of effective decision makers and strategists. These included:

- An ability to resolve strategic dichotomies.
- A depth and diversity of life experiences enabling intuitive judgements.
- A welcoming attitude to the contributions of other people.
- A networking instinct, connecting with all levels of the organisation.
- The confidence to speak up, negotiate and persuade.
- The resilience to make progress despite resistance.
- A talent for using systems thinking when analysing complex operational environments.
- The patience to analyse information from multiple sources and the creativity to synthesise new solutions.
- The vision to conceive of ambitious, but plausible goals, and the ability to inspire colleagues to achieve them.

If you recognise some of these attributes in yourself, that's a good start. What you don't have, others in the team should be able to compensate for. That's how great teams are built. (Chapter 7 also listed some of the unwanted characteristics in people entrusted with strategy development. It may be instructive to read those again before putting the team together!) Table 12.1 summarises the key roles within a strategy development team for the Five Dimensions Process.

Clearly, the team requires some combination of domain expertise, an awareness of the emerging 'state of the art', and extensive knowledge of the organisation and its capabilities. It isn't necessary for the strategy team leader to possess all of these attributes, although it certainly helps.

In general, senior technology leaders have the experience needed to develop strategy, but their domain-level skills will often be some years out of date. Equally significantly, their awareness of the state of the art (especially emerging technologies) will be constrained by the amount of time they can dedicate to following industry news, research reports, and scientific developments. Consequently, mid-career professionals are often best placed to do most of the strategy development. They can sell it 'up' to organisational leaders and explain it 'down' to those on the front line. In Peter Westwick's

Table 12.1 Strategy development team roles

Role	Description	Attributes
Strategy leader	Tasked with delivering the organisation's technology or engineering strategy.	An experienced individual with broad technical interests (though not necessarily expertise). A strategic thinker. A great facilitator. Could be a professional project manager, or perhaps an 'outsider' (see below).
Domain leader(s)	Representing each of the key domains within the organisation's portfolio of technologies.	Many years of experience working within that domain, and able to encourage their team of domain engineers and technicians to respond with information and ideas.
Domain engineers and technicians	Frontline workers in the key domains, responding to requests from their domain leader.	Strong domain knowledge. Good analysts/researchers. Prepared to speak up.
Business representative(s)	The key point of contact between the strategy development team and the wider organisation.	Knowledgeable about the organisation, its processes and products. Familiar with the business strategy and able to explain it. Could be an experienced business analyst or mid-level manager with interests in technology, but with no direct responsibility for technology or engineering domains.
Outsider	An individual with no personal interest in the outcome of the process. The outsider challenges groupthink and wayward progress (including ethical concerns).	May be a consultant or a trusted friend of the organisation, e.g. a former employee. Smart, creative, confident. Prepared to ask 'difficult' questions and breach internal taboos. Technically literate, but not necessarily a domain expert.

remarkable story of how stealth aircraft were developed, he used the phrase "History from the middle" to describe this practice.[1]

The leaders of each technology domain and their team members will undoubtedly need to contribute, as will one or more representatives from the operational side of the business. Furthermore, strategy consultant Julia Sloan recommends including people from outside the organisation "who have good thinking habits but who come from worlds which are unfamiliar and very different from your own." They offer new and different perspectives, of the kind unlikely to emerge from the groupthink of culturally-aligned colleagues.[2]

Strategy development involves a series of events, particularly workshops, but it shouldn't be necessary for the *whole* team to attend *every* event. To ensure efficiency and avoid over-thinking, the process must involve the smallest number of people necessary for achieving its aims. For instance, front line technical staff only need to be involved in the earlier stages of the process, while Sloan's 'outsider' is probably required to provide inputs during later stages. These task allocations will become more obvious in the description that follows.

Sometimes one person will wear many hats. If the strategy team leader has also been involved in the development of the business strategy, and if they have strong expertise in one or more domains, it's conceivable that they could do a large proportion of the work themselves, particularly in smaller organisations. Indeed, a 'team' could vary in size from a single multi-tasking, multi-domain leader, to a full complement of perhaps ten or more people.

Anyone capable of fulfilling two roles should be highly valued. For instance, the outsider could be brought in to perform the strategy leader role. Similarly, a more hands-on domain leader could perform some of the research tasks which would otherwise be delegated to frontline personnel.

Timing and triggers

When should the team begin its work? More precisely, when should the first iteration of an organisation's technology strategy be created, and what should be the trigger for subsequent iterations?

Here, the status of the business strategy is crucial. Under normal circumstances, the production of a technology strategy should begin within days (if not hours) of the business strategy's approval. Don't wait for it to be published in a glossy document, which could take weeks. The world is changing too quickly, and the business strategy needs immediate support.

What happens if there is currently no business strategy? In these circumstances it is important to gain clarification from the senior leadership whether one can be expected in the near future. If not, don't wait. This is where the business representative on the development team will be required to play a significant role. They must give the best advice possible about the direction that the business wants to take, its expected policies, risk appetites, and so on. Although this is not an ideal situation, it does present a unique opportunity, because the production of a high quality technology strategy will then feed into and influence any subsequently produced business strategy.

It should also be noted that there is an important exception here. Companies that are wholly technical in their focus, often founded by scientists or engineers, and which continue to be led by them, might not distinguish between what they perceive as the business strategy and the technology strategy. Although I would argue that these should be viewed as separate entities, their production may occur simultaneously, with the same people leading both activities. This type of combined strategy development is not addressed directly in this book, but the reader may use the contents of this chapter to inform, and hopefully improve, this all-in-one strategy process.

Once the first iteration of the technology strategy has been delivered, a question arises about the frequency of subsequent revisions, which we might call 'versions'. Should these be periodic and predictable (e.g. annual, bi-annual) or driven by events (e.g. "getting punched in the mouth")? I would argue that changes to the technology strategy must be the latter, i.e. event driven. The following list of possible events is far from comprehensive, but each should be seen as a trigger for strategy revision:

- A new or significantly-amended business strategy is approved.
- Another organisation has been acquired, or will be merged, leading to technological impacts.
- A rival 'dominant design' or a recent scientific discovery will eventually render current products defunct.
- Access to a critical supplier from overseas is lost, e.g. due to government sanctions.
- New technical regulations or international standards will soon be introduced.
- Substantial ethical challenges to production processes have emerged.
- The R&D department is patenting a product with huge commercial implications.
- Influential voices within technical teams are demanding a new version, perhaps due to strategy depreciation, or general dissatisfaction with the current direction of travel.

Technology leaders must use careful judgement when determining when to initiate a new strategy development. For example, if none of the above events has occurred (nor anything similar), then the default period between revisions could be up to two years.

Even the most moribund of technological domains are undergoing constant, if slow, evolution. Don't be lulled by the glacial rate of change. With time, glaciers level mountains. Take a fresh look at the state of the art and any emerging risks. You might be surprised how things have progressed since you last examined the domain closely.

Once begun, every strategy development or strategy revision should be completed in the shortest possible time. For most small to medium-sized organisations, the process described below should take no more than a few weeks. Any longer, and the twin problems of the execution gap and depreciation will emerge.

Process and structure

In *Good Strategy, Bad Strategy* (2017), Richard Rumelt remarks that "Good strategy is not just "what" you are trying to do. It is also "why" and "how" you are doing it."[3] This translates broadly to the strategy development and execution process described in Chapter 3 – the Five Dimensions Process. There are three stages to the process. The first two, labelled *Research* and *Strategising*, lead to the production of the strategy. The third and final stage is the output from the strategy, which we call *Execution*. Only here does the strategy become responsible for tangible changes to the organisation's technological environment.

I would argue that Rumelt's "what" and "how" are more central to the communicated strategy than the "why". The latter may be of interest to people who wish to understand the background to decisions, but for communication purposes it's the "what" and "how" that really matter. Once the strategy development is complete, the "why" can simply be archived.

At all times throughout this process, the strategy development team are encouraged to retain a focus on the five dimensions of technology. This will provide an assurance that each technology and each product type have been thoroughly analysed. As noted earlier, the five dimensions also help with the creation of sub-strategies, where each sub-strategy addresses a single dimension or a combination of related dimensions. The strategy development team, under the guidance of the strategy leader, must design their approach at the very start of the process. The scale of the organisation and the criticality of particular technologies will shape these strategy design decisions.

Ultimately, there can only be one over-arching technology strategy, because all of its sub-strategies are working in concert to support organisational goals. This unity of ideas and actions is critical.

First stage: Researching

The research phase corresponds to the "why" of strategy development. It is about information gathering, analysis, and the synthesis of ideas. There are four types of research activity:

1 An examination of 'where we are today' – the current status of the organisation's technological environment.
2 A careful study of the business strategy and its technological implications.
3 A state of the art review, examining emerging technologies and practices.
4 Analysis of any uncertainties, known challenges, and ideas for navigating the future.

Let's look at each of these in turn.

Where are we today?

Firstly, we need to know where we stand. What is our baseline? What technologies, products, working practices, machinery, facilities, intellectual property, and skills does the organisation have? It's important to list everything that could be of strategic relevance. Also, what is anticipated for the near future? Is there any work in progress?

Many enterprises, especially industrial businesses, will need to examine multiple domains, whereas office-based organisations, such as consultancies and government authorities, may only be concerned with the digital domain. However, it's easy to dismiss the significance of 'low-tech' assets and activities, such as buildings, energy consumption, and vehicles. A truly comprehensive technology strategy may therefore involve many more domains than initially anticipated.

Regardless of organisational scope and scale, this step of the Five Dimensions Process will involve a lot of data collection. Domain leaders, such as the head of IT or a chief engineer, will be required to supply summary data about their own domains. Think of it as an inventory. The strategy team will need to know what assets they have, what they do, and how/why they do it. Here, the five dimensions of technology may be analysed to ensure that everything has been taken into consideration.

Much of this inventorising and itemising can be delegated to frontline staff, who often know more about such matters than their team leaders and department heads. The data should be gathered in summary form, e.g. short documents or spreadsheets. It doesn't need to be pretty, because these files will never be published.

This exercise will be of considerable benefit to the strategy team's domain leaders. Within organisations, technology domains are typically siloed, with little information sharing or cross-fertilisation. For domain leaders, it can be a revelation to learn about the current assets and status of neighbouring, co-domains. From this exercise alone, opportunities for more internal collaboration may emerge. Other members of the strategy team will also benefit from being able to see this data, particularly the business representative(s).

External data will also need to be gathered, and much of this should be readily available in the public domain. It needs to include:

- Current and forthcoming regulations or standards.
- The status of competitors.
- Relevant information about the wider economic and political environment.

The business representative(s), or perhaps the outsider, may be the best candidates for undertaking this externally-focused research. A useful *aide memoire* for this task could be the groups of 'indirect' technology stakeholders described in Chapter 8 (Figure 8.1).

We might also expect the business representative to share research data gathered during development of the business strategy. This might include a value chain analysis, a strategic asset audit, or a PESTLE study (see Box 12.1).

Box 12.1   ANALYTICAL TOOLS AND TECHNIQUES

PESTLE

The PESTLE analysis tool is well-known among business strategists. Its name is an acronym, reminding us that there are six important external factors which must always be taken into consideration when producing an organisational strategy. Here are the six factors, with examples:

Political: government policies, industrial strategies, regulations and subsidies; international collaborations.

Economic: exchange rates; wages; unemployment; regions of high growth, such as India and China.

Societal: cultural expectations and ethics; age distributions; education and skill levels.

Technological: anticipated developments and likely impacts on organisational products and processes.

Legal: employment rights; public liability; health and safety; specific laws in countries where the organisation may be operating (e.g. GDPR, Sarbanes-Oxley Act).

Ecological: natural resource availability; effects of depletion and pollution; climate.

According to Cadle *et al.*, "When using the PESTLE technique it is important to recognise that we are looking for factors that fit two criteria: they are outside the sphere of influence (i.e. control) of the organisation, and they will have some level of impact upon it."[4]

PESTLE examines both the present and the future using qualitative and quantitative techniques.[5] It therefore requires a wide range of research skills and data sources.

Hewitt recommends the use of PESTLE for technology strategy development. He says, "It helps you see what the weather might be, so you know to pack an umbrella."[6]

PESTLE also has alternative uses beyond strategy. For instance, Hopkin describes it as "a well-established structure with proven results for undertaking brainstorming sessions during risk assessment workshops."[7] So, we might say that PESTLE is another tool for navigating uncertainty.

Some of the analytical tools available for supporting this phase of the development are listed later in Table 12.2. However, all of the data captured during these research tasks will begin to depreciate rapidly, so everything described above should be completed quickly (in days, or at most a couple of weeks).

Business strategy input

Concurrent with the previous research step, some members of the strategy team will need to be studying the organisation's current business strategy.

In a sensibly-run organisation, senior technologists and engineers will have participated in the business strategy development. It's important that business leaders understand the capabilities and limitations of technologies when making strategic decisions, and this is only possible if engineers are in the room with the business leadership. An organisation's Chief Technology Officer or Chief Engineer may be unable, on their own, to make contributions of sufficient breadth and depth, so they should be accompanied by domain leaders. If the business strategy can be successfully infused with engineering insights, the subsequent work of developing a stand-alone technology strategy will proceed far more efficiently.

However, for the purposes of explaining this blueprint for developing a technology strategy, we will assume that the business representative is the person most familiar with the current business strategy. It is their job to explain it to the rest of the team.

Other recently produced information which might be available via the business representative are the results of any scenario development work. Scenarios present alternative business futures, and were explained in Chapter 11).

Much of the formal business strategy will be of little or no significance. For instance, matters concerning sales, accounts, or taxation are largely technology-neutral (although computing is usually the platform of choice for these activities). However, where the business strategy addresses topics such as quality control, operations, product development, outsourcing arrangements, relocations, site closures, acquisitions, new geographical markets, partnerships and alliances, to name just a few examples, the implications could be significant. It is the duty of the strategy team to understand these organisational aims and ambitions. Only then can they deliver a technology strategy that underpins the business strategy.

It's conceivable that the organisation will not be in possession of a formally approved business strategy (perhaps due to inept or fractious leadership). In these circumstances the strategy development team, with the help of its business representative(s), must create an unofficial business strategy of their own. This might necessitate interviews with senior business leaders. The absence of a formal business strategy is certainly unhelpful, but a hard working business representative should be able to provide enough information for the team to work with.

Analysing this business strategy will require no more than a few days, involving mostly round table discussions and brainstorming activities within the strategy development team.

State of the art review

Strategies are forward looking. Their time horizons are typically between three and five years, though ten years is not uncommon. (See Table 3.2 in Chapter 3 for examples of time horizons used in real-world strategy documents.) Consequently, the strategy team must be cognizant of forthcoming developments in the key technology domains. Here are some questions to ask:

- What new tools, techniques, and products are emerging?

- What are suppliers saying about forthcoming releases, add-ons, extensions, and updates?
- Is there anything interesting emerging from the internal R&D department?
- Have our competitors patented anything recently?
- Have there been any recent scientific discoveries of interest?

This examination of the 'state of the art' could influence activities such as purchasing, business acquisitions, alliances, R&D, design life extensions, product retirements, recruitment, and staff training.

The review involves domain teams scouring technical and industry publications, recent conference presentations, interviews with leading engineers and entrepreneurs, and the questioning of colleagues. This is also an opportunity to explore some of the foresight techniques described in Chapter 11. The Delphi method is a relatively lengthy exercise, but could be used if there are sufficient funds available. Horizon scanning, however, is much more amenable.

The so-called 'hype cycle' is always a danger. Talk is cheap. Some 'forthcoming' products may be little more than vapourware, designed to raise publicity, attract investors, and test the market. Experienced professionals are impervious to this nonsense, but those who are inexperienced or not directly involved in technology domains (e.g. CEOs and politicians) have a habit of falling for the guff. Even if an exciting new product or technology is based on hard evidence, and offers real prospects, major product releases take much longer to materialise than promised by their sponsors. They also cost a lot more to develop and adopt than originally anticipated. Here's some advice. Stay calm in a technofrenzy. Everything will become clearer after the dust and smoke disperse. Never be rushed into a state of the art technology investment without full due diligence. Indeed sometimes it's better to wait for improved technological maturity (see Box 4.3 *First mover advantage OR Second mover advantage?* in Chapter 4).

Each domain leader must understand what is *probable* and what is *possible* within the time horizon, then share everything with the strategy development team. As this information goes into the mix, it will influence both the strategic vision and the actions needed to deliver it.

Uncertainties, challenges, and ideas

The final research step involves capitalising on the experiences, talents, and strategic thinking skills of the development team.

What can be done to help the organisation navigate its way through the future? All team members will have ideas for improving the technological realm, but they will also have concerns that need to be addressed. Group workshops may be the best way to capture these contributions.

In addition to data gathered in the prior research steps, useful information should also be available from sources such as the organisation's Risk Register (see Chapter 11). If produced correctly, the Register will have incorporated the most significant technological risks. There might even be a benefit in producing a new technology register specifically for this activity.

This step presents an opportunity to invite a wider range of contributors. Personnel from all areas of the organisation could be invited to participate in facilitated workshop sessions. Best practice involves giving a voice to staff who wouldn't normally have the chance to shape strategy. What insights do they have?[8]

Another useful technique involves the blending of a PESTLE study (see Box 12.1), with the well-known SWOT analysis of strengths, weaknesses, opportunities, and threats.[9,10] In other words, create a SWOT matrix for each of the five PESTLE factors.

Meanwhile, the domain leaders should be considering the strengths and weaknesses of their areas of responsibility. What mechanisms do they propose for exploiting those strengths and mitigating the weaknesses?

Some of the ideas that could emerge at this stage have been described in earlier chapters. These include:

- Collaborating with universities (Box 1.1, Chapter 1).
- Ensuring compatibility with other products on the market (Box 2.3, Chapter 2).
- Cancelling failing projects (Box 3.2, Chapter 3).
- Creating a 'lite' product version using the process of 'dennovation' (Box 4.1, Chapter 4).
- Using sensors to "instrument everything" (Box 5.3, Chapter 5).
- Sourcing off-the-shelf supplies, rather than making in-house (Box 6.2, Chapter 6).
- Establishing a knowledge management programme to overcome internal silos (Box 7.2, Chapter 7).
- Breaking the stranglehold of monopoly suppliers and domineering customers (Box 8.3, Chapter 8).

- Future-proofing the design of a product or process (Box 11.3, Chapter 11).

All of the ideas for navigating uncertainty, discussed in Chapter 11 and itemised in Appendix 2, should be part of the conversation.

The team might also want to explore emerging dichotomies, such as whether to:

- Persist with a stable and mature technology, or transition to the 'state of the art' (Box 1.2, Chapter 1).
- Automate a process, or retain a skilled/experienced workforce (Box 2.4, Chapter 2).
- Cloister the engineering staff to improve productivity and morale, or co-locate them within the business to improve visibility and internal relations (Box 3.3, Chapter 3).
- Share the reporting of near-miss operational incidents for quality purposes, or protect reputations and morale by maintaining confidentiality (Box 5.1, Chapter 5).
- Launch a new innovation that cannibalises existing products, or protect current products by suppressing the innovation (Box 6.3, Chapter 6).
- Locate within a technology cluster, or remain geographically independent (Box 7.1, Chapter 7).
- Outsource via offshoring, nearshoring or onshoring, or perhaps retain in-house (Box 8.2, Chapter 8).
- Choose a centralised technical solution, or opt for a more distributed architecture (Box 10.2, Chapter 10).

Among the many tools available to assist with this stage of the 5DP, the following have been described in earlier chapters:

- The Ansoff Matrix, for supporting product innovation (Box 10.1, Chapter 10).
- Real options analysis (Chapter 11).
- Bowtie visualisations for mitigating negative risks and promoting positive risks (Chapter 11).

Not only is there a lot to consider here, but there is a danger that some ideas will clash. This could result in separate engineering teams working to support the strategy, yet inadvertently pulling in opposite directions. Remember, a strategy is defined by its "concerted actions", so these conflicts **must** be resolved before they become enshrined in the strategy. One of the tools for identifying this type of problem is Leavitt's Diamond (see Box 5.2 in Chapter 5). For instance, when changing the technological environment we need to examine the implications for staffing, organisational design, and operational processes? Suffice to say, every significant technology change should be examined for its impact on other technologies.

The research stage of the 5DP is now finished. It hasn't been possible to describe or list every type of data collection or analytical tool. Strategy teams are expected to customise these activities according to the time and resources they have available.

Table 12.2 Some analytical tools supporting technology strategy development

Research step	Tool name	Description	Reference
Where are we now?	Value chain analysis	A decomposition of the organisation's value chain into five primary activities and four support activities. Each activity consists of myriad constituent processes and actions.	Box 1.3 in Chapter 1
	Strategic asset audit	An identification and examination of all assets of strategic value. Strategic assets can be tangible (e.g. laboratories) and intangible (e.g. IP).	Box 3.1 in Chapter 3
	Skills matrix	A simple table capturing the business-critical skills possessed by technical staff. Skill levels are scored, strengths and weaknesses identified.	Box 8.1 in Chapter 8
	PESTLE	Analysis of those political, economic, societal, technological, and ecological factors most likely to have a future impact upon the organisation and its products.	Box 12.1 in this chapter
Business strategy input	Scenario development	A technique for researching and writing fictional alternative futures for organisations. Scenarios test the viability of current strategic thinking.	Chapter 11
State of the art review	Delphi method	A technique for eliciting knowledge, ideas and conclusions from anonymous	Chapters 9 and 11

(Continued)

Table 12.2 (Continued)

Research step	Tool name	Description	Reference
		subject matter experts. The participants engage in multiple rounds of written exchanges, coordinated by an administrator.	
	5D Risk Radar horizon scan	A method for capturing and visualising the likelihood and impact of events affecting a single technology or product over the short, medium, and longer term.	Chapter 11
Uncertainties, challenges and ideas	Risk register	A table used for evaluating the significance of known risks. Each risk is 'scored' by quantitative or qualitative means enabling a prioritisation of key threats and opportunities.	See Chapter 11
	Ansoff matrix	A tool for assisting firms with their product-market analysis and associated strategy development. The matrix maps products, both existing and new, against markets, existing and new.	Box 10.1 in Chapter 10
	Real options analysis	An approach to the design of engineering solutions that empowers future decision makers with additional choices as the operational environment evolves.	See Chapter 11
	Bowtie visualisations	Diagrams representing the activities leading up to a risk event, and its post-event effects. Typically used to manage the activities associated with undesirable events. A variant, known as Positive Risk modelling, visualises desired events.	See Chapter 11
	Leavitt's Diamond	A diamond-shaped visual tool which emphasises the fact that within organisations reflexive relationships exist between four entities: the organisational structures; the work to be performed; the people who do the work; and the technologies used to perform or support the work.	Box 5.2 in Chapter 5

Second stage: Strategising

The strategising phase corresponds to the "what" and the "how" of strategy production. It is because strategies need to be communicated that these should be relatively high level descriptions. Low level detail has no place in a strategy intended to be communicated, understood and remembered.

Vision and objectives

Where are we going? This question is answered by a statement of vision and objectives.

The strategic vision describes the organisation's technological environment X years from now, where X is the chosen time horizon for the strategy. In fast moving domains, such as digital goods and services, the horizon cannot realistically be more than three to five years. Anything beyond that is little more than wild speculation. In less dynamic environments, a five to ten year vision may be feasible. There are few organisations that can realistically offer a vision this far ahead, although Table 3.2 (Chapter 3) features two longer examples. The European Space Agency (ESA) and National Highways both use time horizons of 13 years.

Some organisations even offer a tantalising glimpse of their longer term thinking. For instance, Toshiba's 2018 Technology Strategy presented a conventional five-year horizon, but with an extended vision to 2030, while the ESA discussed some engineering activities 28 years ahead.

Once the principal time horizon has been established, it's necessary to describe the organisation's preferred technological environment upon reaching that horizon. This is the vision: a plausible aspirational description.

How you choose to organise this overall vision is important. It should be comprehensible for non-technical readers (e.g. CEOs) and frontline personnel. It will need to be logically organised; this could be by technological domain, or by individual corporate divisions, or product types, or technology dimensions, or geographical regions. The choice is yours.

Remember that the 'technological environment' goes beyond physical technologies. It can also include such matters as innovation policy, skill profiles, outsourcing, design methodologies, and stakeholder relations. Does the organisation want any of these to be altered or implemented before the end of the time horizon? Here are three vision-type statements from the real-world strategies reviewed in Chapter 1:

Social Security Scotland: "... to create an integrated benefits solution where information is captured once and processed many times."[11]

National Highways: "Eliminate implementation of roadside technology requiring maintenance."[12]

Australian Department of Defence: "Providing resilient global communications, position navigation and timing (PNT) and geospatial intelligence (GEOINT) capabilities direct to ADF users, enabled by a low earth orbit (LEO) SmartSat constellation."[13]

The vision statement must be accompanied by objectives. **Each of these will need to be measurable, or at least unambiguous, so that technical staff know precisely what is expected of them.** Objectives may be captured in one or two sentences. Here are some examples of objective-type statements within the sample strategies:

City and County of San Francisco: Connect residents to high-speed home Internet. Five-year target: 15,000 residents connected. 95% are satisfied or very satisfied with speed and quality of connection.[14]

NASA: By 30 September 2023, NASA will complete commissioning of the James Webb Space Telescope and begin Webb's Cycle 2 observations.[15]

UK Home Office: "To ensure our data is of a consistent quality and can be used by a range of services, we will use metadata standards to clearly define and label each record. This will include information relating to provenance."[16]

It would be unwise to attach priorities to either the vision statements or the objectives. Priorities are susceptible to change, and the overriding goal of the 5DP is to produce a strategy that depreciates slowly. Priorities may be assigned later, during the execution stage.

Visioning, of course, presents a best case scenario. According to Walton and Pyper, "a key limitation of visioning is that it allows for telling only one story of the future and thus may not fully capture all of the uncertainties that are inherent in understanding how the future might unfold."[17] The strategy vision reflects the "official future", to use the expression from Chapter 11. This is also likely to be an optimistic future. Chapter 7 explained the problems associated with optimism bias and the planning fallacy. We mustn't believe that the strategy, as published, will be delivered in full. In truth, it's going to change considerably. Readers of the vision statement need to be reminded that the strategy is alive. It's a living, breathing entity and will be subject to frequent revisions.

But that's okay. As long as changeability is understood, the strategy can be more easily perceived as *a proposal for navigating an uncertain future*.

Writing in the Harvard Business Review's *Guide to Thinking Strategically* (2019), Ron Ashkenas argues that an organisation's strategic vision should be able to fit "on one page", where its content will serve "as a true north to help guide key decisions."[18] Of course, sometimes it may not be possible to confine the vision to a single page, but two or three pages is quite sufficient, even for large organisations.

The strategy's key purpose is to provide **today's** direction for "true north". It provides tactical guidance to employees and contractors, enabling them to work collectively, in a synchronised fashion, in the best interests of the organisation. Tomorrow is another day. Uncertainty may strike. If that happens, the strategy can be revised, as explained later.

Delivery

The vision statement described, at a relatively high level, where the organisation wants to get to. This means we've done the "what". Now let's address the "how".

How are we going to 'engineer' the delivery of the vision and its objectives? What mechanism is being proposed? These answers are significant because, in the words of Grant and Jordan, "a strategy that has been formulated without taking account of its ability to be implemented is a poorly formulated strategy."[19] Reversing this logic Ashkenas advises us to "make sure that your various projects and initiatives have a direct line of sight to your strategic vision."[20]

Once again, in order to minimise depreciation, we are only concerned with high level descriptions and explanations. The most important characteristic of a delivery statement is not its technical detail, but its qualities of coordination. It is far more important that it describes a "package of concerted actions" (from the earlier definition of strategy).

Rumelt argues that "coordination of action provides the most basic source of leverage or advantage available in strategy."[21] A clever metaphor from athletics is introduced by Grant and Jordan. The members of a sprint relay team may have the common goal of reaching the finishing line first, but this doesn't prevent them from dropping the baton due to poor team coordination.[22] So, a lot depends upon getting these concerted actions right.

Each of the objectives described in the earlier vision statement must be addressed. The delivery statement focuses upon individual chunks of work, their sequences, and the resources needed to implement them. Logically there will always be three types of action: creating, altering, and erasing. In other words, your strategy is aiming to change the technological environment, either by introducing something new (e.g. a product, or a team), amending something that already exists (e.g. a policy, or a software application), or completely removing something from the environment (e.g. an ageing asset, or failing outsourcing contract). For instance, projects can be started, adjusted, or cancelled, and systems can be built, re-architected, or decommissioned.

The strategy development team will need to quickly examine and agree upon these delivery mechanisms. It won't be possible to produce either a full business case or cost-benefit analysis for each activity. That level of detail comes later during the execution stage. We're simply looking for a package of initiatives which complement one another, each with a clear 'blood line' to the business strategy.

Like the vision statement, your statement of delivery should be a quick, accessible, but informative read, between one and three pages long.

Three examples of real-world delivery statements, from the strategies reviewed in Chapter 1, are included in Appendix 3.

Testing the strategy

The vision and delivery statements reflected the organisation's 'official future'. However, as explained in Chapter 11 this is only one of many possible futures. This raises the question of how resilient the new strategy will be if, as is likely, the organisation experiences an *alternative future*?

This is the moment at which, with sufficient time and resources, a *scenario development exercise* could be introduced. (See Chapter 11 for more information about scenarios.) This process would create two or three scenarios of plausible alternative futures. If scenarios have been used during the development of the main business strategy, these can be re-used here, saving much time and effort.

The development team would be wise to use these alternative futures to test the resilience of the new technology strategy – a practice known as 'wind tunnelling'. If the newly developed strategy is found to be vulnerable when exposed to these alternative futures, a further review and amendment will be needed before its publication. However, if the strategic vision, objectives and delivery statements are found to be compatible with these scenarios, then the technology strategy should be considered sufficiently robust to survive the onslaught of uncertainty (at least until the organisation encounters an entirely unexpected re-calibrating event).

Having passed the scenario test, the strategy is now ready for communication.

Box 12.2   STRATEGIC AND TACTICAL MOVES

Declaring war on costs

In general, there is more to be gained from a focus upon success and growth, than from an obsession with costs. However, technology costs are more than capable of posing a threat to the viability of organisations, their projects and products. As such, they have strategic significance.

Engineering assets and technological processes or systems are expensive to design, assemble, operate, maintain, repair, and decommission. Fortunately, there are many ways to reduce these cost burdens; some have already been mentioned in this book.

In Chapter 3 there were justifications for terminating projects, often on the basis of burgeoning costs. Much later (in Ch. 7), the technique known as *reference class forecasting* was shown to provide foreknowledge (and hence avoidance) of unanticipated project costs.

The newest technologies can be particularly expensive to develop or procure. So-called 'first movers' bear these costs. Ch. 4 described how 'second movers' may avoid being stung.

In Ch. 6 the financial benefits of purchasing off-the-shelf were explained. As a general rule, self-building and customisation are costly activities, so it's worth developing a taste for 'vanilla' products. In the same chapter, the Pareto Principle was also mentioned; we can assume that 20% of costs will account for 80% of value, so the remaining 80% of costs must surely be scrutinised.

Locating within a thriving technology cluster, such as Greater Boston, may seem superficially attractive, but the increased costs of facilities and inflated salary levels should cause second thoughts (Ch. 7). Perhaps it's better to avoid.

The study of stakeholders in Ch. 8 warned against becoming dependent upon monopoly suppliers. This is one reason for the ever-growing popularity of open source software. Outsourcing and insourcing were also examined for their (debatable) cost benefits. Also featured was the concept of vertical integration – the tactic of acquiring upstream suppliers and downstream customers. Integration leads to a reduction in transaction costs, and facilitates more confident bulk ordering.

Process innovation (Ch. 10) is commonly associated with cost-cutting. For instance, the change from batch to continuous flow production methods can have a transformative impact on the bottom line. Similar improvements are possible in the move away from non-standardised, irregular build processes towards design for manufacture and assembly (DfMA).

The *real options* methodology, explained in Ch. 11, showed how longer term costs may be reduced, but only by increasing short term costs. This tactic requires bold management. Conversely, the 'real constraints' approach offers immediate, though probably foolish, savings.

Later, risk management was described as a tool for controlling the costs from unwanted events. Ch. 11 also examined the concept of future-proofing. In products this increases design life, thereby deferring the costs of decommissioning and disposal.

This is a huge topic. Indeed, there are hundreds of ways to cut costs. However, there are some serious caveats. For instance, the description of value chain analysis in Ch. 1 warned that it's safer to cut so-called 'secondary' support activities than 'primary' activities.

If you choose to declare war on costs, it is possible to make a lot of ground in a very short space of time, but there are mines underfoot, so tread carefully.

Communicating the strategy

Congratulations! Your strategy development team has now successfully produced a draft technology strategy. Furthermore, it has good provenance, having been derived from the business strategy and written by senior, experienced professionals. It now faces two significant hurdles: 1) approval from the organisational leadership; 2) sharing with, and influencing the behaviour of, the wider stakeholder community, especially frontline personnel.

Unless the development team are in the fortunate position of being able to approve their own work, it's likely that a board of some kind will need to be convinced of the strategy's merits. Hopefully this will occur with minimal pushback. To enable this, Ethan Rasiel and Paul Friga, authors of *The McKinsey Mind* (2001), offer some practical advice. They use the term *prewiring* to describe the process of ensuring that key members of the approval board are already supportive of the new strategy.[23] Similarly, the enterprise solutions architect, Eben Hewitt, recommends that important presentations to boards are delivered as a *fait accompli*.

> Once there, make sure that you reference the stakeholders' work, credit their ideas, and thank them for their contribution. This is not only honest and proper, but has the pleasant side effect of creating an echo chamber of support in the room.[24]

In other words, dissenting voices are unlikely to be heard at the presentation, because criticism of the strategy would imply criticism of the most senior stakeholders.

Surely, though, if the leadership team has confidence in the people they assigned to produce the strategy, and if the Five Dimensions

Process has been followed diligently, there is no reason to believe that any objections would be raised. Given that the leadership approved the business strategy, it follows that anything derived from it must also be broadly acceptable.

In *Embracing Complexity* (2015) the authors Boulton, Allen, and Bowman discuss the challenge of implementing strategies within complex environments:

> In too many organizations the strategy process only seems to produce documents, and does *not* produce belief and commitment to a way forward for the organization. If strategy is to have any effect it has to influence the day-to-day activities of the people inside the organization.[25]

So now, having gained high level approval, the next task is to communicate the strategy more widely in a way that is both convenient and persuasive. We need to ensure that the wider stakeholder community understands how the organisation proposes to manage its technological environment in the years ahead. That job must begin with immediate effect, because the new strategy is already depreciating.

Chapters 1 and 3 discuss some of the confidentiality which may need to be respected during stakeholder communications. For instance, the approved strategy may contain sensitive provisions which should only be shared on a 'need to know' basis. For reasons of simplicity, we will focus here upon the version intended for most stakeholders, especially those staff whose job it will be to execute the strategy and make tactical decisions on a daily basis.

Given that employees in larger organisations are likely to be separated by location, time zones, and even shift patterns, a variety of methods will need to be used for these communications. Face-to-face presentations and explanations are desirable, but not always practical. However, a host of other options are available including videos.

One of the challenges with using multiple communication channels (and probably multiple communicators) is version control. How many versions of the strategy will there be and will they be consistent? There could, for instance, be two or more of the following: a wordy portrait-style document, a separately produced bullet-pointed presentation, a dedicated web page, and even a slickly-produced video explainer by the Chief Engineer or CTO. I would argue that **it's better to maintain a single, tightly controlled version, in written form**. Any additional communications should be a subset of this official, master version.

For help with selecting an appropriate documentation style, let's return to the 14 real-world strategies reviewed in Chapter 1. Most of these were formatted as portrait-style, printable documents. Seven appear to have been designed for distribution as glossy publications (e.g. Social Security Scotland, European Space Agency). Others were probably intended solely for online or email distribution.

The remaining four documents were in landscape formats (e.g. National Highways, and the New Zealand Ministry of Social Development). This probably indicates that many of their stake-holders were informed about the latest strategy in face-to-face presentations.

One of the advantages of presentation-style documents is their flexibility, combining ease-of-use in traditional face-to-face explanations, online readability, and ease of printing when the strategy is required in hard copy. Furthermore, presentation formats encourage efficiency in the way that ideas and information are communicated. Generally they use fewer words and more visual elements, such as graphs, diagrams, and tables.

The landscape presentation format is therefore ideal for communicating a technology strategy. This single, multi-purpose document helps with version control, avoiding the need to cross-check between different communication tools. Why use different versions of the strategy when a single document will suffice?

In the first stage of this development process conventional text was used for the statement of vision/objectives and the statement of delivery. These should now be converted into a single, easy-to-communicate presentation-style landscape format. This will be the official organisational technology strategy, and subject to strict version control.

Remember: there are no rules here. The Five Dimensions Process is a recommendation, not a set of precise instructions. Strategy development is not a science, it's more of a 'useful art'. A strategically-minded technologist or engineer is smart enough to know how best to adapt the suggestions contained in this book to the unique circumstances of their own organisation. Do your best. It will almost certainly be an improvement over anything that has gone before.

Box 12.3   STRATEGIC DICHOTOMIES

Develop staff or recruit for new skills?

A familiar feature of the technological realm is the constant demand for new skills. Many managers struggle with this challenge, especially when an older technology needs replacing. They must balance their obligations to support the business strategy with the preferences, needs and ambitions of their own staff.

A common dilemma involves choosing between investing time and money in the re-skilling of existing personnel (assuming they are willing to make the transition) and simply plugging the skills gap by recruiting externally. There are numerous factors to consider:

Developing staff: To retain organisational knowledge and experience, it's important to ensure that existing personnel are satisfied professionally, otherwise they may choose to leave. Investing in their re-skilling is good for morale. Not only does it reward loyalty, but the training process offers a change of routine and a short respite from the workplace. This approach also avoids painful 'career discussions' leading to reluctant re-assignments or enforced redundancies. There are downsides, however. In addition to the costs of re-training, time will be lost while personnel make the transition and come up to speed with the new technology. Your re-skilled employee is now just a beginner.

Recruiting for new skills: By recruiting it's possible to instantly acquire advanced technical capabilities. Externally sourced talent brings fresh ideas and novel insights. This can be an expensive approach, however, especially if the technology is 'hot' and skilled professionals are in demand. The contractor/outsourcing route is sometimes preferred over direct recruiting, although this may incur even greater costs. A different and far riskier approach is to buy another company where the desired skills already exist. However, these various forms of external recruitment have the effect of sending a signal to legacy employees that their career development is not a priority. Although some staff may not care about the new technology, others will be eager to make the transition, and may feel slighted by recruitment activities.

Getting the balance right: Within technology and engineering it's important to recruit 'trainable' personnel. In other words, employees must be able to evolve at the same pace as their industry's technologies. Those with skillsets that are both narrow and deep will become a liability in the future. They may be experts today, but will they be prepared to lose that expertise and become 'beginners' tomorrow? We might say that trainability is both a mindset and a competence. Look for people who combine strong expertise with diverse skills and interests. These are sometimes known as T-skills professionals and they help to future-proof organisations, because they're more likely to make the transition to a new way of working.

Every major technology disruption causes pain, but with good personnel management the net benefits should accrue to all parties. Even those who opt to take their legacy skills elsewhere will probably feel more valued and be happier in their next role.

As we move inexorably towards the era of AI augmentation, we might define an 'expert' as "a person happy to work in partnership with a machine", so the forthcoming augmentation era should make technological transitions smoother and less painful for everyone involved.

Revising the strategy

The newly-developed strategy will need to be revised when significant changes occur, either within the business operating environment or in one of the critical technology domains. Some of these revisions will be limited in scale and scope, going un-noticed by most staff. However, other revisions will be substantial and significant. On each occasion, the technology strategy must be updated and its changes communicated.

A new version of the strategy may also require a change to its time horizon. For instance, a hypothetical five-year *Technology Strategy 2025–2030* v.1.0 will become v.1.1 after a minor amendment, and v.2.0 after substantial changes. This resembles software versioning. However, if an amendment is made near the end of a calendar year, the starting date is moved forward, e.g. to *Technology Strategy 2026–2031* v.1.0. This creates a rolling five-year strategy, an "evolving package" always represented by a unique name and version number.

Consequently, by adopting this 5DP methodology, strategy development ceases to be a periodic, highly-resourced activity. It is now operationalised and low-cost. For example, the development of an updated version may only require a single meeting or workshop involving the original strategy team. Of course, there will always be some preparatory work and a small number of follow-up tasks, notably approvals and necessary communications.

Third stage: Executing

The execution of a technology or engineering strategy is a process of indefinite length involving substantial resources. There are probably thousands of case studies available, but let's look briefly at one, involving General Motors (GM) in the US.

Amrit Tiwana explains how, in the early 21st century, GM translated its business strategy into a major technological transition.[26] By 2013 the company was facing an emerging challenge from rival manufacturers incorporating advanced software capabilities into their vehicles. Whereas software had previously been invisible to customers (e.g. controlling the engine management system), it was rapidly becoming a product differentiator. The ubiquitous smartphone had changed public perceptions and expectations about the capabilities of physical products. Indeed the entire product lifecycle was in the throes of a digital transformation, from design processes through to smart manufacturing, sales methods, and maintenance techniques.

GM therefore decided to bring its software development in-house, terminating a multi-billion dollar outsourcing deal with Hewlett Packard. As a consequence, GM needed to recruit 8,000 developers. Tiwana explains the logic behind GM's decision:

> In-house developers are more likely to understand GM's customers, their latent needs and wants, and details about GM's inner workings better than outsiders. The potentially higher costs to do the IT work in-house could be well worth it if a better IT-driven integration between the mechanicals and electronics resulted in more reliable vehicles that customers wanted more than Ford's or Toyota's.[27]

A strategic decision on this scale inevitably triggers a large number of activities. It was explained earlier that all strategic actions fall under three categories: creating, altering, and erasing. In the GM case, these might have included:

Creating: New software development teams; possibly new work sites and data centres, both in the US and abroad (wherever the necessary skills can be found); new policies, procedures and working practices (e.g. software development methodologies); new car interior designs and user interfaces; new maintenance equipment and techniques; new training programmes; new stakeholder relationships, e.g. with suppliers and complementors (such as the manufacturers of in-car entertainment systems); new research into the risks (e.g. data security) and product ethics (e.g. self-driving modes).

Altering: Current team structures and roles; the purpose and layout of existing facilities; current policies and procedures; the design of legacy products; the scope or specifications for existing projects; the content of current training programmes; relationships with established stakeholders including suppliers, complementors, and regulators.

Erasing: The current outsourcing contract; some internal roles associated with contract management; legacy policies and procedures; leases for facilities used by the outsourced developers; older product designs which are too difficult to re-engineer; legacy maintenance equipment; active projects which are now deemed to be unnecessary; and some training programmes will probably have become defunct.

The actions described above constitute a multi-year transition, and these would be performed within a dynamic business/technology environment. It would therefore be necessary to undertake occasional revisions to the strategy. GM's software development proposals were, in reality, a sub-strategy of a higher level corporate technology and engineering strategy. That, in turn, would have been subservient to the main corporate business strategy. At the time of writing GM remains a thriving company, so one assumes that the software strategy was successful.

The complete communications package

It's important to ensure that no gaps have emerged in the strategic information being shared internally. Seven interrogative words determine the questions which must be answered by the various communications:

1 **Why** is action needed?
2 **What** should be delivered?
3 **Which** part of the technological environment is affected?
4 **Where** will this be done?
5 **When** will this be started and finished?
6 **How** will it be delivered?
7 **Who** will be doing it?

Table 12.3 links each set of answers to a form of communication.

In the published strategy, which incorporates the statements of vision, objectives and delivery, the key questions are answered, but only at a summary level. Information about why the strategy emerged in its current form was captured during the initial research stage. This will have been archived for retrieval, if needed, thereby reducing the clutter often associated with traditional strategy communications.

The execution stage involves lower level details concerning precisely what needs to be done within each technology domain,

Table 12.3 How the Five Dimensions Process communicates answers to each type of question

	Communications	
	High/summary level	**Low/detail level**
Why?	Execution instructions to staff	Strategy research materials (archived)
What? **Which?** **Where?** **When?**	Statement of vision and objectives Statement of delivery	Execution instructions to staff
How?	Statement of delivery	
Who?	Not necessary at this level	

where the actions will be taken, when and by whom. These communications are made by managers and team leaders. They're not the responsibility of the strategy development team, because they are not part of the higher level, formally approved strategy.

Visualising the process

Now let's pull everything together into a single diagram. Figure 12.2 shows the main features of the Five Dimensions Process (5DP).

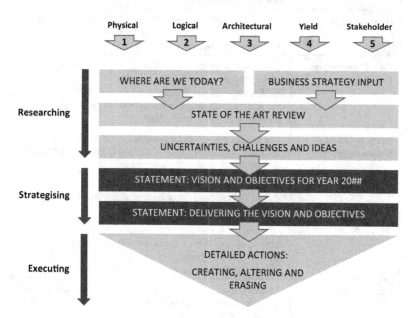

Figure 12.2 The Five Dimensions Process: a method for developing technology strategies

It consists of three stages: researching, strategising, and executing. Throughout every stage consideration must be given to each of the five dimensions of technology. In doing so, the strategy development team can be certain that nothing has slipped through the net. The resulting strategy should be a comprehensive, tightly integrated package.

The strategy needs to engender *trust* in those required to approve and execute it. Rachel Botsman, of Oxford University's Saïd Business School, has examined the contemporary significance of trust, especially in relation to technologies. She defines trust as "a confident relationship with the unknown."[28] When developing a strategy, we are boldly confronting the unknown, and we need everyone involved in executing that strategy to trust in the quality and integrity of its vision, objectives, and delivery methods.

Botsman also says that "trust is an evaluation of outcomes, of how likely it is that things will go right."[29] Of course, in a complex world we can never be certain that 'things will go right', but the 5DP is designed to give us the best chance of achieving satisfactory outcomes. By design, the 5DP embodies trust.

Glossary for this chapter (Items in bold are also defined in the same table)

5DP	An alternative and convenient label for the **Five Dimensions Process**.
domain leader	An employee with responsibility for managing the people and other assets associated with a single technology domain, e.g. electronics, hydraulics, construction, aeronautics, IT.
Five Dimensions Process	A method for producing technology or engineering strategies, described for the first time in this book. It uses the five dimensions of technology to ensure that the developed strategy is comprehensive in its design. It may also be referred to as the **5DP**.
hype cycle of technology	The familiar pattern of high expectations, fuelled by optimism and vested interests, leading inexorably towards dashed hopes and disappointment.
objective	An unambiguous statement of expectations. The objective should be achieved on or before a deadline, e.g. within the strategic time horizon.
PESTLE	An acronym for six important external factors which, it is argued, should always be taken into consideration when producing an organisational strategy. They are: political; economic; societal; technological; legal; and ecological.
state of the art	An expression indicating the most advanced examples of technological development within a particular domain, e.g. the state of the art in biotechnology.

(Continued)

version control	A disciplined method for ensuring that different iterations of a product, e.g. a software application or a strategy document, may be identified without needing to compare contents.
vision	A description of the desired organisational environment at a chosen moment in time, e.g. three years from now.

Notes

1 Westwick, P. (2020) Stealth: The Secret Contest to Invent Invisible Aircraft. New York: OUP. 198.
2 Sloan, J. (2020) *Learning to Think Strategically*. Abingdon: Routledge. 276–283.
3 Rumelt, R. (2017) *Good Strategy, Bad Strategy*. London: Profile Books. 85.
4 Cadle, J., Paul, D. and Turner P. (2014) *Business Analysis Techniques*. Swindon: BCS. 5.
5 McGrath, J. and Bates, B. (2013) *The Little Book of Big Management Theories*. Edinburgh: Pearson. 170–171.
6 Hewitt, E. (2018) *Technology Strategy Patterns*. Sebastapol, CA: O'Reilly. 71.
7 Hopkin, P. (2012) *Fundamentals of Risk Management*. London: Kogan Page. 143.
8 Sloan, *Learning to Think Strategically*.
9 Cadle, Paul and Turner, *Business Analysis Techniques*. 5.
10 Hopkin, *Fundamentals of Risk Management*. 157.
11 Social Security Scotland (2022) *Digital and Technology Strategy 2022–2025*, available at: https://www.socialsecurity.gov.scot/asset-storage/production/downloads/Digital-and-Technology-Strategy-2022-%E2%80%93-25.pdf (Accessed: 03 September 2022).
12 National Highways (2022) *Operational Technology: our 2035 strategy*, available at: https://nationalhighways.co.uk/media/n1edbo0z/operational_technology_strategy_2035_issue-may-2022.pdf (Accessed: 05 September 2022).
13 Australian Department of Defence (undated) *Defence Science and Technology Strategy 2030*, available at: https://www.dst.defence.gov.au/strategy/defence-science-and-technology-strategy-2030 (Accessed: 31 August 2022).
14 City and County of San Francisco (undated) *Information and Communication Technology Plan FY 2022–26*, available at: https://sf.gov/coit-strategy (Accessed: 03 September 2022).
15 NASA (2022) *Strategic Plan 2022*, available at: https://www.nasa.gov/sites/default/files/atoms/files/fy_22_strategic_plan.pdf (Accessed: 02 September 2022).
16 UK Home Office (2021) *Digital, Data and Technology 2024 Strategy*, available at: https://www.gov.uk/government/publications/home-office-digital-data-and-technology-strategy-2024 (Accessed: 04 September 2022).
17 Walton, N. and Pyper, N. (2020) *Technology Strategy*. London (UK): Red Globe Press. 210.
18 Ashkenas, R. (2019) 'Thinking Long-Term in a Short-Term Economy' in *HBR Guide to Thinking Strategically*. Boston (MA): HBR Press. 83.
19 Grant, R.M. and Jordan, J. (2015) *Foundations of Strategy*. Chichester: Wiley. 313.
20 Ashkenas, *HBR Guide to Thinking Strategically*. 83.

21 Rumelt, *Good Strategy, Bad Strategy*. 91.
22 Grant and Jordan, *Foundations of Strategy*. 320.
23 Rasiel, E.M. and Friga, P.N. (2001) *The McKinsey Mind*. New York: McGraw-Hill. 117–118.
24 Hewitt, *Technology Strategy Patterns*. 178.
25 Boulton, J.G., Allen, P.M. and Bowman, C. (2015) *Embracing Complexity*. Oxford: OUP. 161.
26 Tiwana, A. (2017) *IT Strategy for Non-IT Managers: Becoming an Engaged Contributor to Corporate IT Decisions*. Cambridge, MA: The MIT Press. 183–184.
27 Tiwana, *IT Strategy for Non-IT Managers*. 184.
28 Botsman, R. (2017) *Who Can You Trust?* London, UK: Penguin. 20.
29 Botsman, *Who Can You Trust?* 19.

13 Inputs and outputs

Lessons learned and how to apply them

This chapter presents

- A summary of the book's narrative thread.
- Many practical recommendations derived from the narrative.
- An examination of the strategically important discipline of systems engineering.

This chapter establishes

- The centrality of systems thinking to strategy development and execution.

The content of this book has reflected, in part, the path of learning undertaken by the author. It began with a study of around 40 published technology and engineering strategies, 14 of which were reviewed and analysed in Chapter 1. These provided the evidence that current processes for developing formal strategies are deficient – seemingly haphazard in both content and terminology, and devoid of any recognisable best practice. This path of learning led to a plausible standard methodology for developing strategies, known as the Five Dimensions Process.

It is also apparent that the development of technology strategies is ripe for professionalisation. Not only can every technologist and engineer become a better strategist, but some may even choose to specialise in the field of strategy development. This book was intended to support that trend. One route towards professionalisation is described below.

Given that this is the final chapter, it's possible to add some additional value in the form of recommendations. Where adopted, these will help organisations improve their strategy development processes.

Input: The narrative

This was a story that began with a problem and ended with a solution. Along the way, it pulled apart some difficult concepts and

DOI: 10.4324/9781003472919-16

presented new mechanisms for managing the technological realm. Although that's an oversimplification of the book, it has led us to where we are now.

In early chapters, the analysis of strategic 'components' required a deconstruction of *technology* into its five dimensions, denoted by the acronym PLAYS. This enabled five-dimensional approaches to a number of high value activities, including the innovation of products, the identification of risks, and technological foresight.

Families of technologies or products were grouped into virtual entities known as *domains*. These groupings were shown to help with organising the production of strategies.

New definitions of 'strategy' and 'technology strategy' were derived, and the relationship between technology strategy and business strategy explained. Strategies in general were viewed as *packages of concerted actions supporting organisational goals*; these goals are normally embodied in the formal business strategy. The obligation is upon engineering teams to develop their own technology strategies to support these higher level organisational ambitions.

Meanwhile, engineering was described as a solutions-focused profession, responsible for developing much of the world's 'artificiality'. Fundamentally, engineers are designers. They are society's leading professional practitioners of 'design under constraint'.

Consequently, because every technology strategy is a type of artificial construct designed under constraint, engineers already possess most of the skills needed to develop them. This supports an argument for the inclusion of technology strategy development within mainstream engineering education.

The book's narrative then addressed *uncertainty*. Given that strategy development is a forward looking process, uncertainty is the predominant concern. The sources of this uncertainty were shown to be both intrinsic and extrinsic, i.e. both within the remit and control of engineers and beyond their reach. Extrinsic sources of uncertainty are often associated with the complex behaviours of reflexive agents, such as third party actors and the natural environment.

This analysis of uncertainty and complexity introduced new concepts and terminology, such as 'analytical risk', 'paradigm risk', 'entropic technical risk', 'finity', 'disintegrity' and 'vitacausa'. A total of 18 origins of uncertainty were identified and described.

During this focus upon uncertainty the so-called *execution gap* emerged as a critical challenge. This gap represents the time elapsed between a decision and its execution. It correlates with the likelihood that a task will fail to be delivered successfully. The longer the gap, the more opportunity there is for the operational environment to evolve, thereby undermining or *depreciating* the value of the decision.

The net effect of these phenomena is a recognition that formal strategies should not be perceived as 'plans'. **They are better viewed as flexible proposals for navigating the challenges presented by an unknowable future.** Technology strategies must therefore be subject to frequent revisions in response to disruptive, or potentially disruptive, events.

This realisation informed the need for strategy development to be brisk and efficient, and for strategy communications to be short and easily comprehended by personnel at all levels of the organisation. This is essential, because everyone has a role in strategy execution and in the tactical responses to unforeseen events.

Beyond these technical and environmental uncertainties, we must also consider the imperfect motives and behaviours of decision makers. The potential strengths and weaknesses of people involved in strategy development were described in Chapter 7. The virtues we should look for include breadth of experience, organisational knowledge, confidence, assertiveness, resilience, and constructive 'visionary' thinking. Conversely we should seek to exclude decision makers possessed by self-interest, reckless optimism, or a belief that technical solutions are in some way superior to non-technical approaches. The focus must be on outcomes rather than methods.

Stakeholders were another important consideration, because they're involved at every stage of the strategy, project, product, technology, and system lifecycles, from conception through to termination. Significant stakeholders include employees, suppliers, and customers. Marginally less significant are those with indirect relationships to our products and technologies, such as regulators, competitors, complementors, the media, and the natural environment. The ability to understand and empathise with all stakeholders is recognised as a critical skill.

All strategic decisions are underpinned by cultural or moral values. These can be important influences upon stakeholder relations. Ethical objections from stakeholders can severely damage organisational prospects, sometimes leading to project failures. For this reason, a decision making tool called *Ethical Due Process* was introduced.

Strategy development is frequently associated with the concepts of invention and innovation. However, as explained in Chapter 10, the significance of novel ideas and intellectual property is often overplayed by commentators. For instance, it's not uncommon for organisations to achieve success by rejecting technological innovation, preferring more risk averse (*reactive* or *inactive*) approaches. Clearly innovations do occasionally have a strategic role, but this should not be over-played. Nevertheless, all personnel should be provided with opportunities to conceive and develop value-adding ideas. Organisational cultures can facilitate this.

It would not be an exaggeration to say that uncertainty has dominated the book's narrative. Consequently, Chapter 11 helped to organise and describe the many methods available for 'navigating' unknowable futures. Among the many tools and techniques described, three broad approaches were highlighted: *design for uncertainty*, *risk management*, and *foresight analysis*. Collectively, these methods help us to develop strategies capable of absorbing the repeated 'punches' thrown by our complex operational environments.

Finally, the *Five Dimensions Process* was presented. The 5DP is this book's unique contribution to the development of technology and engineering strategies. Its three stages of *researching*, *strategising*, and *executing* ought to produce viable, evidence-based, easily communicated proposals for navigating an uncertain future.

Input: A systems perspective

One of this book's recurring themes is the way that components work together, adding value by transforming inputs into outputs. This is how a 'system' was defined in Chapter 2. It also describes how technologies were analysed into their five component dimensions. This systems perspective lies at the very heart of technology strategy. Many types of systems were described in the book. They included:

- Engineered systems, e.g. motorbikes, genetically modified animals.
- Non-engineered systems, e.g. natural ecosystems.
- Sub-systems of larger systems, e.g. the engine of a ship.
- Systems of systems, e.g. a petrochemical refinery.
- Socio-technical systems (where technologies and people interact in complex, dispersed arrangements), e.g. the civil aviation industry.
- Megatechnical systems (so large and complex that they challenge the capacity of any single organisation to control or fundamentally change them), e.g. the internet.
- Complex adaptive systems (in which entities react to one another and adapt in unpredictable ways), e.g. all systems involving people.

The ability to analyse and understand systemic behaviour, particularly the way that components, sub-systems, and higher level systems interact with one another and evolve, is known as 'systems thinking'. This was described in Chapter 7 as one of the attributes to look for in a technology strategist.

This type of thinker perceives our working environment as an entanglement of engineered and non-engineered systems exhibiting a combination of complex and non-complex behaviours. With good analytical skills, these environments can be disentangled and managed more effectively.

In his book *Technology in Context* (1998), Ernest Braun adopted a systems thinking perspective when describing the "inputs, outputs and impacts" of a domestic washing machine:

> It requires certain amounts of metals, paint, rubber, plastics, electronic components, and energy for its production. These inputs can be followed back further, right to the initial sources of raw materials and to all the stages of processing and transporting them. The machine is then shipped to a customer and, during its service-life, consumes certain amounts of water, electricity, washing powder, other chemicals such as fabric softeners, and spare parts. All the water consumed is discharged into the sewers and has to be treated. This effluent and its impact on the environment can also be followed to its final destination. When the machine reaches the end of its useful life, it will either be dumped in its entirety or partly dismantled and recycled, depending upon its construction and prevailing environmental regulations and conditions.[1]

Where this mindset prevails, success is more likely to follow. According to Pyster *et al.*, Hideo Shima and his team demonstrated this "total systems approach" when developing the bullet train concept in the 1960s:

> From initial stages, it was realized that the *Shinkansen* is composed not only of hardware but also of software, people, and processes – aspects such as traffic control, train crews, and maintenance.[2]

If all technology strategies could be executed as successfully as the Shinkansen, which for more than 60 years has combined high speeds with unmatched levels of punctuality and passenger safety, then perhaps we can begin to anticipate a better future.

Norman Augustine, retired CEO of Lockheed Martin, describes a scenario which captures the essence of systems thinking. He notes that if you ask an aeronautical engineer how to shorten travel times for air passengers, their response will probably involve aerodynamic improvements or more powerful engines. However, a systems thinker would take a more holistic view of the travel process, breaking it down into multiple components. The aircraft, of course, is only one part of the overall system:

> There's the getting to the airport part, finding a parking spot part, navigating the terminal part, ticketing part, processing the baggage part, waiting for security part, waiting to board part, boarding part, and getting to the final destination part. All these parts – and several more – contribute to the speed, efficiency, and performance of the entire system.[3]

When we ask an engineer for a solution, we have every right to assume that our request will be subject to this type of thinking and analysis.

Arup's Jo da Silva, a civil engineer and Fellow of the Royal Academy of Engineering, adopts this systems perspective when reflecting upon contemporary engineering responses to coastal protection:

> If you look at flood defences, we would have defaulted to 'build a seawall'. Now, if you look at coastal engineering and what we are doing, there are much more integrated solutions that make the most of the environmental features, whether those are mangroves or dunes. You combine the natural blue and green infrastructure with physical grey infrastructure, and it is how those two things actually work together that matters.

Instead of focusing upon such engineered artifacts as bridges or roads, da Silva says that "we should be talking about mobility, connectivity and ensuring the flow of goods, services and people."[4] A bridge or a road may be the *obvious* engineering solution, but it doesn't always address the underlying challenge posed by the stakeholders.

Given that the job of an engineer is to conceive, design and optimise solutions within complex environments, it's reasonable to assume that broad-based systems thinking should be taught as a core skill within all university engineering programmes. Of particular importance is the role of complexity, as manifested in the behaviour of people, the economy and the natural world. This type of teaching does exist in some institutions, but it needs to become universal.

Systems engineering

The Second World War saw a rapid growth in systems thinking and analysis. Military planners and designers were especially interested in the human-machine interface, the integration of systems, the coordination of multi-stage supply chains, and the disruption of enemy infrastructures.

In the years that followed, the emergence of computing and more advanced telecommunications changed the landscape of engineering design, leading to ever-more complex arrangements. These elaborate *systems of systems* have required coordination between engineers from different disciplines. For example, it's not difficult to conceive of industries, or individual enterprises, in which chemical, electrical, digital, and mechanical engineering must combine in order to deliver goods and services.

Given this increasing multidisciplinarity, who should be taking overall responsibility for these combined operations? Which engineering discipline is best able to coordinate and manage the others? In response to this question, a meta-discipline has emerged: *systems engineering*.

It wasn't until 1990 that the first professional body, The National Council on Systems Engineering (NCOSE), was set up. This soon became the International Council.[5] Today, INCOSE remains the pre-eminent institution. Systems engineering is defined by INCOSE as:

> A transdisciplinary and integrative approach to enable the successful realization, use, and retirement of engineered systems, using systems principles and concepts, and scientific, technological, and management methods.[6]

In its *Systems Engineering Handbook* (2023), INCOSE describes ten types of industrial systems of systems, which it refers to as "product sectors" and "application domains". These are: automotive systems, biomedical and healthcare systems, commercial aerospace systems, defence systems, infrastructure systems, oil and gas systems, power and energy systems, space systems, telecommunication systems, and transportation systems.[7]

Systems engineering is a discipline that will probably become synonymous with the 21st century as we increasingly merge our engineering solutions into comprehensive, boundaryless systems.

Systems engineers

According to INCOSE,[8,9] the distinctive characteristics of the systems engineering profession include:

- The optimisation of whole systems, rather than a focus upon the optimisation of individual sub-systems or components.

- The management of competing demands from individual systems within higher level combined systems.
- The management of concurrent but asynchronous system lifecycles within the same environment.
- A responsibility for the entire systems lifecycle, from conception to disposal.
- A concern for the boundaries of engineered systems, and their interactions with adjacent human, economic, and environmental systems.

Today, there aren't enough people in our organisations with systems engineering responsibilities. Our societies and economies are desperately short of people capable of performing these roles. The public recognition of the systems engineer is long overdue. Indeed, our lives may come to depend on it.

In July 2020 a Boeing 737 operated by TUI departed from Birmingham Airport (UK) for Palma de Mallorca in Spain. The load sheet, given to the pilots, had under-stated the aircraft's gross weight by 1,244 kg (2,743 pounds).[10] As a consequence, the pilots used a lower than recommended velocity at take-off. Fortunately the flight, with 193 passengers and crew, was able to gain height and arrive safely at its destination. Only later was it discovered that TUI's recently upgraded passenger management software was now underestimating the average weight of female passengers. The application was categorising adult females as children if they'd been registered using the title "Miss". The source of this 'error' was found to be a cultural misinterpretation by the programmers, who were based in a country where "Miss" only referred to young girls.

Civil aviation is a socio-technical system of systems. On this occasion, a group of people with no responsibility for the design, maintenance or piloting of aeroplanes (the developers of ticket-selling software) had acquired the capability to undermine aerodynamic integrity. It was a 'near-miss', in every sense of the phrase.

In his Foreword to *The Paradoxical Mindset of Systems Engineers* (2018), David Long, former President of both Vitech Corporation and INCOSE, wrote:

> Whether we choose to characterize this as the age of complexity or the systems age, the simple truth is clear. Our world is defined by interactions and interdependencies.[11]

The TUI incident is instructive because it demonstrates the necessity for employing engineers inclined towards holistic, end-to-end views of the systems they manage or support. This requirement goes beyond mere systems thinking. It calls for many more people, especially students, to choose the systems engineering profession. In order to better understand this role, let's briefly review the attributes and characteristics of professional systems engineers (SEs).

In the first instance, SEs are expected to have substantial engineering expertise. According to Pyster *et al*.:

> Highly effective systems engineers are *multidisciplinary* by nature – they are experts in a few technologies and system types, and critically, they understand *just enough* about every technology and discipline that are central to the systems on which they work.[12]

The authors also point to the need for strong problem-solving skills, "particularly the ability to focus on root cause rather than proximal cause."[13]

Furthermore, their experience within the workplace should extend to a broad range of technical environments and people-focused interactions. Familiarity with different lifecycles – such as those pertaining to projects, products, and technologies – is also highly valued.[14]

INCOSE lists various non-technical interpersonal skills including mediation and facilitation. When these are combined with an academic foundation in one engineering discipline and a working knowledge of adjacent disciplines, it can be said that systems engineers possess a true 'T-skills' profile.[15]

Given all of the above, it should be evident that SEs possess the attributes to be highly effective technology strategists. Indeed, no professional discipline is better equipped to perform the role of a strategy development leader (as described in Chapter 12).

Systems engineering may be viewed as an attractive career choice for aspiring engineers. It is also an ideal recruitment focus for organisations aiming to develop world-leading technology strategies.

Outputs: The recommendations

By way of concluding this book, here are some actions which, directly or indirectly, should help to improve your organisation's ability to develop and implement successful strategies. They are presented in no particular order, but have been grouped for convenience.

Analytical work

1 Know your strategic assets. Perform a strategic asset audit of the engineering environment.

2 Know your risks. Analyse technology and product risks in each of the five dimensions. Use a 5D Risk Radar horizon scan for each technology or product. Compile a technology risk register. Ensure that its results are incorporated within the main organisational Risk Register.
3 Know your projects. Scrutinise every business case. Look for exaggerated claims and take disciplinary action against those who make them. Use reference class forecasting on major projects in order to acquire more accurate estimates of duration and budgets.
4 Use *real options* analysis to deliver advantages over the longer term, particularly when designing high value products with uncertain futures.

Technological goods and services

1 Use flexibility, scalability, and modularity to ensure that products are better able to navigate uncertainty.
2 Using the 'five dimensions' as your guide, innovate new products and discover improvements to existing products.
3 Examine mature products for featuritis (i.e. over-specification leading to reduced usability and reliability); consider *denno-vating* features in order to create 'lite' versions.

Personnel, their development and job satisfaction

1 Look for strategy-friendly attributes in all recruits, including trainability, breadth of work/life experience, and a good grasp of systems thinking.
2 Introduce formal training in systems thinking and in the underlying principles of systems engineering.
3 Recruit one or more qualified systems engineers. Give them responsibility for the integrated management of internal systems.
4 Support experienced engineers in their quest to become certified systems engineers.
5 Introduce basic training in technology ethics, risk management, and complexity theory.
6 Create and maintain a skills matrix for each team or department. Use it to strategically manage the future skills profile of your organisation.
7 Provide a range of internal opportunities for technical personnel to engage in product and process innovation, e.g. lab space, project funding, and support for entrepreneurial spin-outs.

8 Consider the benefits and disbenefits of *cloistering* technical teams. Look at the implications for quality, productivity, data confidentiality, and IP protection.
9 In order to learn from significant errors made by colleagues, introduce a no-blame, near-miss reporting culture.
10 Ensure that experienced engineers are invited to participate in pre-acquisition due diligence activities.
11 Build collaborative working relationships between technical teams and core business personnel.

General good practice

1 Minimise all execution gaps by implementing decisions at the earliest opportunity. Where substantial delays occur, re-evaluate the decision prior to execution. Explore whether longer projects can be deconstructed into shorter ones.
2 Apply *Ethical Due Process* to any potentially controversial activities or products.
3 Build relationships with local universities in order to benefit from specialist facilities and dedicated student research projects (i.e. free consultancy). Meanwhile, identify and recruit the best students.
4 Terminate any failed or 'zombie' projects (i.e. those reducing in value, yet refusing to die).
5 For non-critical activities use only off-the-shelf 'vanilla' products. Rather than customising products to fit long-established procedures, try adjusting those procedures to fit standardised products.
6 Help to shape the external technological environment by participating in industry associations and standards-setting institutions.

Technology strategy development

1 Obtain senior leadership support for your organisation's first (or next) strategy development using the Five Dimensions Process.
2 Notify clients of your organisation's competence in delivering technology and engineering strategies using a standard methodology (i.e. the 5DP).
3 Assign professional systems engineers to lead strategy development teams.
4 Ensure that experienced engineering personnel are 'in the room' during the development of every new iteration of the business strategy.

Navigating to success

During early research for this book I wanted to understand the true essence of strategy, but from an engineering perspective. When communicating such difficult concepts, it's often helpful to use a metaphor. An analogy was needed that could represent the challenge of pursuing moving objectives within dynamic environments.

As we know, this challenge is exacerbated by the complex behaviour of other systems beyond our control, including natural systems.

The most appropriate metaphor I could find was that of a ship's captain seeking to rendezvous with another ship, just visible on the horizon.

The captain has an able crew and the use of various control mechanisms, including a rudder and throttle. However, there are many variables, including the wind, the currents, the waves, mechanical reliability, and the performance of individual crew members. Most of these are difficult to analyse and predict with confidence.

Meanwhile, the rendezvous objective, the ship on the horizon, is also subject to the same variables. At time T=0 it will be at Position A, but by T=1 it could be at Position B, or even Position C. Imperfect attempts can be made to determine these positions using combinations of available data and experiential judgement.

The captain's "package of concerted actions" will be in flux, requiring frequent revisions. This is not a single strategy, but a sequence of strategies (version 1.0, version 1.1, etc.), each consisting of a proposal for reaching the objective. Each version of the strategy may be satisfactory at the moment of conception, but depreciates rapidly thereafter as the wind or currents change direction, or as the captain of the other ship makes unanticipated changes of course.

Sometimes the rendezvous will not be achieved - the strategies will have failed. However, with the right training and experience (and the mindset of a systems engineer) the captain should be able to complete the objective. The captain's decisions will have been vindicated and the sequence of strategies judged a success.

Glossary for this chapter (Items in bold are also defined in the same table)

INCOSE	The International Council on Systems Engineering, the leading professional body for **systems engineers**.
systems engineer	An experienced, highly skilled professional engineer specialising in the management of systems of systems.

Notes

1 Braun, E. (1998) *Technology in Context*. London: Routledge. 140.
2 Pyster, A., Hutchison, N. and Henry, D. (2018) *The Paradoxical Mindset of Systems Engineers*. Hoboken: Wiley. 117.
3 Madhavan, G. (2016) *Think Like an Engineer*. London: Oneworld. 51–52.
4 Kenward, M. (2019) 'Structures for a Sustainable Society'. *Ingenia*, Issue 80, 38–42.
5 International Council on Systems Engineering (2023) *Systems Engineering Handbook: A Guide for System Life Cycle Process and Activities* (5th ed.). Hoboken: Wiley. 3.
6 BKCASE (2023) 'Guide to the Systems Engineering Body of Knowledge (SEBoK), version 2.8'. Available at: https://sebokwiki.org/wiki/Guide_to_the_Systems_Engineering_Body_of_Knowledge_(SEBoK) (Accessed: 03 November 2023).
7 International Council on Systems Engineering, *Systems Engineering Handbook*. 244–259.
8 INCOSE UK (2020) 'Systems Engineering Competency Framework Z6 Issue 1.1'. Available at: https://incoseuk.org/Documents/zGuides/Z6_Competency_july2020_issue1.1_pdf_web.pdf (Accessed: 03 November 2023).
9 International Council on Systems Engineering.
10 Air Accidents Investigation Branch, *AAIB investigation to Boeing 737-8K5, G-TAWG 21 July 2020*, Available at: https://www.gov.uk/aaib-reports/aaib-investigation-to-boeing-737-8k5-g-tawg-21-july-2020 (Accessed 10 November 2023).
11 Pyster, Hutchison, and Henry, *The Paradoxical Mindset of Systems Engineers*. Foreword.
12 Pyster, Hutchison, and Henry. 2.
13 Pyster, Hutchison, and Henry. 18.
14 Pyster, Hutchison, and Henry. 147–153.
15 International Council on Systems Engineering. 262–263.

Appendices

The following appendices provide supplementary information for the reader.

- **Appendix 1** contains the 'five dimensions' theory of technology, referenced in Chapter 2.
- **Appendix 2** is a table itemising most of the ideas for navigating uncertainty described in this book. Many of these are referred to in Chapter 11.
- **Appendix 3** presents short extracts from three, real-world strategy delivery statements.
- **Appendix 4** itemises the *Analytical tools and techniques*, the *Strategic and tactical moves*, and the *Strategic dichotomies* which have been featured throughout the book.

Appendix 1

The 'five dimensions' theory of technology

The following theory of technology was developed by the author during research for this book. It was needed because, as explained in Chapter 2, no viable theory appears to exist.

The resulting definition supports ideas in many of the subsequent chapters, including those addressing uncertainty and innovation.

The theory

What is a technology? How do we differentiate between a technology and a non-technology? Are there any criteria we can use to answer these questions?

It is my assertion that all technologies are 'designed' entities. By this I mean that they bear the imprint of human agency. They have been created by people. They are artificial and unnatural.

All technologies possess five key attributes. These are the necessary and sufficient conditions for any entity to be called a technology. I refer to these attributes as 'dimensions'.

The five dimensions of technology are:

1 Physical
2 Logical
3 Architectural
4 Yield
5 Stakeholder.

The acronym **PLAYS** may be used as a shortcut. These dimensions are not mutually exclusive. There are overlaps. However, it seems evident that everything we call a technology exhibits all five dimensions. If a single dimension is missing, the entity cannot be called a technology. Let's examine each dimension in turn:

Physical

Every technology has a physical dimension. Some aspect of the technology must exist in the material world. It has mass.

In common parlance this interpretation is valid, because the label 'technology' is rarely used for a non-physical entity, such as a theory, idea, formula, procedure, patent, skill, or body of knowledge. To do so would be incorrect according to this theory. For instance, a patent is not a technology because it consists only of words and diagrams. It has no capability to perform a function.

Science historian George Basalla agrees:

> At every point technology is intimately involved with the physical, with the material; artifacts are both the means and the ends of technology. The three-dimensional physical object is as much an expression of technology as a painting or a piece of sculpture is an expression of the visual arts.[1]

The technology may consist of a single physical component (e.g. a spring or a paperclip) or it could be a complex system with thousands of physical parts.

What about natural physical entities, such as rocks, plants, and animals? Can they be technologies? A physical entity in its natural state, if devoid of any human design, *cannot* be a technology. The human heart is clearly a wonderful machine, but it's not a technology. However, a natural entity which has been adapted by humans can be transformed into a technology. For instance, the domestication of the horse was hugely transformative for humanity. For thousands of years it was our most capable motive force enabling riding, carrying, and pulling. A selectively bred horse is therefore a technology.

Humans are not designed to serve a purpose. Therefore we cannot describe ourselves as technologies, but people can perform the role of components within multi-component systems, e.g. by operating machinery. As Professor Maarten Franssen of TU Delft explains, "it is justified to model them as deterministic subsystems like any hardware device."[2] The use of living things as components, or *biocomponents*, is discussed in Chapter 4.

Logical

Every technology has a logical dimension. This logic represents its core functionality or purpose. Often this logic will exploit natural phenomena such as inertia, friction, biological cell division, surface tension, or a chemical reaction.

It should be possible to describe the logic within a single sentence. For instance: "A glass window exploits attributes of transparency and strength to illuminate interior spaces with natural light, and provide exterior views, while offering protection from ingress by the wind, rain, dust, and so on." An entity with no apparent purpose is not a technology.

Although the words we choose to describe the logic are constrained by language, the core logic is always identifiable.

However, the detailed operational logic may be more extensive than the core logic, due to variations in the way that a single technology can be used. For example, a window may feature louvred vents and dirt-resistant coatings, but these are not 'core' to its mission. In many contemporary products, much of the operational and core logic is embodied in software.

Architectural

Every technology has an architectural dimension. An architecture is the intelligent combination and integration of the physical and the logical to produce a functioning or purposeful arrangement. Multiple alternative arrangements are possible. These are subject to the constraints of available materials and the core logic.

Different purposes may be served by different architectures. Some may be optimised for energy efficiency, others for cost, aesthetics, precision, and so on. In 19th century Birmingham, which at that time was the centre of Britain's metalworking industries, Karl Marx discovered that 500 different kinds of hammer were in production.[3] It's not hard to imagine hammer variants for jewellers, cobblers, carpenters, farriers, and so on. Each has the same core logic of a hammer (kinetic energy transfer), but a different architecture.

To emphasise this point, a pile driver on a construction site bears no resemblance to a jeweller's hammer, yet it shares the same logic of transferring energy via directed blows. They are clearly both hammers. Their architectural differences were determined during the design process in response to very different sets of specifications.

Yield

Every technology has a yield dimension. The yield is the technology's output as it delivers value to one or more stakeholders. As Arthur describes it, "A technology does something. It executes a purpose."[4]

An entity only becomes a technology when it is able to execute and deliver its yield. As examples, a hammer delivers blows, a filament emits heat and light, a bridge enables crossings, a computer processes data, a ship undertakes journeys over water.

It should always be possible to quantify the yield in some way. For example, the yield of an aeroplane may be measured in take-off and landing cycles, or hours of operation. This quantification may require some imagination. For example, bridge crossings could be counted from tolls. Yield quantification often features within 'design life' planning. A car's design life could, for example, be 200,000 km or 10,000 journey cycles.

Technologies are human constructs designed with a purpose in mind. Consequently, if there is no purpose, there can be no value. More broadly, if a technology loses its ability to deliver value (e.g. due to a component failure), or if the value of its yield reduces to zero (e.g. caused by the absence of beneficiaries), then it ceases to be a technology.

Stakeholder

Every technology has a stakeholder dimension. We are concerned here with the stakeholders who benefit from the technology's yield, such as owners and users.

A functioning technology might eventually lose all of its beneficiary stakeholders. An entity devoid of stakeholders cannot be a source of value, and therefore cannot be a technology. Although in perfect working order, it will have become 'defunct'. A defunct technology is not a technology.

Here is a more succinct version of this theory:

A DEFINITION FOR *TECHNOLOGY*

A technology is a designed entity consisting of an integrated physical and logical architecture yielding stakeholder value.

Its five 'dimensions' have the acronym **PLAYS**. These are the necessary and sufficient conditions for being a technology. Therefore, any entity exhibiting all of the PLAYS attributes *must* be a technology. For this theory to be valid, there can be no exceptions.

This gives us two different but commonly used meanings of the word *technology*. Both are nouns:

1 A group of related entities, each of which fulfils the PLAYS criteria, but possibly with varying architectures. Examples: the technologies we call "hammers", or "electric batteries", or "rockets".
2 A collective term for all technologies and engineering practices available to a culture or organisation. Examples: "I have been reading about the history of technology", or "in 1855 George Wilson became the University of Edinburgh's first Professor of Technology."

To support this definition, Table A1.1 examines a selection of artificial entities and their 'dimensions' according to this theory.

Table A1.1 Artificial entities and their 'dimensions'. Although each entity is artificial (i.e. bearing the imprint of human intelligence, or design) this does not imply that it's also a technology

Entity	Five dimensions					Technology?
	Physical	Logical	Architectural	Yield	Stakeholder	
Hammer	✓	✓	✓	✓	✓	Y
Nail	✓	✓	✓	✓	✓	Y
Antibiotic	✓	✓	✓	✓	✓	Y
Patent	X	✓	X	X	✓	N
Chair	✓	✓	✓	✓	✓	Y
Electric motor	✓	✓	✓	✓	✓	Y
Farm (a system)	✓	✓	✓	✓	✓	Y
Farming (associated systems)	✓	✓	X	✓	✓	N
Domesticated crop or animal	✓	✓	✓	✓	✓	Y
Ship	✓	✓	✓	✓	✓	Y
Ship in dry dock for repairs	✓	✓	✓	X	X	N
Chemical compound	✓	✓	✓	✓	✓	Y
Office building	✓	✓	✓	✓	✓	Y
Brick wall	✓	✓	✓	✓	✓	Y
Wind turbine	✓	✓	✓	✓	✓	Y

(Continued)

Table A1.1 (Continued)

Entity	Five dimensions					Technology?
	Physical	Logical	Architectural	Yield	Stakeholder	
Turbine blade	✓	✓	✓	✓	✓	Y
Gene editing (a process)	✓	✓	✓	✓	✓	Y
An edited gene (a tool)	✓	✓	✓	✓	✓	Y
Written language	✓	✓	✓	✓	✓	Y
Spoken language (e.g. English)	X	✓	X	✓	✓	N
Computer	✓	✓	✓	✓	✓	Y
Software	?	✓	✓	?	✓	N
Algorithm	X	✓	X	✓	✓	N
Faulty computer – no power	✓	X	✓	X	X	N
Mouse trap	✓	✓	✓	✓	✓	Y
Dinosaur trap	✓	✓	✓	X	X	N

Notes for Table A1.1:

- A *patent* is a carefully-worded description of a proposed technology. It may be argued that a patent has a logical dimension, but because it lacks physicality it has no architecture. A patent is not a technology.
- The *ship in dry dock for repairs* is devoid of the ability to deliver value (as a transporter of things over water). We might say that its physical architecture and logic is still valid, but it has no yield. It is currently not a technology, although when it refloats it will become a technology again. If, on the other hand, it remains in dry dock to become a museum, then it could be called a building, which is a different type of technology.
- A *brick wall* nearly fails as a technology because its yield is difficult to quantify. For this reason, most people would probably not classify a wall as a technology. However, I've chosen to do so by quantifying a wall's yield in terms of its longevity of success, e.g. "this wall has kept wild pigs off my land for 15 years." Some walls clearly have an identifiable purpose for which their value can be measured. In these circumstances, they must be regarded as technologies in their own right.
- A *farm* can undoubtedly be viewed as a technological system. However, the term *farming* is merely a label for the industry to which farms belong.
- The difference between a *spoken language* and physical *writing* should be self-evident. Akio Morita, one of Sony's co-founders, noted that "Written Japanese is also a simple language to speed-read because to get a quick sense of what a piece of writing is about, all that is needed is a quick scan of the Chinese characters. That is technology, too."[5] Headrick agrees: "One of the most important technologies we have inherited from the ancient civilizations is writing, a means of storing and transmitting information through space and time by inscribing symbols representing things, ideas, and sounds."[6]
- *Software* is an artificial construct associated with the technological realm. However, it has a barely perceptible physical dimension. Here we must distinguish between the software itself and the physical dimension of the technologies which host it, such as storage and processing devices. Furthermore, software's yield is questionable, because it is reliant upon these other technologies in order to function and deliver value to its beneficiaries. Therefore, software is not a technology, it is a logical component.
- The *dinosaur trap* could be a useful technology if dinosaurs were available for trapping. However, because there are none in

existence, it's impossible for the trap to generate a yield. There will be stakeholders, such as the maker of the trap and the supplier of materials, but these are not beneficiaries of the trap, and the device itself is just a curiosity. It's not a technology.

• In compiling this table I have adopted the position that, as soon as a technology is unable to perform its function or deliver a yield due to some impediment (e.g. a 'ship in dry dock', or 'computer without power'), then it is no longer a technology. The reader is perfectly entitled to disagree with this approach, which is largely philosophical rather than practical. It has no implications for this book, because technology strategists have a much broader scope of interest, including technologies that don't yet exist (e.g. R&D considerations) and those which have recently become defunct (e.g. decommissioning and disposal plans).

The five dimensions theory is used throughout this book as a tool to support the development and execution of technology strategies. For example, PLAYS could help us to dissect technologies with the aim of innovating enhancements to them. The five dimensions are also central to the template for producing formal technology strategies, described in Chapters 3 and 12. This is why it is called the *Five Dimensions Process*.

Notes

1 Basalla, G. (1988) *The Evolution of Technology*. Cambridge (UK): CUP. 30.
2 Franssen, M. (2010) 'Roles and Rules and the Modelling of Socio-Technical Systems'. *Philosophy of Engineering*, Vol. 1. Royal Academy of Engineering, London, June 2010. Available at: https://www.raeng.org.uk/publications/reports/philosophy-of-engineering-volume-1, 45–53.
3 Basalla, *The Evolution of Technology*. 2.
4 Arthur, W.B. (2010) *The Nature of Technology*. London: Penguin. 29.
5 Morita, A. (1987) *Made in Japan*. London: Collins. 234.
6 Headrick, D.R. (2009) *Technology: A World History*. New York: OUP. 32–33.

Appendix 2

Ideas for navigating uncertainty

There are countless ways to navigate uncertainty in the technological realm. Many have been mentioned in this book, sometimes only briefly. This table identifies most of them (Table A2.1).

Table A2.1 Examples of the many navigation methods mentioned in Chapters 1–11 of this book

Ch.	Navigation	Description
2	using established design methodologies	Good quality design minimises the uncertainty associated with new products, especially their usability and technical performance.
2	forward compatibility	Ensures product longevity within a technological ecosystem in which other products are evolving.
2	systems thinking	By understanding the nature of systems, the system lifecycle, and system interdependencies, decision makers are better able to foresee their evolution.
2	safety engineering	An engineering branch of the risk management profession. Safety management practices are used to navigate uncertainty, preventing unwanted events.
3	focus on quality	Increased product reliability improves stakeholder confidence in future performance.
3	mature products and designs	Proven designs and mature/established products minimise uncertainty, not only because of their proven reliability, but also due to the abundance of information and skilled people available to operate and support them.
3	explaining future technological directions to suppliers	Large organisations, such as the US Department of Defense, can improve the pipeline of future products by notifying suppliers of the technological paths which they, as the customer, wish to follow.
3	synchronising strategies	The technology strategy should be derived from, and synchronised with, the business strategy. Any divergence is potentially disruptive to the organisation.
3	addressing all five dimensions	The reason for analysing all five dimensions of technology is to ensure that no surprises emerge from one of the overlooked dimensions.
3	revising strategies	Strategies begin depreciating as soon as they are written. The operating environment is guaranteed to change in unforeseen ways, so occasional revisions to the strategy must be undertaken.
3	sharing strategies with staff	Day-to-day tactical decisions help to support the strategy. This cannot happen if it has not been shared with frontline personnel.

3	campaigning or lobbying	Pro-actively influencing political institutions increases the likelihood of favourable policies, laws, and regulations.
3	strategic asset audit	An important source of knowledge about key assets. Information gaps could introduce unwelcome surprises at a later date.
3	isolating technical teams	Physical 'cloistering' minimises interference from other groups in the organisation, arguably leading to greater productivity, improvements in quality, and more creative engineering outputs.
4	root cause analysis	Understanding the causes of unexpected events will help to anticipate, and perhaps prevent, re-occurrences.
4	piloting and testing	Pre-launch evaluation techniques are essential for minimising product uncertainty. "What can't be tested, can't be trusted."
4	going 'lite', or dennovating	Removing unnecessary or unwanted functionality reduces the likelihood of technical faults and user errors.
4	excluding life forms	There is a direct correlation between the removal of life forms from engineered systems and their overall reliability. However, absolute exclusion is near impossible because people perform roles designing, building, operating, maintaining, etc.
4	focusing on human factors	Minimise the uncertainty associated with humans via training, ergonomics, medical assessments (e.g. eye tests), the use of incentives, and so on.
4	sensors plus leading indicators	Analysts need well-designed reporting mechanisms for gaining insights into future events. Electronic sensors are often the source of this data. Leading indicators often rely on data gathered by electronic sensors.
4	insourcing	To reduce uncertainty, it is often believed that critical supplies should be delivered by visible, directly managed in-house teams. (This contradicts the outsourcing ideology.)
4	outsourcing	To reduce uncertainty, it is often believed that critical supplies should be delivered via third parties in a managed contractual relationship. (This contradicts with the insourcing ideology.)
4	maintaining trade secrets	Controlling intellectual property via secrecy (rather than simple legal protection) reduces the likelihood of IP theft and copying.

(Continued)

Table A2.1 (Continued)

Ch.	Navigation	Description
4	shortening execution gaps	If the gap between a decision and its execution is minimised this should maximise the likelihood of a successful outcome.
4	efficient integrations	Mergers frequently fail, so the technical integration of merged organisations must be achieved quickly (due to the execution gap) and comprehensively, in order to eliminate future technical debts.
4	pre-merger due diligence	By highlighting the strengths and weaknesses of an acquisition target, post-merger problems can be mitigated. It enables better pre-merger planning of the post-merger integration.
4	moving second	Those who quickly adopt emerging technologies are more exposed to uncertainty. Second movers benefit from the lessons learned by observing the experiences of first movers.
5	project management methodologies	Numerous methodologies have been developed for maximising both the likelihood of successful project deliveries, and the long-term viability and integrity of the resulting product.
5	modelling and extrapolation	Analytical techniques can reveal where trends are heading, and how quickly. We can also learn how systems will respond when inputs and variables change. (However, neither modelling nor extrapolation can fully address the intrinsic uncertainties of complex adaptive systems.)
6	failure modes and effects analysis (FMEA)	One of many established tools for pre-empting problems with products and technical systems.
6	maintenance regimes	Periodic maintenance, using visual checks and the timely replacement of parts, reduces the probability of failures.
6	agile development methods	Agile methodologies shorten 'execution gaps' via the use of frequent delivery-focused 'sprints'.
6	choosing 'vanilla'	Off-the-shelf, non-customised products are likely to be more reliable, user-friendly, and manageable than those that have been customised or self-built.

7	**knowledge management**	Structured organisational programmes for sharing knowledge across internal boundaries and between experienced and inexperienced personnel can be a mitigation for some forms of uncertainty, e.g. associated with the loss of a long-serving employee, or business recovery planning.
7	**leadership vision**	Establishes a shared direction of travel and limits the amount of organisational drift. An important early stage of strategy development.
7	**focusing on outcomes over processes**	The captain of a ship maintains a desired course using frequent adjustments, not by following a rigid plan or written procedure. In rapidly changing, complex environments, destinations can only be reached when the focus is on outcomes, not processes.
7	**recognising and responding to decision-making weaknesses**	Flawed psychological traits among decision makers, such as the sunk costs fallacy, optimism bias, and the endowment effect, must be recognised and countered.
7	**reference class forecasting**	Evidence-based, realistic estimates of the time required to deliver large, complex projects. This evidence is drawn from a database of historical projects (the references).
8	**understanding stakeholders' needs, motives and capabilities**	Who are the relevant stakeholders, and what are their motives? What capabilities do they have to influence the future?
8	**skills matrix**	A mechanism for ensuring that the skills required today, and in the near future, are adequately distributed among the technical teams.
8	**trainable/adaptable people**	Future-proof the workforce by recruiting people who show evidence of being both trainable and receptive to new ways of working.
8	**reducing dependency on powerful suppliers**	Monopolistic or dominant suppliers must be carefully managed. Mitigation methods include product re-design, multisourcing, insourcing, and upstream vertical integration.
8	**reducing dependency on powerful customers**	Dominant customers must be carefully managed. Mitigation methods include designing new products for new markets (diversification), and downstream vertical integration to create captive markets.
8	**collaborations and alliances**	Sharing capabilities and risks with other organisations minimises the exposure to uncertainty, while enhancing the possibility of exploiting new opportunities.

(Continued)

Table A2.1 (Continued)

Ch.	Navigation	Description
8	**contributing to new standards**	By participating in standards-setting bodies, organisations can ensure that future standards will be compatible with their technology strategies.
8	**participating in trade associations**	Shaping the development of a sector by influencing the policies and actions of its representative groups and associations.
8	**technology roadmaps**	Roadmaps assist internal and external stakeholders in understanding the preferred direction of travel and the timings of new product launches, product retirements, etc. (However, the future rarely resembles the roadmap!)
8	**engaging with local communities**	Community relations that are stable and mutually supportive help to secure the longevity of industrial facilities.
9	**ethical pre-emption**	Avoiding future ethical challenges through the use of analytical approaches to ethical decision making.
9	**design for decommissioning**	Avoiding unexpected challenges during end-of-life processes.
10	**IP legal protection**	Creates a form of monopoly aimed at blocking rivals and guaranteeing financial returns from future commercialisation. (Contrast this with the alternative approach of using trade secrets.)
10	**incremental innovation**	As the external operating environment changes, products can be adapted and improved in small steps, removing the possibility that an unbridgeable technological gulf will emerge.
10	**foresight techniques**	Decision makers need better information about possible future pathways. These are provided by tools such as horizon scanning, trend analysis, the Delphi method, and scenario development.
10	**the precautionary principle**	If a new technology or product could introduce significant ethical challenges, greater certainty may be achieved by postponing or abandoning its introduction.
11	**simplicity**	By reducing complexity, we reduce uncertainty.

11	changeability	The future of a product, system or organisation will be more certain if it has two attributes: flexibility in response to external changes; adaptability in response to internal changes. Designs should be robust, scalable, and modifiable.
11	modularity	A design approach which involves integrating semi-independent functional units. This offers the benefits of upgradeability, repairability, extensibility, and so on.
11	real options	Future management options may be 'purchased', i.e. embedded in engineering designs. Real options enable managers to choose between two or more possible paths when the original specifications change, e.g. demand increases or new regulations are introduced.
11	risk management	A formal discipline for navigating uncertainty through the anticipation of possible events (both good and bad). Resources are allocated to either: a) reduce the possibility and scale of negative impacts, or b) increase the possibility and scale of positive impacts.
11	HAZOP study	A highly structured, comprehensive analysis of a complex industrial system with the aim of anticipating and mitigating all weaknesses and potential failures.
11	Bowtie diagram	A visualisation of the activities leading up to a risk event, and the post-event effects. Originally designed to capture negative events, it also includes a variant known as Positive Risk diagrams.
11	horizon scanning	A method for capturing and visualising the likelihood and impact of uncertain events over three horizons: the short term, medium term, and longer term.
11	Delphi method	In its original form, a tool designed to draw upon the opinions of anonymised experts in order to establish the approximate dates when foreseeable technologies would become commercially viable.
11	scenario development	A technique for researching and writing fictional organisational futures, with the aim of testing the viability of current strategic thinking.

Appendix 3

Strategy delivery statements

This appendix presents three extracts from real-world technology strategies. These extracts could be described as 'delivery statements', as explained in Chapter 12. They describe how the vision and its objectives will be delivered. The level of detail indicates, at a high level, future actions and their sequencing.

Note: These statements are presented for information only, not as exemplars of best practice.

European Space Agency (2019)[1]

ESA is

- Proposing a formal zero debris approach for ESA missions.
- Adding extra requirements for Copernicus expansion missions to prepare satellites to be removed by an external servicer in case of failures in orbit.
- Demonstrating active removal of space debris by 2025.
- Preparing steps to make all ESA missions environmentally neutral.
- Developing the technology that allows all ESA missions to be risk neutral by 2030.

To achieve this target, ESA is developing technologies to eliminate the creation of new debris (such as Cleansat technologies, demisable components, end-of-life deorbiting technologies, retrieval interfaces), technologies for active space debris removal (such as advanced GNC for close proximity operations, in-space robotics), in-space servicing, space debris surveillance and characterisation technologies.

Dundee City Council (undated)[2]

The DCC Technology Strategy Roadmap provides a sequence of high-level activities that will take DCC through the planning and iteration of the Cloud-based Platform (Digital) Architecture and related data model, to the target digital, future state. Whilst much of the strategy may be developed through adoption of an agile development methodology, at the outset DCC will benefit from a high level structure and phasing of activities. The phasing provides an outline structure for the technology transformation stage, highlighting major aspects such as:

- Approval of the strategy and roadmap.
- Introduction of a Change Management Policy.
- Introduction of a Performance Management Framework.
- Implementation of cloud-based collaboration and productivity solutions.
- Implementation of a Project Management Office.
- Audit the Application portfolio.
- Migration of server hardware to fully resilient data centres.
- Review the Education IT provision model.
- Integrate Health and Social Care processes.
- Developing a cloud migration plan for applications.
- Incorporate Security, Risk and Compliance.
- Staff skills assessment and reskilling.
- Consider new technologies e.g. AI, Robotics.

New Zealand Ministry of Social Development (2022)[3]

Foundations Establishing the foundational tools and capabilities that must be in place before we commence our transformation.

Horizon 1 Delivers value with a focus on digital, service, and process redesign for employment, students, and seniors, early response, and putting in place the foundations for the service model.

Horizon 2 Delivers value with a focus on service and process redesign for working age income support and embedding the service model.

Horizon 3 Delivers value with a focus on full modernisation of the underlying technology, business processes, and service model optimisation.

Horizon 4 Delivers value with a focus on partner enablement and expansion of the service model.

Notes

1 European Space Agency (2022) *Technology Strategy*, available at: https://esamultimedia.esa.int/docs/technology/ESA_Technology_Strategy_Version_1_0.pdf (Accessed: 06 October 2023).

2 Dundee City Council (undated) *Information Technology Strategy*, available at: https://www.dundeecity.gov.uk/sites/default/files/publications/dcc_it_strategy_final.docx (Accessed: 03 September 2022).
3 New Zealand Ministry of Social Development (2022) *Technology Strategy*, available at: https://www.msd.govt.nz/about-msd-and-our-work/publications-resources/corporate/msd-technology-strategy.html (Accessed: 04 September 2022).

Appendix 4

Tools, techniques, strategies, tactics, and dichotomies

The first three sections of this book included a number of break-out boxes. These featured stand-alone content that were intended to be both informative and thought provoking. Most of the break-out boxes were presented under three headings: *Analytical tools and techniques*, *Strategic and tactical moves*, and *Strategic dichotomies*.

This appendix itemises the contents of these boxes.

Analytical tools and techniques

In order to support a strategic decision, it may be necessary to engage in structured analysis involving some recognised tool or technique. A selection of useful examples were featured in this book, and are listed in Table A4.1.

Table A4.1 References for each analytical tool and technique

Chapter	Box no.	Title
1	1.3	Value chain analysis
2	2.1	The Double Diamond Design Process Model
3	3.1	Strategic asset audit
4	4.2	Leading indicators
5	5.2	Leavitt's Diamond
6	6.1	Failure modes and effects analysis (FMEA)
7	7.3	Reference class forecasting (RCF)
8	8.1	The skills matrix
9	9.4	The RACI matrix (of ethical obligations)
10	10.1	Product innovation and the Ansoff Matrix
11	-	-
12	12.1	PESTLE
13	-	-

Strategic and tactical moves

Professional strategists need to be familiar with established strategic moves and tactics. Those listed in Table A4.2 were described and explained in the book.

Table A4.2 References for each strategic and tactical move

Chapter	Box no.	Title
1	1.1	Collaborating with universities
2	2.3	Exploiting compatibility
3	3.2	Terminating projects
4	4.1	Going 'lite', or *dennovating*
5	5.3	"Instrument everything"
6	6.2	Choosing vanilla
7	7.2	Exchanging knowledge
8	8.3	Weakening the hold of monopolists
9	9.2	Ethical by design, ethical by default
10	10.3	Invoking the precautionary principle
11	11.3	Future-proofing
12	12.2	Declaring war on costs
13	-	-

Strategic dichotomies

Technologists and engineers occasionally reach a 'fork in the road'. We may call this a dichotomy. Some of these difficult choices, or *strategic dichotomies*, were examined in the text. They're listed in Table A4.3.

Table A4.3 References for each strategic dichotomy

Chapter	Box no.	Title
1	1.2	Technology stick OR Technology twist?
2	2.4	People OR Machines?
3	3.3	Co-location OR Cloistering?
4	4.3	First mover advantage OR Second mover advantage?
5	5.1	Suppress failure OR Highlight failure?
6	6.3	Disrupt and cannibalise OR Protect and suppress?
7	7.1	Locate in a cluster OR Locate independently?
8	8.2	Offshoring OR Nearshoring OR Onshoring?
9	9.3	Satisfying client wants OR Satisfying client needs?
10	10.2	Concentrated solutions OR Distributed solutions?
11	11.2	Risk aversion OR Risk taking?
12	12.3	Develop staff OR Recruit for new skills?
13	-	-

Acknowledgements

As this is my first book, its antecedents go back nearly three decades. Of the many people and institutions I've had the good fortune to know, those that had the greatest influence upon its content and production are recognised below.

Firstly, I'd like to acknowledge the people who provided professional opportunities. Without their favourable interventions this book would not exist. The story begins at General Electric in the 1990s where the actions of Jo Norman, Bob Brannock, Duncan Towner, and Peter Campbell created a solid platform for everything that followed. GE was the source of my workplace education in technology and risk management. It was also inspiring to be part of a respected international engineering business with great principles. After GE, the Edinburgh-based charity Challenges Worldwide supported my early interest in consulting practices through formative project assignments in Asia and Africa. Risktec Solutions (now TÜV Rheinland) then offered a string of project-based opportunities, enabling me to learn more about engineering, the education of engineers, and the management of technological risk. At Risktec, Alan Hoy, Vicky Billingham, and Mel Davies deserve special thanks. Steve Lewis was especially supportive.

I'd also like to acknowledge a number of former colleagues and friends who gave invaluable support at key moments. Peter Bhattacharya, Chris Adams, Gary Connolly, Odhran McCloskey, Mary Reidy, Sheryl Hurst, and Richard Popplestone all offered their time, sharing impressive knowledge and skills.

Those who contributed to my education, either through teaching or by opening doors (both physically and metaphorically) include the following. In Wales, Michael Foley. In London, Ben Pimlott and Helen Margetts. In Cambridge, Bill Nuttall, David Reiner, and Peter Guthrie. Collectively their marking, feedback, reading recommendations, academic references, course contents, programme management skills, and research opportunities, had a transformative effect upon my professional and educational progress. It's also right to thank the institutions, notably the now-closed Central Manchester College, the University of Wales (Aberystwyth), the University of

London (Birkbeck College), the University of Cambridge (Judge Institute, Department of Engineering, and Darwin College), and Massachusetts Institute of Technology (via the Cambridge-MIT Institute). I retain a close attachment to all of these places.

Early reviewers of the manuscript, each of whom supplied vital feedback, were Margaret Grzegorczyk, Pantea Lotfian, Ivan MacTaggart, Renee Robins, Jost Schatzmann, and Patrick van der Duin. Their criticisms, insights, and pointers were gratefully received.

Prior to publication, written endorsements were received from three experienced and authoritative practitioners. Representing the systems engineering profession was Alan Harding, a former President of INCOSE. Meanwhile, through my membership of the Institution of Engineering and Technology (IET) I had the good fortune to connect with two experienced engineers, Benjamin Cowan and Gavin Lewis, both of whom were generous with their time and feedback.

A more disparate group of contacts – Julia Sloan, Thomas Bohné, Andrew Keevil, Paul Roberts, Jonathan Rosenhead, Geoff Royston, and George Stowell – each contributed to the book's progress via digital correspondence.

Above all, Bill Nuttall, now Professor of Energy at The Open University, and a former leader of the Technology Policy Programme at Cambridge, represented the critical link between formal education, professional practice, and the book's realisation.

All of these people, and their institutions, fully deserve to be acknowledged for their contributions. Nevertheless, I take absolute responsibility for any factual errors, omissions or inconsistencies in the text. The book's strengths are all theirs. Any weaknesses are unequivocally mine.

Index

Printed in the United States
by Baker & Taylor Publisher Services